AN INTRODUCTORY
HISTORY OF
ENGLISH EDUCATION
SINCE 1800

BY

S. J. CURTIS, M.A., Ph.D.

FORMERLY READER IN EDUCATION IN THE UNIVERSITY OF LEEDS

AND

M. E. A. BOULTWOOD, M.A.

SENIOR LECTURER IN EDUCATION IN THE UNIVERSITY OF LEEDS

UNIVERSITY TUTORIAL PRESS LTD
9-10 GREAT SUTTON STREET, LONDON, E.C.1

By Dr S. J. Curtis
and M. E. A. Boultwood, M.A.

A SHORT HISTORY OF
EDUCATIONAL IDEAS

By Dr S. J. Curtis

HISTORY OF EDUCATION
IN GREAT BRITAIN

AN INTRODUCTION TO THE
PHILOSOPHY OF EDUCATION

UNIVERSITY TUTORIAL PRESS

Published 1960
Second Edition 1962
Third Edition 1964
Fourth Edition 1966
Reprinted 1967

PRINTED IN GREAT BRITAIN BY UNIVERSITY TUTORIAL PRESS LTD, FOXTON
NEAR CAMBRIDGE

PREFACE

DURING the past two decades events in the world of education have marched with speed and dramatic sequence, heralding changes and controversies which will affect the lives of coming generations. Those who seek an understanding of new problems through a study of the 1944 Act and subsequent developments will achieve little but doubt and perplexity if they ignore those other changes and controversies which have shaped English education through many eras.

This book is designed to aid the purposeful study of contemporary education, not only by tracing the development of the main institutions existent to-day, but also by indicating the relationship of this development to changes in opinion and theory on education. Such relationships are often perceptible only from the long view. The account given herein takes as its starting point the beginning of the nineteenth century when the nation was almost ready to accept those ideas which won State aid for schools long before the achievement of universal education.

We have written this book for all those who are interested in a subject which we find engrossing, but we appreciate that the majority of readers will be teachers and intending teachers. Therefore we have had in mind the needs of students in training. With the addition of a third year to the initial course of the training college, it is envisaged that many students may have opportunities to read more widely than their predecessors. We hope that this book will be a help to these students, that it will guide them in their search for an understanding of the great service they are to join, and that it will stimulate them in the formation of their own opinions and philosophies.

NOTE TO THE FOURTH EDITION

Since 1960 educational changes have been accelerating to such an extent that we are in a decade in which a veritable revolution of the educational system of this country has begun. Three major reports have been issued, and in the future the Plowden Committee will complete the survey of education in Great Britain. The present edition aims at providing a summary of the Crowther, Newsom, and Robbins Reports and the changes which have already taken place under the present Government.

S. J. C.

M. E. A. B.

iii

CONTENTS

AN INTRODUCTORY HISTORY
OF ENGLISH EDUCATION SINCE 1800

CHAPTER I

ENGLISH SCHOOLS IN 1800

What facilities existed at the beginning of the nineteenth century for poor children to obtain elementary education and for well-to-do parents to send their children to secondary schools? The answer to the first part of the question depends to a certain extent on locality. Schools were unevenly distributed and, on the whole, parents who lived in south-eastern England had better opportunities for securing elementary education for their children than those who lived in the rural districts of the North and West, and English children were more fortunate than Welsh. The shifting of population which resulted in the development of new centres of industry after the middle of the eighteenth century had left many districts of England and Wales very ill-provided with any kind of school.

Charity Schools

Even in areas where there was a more adequate provision of schools, many poor parents were unable to take advantage of it. Wages were low and, as a consequence of the war with revolutionary France, the cost of food and clothing was soaring. As soon as children reached the age of five or six they were sent to mines and factories to work for long hours in unhealthy surroundings in order to supplement family earnings. One has only to read the reports of factory inspectors in the early decades of the nineteenth century to realise the appalling conditions under which young children worked at an age when they would now be leading a happy, healthy life in the infant or the junior school. Very few children of working-class parents who were fortunate enough to be able to attend school could remain there after nine or ten years of age. It was imperative for them to ease the family budget by their earnings. Hence one can say in general terms that not only were there insufficient schools, but only a small proportion of children of school age, about one in thirty, received any organised education.

The types of elementary school varied greatly. In London and the large towns, and in certain rural districts such as Lincolnshire, parents could send their boys and girls to a charity school. Some of these schools might be described as private charity schools. Local landowners of benevolent disposition had endowed schools during the latter seventeenth and eighteenth centuries to which children were admitted either freely or on payment of fees amounting to a few pence a week. It has been estimated that about 1,000 of these schools existed. A school of this type was founded by Catherine and Mary Ingilby in 1702 at Ripley, near Harrogate.

The schoolmaster was to be a member of the Church of England and "a layman of sober life and conversation, able to teach and instruct youth in reading English, writing and the common and useful rules of arithmetic—and once every week cause his scholars to learn the Church catechism". A similar school was endowed by Admiral Long in 1760 at Burnt Yates in the same parish. Both schools now function as junior mixed and infant schools.

An interesting example from Surrey is the school at Newdigate, near Dorking. In 1661, the Rev. G. Steere, Rector of the parish, left provision for maintaining a school. "I leave the Parish of Newdigate for ever, a school house, which be built upon part of the land called 'Clarke' for the teaching of younge persons at and in the said school house, and not for a place of habitation for any person or persons, and to be maintained by the parish for such use, and I charge my other lands with an annual payment of £6 13s. 6d., for the catechizing, teaching and instruction in reading, writing and other good learning forever of four young persons, born in the Parish, sons of goodly parents." [1]

A larger number of charity schools was the result of the efforts of the Society for Promoting Christian Knowledge. The S.P.C.K. was founded in 1698. Helen Wodehouse points out that the procedure of the S.P.C.K. was influenced by the idea of the joint stock company. What was not possible for any one individual to achieve through his own resources could be realised by small subscriptions paid by a large number of people. In addition funds were raised by collections at annual charity sermons preached by well-known dignitaries of the Church.

The immediate cause of the foundation of the S.P.C.K. was the widespread alarm at the degradation of morals which followed the Restoration of 1660. The original founders were Dr Thomas Bray

[1] W. H. Chouler, *The Birth and Growth of a Village School, 1660-1955.*

and four laymen, and the scheme was supported by the Archbishops, Bishops, and many of the gentry. As well as stimulating
the foundation of charity schools, the S.P.C.K. published and distributed Bibles, Prayer Books, and tracts at half the cost of printing,
the deficiency being made up from the Society's funds.

The movement aroused great enthusiasm. It also provoked
opposition in some quarters, especially in the earlier years of the
eighteenth century when the authorities thought it was favourable
to the Jacobites. Mandeville attacked the education given in the
schools on the grounds that it gave poor children ideas beyond their
station in life thereby making them discontented with their lot.
He rather unjustly accused the S.P.C.K. of not giving sufficient care
to children after they left school. The movement was not confined
to the Established Church, but was also favoured by Isaac Watts
and many Dissenters.

The curriculum included religious instruction based on the
Catechism, the three R's, and, in many schools, instruction in various
trades. Thus sewing and spinning were advocated for girls, and
at Hatton Garden boys were taught the art of navigation. At St
Andrew's, Holborn, the boys received a training in gardening and
the girls in household work. Some of the schools remained as day
schools, while others developed into boarding schools. In most
of the schools the pupils were provided with a distinctive uniform.

The charity schools were the first institutions to provide education on a large scale for both sexes. The S.P.C.K. not only built
new schools, but took over some of the existing private charity
schools which had fallen upon bad times. Each school was maintained by the local inhabitants, but received advice and assistance
from the S.P.C.K. The Society also anticipated many modern
developments. Thus quite early it considered a scheme for the
training of teachers and the inspection of schools, but, evidently,
financial stringency prevented fulfilment of the scheme. In spite
of what Mandeville asserted, considerable interest was taken in
pupils after they had left school. Boys were apprenticed to a variety
of trades and girls to be seamstresses or to enter domestic service.
Up to 1733, 7,139 boys and 1,383 girls had been apprenticed and
3,366 boys and 3,873 girls were in domestic service of one kind or
another. Occasionally former pupils were given the means to set
up in trade themselves.

After the middle of the century the movement lost its initial
enthusiasm and entered upon a period of decline. The number

of schools is difficult to ascertain accurately, but the statistics for 1758 report that in England and Wales there were 1,329 schools with 23,421 pupils (19,506 boys and 3,915 girls). In addition there were the Welsh circulating schools, which numbered 218 with 9,834 pupils, some of whom were adults.

The problem in Wales was made more difficult because of the hilly nature of the country and the large number of scattered homesteads. This was met by the device of the circulating school associated with the Rev. Griffith Jones. He thought that the only practical solution lay in itinerant schoolmasters who would move from one district to another. It was stipulated that the medium of instruction should be Welsh and not English. By the time of Griffith Jones's death in 1761 it is estimated that 150,512 persons between the ages of six and seventy had been taught to read the Bible in Welsh.

Many of the charity schools were very small and contained less than twenty children. Towards the end of the century quite a number of schools closed, but others remained and were handed over to the National Society. After 1902 those which still survived became, with other National schools, non-provided schools, and after 1944, voluntary schools. A few of the larger schools developed into secondary grammar schools. This happened to the school of St James, Westminster, which was founded in 1699 as a day school. After 1725 it became known as Burlington School and was reconstituted as a boarding school. In 1876 it was approved as a Middle Class school, and a subsequent reorganisation in 1906 resulted in its establishment as a girls' day secondary school.

Schools of Industry

As early as 1675, Thomas Firman erected a spinning factory in which children of four or five years of age were taught to read and spin. The philosopher, John Locke, in 1697 advocated a similar type of school for pauper children. A few schools of industry were set up in the early part of the eighteenth century, but it was not until factories began to multiply that they became more numerous.

These schools were not unlike the charity schools, with an industrial basis. The boys were taught useful occupations such as gardening, carpentry, cobbling, and printing; the girls spinning, knitting, sewing, and straw-plaiting. The produce of the pupils was offered for sale and the money obtained was used for the maintenance of the school. If the child's earnings exceeded the cost of his keep, he was given a cash payment.

The idea was to make the school self-supporting. It was always a temptation to the head of the school to neglect the educational and stress the occupational aspect in order to cover expenses. On the whole, boys' schools were not as successful as girls' schools. The products of the boys did not command as ready a sale as those of the girls. As the change to factory conditions accelerated, the demand for child labour became so great that parents preferred to send their children to work in the mills and mines. Even foundlings and orphans were insufficient to keep up numbers in the schools of industry. Girls' schools were better attended than boys', and Mrs Trimmer advocated establishments in which girls could be trained to make and mend their own clothes and undertake plain sewing for people who lived in the neighbourhood.

Sunday Schools

By 1780 the influence of the charity schools had greatly declined and the effect of the industrial changes was becoming very noticeable in the rapid growth of population in the new industrial areas. Although the demand for child labour brought thousands of children into the factories, there was still one day in the week in which most children were free. It was their wild and mischievous behaviour on Sundays in the City of Gloucester which brought about the Sunday School movement, generally associated with the name of Robert Raikes.

He was not the first person to conceive the idea of the Sunday School, and even in Gloucester it appears that the first school of this kind was the work of his friend, the Rev. Thomas Stock. There are isolated instances of Sunday Schools which were founded at an earlier period. Thus John Wesley had experimented with a Sunday School at Savannah in 1737, and in 1763 one was established at Catterick, Yorks., by the Rev. Theophilus Lindsey.

Raikes was influenced by the lawless behaviour and the squalid life of the children engaged in the pin industry of Gloucester. He had already performed notable work in alleviating the terrible conditions of the prisoners in the Gloucester gaol, and in his newspaper, the *Gloucester Journal*, he testified that "the farmers and other inhabitants of the towns and villages receive more injury in their property in the Sabbath than in all the week besides; this in a great measure proceeds from the lawless state of the younger class who are allowed to run wild on that day free from restraint". However true this may have been, it appeared to Raikes that the most effective way of preventing the children from growing up into habitual criminals was to occupy them on Sundays and bring them under Christian influence. With these intentions, Raikes opened his first Sunday School in 1780. The school was also open on week-days for those who were able to attend.

Raikes was able to publicise his ideas through the medium of his Journal, and hence it can be claimed quite justly that he was the pioneer of the Sunday School movement. At the beginning he showed a lack of understanding of children, but he soon discovered that harsh methods of keeping order were not successful and that children are attracted by a kind firmness. The movement spread throughout England during the next decade, and by 1795 nearly a quarter of a million children were attending Sunday Schools.

At first the movement was supported by all denominations and the Sunday School Union, founded in 1803, had a committee composed of both Churchmen and Dissenters. The schools taught reading and spelling as a prelude to reading the Bible, but in many schools secular instruction was given as well. Raikes paid his teachers, but, as the movement extended, the tendency developed of replacing the paid teachers by voluntary workers and confining the instruction to religious subjects.

The Sunday Schools met with opposition from some quarters. The Reign of Terror in Paris caused many people to believe that similar atrocities might take place in England if poor children were educated above their stations in life. One of the individuals who was greatly influenced by the movement was Hannah More, who, with her sister, left London in 1785 to live in the Mendip parish of Cowslip Green. She encountered opposition from ignorant parents who needed to be convinced that she was not securing their children to sell as slaves to the planters of the West Indies. Eventually, the movement overcame opposition. One of its strongest supporters was Mrs Trimmer, a devoted if rather narrow-minded Churchwoman. She not only encouraged the establishment of Sunday Schools and schools of industry, but busied herself with writing story books and primers for children.

The Sunday School movement of the eighteenth century was significant not only because of what it actually achieved, but also for the ideal towards which it pointed the way, that of universal popular education. Sir James Kay-Shuttleworth, writing nearly half a century later, declared: "It is also important to observe, that the development of Sunday Schools for the poor proceeded with gigantic strides . . . The idea of education for the poor sprang from a religious impulse . . . it regarded the school as a nursery of the Church and congregation, and confided its management to the chief communicants, to the deacons, elders, and class teachers. Thus the Sunday School became the type of the daily school".

The movement played a very important part in the development of elementary education in Wales. When Griffith Jones died in 1761, he left £7,000 to his friend, Madam Bevan, to carry on his work, and she, in turn, bequeathed her property in 1779 to the Welsh circulating schools. The will was disputed, and by the time the Court of Chancery decided in support of the will, the schools had practically disappeared.

The Sunday Schools took the place of the circulating schools. The pioneer of the Welsh movement was the Rev. Thomas Charles of Bala. His work led to a widespread demand for copies of the Welsh Bible, but in spite of the fact that the Established Church initiated the Sunday Schools, the Church in Wales failed to grasp the significance of the movement. The Methodists realised the opportunities presented and hence Nonconformity rather than the Established Church played the major part in shaping Welsh education.

Voluntary effort working through the philanthropic societies was confronted by serious difficulties in the task of providing elementary education for poor children. The funds available were quite inadequate and the scarcity of experienced teachers was an additional obstacle. The problem was, on the one hand, to make the best use of the teachers available, and, on the other, to find the most economical method of organising and maintaining a school. These account for the popular support given to the schemes advocated by Andrew Bell and Joseph Lancaster.

Joseph Lancaster (1778-1838)

Lancaster was the son of an old soldier who had taken up the trade of a sieve-maker. His schooldays started in him a love of reading, and when a book on the slave trade came into his hands his enthusiasm led him to run away from home to teach negroes in Jamaica. He was brought back, and then decided to become a dissenting minister, but before he had finally made up his mind, he was attracted by the Quakers and became a member of the Society of Friends. As the Society had no paid ministers he had to look elsewhere for support and his natural love of teaching led him to adopt the calling of an usher, first in a boarding and then in a day school. This did not satisfy him because he longed to have a school of his own.

His first school was held in an outhouse belonging to his father, and it was so successful that in 1801 he established a school in Borough Road. Lancaster was a born teacher who attracted ever growing numbers of pupils, and this led him into financial difficulties. There were too many boys for him to teach and he could not afford to pay assistant masters. The result was that he hit upon the idea of employing monitors, that is, making use of older children to teach the younger. This was not an original idea although Lancaster believed it was. Years earlier it had been in use at Winchester College, Manchester Grammar School, and other grammar schools. Robert Raikes had used a similar method in his educational work in the prisons and in his Sunday Schools.

It seems that Lancaster knew nothing of these earlier experiments and claimed that he had discovered a new method of running a school with the minimum of cost. He described his scheme in a pamphlet entitled *Improvements in Education*, 1803, but by the time it had run into a third edition in 1805 it became a fairly good-sized book. Lancaster knew how to advertise and it was not long before he secured the patronage of George III. This stimulated his natural vanity and his reckless, extravagant nature led him to spend more than he could afford.

He was arrested for debt, but was soon released on a technical point of law. He had built two schools, a training college for teachers, and had established a printing press and a factory for making slates. These ventures plunged him still further into debt. Matters were not helped by his love of display, his personal extravagance, and his complete inability to handle money. Eventually his supporters helped him to discharge his debts and formed the Royal Lancasterian Society in 1808.

Lancaster was, however, unable to profit from his experiences and the committee of the Society strove vainly to limit his expenditure. In 1812 the Society was reorganised as the British and Foreign School Society, and Lancaster was forced to accept the position of superintendent of the Borough Road school at a salary of £365 a year. In 1814 he resigned this office in the hope that his friends would support him in new ventures. They withheld their support and he left England in 1818 for the United States. He died in New York in 1838.

Andrew Bell (1753-1832)

In many ways Bell was the exact opposite of Lancaster. Whilst the latter was always in debt, the former had a genius for making money. After a very unhappy time at school, Bell entered the University of St Andrews in 1769. He accepted a teaching post in Virginia, but the War of Independence necessitated his return to England in 1781. After spending some time as a private tutor, he was ordained by Barrington, Bishop of Salisbury (later Bishop of Durham and a warm supporter of elementary education for the poorer classes).

Life as a clergyman in the Episcopal Church of Scotland did not offer sufficient outlet for his ambitions and he resolved, like so many other young men of the period, to seek his fortune in India. Before leaving this country he persuaded the University of St Andrews to grant him the degree of Doctor of Medicine. Within a short space of time he collected a number of regimental chaplaincies and was appointed superintendent of the Military Male Asylum in Madras. This was a school for the orphan sons of soldiers. Like Lancaster, Bell was a born teacher who threw himself heart and soul into his work.

It was in Madras that he came across a native teacher who made use of sand for teaching his children writing. Bell thought that this was a good method, but when he tried to introduce it into the Asylum he was met by the strong resistance of the assistants. He was determined, however, to carry out his plan. He selected John Frisken, an eight-year-old boy, and set him to teach the class. The experiment was successful and Frisken was appointed teacher of the lowest class. This was in 1791 or 1792, some years before Lancaster had adopted the monitorial idea. Bell returned to England in 1795 as a comparatively wealthy man and was given the rectory of Swanage, in Dorset.

In 1797 he published an account of his work in Madras under the title of *An Experiment in Education*. The book ran through five editions, the last in 1814 being greatly enlarged. Bell made the acquaintance of Lancaster, and for a time the two men exchanged views. Then Mrs Trimmer interfered. She resented the success of Lancaster, whose schools were undenominational, and she published a pamphlet in which it stated that Bell had originated the monitorial system and Lancaster had copied it. There is little doubt that both men had acted independently in adopting the system. This produced a rift between Churchmen and Nonconformists, which, though unimportant at that time, was really the beginning of the acrimonious struggle between the two parties which was so disastrous in later years to the cause of national education.

In 1811 the National Society for Promoting the Education of the Poor in the Principles of the Established Church was formed and took over much of the work previously carried out by the S.P.C.K. After several promotions, Bell was given a prebend's stall in Westminster Abbey. Later his health failed and he died in 1832, leaving a considerable fortune.

Monitorial Schools

The schools of Lancaster and Bell had many points in common. Both men adopted the monitorial system. Lancaster boasted that under his plan it was possible for one master to teach a thousand pupils. Bell went one better in his assertion that under his system one master could conduct ten schools of a thousand if the premises were close together. The keynote of both systems was cheapness. The annual cost of teaching a child in a Lancasterian school was 7s. 6d., and in a very large school this amount could be still more reduced. It was estimated that in a National school of 500 pupils the cost per head was 4s. 2d.

In both systems the sand-tray was used for teaching the beginnings of writing and numbering. With older children slates and reading-cards were employed. The print of the latter was sufficiently large for the whole group to see it. The object was to save expenditure on books which would have to be replaced at frequent intervals. Lancaster's methods were more regimented than Bell's. He developed an elaborate organisation in accordance with his motto, "A place for everything and everything in its place". Pupils were marched to their places and desks. Each pupil had a number and the same number was used for his hat nail, his desk, and his slate. In addition to teaching monitors, there was a small army of other monitors for ruling paper, mending quill pens, registration, and other duties.

Lancaster classified his pupils according to their attainments into eight classes for reading and twelve for arithmetic. Thus, class one in reading was called the ABC class; classes two to five taught words of two letters ranging to five or six letters in the fifth class, and classes six and seven were occupied in reading the Testament and the Bible respectively. The senior class consisted of the best readers.

The method of teaching the letters was based on similarity of form, *e.g.* letters which depended on lines, such as H, T, E, were followed by those depending on angles, such as A, V, N, and, finally, those which involved circles or curves, O, C, B, S. The groups under the charge of a monitor varied in number from twelve to twenty according to the size of the school. The monitorial school was conducted in a large oblong room, sometimes partitioned to separate boys from girls.

Running down the centre of the room was a line of long desks which were used for writing. On each side there was a space marked out by a series of studs arranged in semicircles for the pupils and a larger stud for the monitor. In one room in the Salt Grammar School, Shipley, Yorks., which was originally conducted as a monitorial school, the studs remained until quite recently. Bell's system was more flexible than Lancaster's. There were fewer monitors and larger classes. The desks were placed near to the walls, leaving the centre free for monitorial groups. This was marked out in hollow squares for the classes. In both systems the monitors were pupils drawn from the upper classes who received the lesson they had to teach from the master and then passed it on to the pupils.

Bell and Lancaster believed in appealing to the spirit of emulation. They deprecated severe physical punishment and relied mainly upon rewards and censure. The head monitor or inspector examined the classes at regular intervals and promoted those who were efficient to the next class. When he was promoted the pupil received a prize, usually a small picture. Lancaster wrote: "It is no unusual thing with me to deliver 100 to 200 prizes at the same time. And at such times the countenances of the whole school exhibit a most pleasing scene of delight: as the boys who obtain prizes commonly walk round the school in procession, holding the prizes in their hands, and an herald proclaiming before them, 'These good boys have obtained prizes for going into another class'. The honour of this has effect as powerful, if not more so, than the prizes themselves".[1]

[1] *Lancaster's Improvements and Bell's Experiment,* ed. David Salmon, p. 36, C.U.P., 1932.

For cases of serious misbehaviour, Lancaster invented some very ingenious forms of punishment, *e.g.* a wooden log of four to six pounds in weight was worn round the shoulders as a pillory or the boy's legs were fastened together by wooden shackles in order to keep him from wandering. Sometimes a pupil was put into a cage which was hauled up by a rope passing over a roof beam. If a boy came to school with a dirty face, a girl was appointed to wash it and administer slaps as she did so.

Apart from the taint of cheapness which was to be characteristic of elementary education for many generations to come, the monitorial method was essentially mechanical. Its sponsors rather gloried in this. They were living in an age in which the introduction of machinery had revolutionised the processes of industry. Looking backwards, we of the present age can see that little education apart from mere instruction could have been given by other children only a year or two in advance of their pupils. Nevertheless, the work of Bell and Lancaster represents a sincere attempt to provide through voluntary effort education for children of the poorer classes, and it also proved that the task was beyond the capacity of the philanthropic societies unless some form of state aid was forthcoming.

Private Schools

One other source of schooling was available for children whose parents could afford to pay the few pence demanded each week. This was provided by private schools. Some of these aspired to give a secondary education, but the majority provided only an elementary education of some kind. A number of private schools, termed in later official reports "private adventure schools", were taught by masters who had failed in every other occupation or who earned a living by mixing teaching with cobbling or some other trade. Some were ex-soldiers, and since no pensions were paid in those days they had to find a means of earning a living. By far the greater number were Dame schools conducted by women, often widows, as a means of securing a rather precarious livelihood. Often the mistress was nearly as ignorant as the children she taught. It would, however, be a great mistake to regard all private schools as inefficient. There were some, like that taught by Mrs. Barbauld, which endeavoured to provide a really sound training, but the majority of them were rather inefficient babyminding establishments.

Ragged Schools

Finally, the so-called ragged schools were developed to provide some kind of education for the really destitute. John Pounds, of Portsmouth, is usually regarded as the pioneer of this type of school, but it was not long before a society was formed to deal with this problem. Many of the ragged schools continued to exist beyond the middle of the nineteenth century.

Grammar Schools

The well-to-do parent had a number of choices open to him. In the first place there were the endowed grammar schools, many of which were of ancient foundation. The earliest grammar schools developed in close connection with the establishment of the cathedrals and collegiate churches. It is generally agreed that the first English grammar school was the school of Canterbury, founded by Augustine soon after the conversion of the people of Kent. It is now the King's School, Canterbury, which owes its name not to Ethelbert, King of Kent, but to Henry VIII who refounded it after a short lapse at the Reformation. It seems that the school of York, now St Peter's School, is our oldest continuous school, dating at least from the middle of the seventh century.

Augustine was faced with the problem of providing English priests and singing boys for the services of the Church. Since Latin was the universal language of the Western Church, and, indeed, of all educated people, the study of Latin grammar was necessary not only for the clergy but also for what we should now call civil and local government servants, who came into existence with the feudal system. It is interesting to note that in medieval times the study of Latin was just as vocational as engineering or mining science at the present day. Hence these early schools became eventually known as grammar schools. The schools which concentrated on training the boys in singing the services of the Church were known as song schools.

The important point is that the first English schools were founded through the efforts of the Church and continued under its control until long after the Reformation. The Church maintained its control partly because the religious instruction given was supervised by the Church and partly because every grammar school master had to be licensed by the bishop. In addition, until fairly late in the medieval period, all schoolmasters were clerics.

Other grammar schools originated in connection with monasteries, trade or craft gilds, or with chantries. All monasteries maintained schools for their novices, but some, like Westminster and St Albans, possessed a grammar school attended by boys from without. Others grew up in connection with craft or devotional gilds. These were taught by the gild priests, but they were grammar schools and did not in any sense provide a vocational training. An example is the grammar school of Stratford-on-Avon which was attended by Shakespeare and which sprang from the craft gilds of the town.

Perhaps the most important source of schools in the later Middle Ages was in the chantries. Chantries were endowed by pious benefactors and a priest was appointed to pray for the soul of the founder and other named persons. Thus Thomas Clarell, Vicar of Leeds (1430-69), endowed a chantry in the parish church and a priest was appointed to "pray for the soule of Kynge Edward the iiijth and Quene Elizabeth, the founder's soule and all Christen soules, and to do dyvyne service".[1] In a large number of chantry endowments it was stipulated that the priest should teach a school which was sometimes an elementary but more often a grammar school. At the Reformation, when monasteries, chantries, and religious gilds were dissolved, if the keeping of a school was laid down as a duty of the chantry priest, it was in most cases permitted to continue.

In the Middle Ages the curriculum of the grammar school included not only Latin and religious knowledge but also logic and rhetoric (the art of public speaking and writing official letters). At some of the grammar schools, *e.g.* Canterbury, pupils paid fees for their instruction, but a large number were designated as free schools. There has been much controversy about the meaning of this term, but it seems most likely that a free school received all or a stated number of pupils and instructed them freely. It also seems that some elementary schools, because of their endowment, were able to admit scholars without payment of fees.

The Renaissance resulted in the introduction of Greek, a wider study of classical writers, and the use of printed books. Formerly the only manuscript available belonged to the master, so that the teaching was purely oral. The Reformation resulted in the discontinuance of many grammar schools. The inhabitants of the districts

[1] The Leeds chantry may have furnished additional endowment for Leeds Grammar School, since there are references to a schoolmaster at Leeds dating back for at least two centuries before this time.

served by the school felt the loss and often petitioned the Crown and secured a charter for the refoundation of the school. Many of the schools which bear the name of a Tudor monarch are refoundations of previously existing schools. In these schools, the master and usher (assistant-master) were required to conform to the doctrine of the Established Church and much stress was placed on the religious instruction given.

By the end of the eighteenth century, the grammar schools as a whole were in a sorry state. As a result of the fall in the value of money, many endowments which had yielded sufficient to provide a reasonable stipend for the schoolmaster no longer did so. Some schools either closed or sank to the status of inefficient elementary schools. Others, being bound by their statutes or the will of their founder, could not provide anything beyond a classical education and were unable to include such subjects as modern languages or mathematics, which were in demand in an age of great commercial and industrial expansion. The attempt to introduce additional subjects was foiled by the decision in the Leeds Grammar School case of 1805.

Lord Eldon, then Lord Chancellor, ruled that since Dr Johnson had defined a grammar school as an institution "for teaching grammatically the learned languages", he could not sanction the introduction of any other studies. This decision effectively checked the tendency, except for those large grammar schools that had sufficient funds to obtain a private Act of Parliament to authorise the introduction of subjects not mentioned in the foundation deeds. Thus Macclesfield was able to obtain the authority to establish a modern free school in addition to the grammar school. It was not until the Grammar School Act of 1840 that governing bodies were free to introduce subjects other than those provided for in the foundation.

The decline in the value of the income derived from endowments had a significant effect upon the schools. Most grammar school masters were driven to supplement their stipends by admitting fee-paying pupils or by receiving boarders who were given private coaching. The tendency was to neglect the free scholars and to restrict their instruction to the subjects mentioned in the foundation statute. If a free scholar wished to learn arithmetic, geography, or some other subject, he was required to pay fees. A further consequence was that in all but the larger and more wealthy schools the buildings were neglected and the equipment was often most inadequate.

The existence of a number of free places in grammar schools did allow children of poor parents to enter if the parents were able and willing to keep their boys at school and if they desired a classical education. As we have seen, very few poor children could, or wanted to, take advantage of this, so that the term "free school" was becoming a misnomer. The grammar schools, therefore, in the main, catered for middle-class pupils whose parents were able to pay fees.

Public Schools

Wealthy parents had the option of sending their sons to a public school. Some public schools are medieval foundations; others were founded or refounded in the post-Reformation period. Originally the public schools differed little from the grammar schools; in fact, they were grammar schools. In the medieval period the foundations of such schools as Winchester and Eton were on a larger and more magnificent scale than the rest of the grammar schools. Moreover, whilst many grammar schools were only concerned with boys from the near neighbourhood of the school, Winchester and Eton opened their doors to pupils from all parts of the kingdom. Hence the majority of the public schools developed as boarding schools. Two post-Reformation schools, St Paul's (probably a refoundation), and Merchant Taylor's, were day schools.

In the Middle Ages the term "public" was used occasionally in connection with grammar schools and there seems to have been no fixed meaning attached to it. During the sixteenth century it was used to denote the distinction between school and private tuition. Thus, in Canon LXXVII of 1604, it is stated: "No man shall teach either in public school, or in private house, but such as shall be allowed by the bishop of the diocese or ordinary of the place, under his hand and seal". The latter part of the sentence refers to the requirement of licensing schoolmasters.

The next development consisted in distinguishing between public grammar schools and private schools which were conducted for profit. Thus Charles Hoole, on the title page of his *New Discovery of the Old Art of Teaching School*, 1660, described himself as "Teacher of a Private Grammar School in Lothbury Gardens, London". Another example is afforded by Ralph Thoresby, the topographer and historian, who stated that he received part of his education from "the Reverend Mr Robert Garnet, M.A., of Christ's Col., Cambridge, at a private grammar school at the North-end of the great Stone-Bridge". This school, although it might have had some affiliation, was not the Leeds Grammar School.

In the work previously mentioned, Hoole distinguished between the "great" or collegiate schools, "classical" or grammar schools, and "mixed" schools which provided a curriculum for elementary scholars and also for grammarians. In the eighteenth century the great schools became known as public schools. R. L. Edgeworth, in *Practical Education*, 1798, recommended that parents who could afford it should "send their children to large public schools, to Eton or Winchester; not to any small school, much less to one in their own neighbourhood". The next step was to limit the term to certain great schools, and by the end of the first quarter of the nineteenth century, it was generally recognised that the public schools consisted of the seven large boarding schools, Winchester, Eton, Westminster, Charterhouse, Harrow, Rugby, and Shrewsbury, and the two day schools, St Paul's, and Merchant Taylor's. During the course of the next hundred years we shall see that this list became greatly extended.

At the beginning of the nineteenth century the public schools were in as distressing a condition as the grammar schools. Their curriculum was also just as much restricted, and the moral state of the schools came in for much criticism. The picture of life at Rugby presented in *Tom Brown's Schooldays* is a true one, and the poet Cowper, who had been educated at Westminster, wrote: "Great schools suit but the sturdy and rough". The administration of the schools was chaotic; they were understaffed and the boarding arrangements were unsatisfactory. It was a common complaint that the food was insufficient and badly cooked. After lesson periods and prep., the boys in some schools were herded into the dormitories and locked in. The doors were not opened until it was time to rise for breakfast. Bullying and fagging were universal. It does not seem that on the whole boys objected to fagging for they took it for granted that the younger pupils ought to look after the wants of their seniors.

Accounts of life in the public schools show that order was maintained by flogging. Many legends grew up about Dr Keate at Eton. It was said that on one occasion he flogged the boys sent to him as Confirmation candidates. The mistake occurred because the list of candidates was on a sheet of paper the same size and shape as the punishment slip. There was, however, some justification for the harsh rule of the birch. The scandalous understaffing of the schools produced a serious disciplinary problem. Thus Keate was obliged to teach the upper fifth and sixth forms together, a total of about 170 boys. The only illumination available in the long upper schoolroom was provided by a few candles, and in the dim light of a winter afternoon the boys amused themselves by humming tunes and throwing bread pellets at one another. Under such conditions, it was almost impossible to keep order without recourse to harsh measures, and the belief grew amongst schoolboys that masters were their natural enemies and that it was a creditable thing to deceive them by lying or cheating.

One is not surprised to find that there were frequent revolts in the schools. Winchester, Eton, and Rugby were troubled in this way. In 1818 five boys smashed Keate's desk with a sledge-hammer. They were discovered and flogged, and in his diary Keate reported that "the boys are as quiet as lambs". The last rebellion at Eton took place in 1832. Perhaps the most serious disturbance was at Rugby in 1797 when troops were summoned and the Riot Act read.

Private Tutors

It is not surprising, therefore, that many parents shied from sending their sons to the public schools. The records of the schools show that in most of them numbers fluctuated considerably. When an able Head such as James at Rugby, Butler at Shrewsbury, Barnard at Eton, or Thackeray at Harrow, was appointed, numbers increased and then fell rapidly if the successor was of an inferior type. A century before this time, John Locke had strongly criticised the harsh and brutal life of the public schools and had advised wealthy parents to place their sons under the charge of a private tutor, who, when his pupils reached later adolescence, accompanied them on the Grand Tour of Europe. It was thus that many of the polished gentlemen scholars of the eighteenth century, such as the "elegant" Earl of Shaftesbury, a pupil of Locke, were produced.

Nonconformist Academies

There were, however, other alternatives to the public schools. The Nonconformist academies offered an education based on more generous lines than that to be found in either the grammar or the public schools. The academy tutors were men who had been expelled from the older universities after the Restoration and who, in spite of the laws aimed at Protestant Dissenters becoming school-masters, undertook the training of candidates for the ministry.

Other pupils were also admitted and they included Churchmen. At first the penal laws necessitated constant shifting of premises, but as the eighteenth century wore on greater toleration was exercised.

The academies offered an almost encyclopaedic range of studies. In addition to the classical languages, history and geography, modern foreign languages, mathematics, the natural sciences, logic, drawing, bookkeeping, and many other subjects were taught. One of the most famous was the academy at Warrington, 1757-86, at which Joseph Priestley, the discoverer of oxygen, lectured. Many eminent men were educated at the academies. Samuel Wesley, the father of John Wesley, and Daniel Defoe, the author, studied at Newington Green, and Secker, later Archbishop of Canterbury, and Joseph Butler, afterwards Bishop of Durham and the greatest moral philosopher of that age, were pupils of the academy at Gloucester. In 1779 the restrictions upon Dissenters keeping school were removed and the need for the older academies disappeared.

Private Academies

The success of the dissenting academies resulted in the opening of numerous private academies run by private persons. Some of these were indifferent, but others reached a high standard of efficiency. An example of the latter type was an academy opened by Randall in 1740 at Heath, near Wakefield. This was a large boarding establishment, staffed by nine masters, which offered a wide selection of studies.

The curriculum consisted of English grammar and literature, Latin, Greek, French, mathematics, geography and the use of globes and maps, chronology and history, geometry, astronomy, natural philosophy (science), bookkeeping, surveying, navigation and fortification, ethics, metaphysics, dancing, fencing, and drawing. Pupils studied a group of related subjects according to whether they were proceeding to the universities, seeking a business career, entering the Army or Navy, or living the life of a country gentleman. Boarding cost ten guineas per annum and tuition fees depended on the group of studies selected.

Education of Girls

The Heath Academy was typical of the better class of private academy. There were some which were extremely inefficient, and the worst type was described by Dickens in Dotheboys Hall. On the whole the academies provided a training much superior to that given by the grammar schools. Many of them possessed adequate buildings, and in accordance with the advice given by Locke, they were sited in healthy districts. The grammar schools did not admit girls (in a few exceptional cases, like Rishworth, girls followed a shorter and inferior course compared with the boys), but many academies for young ladies came into existence in the latter years of the eighteenth century. These also varied greatly in efficiency; they tended to emphasise accomplishments such as deportment, music, drawing, dancing, and fancy needlework, rather than sound learning, but unless parents could afford the services of a private governess, they provided the only opportunity for girls to obtain an education other than elementary.

One can summarise the educational position in England at the beginning of the nineteenth century as follows. The provision of elementary education was hopelessly inadequate. What was available was the result of religious and philanthropic effort and it touched only a minority of children of school age. Secondary education, as represented by the public and grammar schools, was in most cases of poor quality and out of touch with contemporary needs. The academies certainly offered a more varied training, but they had little effect on the grammar schools. In both elementary and secondary education, however, there was some indication of reform. In the case of the former, financial resources restricted any great expansion, but a large section of the public was opposed to state assistance.

SUGGESTIONS FOR FURTHER READING

S. J. Curtis, *History of Education in Great Britain*, sixth edition, U.T.P., 1965. Chapter IV, pp. 110-32, Chapter VI.

Frank Smith, *A History of English Elementary Education, 1760-1902*, University of London Press, 1931. Chapters I-III. This book is now out of print, but can be obtained from most libraries.

H. C. Barnard, *A Short History of English Education from 1760 to 1944*, University of London Press, 1947. Chapters I, II, VI.

Lancaster's Improvements and Bell's Experiment, ed. David Salmon, C.U.P., 1932.

CHAPTER II

ENGLISH EDUCATIONAL THOUGHT BEFORE 1800

British educational thought has always been rich and vigorous, at least since the Dark Ages when scholars such as Bede, Alcuin, Dunstan, and Aelfric laid the foundation on which many sincere forward-thinking educators were to build. Some of these first thinkers were brave men in that they often had to take a stand against those dogmas of their own faith which were then binding true scholarship to the ignorance and superstition of the times.

Educational theory is truly effective only when it is ahead of current practice but not so far removed from it as to seem impracticable and visionary. When we look back at pre-Renaissance ideas in England, we are impressed by their narrowness, their omission of psychological considerations, and their ignoring of democratic principles. When, however, we study how boys and girls were brought up at that time, we appreciate how much more enlightened were the thinkers than the parents and teachers.

There were two main types of education in England in the Middle Ages and through the Renaissance period. One type was designed for the production of an adequate number of officials to conduct the affairs of the community. A boy could gain such an education by attending a grammar school either as a fee-payer or as a "poor scholar", and by proceeding to university either as a private student or as a scholarship holder, or as the protegé of a rich nobleman, priest, or tradesman. Although ostensibly aiming at the inculcation of godliness and wisdom—for there was always the chance of an occasional future bishop emerging—this type of education was basically utilitarian in its concentration on the Latin tongue, the official international language, for much the same reason that the three Rs are stressed to-day. The boy studied Latin from the age of seven or even earlier, and by the time he reached university he could read, write, speak, and argue in Latin, but had learned little of his contemporary world because his reading was limited to religious doctrine and the inaccurate, out-of-date histories and geographies of the ancients.

The second type of education was the training of the young gentleman and gentlewoman in noble households. This education

21

in chivalry was a severe, often cruel, process. The young people of a noble family were sent off to another castle or manor house for several years, and it was customary that they should be treated at first as menials in the household, only gradually being admitted to the activities and pursuits of the family itself. Thus they learnt through experience the routine and problems of running a large household and estate, and they became adept by practice in the skills and accomplishments of lords and their ladies—hawking, dancing, dicing, "making a leg", and "riding the high horse". Manners, morals, and religion were learnt by habituation rather than by instruction. Indeed, book-learning itself would play little part in a child's education, although it was deemed advisable for the little gentleman to acquire a fair familiarity with Latin, the language of State and Church.

Outside these two categories most children received no education at all except what they gained in the normal battle of life— through family chores and duties, and through the experience of learning a job, either as apprentice to trade or industry, or as farm labourer or servant.

Our brief survey of English educational thought before 1800 can include only those leading works which have gained wide recognition. The humanists of the Renaissance produced the first great educational literature. The group of great men who developed their ideas at the end of the fifteenth century were not all English, but several of them belonged to the circle inspired by John Colet and Sir Thomas More. These two, the one a priest and an Oxford don, the other a noble scholar, deserve recognition as educators although they wrote little specifically on the subject.

John Colet (1467-1515) set an example in his personal life and attitude to the clerics and teachers of his age. Although a Roman Catholic to the last, he is usually regarded as a leader of the Reformation in England in that he believed in the pursuit of learning with the object of gaining personal understanding of the Holy Word. He taught many young men to read and study deeply those Scriptures which the recent invention of printing had made more accessible to the community. His contribution to education is fourfold; first, in emphasising the need for personal thought and judgment based on systematic study; second, in setting an example in simple, good, and kindly living during a period of exuberant luxury and extravagant vice; third, in giving inspiration to a multitude of students such as Erasmus, the Dutchman, and Vives, the Spaniard;

fourth, in founding St Paul's School. This school aimed to train boys in intelligent thought rather than in mere routine skill in reading and writing. However, they were to be taught by kindly methods in contrast to the harsh severity accepted as necessary at the time.

Colet's friend, Sir Thomas More, brought the spirit of the Italian Renaissance into English lay society. While fostering the appreciation of art and literature and of human achievement in general, More's attitude did not condone the extravagances of Southern Europe, but rather instigated the enjoyment of wide learning and experience. From this sprang speculation on the way towards the happier community—speculation which inevitably involved theories on the improvement of education. More's great work, *Utopia*, not only reflects his discipleship of Plato, but also points a firm way for English education. His insistence that children should be taught in their native tongue, and should learn to use it well, was reiterated by his disciples and widely accepted during the sixteenth century, so that by Shakespeare's time, England was ahead of the rest of Europe in this respect.

A member of More's pleasant household school made the first major contribution in English to educational literature. This book was *The Governour*, and the author, Sir Thomas Elyot (c. 1490-1546), a protegé of the great Cardinal Wolsey, who himself wrote an educational treatise and founded a college. Elyot wrote of the education of his own class of society—education for responsibility and leadership. He was not so much an innovator as an interpreter of classical thought, especially the ideas of Quintilian, who described the schooling of upper-class Roman boys.

Elyot's attitude reminds us that the best minds had already rejected the harsh methods prevalent in his day, and that language teaching was not intended to degenerate into the notorious "grammar grind". Elyot's scheme is based on the assumption that individuals differ in capacities and abilities, so that the education of those who will become officials and leaders of the State should be designed to allow these differences to be developed and fostered. Infant education should be based on the classical tradition—training in good habits, and protection from evil influences and extreme experiences. Greek and Latin were so important to the development of the young gentleman that teaching must begin at seven or even earlier. Petticoat influence should be removed at this stage and a gentle old scholar should guide the boy through his learning, making study enjoyable but insisting on fluency in Latin speech. Elyot stresses the importance of Greek, even at this early stage, and, indeed, his mention of music and gymnastic indicates his allegiance to the great Greeks, but reminds us that he and many of his successors ignored the unbalancing of the Greek curriculum by their imposition of a heavy language requirement.

In adolescence, however, the boy should take up logic, rhetoric, geography, and, later, history and philosophy—all to help in the pursuit of the wisdom of the ancients by interpreting truly their writings. The tutor should not only demand and exemplify the highest conduct, but would also teach far more than mere language rules and techniques. Elyot deplores the low state of the teacher of his day, and puts forward the evergreen argument that if payments were higher, quality would improve.

Roger Ascham (1515-68), a Yorkshireman, gave us our next considerable educational writing. He inherited the Colet-More-Elyot tradition and sought to explain how Greek and Latin could be made truly educative. He was at one time tutor to Princess Elizabeth, and served her as a secretary after her accession to the throne. In his *Scholemaster*, not published until after his death, he argues that facility in the classical languages should lead not only to the imitation of good style, but to the more important search for worthy ideas. He gives practical suggestions on methods and material for the teaching of Latin in the grammar school. He advocates mild discipline, in fact, the school should be "a sanctuary against fear". Several treatises in similar vein appeared in the course of the next century.

One of the most interesting writers is Richard Mulcaster (1530-1611) who inherited the humanist tradition not only in his own education, which made him a noted scholar in Greek and Hebrew, but also in his Mastership of Colet's own school. While insisting on a high standard in Latin, Greek, and Hebrew, Mulcaster emphasised much more strongly than his precursors the need for the good teaching of English. Indeed, it appears at this stage of history that he made a great stride forward in advocating and practising the postponement of other languages for several years in order to give time to the teaching of English.[1] An important factor in this modification of opinion was the growth of nationalism in Elizabethan times. A somewhat awe-inspiring schoolmaster, Mulcaster nevertheless believed that children need not find learning

[1] Mulcaster, R., *The Elementarie*, 1582.

painful—a good teacher ought to be able to maintain high standards without pressing his pupils too hard or treating them harshly.

He regards the training of teachers as essential and he repeats Elyot's plea for the raising of the teacher's status. In many ways Mulcaster has a better understanding of classical education than his predecessors, for he recognises the true function of gymnastic, and, later, mathematics, while in his own school rhetoric was practised in the form of drama and mime. Moreover, he recognises, with More, that girls should be educated, and even puts forward the idea of education for all.

During the latter part of Mulcaster's career, a new spirit was growing in English life and thought, a spirit caught and fostered by his contemporary, Sir Francis Bacon. Before considering the latter's contribution, however, it is necessary to indicate that many educational writers of the seventeenth century did little more than repeat, or very slightly modify, the ideas of Tudor writers on upbringing and schooling. Thus the Leicestershire schoolmaster, John Brinsley (1585-1665), put forward, in his three books, ideas expressed by one or another of his precursors. His curriculum was limited to Latin, Greek, Hebrew, and Religion, with attention to English and arithmetic. His methods were kindly, his aim true understanding rather than rote learning, and his complaint the ignorance and severity of contemporary schoolmasters. The main signs of a slight movement forward are, first, his insistence that good methods and "a right order" of teaching could be taught to intending schoolmasters,[1] and, second, his concern for the health and welfare of his individual pupils. His description of the condition in which some boys arrived at school after long walks in English winter weather, is evidence that many boys from humble homes were attending grammar schools by this time.

Even without the evidence we have of the foundation of many new grammar schools, we should be able to assume from hints given by other writers that more and more boys were attending schools. One sign of the prosperity of the public schools is that they gained the service of eminent men such as Sir Henry Wooton (1565-1639), who, as Provost of Eton, drew to the school many rich and noble boys who might have remained at home in an earlier age. Although in touch with the new lines of thought—being a friend of Bacon— his brief writings on education express no objection to the traditional curriculum. We can only assume, through his references to

[1] Brinsley, J., *A Consolation for our Grammar Schooles*, 1622.

contemporary artistic, literary, and scientific studies, that he probably enabled his pupils to follow these pursuits according to their interests. The great Boyle and other scientists were at Eton during his headship. The main indication of progressive thought in his writing is his view that even in a large school with large classes, it is possible and necessary for teachers to study the needs, capacities, and characteristics of individual pupils. With this end in view his custom was to invite boys to meals in his own house.

The many new and flourishing private schools may possibly have set in motion the slow encroachment of "modern" subjects in the curriculum. They were not bound by statutes to Greek and Latin, but on the other hand their patrons demanded the recognised education of the times for their boys. Thus we find a popular, much travelled master such as Thomas Farnaby (1575-1647) writing classics textbooks instead of breaking new ground with a modern geography book, while even Samuel Hartlib (1600-62), who is usually considered an apostle of the new education, wrote *A True and Readie Way to learn the Latin Tongue*, for which he sought inspiration from the old humanists such as Montaigne.

The most famous of all of these traditionalists is John Milton (1608-74), the poet, who, with hardly a year's experience of teaching a small class of children, was persuaded by Hartlib to write an essay on education. This famous *Tractate of Education*, published in 1644, ignores the education of girls and omits primary education. This is perhaps as well, for Milton's curriculum for boys from twelve to sixteen is dominated by the classical languages. While paying lip service to the value of other subjects—mathematics, science, agriculture, and geography—he envisages no other way of learning them than through the writings of the ancients. Not until after the age when most children now leave school would Milton's pupils enjoy those practical studies and real experiences which later theories emphasised as essential to basic education. Yet Milton is usually quoted as the advocate of a balanced liberal education. Such a reputation is not justified by his *Tractate* as a whole, but may perhaps be allowed to rest on the few well-expressed comments which modern educators so love to quote. It is certain that he knew of the new ideas on curriculum and method, and he may even have tried them out himself. In another ten years' time he might have written an essay worthy to rank with his poetry.

In spite of the growing popularity of the new ideas and new subjects, the old attitude still persisted; *Lily's Grammar* (written by

Colet, Erasmus, and Headmaster Lily) was still the chief school textbook. Die-hard schoolmasters wrote on education in the old vein—Obadiah Walker, for instance, whose publication of 1673, *Of Education, especially of Young Gentlemen*, advocating by no means gentle methods to achieve high standards in the classics, was reprinted several times in the eighteenth century. If the publishers found this profitable we may assume that many a Georgian teacher absorbed this advice.

Even new ventures, new educational experiments founded on the new scientific spirit, often felt the dead hand of tradition. For instance, Christ's Hospital Mathematical School was founded in mid-century to teach future seamen modern subjects, but the pilots of the experiment insisted that the necessary scientific textbooks should be written in Latin, and that ancient Latin histories and geographies should be studied.

Enough has now been said about this phase of educational thought and practice to show how that which was new and fresh in the days of Colet had now become a virtual impediment to progress. Colet and his kind had sought to restore the Greek idea of liberal education by giving the youngster the tools with which he could fashion his own mind and eventually pursue truth and gain judgment by the intellectual processes demonstrated in the best of the classical authors. That only the fittest could survive this process is a reflection, not on the imagination of its English pioneers, but rather on the inadequacies of the human material, whether pupil or teacher, and on the absence of a science of child psychology, or, indeed, of any really organised science.

To find the entry of science to the educational scene we must return to Sir Francis Bacon (1561-1626) and his influence on seventeenth-century thought. Bacon was no great philosopher, but he was an intelligent, quick-witted man of the world and a statesman who made something of a hobby of scholarship. His successful efforts to become leader of an English intelligentsia may well have served to compensate for the frustration and downfall awaiting any unwary Elizabethan politician. His first ten essays— including *Of Study*—were published the year he became an M.P. The following year, 1598, he was arrested for debt. Real political success did not come until the reign of James I. *Advancement of Learning* was published in 1605, two years after he received his knighthood; *Novum Organum* appeared three years after his rise to the Lord Chancellorship. Within a few months he was dismissed in disgrace, and spent his last years in retirement. During the next three years he started, but left unfinished, *New Atlantis*, a sketch of an ideal state. He also prepared an augmented version of *Advancement of Learning* in Latin. Undoubtedly this latter publication was instrumental in spreading his influence throughout Europe, Latin being the universal language, but there are other reasons for the recognition he gained.

The western world was, in fact, just ready to take up a new attitude towards the natural environment which had assumed a growing importance since men had travelled, discovered, and conquered almost to the ends of the earth, and in the process, had proven true those scientific theories of old pioneer scientists—Roger Bacon, Copernicus, Galileo, and their kind. A great deal of information about the natural world had been collected, but it was unchecked, unclassified, unusable. Now came a recognised leader of men in both worldly and intellectual spheres, proclaiming that scholars were too preoccupied with literature dating back to an earlier stage of human knowledge and concentrating on verbal methods of developing the human mind. Scholars need not be ashamed to turn to humbler human experiences for the beginning of knowledge. To students on the Continent, Bacon was indisputably a scholar in the accepted sense, and yet one who could show a new attitude to natural phenomena to be scholarly. His writings expressed ably and with vigour the need of the contemporary world for scientific research. It was inspiring to be told that the discovery of the true nature of God's work would involve the highest in man's intellect. It was interesting to follow the writer's methods of careful observations of the exact facts of natural phenomena; it was exciting to try experiments with natural objects.

To students in England, and to Bacon's personal acquaintances, he was much more than a convincing writer, he was a leader, an enthusiast who showed the way. Like greater scientists of history he lost his life through experiment. During a coach drive on a snowy day he wondered whether snow would preserve meat. Without more ado he stopped to buy a hen, had it drawn by the woman vendor, and then stuffed the body with snow with his own hands. He caught a chill from which he did not recover. This was the spirit which later moved young Oxford students to pursue their modest scientific work as a hobby, and to meet for informal discussions from time to time. More conservative elements in the community looked askance at their wildness, especially when they ventured to predict the blessings science would bring—as when John Wilkins, Oxford don, wrote with gusto on the various possible ways of reaching the moon. However, these "cranks" and their successors were eventually recognised as serious contributors to human knowledge, by the granting of the Royal Society's charter in 1662. Throughout this period, teachers and educational thinkers were among those who gave keen support to the movement.

Largely owing to the activities of the same Samuel Hartlib mentioned earlier, the middle of the century is rich in educational writings which reflect the new attitude towards knowledge and learning. Their limited impact on prevailing practice is explained partly by the strength of tradition and partly by the accidents of history. The outbreak of the Civil War caused the abandonment of ambitious plans designed to reform the whole of education. The Restoration brought to an end the moderate change and experiment which was developing well during the Commonwealth period.

Nevertheless, this phase of educational thought has great significance. Its strength lies not so much in its immediate derivation from Baconian ideas, but rather in its growth under a foreign stimulus. It will be remembered that hitherto short shrift has been given to foreign thinkers, even if they developed their ideas in England—as, for instance, Erasmus and Vives. In the case of Hartlib and his friend, Comenius, however, an exception must be made because they are the chief instigators of the plans for the reform of education.

Comenius (1592—c. 1670), a Moravian exile, had won fame as an educator through a Latin textbook he devised to make learning easier and to give elementary knowledge of natural phenomena. A keen disciple of Bacon, he found himself working out in his mind an impossibly ambitious and visionary scheme for the betterment of all mankind by education. Hartlib was a Pole who had settled in England and had been instrumental in getting Comenius's textbook published in England. Having experimented in running a private school, he was more than a little interested in the ideas mentioned to him confidentially by Comenius in his letters. He had already met John Dury, a Scotsman who was working for the unification of the Protestant churches, the reform of schools, and the establishment of teacher training. Thus, when Comenius described his *Pansophia*, Hartlib published a resumé of it in this country—incidentally, without the author's permission.

This *Praeludia* of 1637 aroused an interest which grew so much in the next four years that Comenius came to England in 1641 to lead his many supporters in the establishment of a Pansophic College—Bacon's Solomon's House—and in the foundation of enough schools to educate all English children. His great vision was of a world united in brotherhood by a universal knowledge of nature, men, and things, a state to be brought about by a "Universal College" where all knowledge could be collected and classified and where teachers could be trained, "Universal Books", to be written by teams of scholars on all subjects and in all languages, "Universal Schools"—education for all, men and women alike, and a "Universal Language", a new international language to be invented to replace Latin.

The events of history, and the English concentration on science itself, prevented the extensive circulation of Comenius's greatest work on education—the *Didactica Magna*, a lifelong task. As the ideas in practical teaching were thus lost to us, it is not relevant to consider them. It is sufficient to say that the best of English writers put forward some of his main points—the need for gentleness and love in teaching rather than cruelty, the desirability of good physical conditions in the school, the need for the widening of the curriculum, the need for teaching the vernacular at the elementary stage, the need for sense experience—following Bacon—as the basis of all learning; perhaps, above all, the need for teacher training and the development of a didactic art—the right way of teaching.

Among the English disciples of Comenius there were others besides Hartlib and Dury who wrote articles and treatises which may have helped many a schoolmaster to teach better. One of the best known is Hezekiah Woodward (1590-1675), a Puritan divine, who wrote *Of a Child's Portion* and several other books in which many Comenian ideas are accepted and confirmed. Another was Sir William Petty (1623-87), a brilliant, scientifically-minded administrator, who, while still a young man, wrote for Hartlib an article outlining a Comenian type of education. Petty also indicated in his diaries that he believed in a wide curriculum for both boys and girls. Probably as a result of these works the idea of universal education was well known in this country by the end of the century when, in 1698, the Society for the Propagation of Christian Knowledge was formed with the object of setting up schools for poor children. Unfortunately, the curriculum of these schools was restricted to the teaching of reading, religion, and some simple handwork.

John Locke

In the meantime one of the most famous English educational thinkers was developing his ideas and writing a great philosophical work, *Essay on the Human Understanding*. John Locke (1632-1704) combined a medical man's interest in physical welfare with a scientist's enthusiasm for new knowledge. Locke suffered the traditional gentlemanly education, and as a result, hated school and despised universities. He became involved in political activities, not through real interest but through the influence of his friend and patron, the Earl of Shaftesbury, whose own disgrace led to Locke's exile on the Continent for several years. He wrote most of his *Essay* during this time, and also wrote to a friend in England those letters which were eventually put into book form, the famous *Thoughts on Education.*

Locke's ideas demand fuller consideration than those of earlier writers because, as he was a famous philosopher, his educational doctrine was recognised and highly respected throughout the eighteenth century, although it is to be feared that few teachers and tutors carried out these ideas in practice.

While there are indications in his non-educational writings that Locke recognised the need for universal education, his *Thoughts* are on the education of young gentlemen. His short essay on *Working Schools* does not persuade us that his sympathy with the poor was either deep or understanding. He suggests that poor schoolchildren should be fed on water gruel and should work at some industry part of the day to minimise the cost of education to the community.

Like Comenius and all Baconian realists, Locke emphasises the function of individual experience in building up knowledge and human powers. Thus education should be concerned with the organisation of experience. "Nine parts of ten are what they are by their Education", writes Locke. Educative experiences should be physical as well as mental and spiritual, he argues. "A sound Mind in a sound Body" are the opening words of his *Thoughts*.

Early Lockian education is mainly a question of training in good habits, physical, mental, moral, and social. This was already a very old idea handed down from Plato, but Locke added his own unique contribution by suggesting that habit formation should involve a "hardening process". This was partly a shaft aimed at the careless, luxury-living parents of the time, and partly a way of developing character as well as health. Unhygienic, elaborate clothes were to be dispensed with—in fact, the child should have thin, simple clothes, a hard bed, and a frugal diet. He was to be made tough and adaptable by wearing leaky shoes, by missing meals, by being aroused suddenly from sleep, and by being confronted with ugly and frightening objects.

Even when very young, the boy could be trained to think and reason about the events and problems of his daily life. "When I talk of reasoning," writes Locke, "I do not intend any other but such as is suited to the child's capacity and apprehension". While the boy's life should be simple to the point of austerity and discomfort, he should, at the same time, have a full range of social experiences within the home as he grows from infancy. While the main aims of education are virtue and wisdom, breeding comes next, before the acquisition of knowledge. In days of exaggeration and affectation, Locke hoped to see a younger generation with simple, easy good manners. The home atmosphere was to be free and happy, for although a father should inspire "awe" in his children, there should be no harshness—in fact, neither punishments nor rewards, which lead to deceit and to good behaviour for the wrong motives. An important factor in the development of children was the free play which should be encouraged by parents or tutors, especially in the direction of "educational" activities. All these requirements placed a great responsibility on home and teachers. Early childhood was to be protected from undesirable influences in the outside world—the coarse speech and rough behaviour of servants, the affectations, the exaggerations of polite society, the grossness and immorality which was common at all social levels. Locke's aim was a self-disciplined, rather austere, yet socially poised and correct, Christian gentleman. Thus the influence of father and tutor was all important. Both were to set the boy the highest examples of conduct and attitude. The tutor should be not only a fine scholar, but also a man of great integrity who had already faced and resisted worldly temptations. One of his main tasks would be to introduce the adolescent to the world, for, writes Locke, "The only fence against the world is a thorough knowledge of it".

Learning, the least important aim of education, was to be concentrated on those parts of human knowledge most relevant to contemporary life. Early learning was to be as far as possible through experience—now called "activity methods"—and the work was to be arranged and timed so that the pupil attempted only that which was within his capacity. Moreover, studies were to be made enjoyable, although good habits were to be inculcated from the first—the pen was to be held in a certain way for writing; reading was to be confined to moral stories and books expressing noble ideas in the best literary style. Training in speaking in English and French should come quite early in childhood. This introduction of French conversation is an innovation which reflects a new contemporary interest. Many gentlemen had spent years of exile in France and many Frenchmen came to England during the eighteenth century. Some of these latter became teachers of French, visiting both private and grammar schools, to teach those children whose parents wished them to have this extra accomplishment.

It was too early for the complete rejection of Latin. Locke describes it as "necessary to a gentleman", but suggests that while learning Latin, boys could learn "parts of knowledge of things that fall under the senses". He makes no acknowledgment to Comenius or other writers for this idea. The grammar and compositions, belonging to traditional Latin teaching, ought to be left to the mature student, in Locke's opinion.

Locke's realist attitude is exemplified by his curriculum. The reduction of time given to Latin, Greek, and Hebrew should facilitate the introduction of mathematics, contemporary history and geography, and elementary science, but his comments on the content and methods to be used indicate an understanding of the development of science more limited than that of Bacon, and an appreciation of the abilities and needs of children far inferior to that of Comenius. Apparently little more than reading facts and listening to lectures is involved during childhood and adolescence. The young man, however, may try a variety of crafts, gardening, iron-work, carpentry, engraving, stone-polishing, optical-glass polishing, and accountancy. These pursuits are not suggested for the demonstration of scientific principles but for the profitable use of leisure time in this era of gaming and profligacy. Social accomplishments, however, were to have a positive value, particularly dancing, which, according to Locke, was essential throughout education. Locke's attitude to professionalism in music, fencing, riding, and craftwork indicates the incompleteness of his break with the classical tradition.

Apart from his plea for "well regulated liberty" in child education, Locke's most important contribution to educational thought is perhaps his insistence on the need for each person to train his own "understanding" by constant practice in the comparing, contrasting, and weighing up of other men's ideas and points of view, whether written or spoken, whether ancient or contemporary.

Before the trends of thought on education in 1800 can be appreciated, the influence of foreign writers of the eighteenth century must be taken into account. During the century many translations, particularly from the French, were published in this country and thus played their part, not only in provoking thought on education, but also in stimulating a wider interest in the contemporary world and its many tongues. French and geography were established as of educational import by the end of the century.

Of the several writers on education two are particularly worthy of mention in this brief survey. During the first part of the century the writings of Fénelon (1651-1715) served as a kind of complement to Locke's *Thoughts*. Whereas Locke was mainly concerned with the education of boys, Fénelon's *Traité de l'Education des Filles* suggested how girls could be educated to become intelligent, modest, prudent, and domesticated wives and mothers and yet, at the same time, acquire facility in polite conversation and fashionable accomplishments. His arguments favoured a wider curriculum—both intellectual and practical—than had hitherto prevailed, and it is not surprising that English ladies took their *Traité* to their bosoms and eventually produced their own imitations and interpretations.

To the second half of the century belongs the name of Jean Jacques Rousseau (1712-78), whose two main works, *The Social Contract* and *Emile*, were translated into English soon after their publication in 1762. Although these works aroused storms of controversy, reflected in much of the non-educational literature of the period, the full appreciation of their educational significance had to await another era. Their main value at that time was in shattering complacency and stimulating critical thought, which soon led to the evaluating of the nation's scrappy and outworn educational system—if such it could be called.

Rousseau, by his own confession, rose from poor apprentice to famous savant by a series of episodes, mostly unedifying and sometimes sordid. His experience, his undoubted intelligence, and his mercurial temperament led him to two main conclusions about human life. These are expressed pithily and pertinently in the opening words of his two major works. "Man is born free, but everywhere he is in chains," he thunders in *The Social Contract*. "Everything is good as it comes from the hand of God. Men meddle with it and it becomes evil," he complains in *Emile*.

Rousseau was an admirer and disciple of Locke, and the difference between their educational ideas is not as great as some writers have suggested. Much of *Emile* is a restatement of "The great Mr Locke's" views, but Rousseau chose to hammer home his points, particularly the pupil-teacher relationship and the nature of "experience" by suggesting conditions so extreme as to seem contradictory to the common sense of Locke.

Accepting Locke's argument that human beings are, from birth, moulded by their experience, Rousseau developed his concept of the "heavy yoke of necessity". Man may be born free, but immediately after birth his contacts with the physical world begin to impress upon him that he is no longer free. He is controlled by nature—by time, space, substance, the laws of science—and by his own human nature. These chains he cannot escape, so that part of his education, his maturing, is learning how far they are inescapable, of learning how to accept these controls without bitterness and frustration in order that his spirit may concentrate on higher matters. Part of his natural environment is, of course, the rest of mankind.

In *The Social Contract* Rousseau is concerned with the degree to which the individual should accept philosophically the control of his life by other men. In a State where tyranny and serfdom prevailed, and where the abuse and persecution of men by other men was common at all levels of society, the individual's chance of achieving a mature personality was indeed small. Most people, weighed down by their chains, could not even obtain enough food. How could they resign themselves to such a burden? Why should they, when others had more than enough? Man's ability to throw off the chains of the physical environment may be limited, but he has the power to cast off the shackles forged by his fellows. First he must reconstitute the society in which he lives. He must enter into an agreement with the rest of the community that all members must have equal opportunity of freedom. The chains forged by men to control men must be reduced to the slenderest needed to bind together an orderly society. In fact, each man must voluntarily limit his own freedom in order to live in society without encroaching on the freedom of his neighbours. Thus he makes the social contract, so that, in resigning himself to his "burden of necessity", he may seek emotional and intellectual maturity and enjoy the freedom from want and fear which is his birthright.

Having shown the evils of contemporary society to be the root of mankind's plight, Rousseau, in *Emile*, gives to the educator the task of producing the mature citizens of the *Contract*. Contemporary education, except the informal training of the labourer's home, was arid and harmful. Years earlier he had condemned the "absurd" system of education which served only "to adorn our wit and corrupt our judgment",[1] and now he described a kind of education which, being based not on books and words but on real experience, would gradually give the young human being an intellectual understanding of the limits of his bondage and of his freedom. Although from the orthodox readers' viewpoint a childhood without book-learning would be sadly mis-spent, Rousseau claims that the abolition of formal teaching for the first twelve years would leave time for the child to learn through real experience the true weight of the "yoke of necessity". Although Rousseau asserts that Locke was wrong in wishing to train the reason in childhood, each experiment he himself would "stage-manage" for the pupil was designed to teach a lesson by making the youngster think for himself. "I must control myself if I am not to be controlled by things and men", the child will decide as a result of his experiences in carefully contrived situations. Having been subjected to Locke's "hardening process", he will soon realise that he may have the freedom of health and strength if only he follows certain rules of eating, sleeping, and exercising. He can enjoy measures of comfort and pleasure if he complies with rules of common sense and courtesy. If he breaks a window, he must endure the draught and discomfort; if he destroys the gardener's prize beans, he must suffer the sorrow of seeing his own garden desecrated. In stressing, like Locke, the importance of sense experience in education, Rousseau overlooked that such lessons were not learned entirely through the senses and emotions. If the intellect were not brought to bear on experience, the same mistake would be repeated until the intellect were fit to cope with it. Learning at this level is not a mere matter of reflexes, although "Man's first reason is a reason of sense-experience".[2]

In emphasising that personal investigation and exploration of the environment is an essential part of education, Rousseau painted the picture of a country estate with a lone pupil and a solitary tutor. This has been interpreted as a withdrawing of the child from society until the normal years of schooling are practically over. Yet the

---

[1] *Discourse on the Arts of Sciences*, 1750, p. 147.
[2] Rousseau, J. J., *Emile*, p. 90, Everyman Edition.

human element is always present in Emile's environment; it is only the vicious society of Rousseau's France that is excluded. True, no mention is made of the impeccable family which always seems to hover in the background of Locke's *Thoughts*, but such a family was created by Rousseau in another book, *La Nouvelle Hélorise*. This family—rather more acceptable than Locke's, because the mother is credited with intelligence—must be taken into account in evaluating Rousseau's ideas on education.

Thinking Englishmen found many disturbing—even shocking—concepts in Rousseau's writings. If there were no original sin, if the child were born good and his first impulses were always right, how could they condone the harsh, cruel discipline still imposed in a great many schools? If it were true that children developed best in following their own interests, running, playing, exploring the land-scape, trying to make things, then of what use was an education which still gave most time to Latin and Greek and none at all to science, handicraft, and physical exercise? If it were true that the evils and abuses of the day could be avoided in a society of well-educated people, how could they tolerate the lack of provision of education for millions of Englishmen?

Eighteenth Century Educational Ideas

Locke's influence on later minor educational writers was wide-spread and long-lived, but it was rarely profound. Many works, in the first half of the century, repeat Lockian strictures on the need for habit training, on the evils of school education, on the ineffi-cacy of harsh methods, and on the value of a wider curriculum. Occasionally, the dangers of untrained judgment are mentioned. By mid-century the time was ripe for change and criticism. One important new development was the growing concern for girls' education—in which Locke had shown no interest. One of the earliest attempts to break the spell of Locke was Thomas Sheridan's contention that the philosopher's theory was "only an attempt to mend and patch our present systems". The book, *British Educa-tion*, in which this was written, was published in 1756, six years before Rousseau's *The Social Contract* and *Emile* burst upon the world. Some of Sheridan's ideas appear to be related to those of Hartlib's circle, a century earlier. He writes of a "right" way of education and suggests a wide curriculum based on English for the elementary school, and vocational training in a kind of multi-lateral secondary school, which should provide preparatory courses for the Law, the Army, the Church, Estate Management, and Trade. By the time his *Plan of Education* appeared in 1769, Rousseau had denounced the decadence of society, but Sheridan's views on the relationship of State and education seem to be an independent and genuine development of his former thesis. He regards Lockian methods as inadequate for the production of good citizens.

Although in the second half of the century several fine thinkers —David Williams, John Ash, and Joseph Priestley among them— re-stated Locke's ideas, the stimulus given by Rousseau to educational thought had caused movements both to the right and to the left. Representatives of the traditionalists are Vicesimus Knox and William Barrow, who, at the end of the century, favoured a return to the classical curriculum and its aims. The innovators were people like the Edgeworths and their friends who were prepared to try out new ideas and to introduce a wide range of activities into education.

SUGGESTIONS FOR FURTHER READING

Curtis and Boultwood, *A Short History of Educational Ideas*, 4th edition, U.T.P., 1965. Chapters VI, VIII, IX, X.

E. T. Campagnac, *Mulcaster's Elementarie*, Clarendon Press, 1920.

J. Needham, *The Teacher of Nations*, C.U.P., 1942.

J. Locke, *Some Thoughts on Education*, Ed. Quick, C.U.P., 1895 (or in Adamson's *Educational Writings of John Locke*, Longmans Green and Co., 1912).

W. Boyd, *From Locke to Montessori*, Harrap, 1917.

Emile for To-day, Heinemann, 1955.

Helen Wodehouse, *A Survey of the History of Education, Part I*, Arnold, 1925.

CHAPTER III

IDEAS ON STATE INTERVENTION IN EDUCATION

Although a few writers had referred to the advantages of universal education before the days of Comenius, it was not until his ideas were seized upon by a group of Englishmen in the 1630s that any significant body of opinion developed in favour of the setting up of a nation-wide school system. The great vision of Comenius—universal college, books, schools, and languages—has already been described. Samuel Hartlib won for Comenius a small but enthusiastic band of followers of varied religious and political convictions. From 1636 Hartlib and Dury, in correspondence with Comenius, worked as a team, Hartlib "the solicitor of human learning for the reformation of schooles" and Dury "to promote the councells of peace ecclesiastical". In 1640 the Speaker in his Sermon before the House of Commons, referred to the efforts of Hartlib and Dury and urged that their help be sought. Within four months Parliament had set up a Committee to enquire into schools. Comenius, hearing of this, told his friends, "They are eagerly debating on the reform of schools in the whole kingdom in a manner similar to that which my wishes tend, namely, that all young people should be instructed, none neglected".[1] Hartlib, representing a group of M.P.s, sent off an invitation to Comenius, who arrived in England in September 1641, believing that he had been invited officially by Parliament.

The outbreak of the Civil War the following year drove Comenius from England, and during the next few years education suffered through the dislocation and hazards of wartime.

Nevertheless, the Parliamentarian party gave attention to education in the areas which came under its control, using for this purpose funds drawn from the sequestered estates of their opponents. One of the earliest cases of this political intervention was in 1644 in Cheshire, where the local authorities were granted powers to eject all "scandalous" schoolmasters and to appoint their own candidates.[2] From 1649 onwards it seems that Parliament, opening with

[1] Young, *Comenius in England*, p. 63.
[2] Firth and Rait, *Acts and Ordinances of the Interregnum, 1642-1660*.

39

a discussion of education, gave much attention to the improvement and extension of schools and made grants of money. The Commissioners administering the funds of confiscated estates had power to found new schools,[1] and there was a similar development in Wales under the Commissioners for the Propagation of the Gospel in Wales.[2]

There is also evidence that the State, during the Commonwealth, encouraged educational writers, theorists, investigators, and research workers by granting money for suitable projects.[3]

After the Restoration, although Charles II was pleased to consider himself a patron of education and a founder of schools,[4] the extension of education was halted. Grammar schools fell into disfavour as likely breeding places for sedition, and there was no further use of public funds for elementary education. It was through individual philanthropy and by group endeavour that the new type of elementary school developed—the charity school of the eighteenth century. There were also many private schools and academies run illegally for a long time by Nonconformists of one kind and another.

Nevertheless, the seed had been sown in the field of educational ideas. In 1656 Harrington, in his *Oceania*, had affirmed that education was important for the well-being of the State and that the latter should make education compulsory and should control the schools through magistrates possessing power to punish parents who did not send their children to school. William Dell in the same period had asserted, in *The Right Reformation of Learning*, that education was the State's responsibility—that there should be more schools and a wider curriculum. George Snell, a schoolmaster, had written a treatise suggesting the setting up of a Standing Committee of State to deal with education—to superintend schools throughout the country and to found, in each large town, a college where all arts and sciences, including farming and hygiene, would be taught in English.

Although John Locke, while a young man, must have heard these suggestions discussed by his friends and acquaintances, his writings during the next three or four decades do not indicate that

---

[1] *E.g.* Halesowen, 1652.

[2] *E.g.* Merioneth.

[3] *E.g.* £100 and the cost of a journey to Scotland granted to Fitzpayne Fisher for the purpose of writing a treatise for use in schools. (*Calendar of State Papers, 1652.*)

[4] *E.g.* Bradford Grammar School and Christ's Hospital Mathematical School—but both had been founded earlier.

these ideas had ever appealed to him. His short essay on *Working Schools* recommended not national effort but local enterprise. Moreover, the reasons for the setting up of parish working schools were to be economic rather than philosophic or philanthropic. Far too many people lived "on the parish", in Locke's opinion. Parochial authorities could reduce the outlay on "relief" by freeing poor parents from the burden of looking after their children, so that mothers could work, and fathers could make earnings go further. The schools were to be for those children of three to fourteen, who belonged to families seeking "relief". Money given to parents was often spent at the alehouse, but the provision of supervision and food for the children instead of financial aid, would obviate this problem.

Thus the children would come regularly to school because they needed the food provided there—although this was but bread and water. They would be required to attend Church on Sundays and to work at a money-earning occupation on week-days—at spinning, knitting, or other handicrafts, according to the materials and trades of the local area. This kind of life would not only enable the school to produce marketable goods, but would also give the children training in good habits, morals, and working methods. Thus the schools would be self-supporting, and their pupils would become wage-earners rather than relief-drawers. The guardians of the poor should direct the schools and should pay teachers' salaries out of the poor rate. Locke's mention of "schoolmasters or dames" seems to indicate that reading and writing should be taught.

Public responsibility should extend to a kind of "after-care". The gentlemen, farmers, and craftsmen of the district should be required to take apprentices from the working schools without premium. As the boys would be bound to their masters until they were twenty-three, they would thus give several years of trained, skilled work which would "make amends for the usual sums". An interesting additional function of the schools would be to teach crafts to any adults who might wish to learn. Materials for all vocational activities should be provided from public funds.

Although Locke's suggestions for this limited measure of public education were not followed, most of the charity schools set up from this time onwards did attempt to provide some vocational training. Nearly a century later the name "working schools" was revived by the redoubtable Mrs Trimmer—but her schools were still "private" in origin and supervision. The development of elementary education through private effort during that century may owe something to the State's indirect subsidising of private endowment through the functioning of the Mortmain Act of 1696. This Act, in restoring the King's power to grant "licences in Mortmain", pointed out "the advantages to learning of founding and granting lands to colleges and schools". As a result, many men during the next forty years sought licences to bequeath land and property for the foundation of schools, thereby gaining exemption from taxation on that property. Thus many endowed, non-classical schools came into existence before 1736, when another Mortmain Act tightened up the procedure of making gifts for charitable purposes "on account of the great increase in the alienations made by languishing and dying persons to the disinherision of their lawful heirs".

The eighteenth century was not undisturbed by controversy on the whole question of extending education. No doubt there were many who were as unfavourably impressed by the charity school movement as Bernard de Mandeville, a Dutchman, who published an essay on that subject in 1723.[1] Not only did he consider the schools merely "in fashion the same as hooped petticoats", he also thought they would breed vice and discontent among the lower classes, whose continued subservience and honesty—best preserved by ignorance—were esential to the social and economic stability of the nation. His comments on the ulterior motives of the clergy obviously rest on personal prejudice, but he spoke for many Englishmen when he asserted, "Nothing should be taught for nothing but at Church".

Rousseau's publications of 1762, although soon translated, gave no clear-cut directive on the question of State intervention in education. The *Contract* and *Emile* suggested that as society was so decadent, no education provided by its Government could avoid inculcating the old fallacies which had helped to bring about this condition. There is no doubt, however, that Rousseau believed State education to be essential, but he found himself in the same cleft stick as Plato when faced with the problem of first bringing about reform or revolution in society. Of public education in Geneva, his native State, he wrote, "I received this public education, not indeed in the shape of formal instruction, but of traditions and maxims which, however, handed on from generation to generation, gave to my early boyhood the knowledge which it required and the

[1] Included in *Fable of the Bees or Private Vices versus Public Benefits.*

feeling which it needed".[1] Needless to say, he was not so critical of Genevan society as he was of Louis XIV's France. Ten years after *Emile* appeared, he wrote more about public education in his *Consideration on the Government of Poland*. Had these views been made known in England they might have won more converts than did his earlier works. As his main object was to persuade Poland to inculcate Polish nationalism, he gave little attention to the question of universal schools, but he insisted that a committee of the State's best men should be set up to devise and conduct a national system of education, and to be responsible for the employment of teachers and the provision of schools and games centres. It is interesting that he saw the State school teacher as a married man "distinguished for character and probity as well as for good sense and intelligence and destined after a certain period for other occupations not more important or more honourable—for that is not possible—but less exacting and of greater repute".

As Emile's tutor was not unlike Locke's paragon in learning, devotion, and understanding, it is not surprising that Rousseau was concerned for the status of the teaching profession as a whole. In England, ideas on the extension of education were similarly linked with pleas for improvement in the quality and status of teachers. It was no foreign inspiration which caused Oliver Goldsmith to write, "The care of our children, is it below the State? . . . For the State to take charge of all its children as in Persia or Sparta, might at present be inconvenient, but surely with great ease it might cast an eye to their instructors".[2]

During the second half of the century, English opinion in favour of a wider school system was led by several eminent thinkers who, although they might not agree as to ways and means of achieving this, were firm in their condemnation of the inadequacy of the existent provisions. A pioneer in this movement was Adam Smith (1723-90), whose views on education were but incidental in the economic theory for which he is remembered. After proceeding from a Scottish university to Oxford, he accepted the tutorship of a young nobleman whose educational trip to the Continent enabled Smith to meet some eminent thinkers, including Rousseau. He was a lifelong friend of the philosopher, Hume, and it is his influence rather than Rousseau's which can be traced in *The Wealth of Nations* which appeared, aften ten years' work, in 1776.

[1] Letter to Dr Tronchin, 1758.
[2] *The Bee and Other Essays* (1759), p. 130, O.U.P., 1914.

As a political economist, Smith advocated the performance by the Government of duties which could not be done so well by individuals. One of the duties he had in mind was the provision of education for the working classes, whose moral and physical deterioration Smith attributed to the deadening routine activities of the factory system, and the division of labour fostered by the Industrial Revolution. He believed that State education would build up resistance to superstition and "enthusiasm"; moreover, it would help poor people to become orderly and self-respecting. "They feel themselves each individually more respectable," he wrote, "and more likely to obtain the respect of their lawful superiors."

Adam Smith argued that an educated populace would be capable of recognising mischief-making propaganda and, therefore, would be unlikely to succumb to mass hysteria or to anti-Government agitation. "In free countries where the safety of government depends on favourable judgment, which the people may form of its conduct," he wrote, "it must surely be of the highest importance that they should not be disposed to judge rashly or capriciously concerning it."[1] It might well be assumed that Smith had in mind a full and thorough education for all, but in fact he suggested only the three R's and some physical occupation. He probably took the charity school as his model, for as an economist he was concerned with costs to the State. "For a very small expense," he asserted, "the public can facilitate, can encourage, and can even impose upon almost the whole body of the people, the necessity of acquiring those most essential parts of education."

He envisaged the setting up of small schools in parishes and districts, not free, but charging fees so low "that even a common labourer may afford it". Even as the parents should be required to make an effort, so should the teachers, who would receive only part of their salaries from public funds, the rest being covered by fees paid by their pupils. This measure to ensure that teachers did not neglect their work is, perhaps, a reflection on the average grammar school teacher of the period. There remained the problem of ensuring that pupils would attend schools. There was to be no immediate compulsion, but as each trade and profession would be required to establish an entrance examination, the parents would see the necessity for sending children to school.

[1] *The Wealth of Nations*, Book V, Chapter I.

During the two decades which followed the publication of Smith's major work, another movement for the education of the poor was launched and steered to success. The greatest Sunday School pioneer—although not the first—was Robert Raikes (1735-1811), a Gloucester publisher, perhaps the first man to use press propaganda for wide assaults on public opinion. Having penetrated the local gaols to help the prisoners, he became convinced that "extreme ignorance was the principal cause of those enormities which brought them to the deplorable situation precluding all hope of any lasting or real amendment from their punishment". Prevention, then, would be better than cure, so he considered the conditions of the children of the labouring classes—such children as those ragamuffins who disturbed his work by shouting and swearing outside his windows. By this time very few young people enjoyed the advantages of the apprenticeship system, which had previously guaranteed the survival of a partially-educated working class. As the new industries, such as the pin factories of Gloucester, claimed the children on week-days, Raikes ventured to collect groups together at the Cathedral on Sundays. Finding that the dispensation of sweets and small gifts won a relatively clean and subdued following, he determined to raise enough money "to procure masters and mistresses for a large number of children of both sexes to be educated".

From 1780, when Raikes's first school was opened in Sooty Alley, Gloucester, the rapid growth of Sunday education in the face of much criticism and opposition was proof enough, not only of the power of press propaganda but also of the general temper of the British people at this time. More education was desirable rather than dangerous. Elementary education would lead people back to piety and would encourage social regeneration. Whether Jean Jacques Rousseau or the growth of industrial population was the more influential in the development of this attitude matters less than that a philanthropic movement pointed the way to State participation in education. Raikes, by insisting on the need for paid professional teachers, set a standard which was not widely maintained. The remarkable collaboration of Church and Nonconformity in the Society for the Establishment of Sunday Schools in the Different Counties of England devoted some money to teachers' salaries, but there was a strong body of opinion in favour of voluntary instruction. In spite of the wider acceptance of the belief that all should learn to read the Bible, more liberal ideas on elementary education were not widespread even among those who worked on behalf of the charity and Sunday schools. Thus the Society for the Establishment of Sunday Schools forbade the teaching of writing and arithmetic on Sunday, although, eventually, these activities were permitted to adult students who had already learnt to read.

Some influential men were as hostile as Viscount Byng, who said in 1787, "I have met some of the newly-adopted Sunday Schools to-day . . . I am point blank against these institutions; the poor should not read, and of writing I never heard for them the use". Raikes himself envisaged no limits of caste or expediency. He employed many teachers and devised a monitorial system for the practising of elementary reading skills. He did not reach the idea of State education, but he knew that Sundays and odd minutes on week-days were inadequate for the fulfilment of his aim: "To raise up among the lowest of the people a new race taught at an early period the happiness of thinking on that which is good, and bringing those thoughts into action in the several duties which Christianity enjoys".

While Raikes and his like were pushing ahead with practical schemes for extending education, the intelligentsia disputed the question of the State's part in the instruction of its members. Thomas Paine, the famous author of *The Rights of Man* (1792), maintained in his treatise, "A nation under a well-regulated Government should permit none to remain uninstructed. It is monarchical and aristocratic government only that requires ignorance for its support".[1] Published at a time when the horrors of the French Revolution had produced the inevitable reaction in this country, the book was not likely to dispose the authorities favourably towards education, but Paine's arguments are interesting. Differentiating between Society and Government, he pointed out that the latter, although but an evil necessity, had great powers for good. Its duty was to choose right courses of action such as, in the case of education, an amendment of the Poor Law increasing relief to £4 a year per child up to the age of fourteen so long as these children were sent to school. Paine makes a nice discrimination between these poorest of the poor and a slightly higher social rank qualifying for additional poor relief to the tune of ten shillings a year each child for six years to pay school fees, and half a crown for paper and spelling books. It is perhaps not lacking in significance that even at the end of the century an advanced thinker did not suggest a full system of State education. He was content that

[1] *The Rights of Man*, Part II, Chapter V.

members of society should provide schools and the State's task was to devise means of filling them.

Paine, of Quaker upbringing and radical tendencies, had himself tried schoolmastering among a variety of other vocations. This may explain his attitude towards schools and the proposal of a scheme which would obviate the need for State ownership and control. The views he expressed on other aspects of polity, however, were extreme enough to involve his publishers and supporters in heavy penalties, but he himself slipped off to France where he was made a deputy to the National Convention of the revolutionary government. Thus it is probable that the average Englishman dismissed his suggestions on education along with his more combustible ideas.

Some of his main arguments, however, were circulated by a less dynamic writer who deprecated the use of violence in social and political reform. Yet William Godwin was both republican and atheist when he published, in 1793, his *Enquiry concerning Political Justice*, which won him fame and a small fortune. Godwin, son of a dissenting minister, had also taught in schools, but now, at thirty-seven, he was a member of a group of intellectuals—all radicals and free-thinkers—who were sympathetic towards the French revolutionaries. The *Enquiry* was subversive of all government and laws —even marriage, "the worst of all laws"—and its immunity from prosecution was due mainly to its cost, for, as Pitt commented to the Privy Council, "A three guinea book could never do much harm among those who had not three shillings to spare".

Godwin went even further than Paine in his distrust of the State. He admitted no hope of good proceeding from State effort and, therefore, he was violently opposed to State interference in education, even in a limited or indirect form. He disapproved of the control of a large proportion of schools by the Church of England and other denominations, but he considered the contemporary situation preferable to a State-controlled system. The inculcation of religious dogmas would be replaced by the imposition of party political dogmas. "Government will not fail to employ it to strengthen its hand and perpetuate its institutions," he wrote. "Their views as institutions of a system of education will not fail to be analogous to their views in their political capacity." [1] The development of free enquiry would be checked, and thus the

[1] *Political Justice*, Chapter II, p. 298.

individual's progress towards protection and happiness would be prevented.

Large schools and universities had already revealed the dangers which would be intensified in a national system. "They actively restrain the flights of the mind", Godwin asserted, "and fix it in the belief of exploded errors." "It has frequently been observed of universities . . . that the knowledge taught there is a century behind the knowledge which exists among unshackled and unprejudiced members of the same community."[1] He believed in the small school and individual tuition, for his concept of education was not free from Rousseau's influence. "The native activity of the mind" was to be stimulated, and this involved self-development. "This whole proposition of a national education", he claimed, "is founded upon a supposition . . . that unpatronified truth is inadequate to the purpose of enlightening mankind."[2]

Education proceeds in three ways, Godwin thinks, firstly through the normal fortuitous experiences and contacts of everyday life, secondly, by communication from teachers, and, thirdly, through living under a certain form of government, which experience in itself brings about a modification of ideas. Thus the teacher's function is all-important. He has the power to mould his pupils, but he also has the duty of providing an environment which will foster intellectual and moral development. He can awaken the desire for knowledge by the provision of proper motives. In helping the pupils to understand and appreciate their own motives, the teacher will intensify their power and so aid the pupils' natural "perfectibility". Godwin had no use for Rousseau's methods, which in a later work he dismissed as "a series of tricks, of which the master holds the wires, and the scholar is never to suspect in what manner they are moved".[3] At a time when the Sunday School movement was expanding by the extensive use of voluntary unskilled teaching, it is hardly surprising that Godwin could not see his ideal "preceptor" as a mass-produced, mass-controlled cog in a State machine.

The main theme of *Political Justice* was human equality, a doctrine which Godwin himself eventually rejected. The repercussions of its publication were many, but perhaps the most significant was the treatise by T. R. Malthus, published in 1798. This famous *Essay on Population* was a young Cambridge don's answer

---

[1] *Political Justice*, Chapter II, p. 294.
[2] *ibid.*, p. 296-7.
[3] *The Enquiries*, p. 106.

to Rousseau and Godwin, a refutation of their doctrine and at the same time a plea for universal education.

Malthus postulates the control of human societies by natural laws. There is a natural tendency for population to increase and strain the food resources of the community, but natural checks operate to equalise the situation. The death-rate increases through disease, malnutrition, dirt, overcrowding, wars, pestilence, and famine. Malthus did not state that poverty is necessary and incurable. He contended that it could be kept in bounds by individual effort and group common sense. He did not think the latter quality had been a characteristic of his own society. Benevolence and charity had been lavished so indiscriminately on the ignorant poor that their degeneration was accelerated by dependence and the lack of incentive to develop will-power and foresight. In the evils of the industrial areas, the natural law could be seen working. The nation was not achieving greater equality, but less, because the population was outstripping national resources. The only true remedy was to abolish the palliative of charity and to substitute the permanent asset of literacy. Only through education could the poor learn to fight for self-respect, self-regeneration, and self-support. "In their education, and in the circulation of those important political truths that most nearly concern them . . . are perhaps the only means of really raising their condition and of making them happier and more peaceful subjects." [1]

Malthus was extremely sceptical of the value of Sunday Schools, deeming it "a great national disgrace" that the education of the poor should be not only so inadequate in quality and quantity, but also in the hands of private individuals and organisations who could bias the teaching as they chose. Thus it seems clear that the political economist envisaged a State system of education. He had no fear lest learning should harm the country by breeding discontent. He had faith in the uplifting of the poorer classes through the enlightened efforts of its own individual members. It cannot be doubted that he spoke for many Englishmen and convinced many more.

The advocates of national education were not united in their motives and beliefs. Some were philanthropists, others economists, social reformers, and teachers. The untimely death of Mary Wollstoncraft Godwin in 1797 took from the scene of battle a brilliant mind whose *Vindication of the Rights of Women* (1792) included

[1] *Essay on Population*, Book IV, Chapter IX.

an appeal for co-educational national schools which would have better teaching than that dictated by parents, and smaller classes than those in profit-making private schools. She envisaged a wide curriculum, including nature study, history, elementary science, and plenty of physical exercise. The young Joseph Lancaster was making his own experiments in teaching at the turn of the century, and in his *Improvements in Education* (1803) blamed sectarian rivalries for the absence of a system of national education.

One of the most important names in the campaign is that of Jeremy Bentham (1748-1832), a political philosopher of some brilliance—he had learnt Latin at four years of age, and had graduated at fifteen. He was the first apostle of the cult known as Utilitarianism which was based on the assumption that human behaviour is determined by pain and pleasure. "They govern us in all we do, in all we say, in all we think", he asserts. "Every effort we make to throw off our subjection will serve but to demonstrate and confirm it." The subjection of man must be accepted as a basic principle, he maintains, and should be *used*, not avoided, in the task of improving human happiness. As men inevitably choose what seems to be the pleasant and avoid the unpleasant courses of action, social organisation must take advantage of this principle.

In his *Principles of Penal Law* of 1802, Bentham proposed that education provided by the State should be a means of showing people the alternatives to the "pleasures" of crime and immorality. "Education is only government acting by means of a domestic magistrate", he writes. ". . . but in requesting education as an indirect mode of preventing offences, it requires an essential reform. The most neglected class must become the principal object of care. The less parents are able to discharge this duty, the more necessary it is for the government to fulfil it. It ought not only to watch over orphans left in indigence, but also over the children whose parents no longer deserve the confidence of the law with regard to this important charge—over those who have already committed crimes, or who, destitute of protection and resources, are given up to all the seduction of misery. These classes, absolutely neglected in most States, become the hotbeds of crime."

During the next few years, Samuel Whitbread (1758-1815), Member of Parliament and brewery owner, worked out his ideas on Poor Law reform, and in 1807, when the menace of Napoleon was temporarily removed, he brought forward his Poor Law Bill, a comprehensive measure including the establishment of a system of free education. Prospects were bright and public interest high. The scheme of education was extracted and presented as a Parochial Schools Bill to provide two years' free education for children between seven and fourteen whose parents could not afford to pay fees. Unfortunately, the time proved unripe, but although Whitbread's scheme was dropped, there were now plenty of other enthusiasts to carry on the struggle.

Jeremy Bentham proposed in 1809 that the vote should be denied those who could not read. He was a determined advocate of Parliamentary reform, but he foresaw that such reform could not be effective if the electorate remained ignorant. He wrote, "From two or three months' social pastime, at the hours of repose from work, would give it (the vote) to all adults in whose eyes the privilege were worth that price; and he in whose eyes it were not worth that price, could not, with much justice, complain at the not having it".

Bentham gave little attention to the possible methods of universal elementary education. It was to be moral, intellectual, and vocational—probably the curriculum of the charity school and the organisation and method of the new monitorial schools of Bell and Lancaster. His concept of the State secondary school was more definite.[1] It was to be "chrestomathic", that is, for *useful* learning as opposed to the decadent and illiberal liberal education of grammar school and university. The curriculum was to embrace the whole range of human knowledge and activity. The organisation was to be rather like that suggested for the modern comprehensive school, each pupil belonging to a number of groups according to his varying abilities in different subjects. The monitorial system was to be used, under the supervision of a headmaster who, from the ivory tower of his circular "panopticon" school, could survey at a glance the multifarious activities.

Although the chrestomathic school did not materialise, Bentham continued to consider the question of State education, and in 1827, his *Constitutional Code* contained the proposal that applicants for government posts should have reached a certain standard in State schools and should be subjected to competitive examination in subjects related to the intended official work. The repercussions of this suggestion are obvious in our Civil Service system. Bentham's influence was considerable and many of his suggestions were

[1] *Chrestomathia*, 1816.

accepted by leading politicians, such as the forceful Lord Henry Brougham.

Lord Brougham (1778-1868), whose efforts on behalf of national education and in connection with the foundation of London University are described elsewhere, was a brilliant and far-sighted thinker on education, whatever may have been the arrogance and peculiarities of his personality. Starting his career as a lawyer, he entered Parliament at thirty-two and was perhaps the leading figure in the great movement for Parliamentary reform. When his party lost power two years after the Reform Bill, the virtual retirement of Brougham followed—a great loss to English public affairs, for he had been concerned not merely with political reform, but had helped George Birkbeck to found the Mechanics' Institute in London in 1824, and had secured the establishment of the Society for the Diffusion of Useful Knowledge in 1825.

His ideas on education embraced not only schools but also further education. Thus he contended that reading could be one of the recreations of the working classes and that, therefore, there was a great need for more and cheaper books, more and better teachers, more and wider opportunities for instruction and leisure. He saw the education of the people as proceeding from the infant school to the elementary school and then to adult schools such as the Mechanics' Institute. He did not advocate State interference with either infant or adult schools, but he agitated for a national system of elementary schooling.

He made many suggestions for improving educational facilities in general—the removal of the paper tax so that cheap books could be produced, the writing of elementary textbooks, the setting up of book clubs and reading circles, the extension of libraries, even to rural areas, the provision of lecture courses throughout the country. He hoped to see the development of infant and adult education through philanthropy, setting an example himself by founding infant schools which offered pleasant and happy conditions. It irked him to know that many charitable funds were devoted to schemes which did not encourage the improvement of the poor. He was convinced that the first task was not to inculcate knowledge, but rather to raise standards in morals, behaviour, and cleanliness, and to develop not only character, but also a spirit of co-operation in the reception of the blessings of education. He thought that the diffusion of knowledge itself would stabilise the nation, but he added a warning: "No such scheme can either take

root or spread over the country so as to produce its full measure of
good unless its support is derived from those who are chiefly to reap
the benefits".

When parliamentary reform was achieved in 1832, the Sunday
School movement had been flourishing for over fifty years and
was now suspected by many reformers of hampering the cause of
national education. Some deplored the use of Sundays for instruction other than the inculcation of morals and religion by voluntary
enthusiasts. Valentine Ward wrote that not only was writing
taught, but also "in some instances arithmetic, if not geography
also".[1] After suggesting that the poor might well learn to write
during their free time on the other six days of the week, he asserted
that so many middle class as well as poor children were attending
Sunday Schools that attendance at day schools was declining, and
children were being sent to work "many years sooner than they
would be if the Sunday Schools were not open as a substitute for
day schools". He advised parents to give their children an adequate
day school education.

In 1833 Robert Southey criticised factory owners for supporting the Sunday School movement, not through conviction of its
value or desirability, but rather as a matter of expediency to preserve the labour supply for week-days. The scale on which similar
instruction was being attempted is shown by the evidence given
before a Select Committee of Parliament in 1834, that Manchester
Sunday Schools were giving such education for five and a half hours
on Sundays and two evenings during the week. One school alone
had 2,700 pupils and 120 unpaid teachers.

From this time onwards, however, this phase of Sunday education declined as a day school system grew up with the help of
Parliamentary grants awarded from 1833 onwards.

SUGGESTIONS FOR FURTHER READING

Curtis and Boultwood, *A Short History of Educational Ideas*, 4th
    edition, U.T.P., 1965. Chapters IX, XV.

L. Stephen, *The English Utilitarians*, Duckworth, 1900.

Sir H. Craik, *The State and its Relation to Education*, Macmillan,
    1882.

H. Holman, *English National Education*, Blackie, 1898.

---

[1] *Observations on Sunday Schools*, Leeds, 1827.

CHAPTER IV

ELEMENTARY EDUCATION IN THE NINETEENTH CENTURY

Early Attempts to Secure State Aid

The ferment of ideas about the subject of State intervention in popular education produced the first of a series of attempts to secure aid from the Government. Samuel Whitbread, in 1807, introduced the Parochial Schools Bill as part of his scheme for Poor Law reform. He had been impressed by the claims of the supporters of the monitorial system that it was possible to educate a child at the cost of five shillings a year. The Bill proposed that power should be given to the vestries or the magistrates to raise money for the establishment or support of parochial schools. The Bill was premature, for Parliament as a whole did not yet believe in popular education.

After a sharp debate in the Commons, during which modifications were introduced, the Bill was rejected by the House of Lords. The main objections were that if the poor were educated they would become discontented with their lot and would be influenced by reading seditious pamphlets. The Archbishop of Canterbury refused to support any scheme which tended to remove the schools from the control of the Church.

Whitbread's successor in the fight for popular education was Mr (later Lord) Henry Brougham, who, in 1816, was successful in obtaining the appointment of a Parliamentary Committee to investigate the state of education in the London area. The Report revealed the utter inadequacy of the provision of elementary education and called attention to the scandalous misuse of educational charities. The Committee was reappointed, and in 1818 a Bill was introduced with the intention of setting up a Royal Commission to inquire into educational endowments. The Commission was severely restricted in its scope by amendments made by the Lords, but the survey of the Commissioners, which lasted until 1837, resulted in the publication of a series of reports which are an extremely valuable contribution to our knowledge of conditions in this period.

Brougham was encouraged to introduce his Parish Schools Bill in 1820. It was opposed by the Dissenters and received but lukewarm support from the Church. In face of the strong opposition, Brougham decided that his wisest course was to withdraw the Bill. One important feature of the Bill was the recommendation of what in later years became known as a conscience clause. It provided an assurance "that the children of sectaries shall learn the principles and attend the ordinances of religion according to the doctrines and forms to which their families are attached".

After this failure, Brougham turned his attention to the field of adult and university education, and the cause of popular education found a champion in Mr J. A. Roebuck. In a speech, 30 July 1833, he proposed a compulsory scheme of education. He said: "In general terms, I would say that I would oblige by law every child in Great Britain and Ireland, from, perhaps, six years of age to twelve years of age, to be a regular attendant at school. If the parents be able to give and actually do give their children elsewhere sufficient education, then they should not be compelled to send them to the national school. If, however, they should be unable or unwilling to give them such instruction, then the State should step in and supply this want by compelling the parent to send the child to the school of the State". It should be noted that this has become a permanent principle in English law.

First Government Grant for Education

After a spirited debate, the Commons decided to proceed no further. Matters, however, could not be left at this stage. The Commons had been elected under the extended franchise of the Reform Act of 1832 and they had received numerous petitions from all parts of the country. Something had to be done about popular education. A few days later, in a half-empty House of Commons, the suggestion of Lord Althorpe to allocate the sum of £20,000 for the purpose of school building was approved by a vote of 50 against 26. The actual wording of this, the first step in State intervention, was as follows: "That a Sum, not exceeding £20,000, be granted to His Majesty, to be issued in aid of Private Subscriptions for the Erection of School Houses, for the Education of the Children of the Poorer Classes in Great Britain, to the 31st day of March 1834; and that the said sum be issued and paid without any fee or other deduction whatsoever".

Important as this step may seem at the present day, it attracted little attention at the time. The conditions of the grant were set out in a Treasury Minute. No grant would be paid until half the estimated cost of building a school had been raised by voluntary subscription. This principle is still observed. The present condition for recognising a voluntary school as aided is that the managers are able and willing to contribute half the cost of rebuilding or improvement. The grant was to be distributed by the National and the British Societies. In order to receive a grant it was necessary for it to be supported by one of these societies. Preference was to be given to applications from large towns and cities.

The grant was generally recognised as an interim measure, and during the next few years the clamour for popular education increased. Parliamentary discussion ranged round the inadequacy of the school provision and the poor quality of the teaching. Many people felt that the answer to the latter problem was to be found in the establishment of colleges for the training of teachers. At this time the only training institutions in England were the model schools of the National and British Societies. A proposal for the formation of a board of commissioners to consider the establishment of training institutions failed to secure sufficient support, largely because of the apathy of Parliament and the hostility of the Church towards the recommendations about religious training in the projected colleges.

Religious Controversy

The antagonism between the Church and the Nonconformists was increasing. It was perhaps unfortunate that the demand for national education coincided with an awakening of spiritual fervour in the Church which had the effect of shaking off the legacy of apathy so characteristic of the eighteenth century. The religious revival known as the Oxford Movement was born, according to Newman, in 1833, when John Keble chose "National Apostasy" as the title of a sermon he delivered at St Mary's, Oxford. For some time, many Churchmen had been alarmed at the policy of the Whig Government which they thought threatened the very existence of the national Church. The agitation for secular education, the admission of Nonconformists to civil rights (1828) and the Catholic Emancipation Act of the following year, convinced them that the Government was hostile to the Church. When in 1833 ten Irish bishoprics were suppressed, it seemed to them that this was the last straw and clearly showed that the Whigs aimed at the destruction of the Church. Hence, Keble contended that the Government had ignored the fact that the English Church was a part of Christ's Holy Catholic Church and was bound by all the fundamental laws of that Church.

Within a few months the *Tracts for the Times* began to appear. They were circulated amongst the clergy, but this was possibly a tactical error since it was some time before they began to affect lay opinion. Many of the clergy who did not follow the Tractarians in doctrinal matters agreed with them in asserting the ancient claim of the Church to the control of education. It is true that the Church represented the majority of the nation, but the Nonconformists stood for a growing and vigorous minority. On the whole, the political grouping of the time was influenced by the religious differences. The Tories were supporters of the Church, whilst the Whigs tended to favour the Nonconformists. There were, of course, many exceptions, but this represented the general layout of the political situation.

Nonconformists opposed the claim of the Church to control education, but for the most part they agreed with the Church that religious teaching ought to be an essential part of education. Only a small minority, as yet, was in favour of a purely secular education. The fact that the National Society controlled by far the greatest number of schools did not cause any serious trouble in the large towns which possessed both National and British schools. In rural districts, however, it was often the case that the parish school was the only one available, and Nonconformists objected to sending their children to be taught the doctrines of the Church of England. In the earlier days of its history, the National Society was liberal in its outlook and was ready to concede what in later days was known as a conscience clause, *i.e.* children whose parents objected to the religious instruction given in the school could be withdrawn during those periods.

One effect of the Oxford Movement was that its followers began to insist on attendance for religious instruction as a condition of entry to the schools. When Newman and some of his associates seceded to Rome, both Evangelicals and Dissenters became greatly alarmed. They thought that the Oxford Movement was disloyal to the Reformation settlement and that the Church was gradually becoming Romanised. Even the loyalty of such men as Keble and

Dr Pusey did not allay their fears. Hence, the religious dissensions assumed an increasingly bitter aspect, and for nearly three-quarters of a century the problem of religious teaching was a serious obstacle to all schemes of national education.

The Committee of Council

Taking into consideration the complexity and difficulty of the situation, the Government concluded that no education bill would stand a chance of Parliamentary approval. Even if it were accepted by the Commons it would probably be rejected by the House of Lords, but it was imperative to do something to satisfy the demand for popular education. Lord John Russell decided to advise the Queen to use the Royal Prerogative in creating a special department of the Privy Council to superintend the grants made by the Government for the erection of schools and training colleges. Accordingly an Order in Council of 1839 set up a Committee of the Privy Council for Education which should consist of not more than five members; the President of the Council, the Lord Privy Seal, the Chancellor of the Exchequer, the Home Secretary, and the Master of the Mint. The primary duty of the Committee of Council was to consider how the annual grant, which it was hoped would be increased to £30,000, should be distributed.

Two other duties were envisaged for the Committee; the establishment of a Normal Training College for teachers and to superintend the compilation of improved school textbooks. Dr Kay (afterwards Sir James Kay-Shuttleworth) was appointed Secretary of the Committee of Council, and it was because of his wise and skilful guidance that this first central authority for education was not only able to continue in existence but increased the scope of its work. The increased grant was passed by a small majority, but there remained the danger for some years that an adverse vote in the Commons might bring the Committee to an end.

The House of Lords protested at the use of the Royal Prerogative. The Queen replied: "I cannot help expressing my regret that you should have thought it necessary to take such a step on the present occasion".

Sir James Kay-Shuttleworth

Dr Kay's career falls into four well-marked periods. He was first a successful physician in Manchester during the great cholera epidemic of 1832. He was shocked at the terrible housing conditions and unsatisfactory sanitation and ventilation to be found in the poorer parts of the city, and became convinced that education would be one of the chief means of combating these evils. His pamphlet, *The Moral and Physical Condition of the Working Classes employed in the Cotton Manufacture in Manchester*, was the stimulus which led some of the most prominent citizens to establish a Statistical Society for investigating conditions in Manchester, Liverpool, and the surrounding districts. This example was followed by the formation of similar societies in London, Leeds, and other large centres of population. The investigation revealed the awful state of squalor to be found in the homes of the poorer people and the utter inadequacy of the dame and private schools.

Dr Kay's work became widely known, and when, as a result of the Poor Law Reform Act of 1834, pauper children in workhouses were obliged to receive instruction for four hours each day, he was appointed an Assistant Poor Law Commissioner in East Anglia and was later transferred to London. This was the commencement of the second stage in his career. His study of the educational methods employed in Scotland and on the Continent convinced him that the monitorial system was a failure. He called it, "Monitorial humbug". His search for an alternative system was ended by the result of a fortunate accident. In one workhouse school he found a boy, William Rush, thirteen years old, who was successfully teaching a class in the absence of the master through illness. Dr Kay was impressed by what he saw and decided that he had discovered what he wanted. This led him to experiment with boy assistants in other workhouse schools.

Such assistants became known as pupil-teachers. They were older than the average monitor, and Kay looked upon them as apprentices to the art of teaching. Further experiments were carried out in the workhouse school at Norwood, which contained upwards of 1,100 children. Norwood became the testing ground for the pupil-teacher idea and large numbers of visitors came to watch the experiment. The excellent work he had accomplished as a Poor Law Commissioner secured for Dr Kay the appointment of Secretary of the Committee of the Privy Council for Education. This part of his career as a senior civil servant lasted until 1849.

Dr Kay realised that little progress could be made in education until adequate numbers of trained teachers were available. When the project for a Government training college broke down on the religious issue, he determined to open a training college in the old manor house at Battersea and to rely upon his own resources for carrying out the experiment. With the aid of his friend, Mr Tufnell, and with his mother and sister in charge of the domestic side, he started the college in 1840. The college was an Anglican institution and was fully residential. It catered for pupil-teachers from schools like Norwood and also for older men between the ages of twenty and thirty. In company with Tufnell, Dr Kay visited the Continent and was so impressed by the schools of Holland and Switzerland that he became convinced that he was on the right track. He was specially interested in the educational developments which owed much to the influence of Pestalozzi and Fellenberg, and incorporated much of the experience he gained into the organisation of the Battersea college.

It was a hard life for the students. They made their own beds, scrubbed the floors, prepared the vegetables, and cared for the garden. He found that many of them had a slender foundation in the academic subjects and their primary need was a thorough training in the elementary branches of knowledge. The curriculum included mensuration and land-surveying, geography, elementary science, accounts, drawing, and music. Lectures on the theory and practice of teaching were given by Dr Kay himself. Although he was fully occupied with his official duties, he managed to live at the college and take an appreciable share in the instruction.

The financial burden of running the college was too great for Kay and his friends, and by 1842 there was a deficit of over £2,000. Dr Kay left the college when he married Miss Shuttleworth and took by Royal licence the name of Kay-Shuttleworth. The Government made a grant for one year only of £1,000, but it was realised that the only way of placing the college on a sound financial basis would be to hand it over to the National Society. This was done in 1843, but the work which had been accomplished was by no means a failure. The example of Battersea stimulated the Church to open more training colleges, so that by 1845 the Church of England had established twenty-two colleges containing, at that date, over 540 students.

The Committee of Council had been charged with the duty of determining "in what manner the grants of money made from time to time should be distributed". It was decided that this duty could only be performed effectively if the schools were inspected and a Minute of Council announced that all future building grants would involve the right of inspection. "The right of inspection will be required by the Committees in all cases; inspectors, authorised by Her Majesty in Council, will be appointed from time to time to visit schools to be henceforth aided by public money: the inspectors will not interfere with the religious instruction, or discipline, or management of the school, it being their object to collect facts and information, and to report the result of their inspections to the Committee of Council." (*Minutes of the Committee of Council*, 24 September 1839.)

The Church was opposed to the Minute and the National Society claimed the right to inspect its own schools. Kay-Shuttleworth wanted to avoid any unpleasantness with the Church and proposed a compromise solution known as the Concordat of 1840, which enabled him to work in co-operation with the Anglican authorities. He took the business of inspection very seriously. A detailed questionnaire was issued for the guidance of inspectors which took into account every phase of the school life. They were to inquire about the tenure and the site of the school house, the heating, lighting, ventilation, and sanitation of the building, the organisation and discipline of the school, the methods of instruction, the number and qualifications of the staff, registration and attendance, the finances of the school, the provision of playgrounds, libraries, and the relations which existed between parents and teachers.

An unfortunate set-back occurred in 1843. Since there was yet no compulsory schooling many of the poorer parents were glad to send their children, as soon as they were out of the infant stage, to work in the mines and factories. Their earnings were a very welcome addition to the family income. From 1802 a series of Factory Acts had been enacted to secure a minimum of instruction for these children, but the law was more often defied than obeyed. Sir James Graham introduced a Factory Bill in 1843, the educational clauses of which were approved by Kay-Shuttleworth. The management of the proposed factory schools was to be largely in the hands of the Anglican Church, though a conscience clause was inserted to make the Bill acceptable to Nonconformists.

As soon as the Nonconformists had time to study the implications of the Bill an intense opposition developed. Graham vainly attempted to win over his opponents, but he eventually decided to drop the Bill. The amended Factory Act of 1844 omitted any reference to religious instruction and concentrated on fixing the hours during which young people of different ages could be employed.

Between the ages of eight and thirteen children were obliged to spend three days or six half-days at school. Every employer was obliged to obtain a certificate from the schoolmaster to the effect that each child had attended school for the prescribed number of hours. This was the origin of the "half-timers", a system which, much to the hindrance of effective education, lingered on to 1918.

The education grant had reached nearly £100,000 a year by 1846, and the Committee of Council felt its position was strong enough to proceed to further developments. In what followed, it is easy to trace the influence of Kay-Shuttleworth. A Minute of 1846 introduced the pupil-teacher system. Certain schools which had obtained a favourable report from Her Majesty's Inspectors were to be recognised as suitable to training pupil-teachers. The period of apprenticeship was five years from the age of thirteen. The young person received a stipend of £10 per annum rising by annual increments to £20. Head teachers were required to give their pupil-teachers one and a half hours instruction each school day. They were rewarded by an addition of five pounds to their salary for the first pupil-teacher, nine pounds for two, and three pounds for every additional one.

At the end of their apprenticeship, pupil-teachers entered for the Queen's Scholarship Examination, and those who were successful were awarded grants of £20-£25 at a training college. The period of training was to be three years, but few students remained for this length of time. Many left at the end of the first year, and it was eventually recognised that the normal length of the training period would be two years. Trained teachers were certificated and could receive proficiency grants, and those with a minimum service of fifteen years were eligible for a retirement pension.

Additional grants were made for school gardens and workshops and also for books and maps. An important Minute was concerned with the management of elementary schools. Each school was obliged to have a board of managers. The constitution of this body and the election of its members depended upon whether the school was Church of England, Roman Catholic, Wesleyan, or a school of the British and Foreign School Society. The Catholic Poor School Society had been formed in 1847 and was eventually recognised as a body which could receive building grants from the Government. The Committee of Council issued building regulations which had to be observed before a grant would be paid.

Kay-Shuttleworth had worked for many years with a very inadequate staff, and eventually the burden began to affect his health. After a partial recovery from an illness in 1848 he found it necessary to tender his resignation in the following year. In recognition of his outstanding services to education the Queen conferred a baronetcy upon him. He was succeeded by Mr (afterwards Lord) Lingen. The resignation of Sir James Kay-Shuttleworth did not bring to an end his services to education. As an elder statesman, until his death in 1877, he made some valuable contributions; as a witness giving evidence to the Schools' Inquiry (Taunton) Commission; as a prime mover in the rebuilding of Giggleswick School and the reconstitution of Sedbergh School; and as an active supporter of the movements for the higher education of girls and the training of secondary teachers. No wonder, then, that Mr W. E. Forster, when he introduced the Elementary Education Bill of 1870, described Sir James as "the man to whom, probably more than any other, we owe national education in England".

The reports of the H.M.I.s, published by the Committee of Council, reveal the totally unsatisfactory state of a large number of schools. The following represents one of the worst type of school. "It was a low-roofed solitary cottage on a hill that overlooked a wide view of the southern part of the county and the eastern of Glamorgan: a bleak place for children to assemble at. When I entered, the young tenants of one desk, in number about a dozen, were all huddled up at one end of it with their heads together examining some object of curiosity. A boy was playing with a stick on the floor. In one corner stood a basin of dirty water and a kettle. On a shelf was a piece of raw mutton in a pie dish. While I was putting down the answers to my questions, I saw a ruddy little fellow with his face half-immersed in his master's mug of beer, drinking eagerly, and watching with upturned eyes the movements of the defrauded pedagogue."

Richard Dawes and King's Somborne

All schools, however, were not like this. Thus Lady Byron's school at Ealing Grove came in for high praise and the school at King's Somborne, in Hampshire, would be counted as efficient from a modern standpoint. It is an example of what could be achieved by an intelligent and enthusiastic educationist. The story of King's Somborne began in 1836, when the Reverend Richard Dawes was appointed Vicar. He had been a Fellow of Downing College,

Cambridge, but had been passed over for the Mastership of the college because he supported the claims of Dissenters to be admitted to the university.

At the time of his appointment he found a grave social problem in his parish. The reformed Poor Law of 1834 had not had time to take effect. For years the farmers had refused to increase the wages of their labourers because they knew that the guardians of the poor would make up any deficiencies through outdoor relief. Hence the labourers were fast losing their dignity and self-respect. King's Somborne was a large village with a population of 1,125 living in the village and in a number of scattered farmhouses. The low wages, coupled with high rents for the cottages, made it necessary for parents to send their children to work in the fields at an early age.

Dawes was convinced that education could do a great deal in improving the condition of his parish, and this belief led him to open a school in 1842. He adopted three guiding principles for the school: it must become self-supporting; it should include all the children of the village; and its aim should be the preparation of the pupils for intelligent participation in the life of the community and in life as a whole. The site of the school was the gift of the lady of the manor. Dawes contributed £500 towards the building and received an equivalent grant from the Committee of Council. When the school opened the staff consisted of a master and mistress who were a married couple, an assistant-master and mistress, and four paid monitors. The latter were replaced in 1846 by six pupil-teachers. The master and mistress had a house and garden and a combined salary of £75 a year.

In the second year the school fulfilled Dawes's first requirement that it should be self-supporting. The fees were a few pence a week for children of labourers and from six to ten shillings a quarter from parents who earned higher wages. The growth of the school was remarkable. It opened with thirty-eight children, and at the end of the fourth year there were 158 on the roll. Dawes insisted on prompt payment of fees. He believed that people do not value what they obtain for nothing. The success of the school was the result of good teaching and a well-planned curriculum. Although many additional subjects were taught the three Rs were not neglected. A full account of the school was given in the reports of the Rev. H. Mozeley in 1848 and that of Matthew Arnold in 1853 and also in pamphlets published by Dawes to explain his system.

Dawes supervised the work of the teachers. He was not a trained teacher himself nor were his teachers superior in attainments to those in other National schools. He brought to the task a long experience of teaching science to undergraduates in which he had to start from basic principles. He had read and digested Rousseau's *Emile* and knew the work of William Cobbett who had undertaken the education of his own children. Moreover, he was a man of high ideals who knew just what he wanted, and had the gift of inspiring others and so aroused enthusiasm in his teachers.

One of the basic lessons taught in the school was the duty of cleanliness. Many parents had not washed their feet since they were children. All pupils had to wash their hands, faces, and necks daily and their feet twice a week. They were taught to clean their teeth and each child had its own toothbrush. Gradually the example set by the children spread to the parents. Every girl possessed a brush and comb and the H.M.I. recorded that when he asked a little girl who failed to answer his question what her pretty head was for, she astonishingly replied, "To brush and comb, Sir".

Dawes disliked the cramming of facts from textbooks. Hence, he devised a method which has a marked similarity to the modern Project. Once a child had mastered the mechanics of reading he was introduced to the finest poetry and prose in the English language. The aim was to make reading a pleasurable activity. Special care was given to written expression. Dawes wrote: "Thus a child in the lowest class but one, when it can write words legibly upon a slate, is told to write the names of its brothers and sisters, of all the things in the house where it lives, of all the birds or trees or plants that it knows, and the like. Another stage in its instruction associates qualities with things. It is told, perhaps, to write down the names of all the white or black things that it knows, of all the ugly or handsome things, or the tall and short ones, or iron and wooden ones. And then, when the child can write sentences, on the uses of things familiar to its observation—it writes of things used for the food of man or animals, used in building a cottage, or as implements of agriculture. Lastly, it is made to exhaust its knowledge of such things by being told to write down all it knows about them: all it knows, for instance, about sheep, or cows, or horses, wheat, iron, or copper, of the village of King's Somborne, or the neighbouring downs and hills, of the farms and holdings in the parish, of the parish roads, of the River Teste which runs through it, of the neighbouring town of Stockbridge, of Hampshire, of the island of Great Britain, of the earth, or of the sun, moon, and stars".

Dawes considered that the geography taught in many schools, which consisted in learning names of towns, capes, and bays, afforded no useful training. The pupils of his school began by associating the points of the compass with familiar landmarks. The school possessed a compass and the pupils were taught how to use it. They were also taught how to read a map and the use of the globe. In learning about other countries emphasis was on the contrast between their physical features and how differences of climate, soil, or mineral wealth affect the life and occupations of the inhabitants. Dawes despised the history books that were available for schools. Instruction in his school started with a visit to local historical remains, e.g. a Roman camp, the Roman road from Old Sarum to Winchester. The school was built on the site of a palace of John of Gaunt and some of its stones were to be found in the school walls. Special attention was given to discussions through which the pupils learnt how people lived at different periods: what their houses, clothing, food, and transport were like.

As one might expect there was an excellent scheme in science and mathematics. Nature study was learnt through direct observation of local plants and trees, the study of birds and their migrations. Under the supervision of the assistant-master the boys kept records of barometer and thermometer readings and used them to construct a chart to show weekly and monthly averages. They also kept a journal in which they recorded noteworthy events in the neighbourhood, such as, the arrival of the first swallow, the coming of the cuckoo, the earliest appearance of pear and apple blossom and the first ears of wheat or barley. The child who furnished any items of this kind was asked to account for the cause of the early appearance.

The physical sciences were taught with an emphasis on the phenomena of everyday life and the experimental approach was encouraged. Dawes wrote: "In subjects of this kind, and to children, mere verbal explanations, as everyone will perceive, are of no use whatever . . . For instance, a teacher may talk to them about a thermometer, and find in the end, they just know as much about it as they did when he began; but if he shows them one, and then grasps it in his hand, telling them to look at the fluid as it rises, or plunges it into hot or cold water, and then lets them see the effect, they then begin to open their eyes in a wonderful manner, light breaks in upon them, and information thus given leaves an impression which in after life they turn to as a source of instruction, by the reasoning powers of their own minds".

During the early stages of this type of teaching the teachers needed a considerable amount of guidance, and Dawes wrote: "The teachers here who at first knew but little of these matters, are now qualified to give instruction in them; to teach the mechanical principles of the tools they use—the spade, the axe, the plough; barometer, pair of bellows; metals varying in volume according to the quantity of heat which is in them, or, as it is termed, expanding by heat and contracting by cold; why one substance feels colder to the hand than another; the way in which metals are separated from their ores; how water is converted into steam and again condensed; how their clothes are dried, and why they feel cold in sitting in wet clothes; why one body floats on water and another sinks; why, on going into the school on a cold morning, they sometimes see a quantity of water on the glass, and why it is on the inside and not on the outside; why, when their ink is dried up, does it leave a substance behind which does not go away". These problems were tackled by the pupils themselves, who conducted simple experiments in order to find answers to them.

In mathematics the older boys learnt mensuration, algebra, and the subject matter of the first three books of Euclid. Actual measurement was ordinarily employed in land surveying and in the carpenter's shop. The inspector reported: "The more advanced boys have a very competent knowledge of the mensuration of the regular figures; of finding the weight of a body from knowing its specific gravity; how the knowledge of the properties of a few simple geometrical figures simplifies all the measurements of the things they have to do".

Dawes's comment on the method was amusing. "To show what an interest this mode of teaching excites in them, I will mention an occurrence which happened a few days ago; writing in my study, I heard a noise of joyous voices, which I found proceeded from half-a-dozen boys, who, after school hours, had come to measure my garden-roller; the master of the school had been teaching them how to find the solid contents of a roller, such as the farmers use in the fields (a hollow iron cylinder), and from knowing the specific gravity of iron to find its weight; my garden-roller occurring to them, they had come to practise on it."

King's Somborne was also noted for its singing. The children organised village concerts and invited their parents. The inspector reported: "Singing is no task to these children; music has found its way to their hearts, a result which I have never met with in an elementary school". Dawes insisted on the children owning their own books and required the older pupils to do home lessons. One mother remarked: "You cannot think, Sir, how pleasantly we spend our evenings now compared with what we used to do; the girls reading and getting their lessons while I am sewing, and their father working with them; and he is so disappointed, Sir, if the evening task is above him, so that he cannot help in it".

Dawes was too able a man to be left with a country vicarage, and in 1850 he was created Dean of Hereford, but the school continued for many years on the lines he had originated. Matthew Arnold gave a glowing account of his visit to King's Somborne when he gave evidence before the Newcastle Commission. At Hereford, Dawes continued his educational work which he extended into the field of secondary education.

Newcastle Commission

That the school at King's Somborne was the exception rather than the rule may be gathered from the report of the Newcastle Commission. There was a growing belief in the 1850s that the increasing amount of money spent on popular education was not being used to the best purpose. The Crimean War had cost the nation about £78,000,000 and the result was a cry for economy. Was the nation obtaining value for the money spent on education? To answer this, Sir John Pakington obtained in 1858 the appointment of a Royal Commission to "inquire into the present state of popular education in England, and to consider and report what measures, if any, are required for the extension of *sound and cheap* elementary instruction to all classes of the people". The operative words are in italics.

The Chairman of the Commission was the Duke of Newcastle and ten assistant-commissioners were appointed to examine sample districts. The Rev. James Fraser (later Bishop of Manchester) was sent to Germany and Matthew Arnold to France to report on elementary education in those countries. Statistical returns were obtained from the United States and Canada. Charity and reformatory schools and those under the Admiralty and War Office were investigated, and the report of the Commission, issued in 1861, contained 127 pages of statistics, but many of these were unreliable because they were based on estimates.

Considerations of space will not permit a detailed account of the findings of the Commission and only certain salient features can be mentioned. Elementary schools were classified as Public, *i.e.* supervised by the philanthropic societies like the National, British and Foreign, and Catholic Poor Schools' Society and which were not run for profit; and Private schools conducted by individuals as a means of earning a livelihood. Most of the private schools were markedly inefficient. On the whole, even in the public schools, the attendance was irregular; the average length of schooling amounted to about four years and only one child in 7·7 attended the schools. The Commission, however, seemed to be optimistic and declared satisfaction with the prevailing system. Elementary education was still regarded as a charity, and because of religious disagreements it was not thought advisable to introduce compulsory elementary education.

The main criticisms were directed to the curriculum and the poor attendance. The fact that most children left school before eleven was noted and the general view was that the basic subjects were being neglected. It was said that the teachers concentrated on the older and brighter pupils. Speaking of the child, Fraser declared: "We must make up our minds to see the last of him, as far as the day school is concerned, at ten or eleven. We must frame our system of education upon this hypothesis; and I venture to maintain that it is possible to teach a child soundly and thoroughly, in a way that he shall not forget it, all that it is necessary for him to possess in the shape of intellectual attainment by the time that he is ten years old". Fraser then outlined what he considered possible in that time. It consisted of ability to spell common words and read a simple paragraph from a newspaper, to write a simple letter, to check a tradesman's bill, and a knowledge of the chief countries of the world. In addition the pupil should have sufficient knowledge of the Bible to understand a simple sermon and enough of the Catechism to understand his duties to God and his neighbour.

Fraser concluded by saying: "I have no brighter view of the future or the possibilities of an English elementary education floating before my eyes than this . . . since we see the last of the boy in school at ten or eleven, it is not said when we see him there first, nor is there any guarantee that we shall see him there at all". This counsel of despair was accepted by the Commission although a minority, amongst whom was Matthew Arnold, were rightly indignant. The general opinion was that more attention should be bestowed on the learning of reading, writing, and arithmetic. Then followed a most significant paragraph. "There is only one way of securing this result, which is to institute a searching examination by competent authority of every child in every school to which grants are to be paid, with the view of ascertaining whether these indispensible elements of knowledge are thoroughly acquired, and to make the prospects and position of the teacher dependent to a considerable extent on the results of this examination."

The Commission made the following proposals. The Government grant ought to be based on the three factors of regular attendance, the state of the school buildings, and a satisfactory report from the inspector. The establishment of local boards of education in the counties and towns with a population over 40,000 was recommended. These boards should appoint a panel of examiners consisting of certificated teachers with over seven years' experience to organise the examinations. Each school should receive a grant from the rates dependent on the examination results. Thus the Newcastle Commission recommended the system which is generally known as Payment by Results.

The Revised Code

In 1856 there had been a reorganisation of the Committee of Council. It now took the title of Education Department and, although it still remained under the Privy Council, a Vice-President was appointed to represent the Department in Parliament. Robert Lowe, the Vice-President, undertook the revision of the Minutes of the Committee of Council so that the relevant regulations about grants and other important matters would be printed in one volume. This was issued as the *Code of 1860.*

Lowe was more of an administrator than an educationist. He agreed in principle with the recommendations of the Newcastle Commission, although he made several important changes in them. He rejected the idea of rate aid for schools because he realised it would involve him in a religious controversy. Also the Revised Code of 1862 made no mention of the local education boards, but handed over the conduct of the examination to the inspectorate. Lowe believed in decentralising education. Grants had previously been paid to individual teachers and pupil-teachers through the Post Office, so that members of the teaching profession were well on the way to becoming civil servants. Now the grant would be forwarded to the managers who would be responsible for paying the teachers. This lessened the amount of administrative work at Whitehall, but it also introduced bargaining between the school managers and the teachers.

When in 1861 Lowe presented the Revised Code to Parliament he was met with such a storm of protest that he postponed its issue until the following year. In its modified form the proposal to examine infants was dropped, the training college grants were to continue for the time being, and the system of Payment by Results was not to be applied to Scotland. In spite of these modifications the general principle remained. Lowe told the Commons: "I cannot promise the House that this system will be an economical one, and I cannot promise that it will be an efficient one, but I can promise that it shall be either one or the other. If it is not cheap, it shall be efficient; if it is not efficient, it shall be cheap".

The Government grant was made dependent on the two factors of average attendance and performance in the examination. A grant of 6s. 6d. per head would be paid if a satisfactory report on children under the age of six was furnished by the inspector. The older children were grouped in six standards and no pupil could be examined twice in the same standard. The subjects tested were reading, writing, arithmetic, and plain needlework for girls. Each child could earn a total grant of 4s. for general merit and attendance. and 8s. for a pass in the three Rs. A failure in any one of the three Rs would reduce the grant by 2s. 8d. Evening schools were accorded similar treatment. The grant per head for each pupil over the age of thirteen was 2s. 6d. for attendance and 5s. for success in the examination. H.M.I.s were issued with detailed instructions about the conduct of the examination.

From a purely monetary point of view the Revised Code was cheap. The Government grant which had reached £813,441 in 1862 had fallen to £636,806 by 1865. A better average attendance was secured. There was a tendency for pupils to remain longer at school, and teachers began to concentrate on the duller children with the inevitable result that the brighter ones were often neglected. As soon as the restriction against certificated teachers teaching both in the day and the evening was removed, evening classes began to develop. The system of distributing the grant to managers prevented the central authority from gaining excessive control over the teachers and so saved English education from the centralisation which was so prominent in France and other European countries. Matthew Arnold considered that there was a marked improvement in school reading books.

So much for the credit side. Kay-Shuttleworth predicted certain adverse features which would follow and in the main he was correct. There was a definite decrease in the number and quality of the pupil-teachers. There was a small addition to the class of certificated teachers, but, on the other hand, the school population had increased by more than 100,000. This resulted in a trend to larger classes; the average of 37·7 pupils per teacher in 1860 had grown to 43·4 by 1866. Some inspectors commented favourably on the Code, but Matthew Arnold showed great courage in pointing out its defects. As an inspector he was not entitled to criticise the policy of the Department and a man less in the public eye might have found himself in trouble. He drew attention to the serious strain which the examination system inflicted upon the children. The teachers realised that their salaries depended upon the number of pupils in their classes who passed the examination so that they used all means to secure the regular attendance of children and their success in the examination. They were sorely tempted to falsify registers and mark children as present who were absent. It speaks much for the high standards of the profession that so few cases of dishonesty occurred.

Teachers and managers were so anxious to secure the maximum grant that children suffering from whooping-cough and other infections were wrapped up and brought to school to sit the examination. The teachers came to regard the inspector as their natural enemy and all kinds of devices were adopted with the object of outwitting him. Some children learnt their readers by heart, and cases were known of teachers who devised a code to signify the answers. Inspectors recorded instances of children reading aloud whilst holding the book upside-down. Even when the Code came to an end in 1897, it took many years to overcome the legacy of the unhappy relations between teachers and inspectors.

One may ask why so great an importance was attached to the examination. In the 1860s it was the only objective test known. The publication of Darwin's *Origin of Species* had drawn attention to the "struggle for existence" and the "survival of the fittest". The universities had started written examinations at the beginning of the century and some years later they were adopted by the Civil Service. Examinations such as the College of Preceptors, 1853, and the Oxford and Cambridge Locals, 1857, had made their way into the secondary schools. An almost pathetic belief in the efficacy of examinations developed and Lowe, who in his politics was a convinced free-trader, agreed that competition was the best form of test.

Since the examination in the elementary school was restricted to the three Rs for grant-earning purposes, other studies tended to be neglected. The liberal curriculum of a school like King's Somborne became a thing of the past. It was only gradually that a wider point of view began to prevail. The first step to mitigate the severity of the Code was taken in 1867, when a complicated Minute was issued which under certain conditions offered grants for "specific subjects" such as geography, history, or grammar. Later the list of specific subjects was extended, but these changes only applied to pupils in Standards IV to VI. In 1875, "class subjects" were introduced, e.g. geography, history, grammar, and plain needlework for girls, and they were made optional for the whole school above the first Standard. Instruction in music, cookery, and drill was encouraged. These changes continued until 1897 when the last vestiges of Payment by Results disappeared. The examination was discontinued and its place was taken by "surprise visits" paid by the inspectors. The point to notice in regard to the steps towards a more liberal curriculum is the absence of any carefully thought out plan. New subjects, either specific or class, were introduced when it was considered expedient to do so, but there was no attempt to view the curriculum as a whole and in its relation to the needs of the child. Often a subject was introduced in a school because of the special interest of the head teacher.

Events Leading to Act of 1870

The nation as a whole did not share the complacent attitude of the Newcastle Commission, and the feeling developed that all would not be well in education until a complete system of elementary education supported by local rates and under local control was established. This was the reason for the formation of the Manchester Education Aid Society in 1864. Two Education Bills were presented to Parliament but were rejected because of the opposition of the Nonconformists, who objected to aiding denominational schools from the rates.

Another national organisation, the Birmingham Education League, was formed in 1869 with George Dixon as Chairman,

Joseph Chamberlain as Vice-Chairman, and Jesse Collings as Secretary. The main support for the League came from the more extreme Liberals or Radicals who believed in free, compulsory, unsectarian education. The supporters of denominational teaching were alarmed at the threat to their schools and formed in opposition to the League, the National Education Union. The result of the clash of views was a Parliamentary investigation of the state of elementary education in Liverpool, Manchester, Leeds, and Birmingham. The inquiry was conducted by Mr (later Sir) Joshua Fitch and Mr Fearon. It revealed a shocking state of affairs. The private schools had not improved since the time of the Newcastle Commission and the facilities for elementary education were woefully inadequate. A considerable number of children of school age were not receiving any kind of organised instruction. The results of the inquiry were typical of conditions in other centres of population. Something had to be done to provide sufficient school accommodation for the whole country, but how was this to be accomplished?

The general election of 1868 had resulted in the return of the Liberals, with Mr Gladstone as Prime Minister. The Vice-President of the Education Department was Mr W. E. Forster, M.P. for Bradford. Forster was well known for his keen interest in education and other social problems. He had married the daughter of Dr Thomas Arnold, of Rugby. The responsibility for introducing a new Education Bill belonged to Forster, but the Birmingham League and National Education Union lost no time in pressing their views on him. Forster rejected the proposals of the League in favour of an idea which had been put forward by Robert Lowe and which had been tried out in New South Wales.

The essence of Lowe's advice was that a complete survey of the educational needs of each district should be made. In areas in which deficiencies were discovered, the voluntary bodies should be given an opportunity to make them good; otherwise compulsion would be brought to bear. Forster's Bill was based on this advice. He suggested that in districts where deficiencies existed, and he thought these would be the majority, the voluntary bodies should be given a year of grace in order to remedy them. At the end of the period of grace the gaps would be filled by the work of School Boards elected by the town councils or, in the case of rural areas, by the vestries. Parents would continue to pay fees up to a maximum of 9d. a week, but those who could not afford to do so would be granted a free ticket.

The first reading of the Bill passed smoothly, but in the interval before the second reading, Mr Dixon and the League found a number of objections, mainly concerned with religious instruction. Forster considered these carefully, and in its final form the Bill was greatly modified. The period of grace was cut down to six months. The School Boards would be elected by those whose names were on the burgess roll of the boroughs, and in the country, by the ratepayers. Special arrangements would be made for the London School Board. The question of religious instruction was settled to the satisfaction of Mr Dixon, who withdrew his amendments, and the Bill became law under the title of the Elementary Education Act, 1870.

Elementary Education Act, 1870

The School Boards, London excepted, consisted of a minimum of five and a maximum of fifteen members. Women had the vote and could sit as members. A system of cumulative voting was adopted which meant that every elector had as many votes as there were vacancies. He could distribute his votes as he pleased, and if he wished he could give all his votes to one candidate. The idea was to preserve the rights of minorities to representation. Thus Roman Catholic electors usually gave all their votes to one candidate to secure his election. In London the new experiment of the secret ballot was tried, and this was eventually adopted in all districts.

The School Boards were given wide powers. They were free to decide whether religious instruction should be given in their schools. In every school a conscience clause operated which enabled parents to withdraw their children from religious instruction if they wished. Hence, religious instruction was given at the beginning or at the end of the school session so that the time-table would not be disarranged. Forster accepted the clause put forward by Mr Cowper-Temple: "No religious catechism or religious formulary, which is distinctive of any particular denomination, shall be taught in the school".

The School Boards were called upon to decide between no religious instruction at all or undenominational teaching based on the Bible. Most adopted the decision of the London School Board, which was influenced by Professor T. Huxley. "In the schools provided by the Board, the Bible shall be read and there shall be given such explanations and such instruction therefrom in the principles of morality and religion as are suited to the capacity of children; provided always . . . that no attempt be made in any such schools to attach children to any particular denomination."

The School Boards could levy a local rate for the building of schools; they could accept the transfer of any voluntary school which desired to be transferred (very few wished for a transfer), and they could acquire land and raise a loan for the building of schools. If they wished, they could make education compulsory in their areas. The London School Board passed a by-law to compel attendance between the ages of five and thirteen, but exemption was granted to children over ten if they had passed Standard V and were obliged to go to work to support their parents. This example was followed by many Boards in the larger towns, but some in rural districts did not make full use of their powers.

There was one clause of the Act which escaped the notice of the League until it was too late to amend it. This was the famous Clause 25 which empowered a School Board to pay the whole or part of the fees of children whose parents could not otherwise afford them. It became obvious in practice that this meant that voluntary schools received most of the money. Manchester, which did not build Board Schools for some years, paid under this clause large sums of money out of the rates in aid of the voluntary schools. On the other hand, in Birmingham the influence of the League was so strong that the School Board refused to apply the clause. Although the League failed to gain complete support for its policy of secular education, it caused a division in the Government ranks which was one of the reasons for defeat in the election of 1874.

Contrary to the belief of many people the Act of 1870 established neither free nor compulsory education. It was a means of filling the gaps, as Forster expressed it. Interest for the next two decades centres on the struggle to make elementary education free and compulsory, and when the requisite school places were provided to see that they were filled and that attendance was regular and punctual. The Boards appointed officers to see that children attended school regularly, and in some districts the local education authority's attendance officer is still called the "School Board man". The Act instituted what is known as the Dual System. On the one hand, there were the Board schools, undenominational and supported by the Government grant, the rates, and fees. On the other, the denominational schools which could not receive rate aid were dependent on the Government grant, fees, subscriptions, and the income from any endowments they possessed. This put them at a great disadvantage.

The six months of grace stimulated the Churches, especially the Anglican and Roman, to great efforts to build new schools. By 1880 the Anglicans had added over a million school places in addition to those which existed in 1870. Churchmen gave most liberally in support of their schools, but they were fighting a losing battle. Forster had calculated that the cost of educating a child would not rise above 30s. per head and that the School Boards would never need to ask for a rate in excess of 3d. in the £. By 1880 the average cost per head in a Church of England school was £1 14s. 10¼d.; in the Board schools, £2 1s. 11¾d. The School Board had the advantage of being able to fall back on the rates to meet an increase in the cost of education.[1] The Church schools at the end of the century were unable to compete on equal terms with the Board schools. Unless it was possible to secure rate aid the number of voluntary schools would steadily decrease.

Lord Sandon's Act, 1876

Before closing this chapter a few words should be said about two other Education Acts and the Cross Commission of 1888. The first of these Acts was known as Lord Sandon's Act of 1876, which gave some relief to managers of voluntary schools by raising the Government grant from 15s. per head to 17s. 6d. and, under certain conditions, it allowed for a still larger grant. Some districts in which no deficiencies existed had not established School Boards. Such districts were ordered to elect School Attendance Committees with the same compulsory powers over attendance as the School Boards. Lord Sandon's Act established a principle which remained in force until 1944. It put the onus on the parent for seeing that his child received adequate instruction in the three Rs, and if the parent did not carry out his obligation he became liable to certain penalties.

Mundella Act, 1880

The position was tightened up by Mr Mundella's Act in 1880, which made the framing of attendance by-laws compulsory for all School Boards and School Attendance Committees. The next step

---

[1] In one district, which is fairly typical, the average cost per head in 1956 was £37.3 in the primary school, £54.7 in the secondary modern, and £70.9 in the grammar school. These figures speak volumes, even taking into account the rise in costs since the war.

was the raising of the school leaving age to eleven without any exemptions in 1893, and to twelve in 1899. In 1891 parents were given the right to demand free education for their children. A special fee grant was made to recompense the schools for loss of revenue, with the result that most elementary schools became free.

Cross Commission

The Cross Commission was a stocktaking of the progress made in elementary education up to 1888. There were sharp differences of opinion amongst its members, and it was thought desirable to issue a majority and a minority report. The majority thought that the voluntary schools should receive rate aid. Another problem confronted the Commission. Children were tending to remain at school after the age of thirteen. A Standard VII was instituted to meet their needs and later ex-standard classes were formed. It became convenient to group the older pupils in one central school, which became known as higher grade school. In rural districts Higher Tops were added to elementary schools. Most higher grade schools organised a science course in order to qualify for the grants offered by the Science and Art Department.

The majority thought that a more efficient type of secondary education could be obtained by developing the endowed grammar schools rather than by supporting the higher grade schools. The minority expressed a view which was eventually to prevail. "We are of opinion that the best security for efficient teaching is the organisation of our school system under local representative authorities, over sufficiently wide areas, with full powers of management and responsibility for maintenance, with well-graduated curricula, a liberal staff of well-trained teachers, and buildings sanitary, suitable and well-equipped with school requisites." The Commission was in favour of raising the school leaving age to fourteen. It recommended that evening schools should no longer be regarded as elementary schools, but should give instruction in science, art, and technology, and offer opportunities for recreation and social life. Their real function was that of an evening continuation school.

Perhaps the most important recommendation was in regard to the training of teachers. The pupil-teacher system was criticised, and it was thought that the training colleges, because of their denominational tests, excluded many promising candidates from the profession. It was considered that the colleges suffered from inbreeding. Most of the staff consisted of men and women who had come from the elementary school, served their apprenticeship as pupil-teachers, and taught in the elementary school, without any opportunity of mixing with those training for other professions. Hence the majority report was in favour of setting up day training colleges in association with the universities and university colleges. The minority attached greater importance to residence than did the majority. The result was that in 1890 the Education Department recognised the day training colleges which were the forerunners of the present University Departments of Education.

SUGGESTIONS FOR FURTHER READING

S. J. Curtis, *History of Education in Great Britain*, sixth edition, U.T.P., 1965. Chapters VII, VIII, IX to p. 313.

Frank Smith, *The Life and Work of Sir James Kay-Shuttleworth*, John Murray, 1923.

H. C. Barnard, *A Short History of English Education from 1760 to 1944*, University of London Press, 1947. Chapters XI, XII, XIII, XIX.

CHAPTER V

SECONDARY EDUCATION IN THE NINETEENTH CENTURY

Public Schools in the Early Nineteenth Century

The condition of the public and endowed grammar schools did not improve in the early years of the nineteenth century, but the public consciousness of the state of degradation into which so many of them had fallen now began to make itself felt. In 1795 the Lord Chief Justice, Lord Kenyon, in giving judgment in regard to a dispute at Skipton Grammar School, summed up the general situation of the grammar schools in the following words. "Whoever will examine the state of the grammar schools in different parts of this kingdom will see to what a lamentable condition most of them are reduced, . . . empty walls without scholars, and everything neglected but the receipt of the salaries and emoluments. In some instances that have lately come within my own knowledge there was not a single scholar in the schools though there were very large endowments to them." Illustrations of this statement abound in N. Carlisle's *Endowed Grammar Schools of England and Wales*, 1818.

By the Grammar School Act of 1840 the grammar schools were freed from the restrictions placed upon them by the will of the founder or the school statutes which usually limited the studies to the classical languages and literature. Grammar school governors were now free to introduce subjects which had not been previously mentioned in the foundation, *e.g.* English language and literature, modern history, geography, elementary mathematics, and modern languages. Some of the more progressive schools took advantage of this freedom, but others, whilst pretending to be classical schools, were nothing more than inferior elementary schools.

The earliest criticisms were directed at the public schools, but the attacks soon became an affair of party politics in which, on the whole, the Liberals attacked and the Tories defended. The exaggerated importance attached to the classics and the neglect of modern studies were emphasised in such periodicals as the *Edinburgh Review* and the *Westminster Review*. The moral aspects of the public schools were severely criticised by Sidney Smith, who was an old scholar of Winchester. He accused them of being hot-beds of vice in which bullying, fagging, and drunkenness were not only tolerated but were general.

Dr Arnold of Rugby

It is only fair to remember that great changes were taking place in the public schools, but during the first quarter of the nineteenth century they had largely escaped notice. The reforms were mainly the result of able headmasters, such as James at Rugby, Barnard at Eton, and Thackeray at Harrow, but the most famous of them were Dr Samuel Butler of Shrewsbury and Dr Thomas Arnold of Rugby. Arnold is more widely known than Butler because of the publicity his reforms received through *Tom Brown's Schooldays* and his life which was written by an old pupil, Dean Stanley. In more recent days Arnold has been severely criticised by Strachey in *Eminent Victorians* and by Bertrand Russell in *Education and the Good Life*. Even if one agrees that many things introduced by Arnold were derived from others, and when allowance is made for the limitations imposed on him by the period in which he lived, it is still true to say that he was one of the greatest influences in creating the prestige now enjoyed by the English public schools.

Arnold drew upon his experience when he was a pupil of Dr Goddard at Winchester, and when he came to Rugby he developed these ideas. After he left the University of Oxford he was ordained and went to live at Laleham, Middlesex, where he did some private tutoring. When the headship of Rugby became vacant in 1828, Arnold's candidature was warmly supported by the Provost of Oriel, who wrote: "If Arnold were elected, he would change the face of education all through the public schools of England".

Rugby, founded by Laurence Sheriff in 1567, had, under the able administration of James, developed from a typical free grammar school to a large boarding school. A few years before Arnold became headmaster the school buildings had been substantially enlarged. Arnold was not an innovator in teaching methods nor did he seek to change the classical curriculum. He believed that the classics were a sound foundation and means for giving a liberal education. He used them as vehicles through which history, literature, philosophy, geography, and citizenship could be taught. Dean Stanley wrote: "Every lesson in Greek and Latin may or ought to be a lesson in English: the translation of every sentence in Demosthenes or Tacitus is properly an exercise in extemporaneous English composition: a problem how to express with equal brevity, clearness, and force in our own language, the thought which the original author so admirably expressed in his".

Arnold was a most inspiring teacher and was able to revivify the traditional classical curriculum. It was, however, as an administrator and a Christian gentleman that he had a lasting influence on public school education. He realised the impossibility of transforming the school by revolutionary methods and decided to build upon and develop whatever was good in the existing system. Hence he did not attempt to abolish the universal custom of fagging but made use of it. He understood the prestige that the sixth form enjoyed and utilised it in the prefect system.

This was not a new idea. Prefects or praepostors, as they were called, had existed at Eton since the days of Elizabeth I. Westminster and Charterhouse had used the older pupils in the same way, but it was Arnold's experience at Winchester which influenced him most and he developed the prefect system beyond what it had been under Goddard. He once told his sixth form: "You should feel like officers in the army whose want of moral courage would be thought cowardice. When I have confidence in the sixth, there is no post in England for which I would exchange this; but if they do not support me, I must go". He took great care in the choice of prefects. If they carried out their duties conscientiously they were supported, but if a prefect failed in his duty, Arnold had no scruples about dismissing him from office. He held regular prefect meetings at which he discussed ways and means of improving the tone of the school. Since his days, prefects have been introduced in all types of school, both day and boarding, and when they have been inspired by such high ideals as those of Arnold, the system has worked successfully. On the other hand, when prefects have been regarded as a kind of police force for the headmaster and staff the system has failed miserably.

Arnold looked upon the school as a community of Christian gentlemen. Unlike Keate, the flogging head of Eton, he trusted his pupils and believed what they said. "If you say so, that is quite enough for me: of course I take your word." It was by putting boys on their honour to tell the truth that the tradition arose that it was a shame to tell Arnold a lie because he always believed it. This did not mean that he dispensed with corporal punishment. He used the rod for moral offences and was quite ruthless in expelling a boy who had an evil influence on his fellows. As he told the school: "It is not necessary that this school should be a school for 300 or even

100 boys, but it is necessary that it should be a school for Christian gentlemen".

He regarded the school chapel as the focal point of the school life and his sermons which gave pupils sound, practical Christian advice had an enormous effect on his listeners. Arnold was not an outstanding theologian, but he knew how to present Christianity to boys and lead them to apply its principles to everyday life. His sudden death in 1842 cut short his work, but his influence not only left a permanent mark in Rugby but spread to other schools through pupils and members of his staff who were appointed to them. It affected the older public schools and also the newer proprietary schools which were modelled on them.

Such schools were the result of far reaching changes which were taking place in the political, social, and economic life of the nation. By the Reform Act of 1832 the middle classes had achieved political power and new careers were open to their sons. The growth of the railways made it possible for more wealthy members of the middle classes to send their sons quickly and cheaply to schools at a distance from their homes. The first of the new schools were day institutions, but through the Arnold influence the later ones were boarding schools. Examples are Cheltenham College, Marlborough College, Rossal School, Wellington College, Epsom, and Haileybury.

Clarendon Commission

The attacks on the public schools were so persistent that in 1861 the Government decided to ask the Queen to appoint a Royal Commission to investigate conditions in the nine large public schools, Winchester, Eton, Westminster, Charterhouse, Harrow, Rugby, Shrewsbury, St Paul's, and Merchant Taylors'. With the exception of the last two all these were boarding schools. The Commission issued its report in 1864. As Lord Clarendon was its Chairman, it is generally known as the Clarendon Commission. The public schools did not take the inquiry in good grace and the Commissioners found it difficult to visit the schools. They obtained most of their information through questionnaires addressed to the headmasters and through interviewing witnesses and obtaining the opinions of those who had special knowledge of public schools.

The Commissioners themselves were ex-public schoolmen and, therefore, with some exceptions, they were in favour of the classical curriculum. They had been impressed by the Prussian Gymnasium which was the creation of von Humboldt, who had been chief of the Prussian Bureau of Education, 1808-10. Humboldt, though a distinguished classical scholar, aimed at blending the humanistic ideals of the classical world with those of modern times. He believed that studies such as history, geography, natural science, religious instruction, drawing, and writing should be added to the main classical and mathematical core. Hebrew and modern languages were regarded as optional subjects. The Clarendon Commissioners were, therefore, ready to recommend a programme on lines similar to those of the Gymnasium.

On the whole they were satisfied with what the public schools were doing and could find little trace of the more serious moral defects which were alleged. They approved the classics as the core of the curriculum, but recommended that more time should be given to English language, modern languages, mathematics, and science, though these should be subsidiary to classics. They thought that the classics were of value in teaching boys their own language. Professor H. Sidgwick criticised this as "the idea that in order that a man may know one thing well, you teach him another".

The Government did not wish to take drastic action with regard to the public schools. The Public Schools Act, 1868, called for a revision of the governing bodies of the schools so as to make them more representative. They were to include members nominated by the Universities of Oxford, Cambridge, and London, and the learned societies. Apart from defining the powers of the new governing bodies the Act refrained from interfering with the curriculum. It left such reforms to the good sense of the schools themselves. Many of the recommendations of the Commission were eventually adopted and the curriculum became more varied and flexible. At Eton, Dr Hornby introduced French, German, history, physics, chemistry, and biology, and the older pupils were given considerable choice in the subjects they wished to study.

One effect of the recommendations was the development of a Modern Side at Harrow. Boys who were allocated to it studied Latin, but also history, modern languages, mathematics, and science. Under E. E. Bowen, the writer of the Harrow School song, *Forty Years On*, the Modern Side became a great success and the experiment was imitated in other public schools.

Taunton Commission

Attention was now directed to the endowed secondary schools and the proprietary schools. The Schools Inquiry Commission was appointed in 1864. It is generally known by the name of its Chairman, Lord Taunton. The inquiry lasted four years and the report was issued in 1868. It was an exhaustive investigation of all types of secondary education and the report was a model of completeness and accuracy. Girls', as well as boys', schools were included, private and proprietary as well as endowed schools. The Commission was extremely fortunate in possessing a number of very able assistant-commissioners, including J. G. Fitch and James Bryce. Matthew Arnold was given the task of inquiring into secondary education in France, Germany, Switzerland, and Italy; the Rev. James Fraser investigated conditions in the United States and Canada; and Mr Fearon inspected the burgh schools in nine towns in Scotland.

The task of the Taunton Commission was more difficult than that of the Clarendon. The latter were investigating schools which provided for the sons of wealthy parents and were concerned with a school population which was largely homogeneous. The Taunton Commission found a great variety of schools which they correctly attributed to social and economic factors that had been emerging since the beginning of the century. Their conclusions took into account both the wishes of the parents and evidence collected from other countries. "Much evidence has been laid before us tending to show that indifference and ignorance of the subject on the part of the parents are among the chief hindrances to education at present. Too often the parents seem hardly to care for education at all. Too often they give an inordinate value to mere show. Too often they think no education worth having that cannot be speedily turned into money. In fact, many parents need education themselves in order to appreciate education for their children, and their present opinion cannot be considered final or supreme."

Nevertheless, the Commission believed that many good schools were almost useless because they supplied one type of education and parents wanted another. A great many parents were dissatisfied with the traditional classical curriculum. "This at least ought to be conceded to them as a general principle, that what they require their children to be taught, that, if it be practicable, shall be put within their reach; what method shall be followed in teaching it, whether anything else shall be taught in addition to it, and, if so, what else— this they would probably be willing to leave to the authorities in charge of the schools."

It was thought that the length of time parents were able or willing to keep their children at school was a criterion of the differences which existed in the so-called middle classes. The Commission, therefore, considered that education ought to be organised through three grades of secondary school according to the average leaving ages of eighteen or nineteen, sixteen, and fourteen, respectively. H. C. Dent has seen in this classification the germ of the tripartite distinction. The first grade, catering for parents who allowed their sons to remain at school until at least eighteen, could be subdivided. One section was nearly identical with those who sent their sons to public schools. They did not wish to interfere with the teaching of the classics as long as instruction in mathematics, modern languages, and science was given. The other section consisted of professional men and the less wealthy country gentry who wished their sons to receive an education at least equal to that they had received. They wished to cheapen education rather than widen it. They were aware of the social value of a classical education.

The second grade of education presented quite a different picture. Some of the parents could afford to keep their sons at school for a year or two after the age of sixteen, but wished them to enter professions, the training for which usually started after that age. Others found that economic circumstances required their boys, when they attained that age, to contribute to the family earnings. The first type of parent was prepared to assign a high value to Latin, both because of its practical and its social value. The second type would barely tolerate Latin and had no use for Greek. Both groups wanted a sound training in mathematics, science, and modern studies.

The third grade of education met the needs of the lower middle classes; tenant farmers, small tradesmen, and skilled artisans. They could not afford to keep their children at school much beyond the age of fourteen. They laid stress on what was called a "clerk's education", which consisted in a thorough knowledge of arithmetic and English. In addition, there could be some instruction in elementary mathematics and natural science. A few were in favour of vocational training, but most preferred a general education. The Commissioners deplored the fact that so few third grade schools existed and pleaded for more of them. This wish was eventually to be met in some measure by the establishment of the higher grade schools. In the larger towns there was room for schools of the first grade, and many of them ought to be boarding schools or with boarding attachments. Such schools would prepare a proportion of their scholars for university entrance.

The investigations of the Commission showed that the supply of secondary schools was woefully inadequate and the distribution of the schools was extremely uneven. A large town, such as Huddersfield, had no endowed secondary school (Almondbury was then outside the town boundary), whilst many of the smaller endowed schools had not only become inferior elementary schools but often interfered with the establishment of really efficient National schools. Some endowments were being grossly misused and many governing bodies seldom met and were satisfied with the low standards which prevailed in their schools. Thus the population of the West Riding was 1,548,299, and it was estimated that 20,533 children should be receiving a post-primary education. Mr Fitch found that the actual number in attendance was 1,836, and in no instance was the available school accommodation fully taken up. Some schools in large towns were doing effective work within limits, but all of them could be improved.

The following examples illustrate conditions in the less efficient schools:

(a) Fitch reported on the school at Easingwold, Yorks., as follows: "I found a school along the middle of which was a partition breast high, dividing the scholars into two groups. The master's desk was fixed in an elevated position and dominated both divisions of the school. He explained to me that the free scholars were on one side and the paying scholars on the other. He had erected the partition, he said, in defence of his own interests, for unless he kept the two classes of pupils—the 'sheep and the goats', as he familiarly called them—habitually apart, the more respectable parents would object to pay, and perhaps remove their children altogether. I learned that while he was bound to admit a certain number of free scholars, it had been his custom to receive others on the footing of private pupils and that even in the playground there was no intercourse between them." It was quite general to find that free scholars were only taught the subjects named in the will of the founder. Parents who wished their children to be instructed in reading or arithmetic were required to pay a fee.

(b) Mr Fearon visited Thame Grammar School (Oxfordshire). He reported: "The *Master* is a graduate of Oxford University. For some years he has taken no active part in teaching. Indeed in some years it can scarcely have been necessary that he should do so: in 1863, for example, when the number of pupils was only half that of the masters. The *Usher* is a Member of the College of Preceptors, but has no other degree or qualification. The *Pupil* was eleven years and nine months old. He was the son of a farmer, and had been two years in the school. He was not learning anything but reading, dictation, and elementary arithmetic. His reading was, compared with that of children in a National school, bad; his spelling, very bad; his arithmetic, bad. No Latin, no French. For this education he was paying two guineas per annum to the master, and one guinea to the usher." The master received £200 and the usher £100 from the endowment.

(*c*) Mr Fearon also visited Ware Grammar School. He noticed the very unsatisfactory attainments of the eighteen pupils and reported on the school house. "The school buildings are most miserable. They consist simply of two small rooms one above the other in a little house which stands at the corner of the old churchyard ... The lower of the two rooms is let by the master to a brewer as a beer-cellar. The brewer's yard and brewhouse adjoin the school— and I am told, that noise and smell from this business are frequently almost intolerable in the schoolroom up-stairs ... The floor is very unsound, and by inspection of the beams in the room below, I doubt if the whole school will not before long fall through into the brewer's cellar ... These premises are totally unfit for their purpose, and do not appear to be worth repair."

(*d*) Sometimes excellent results were being obtained in most unsatisfactory buildings. Mr Bryce visited a school at Bispham. The school was an old house with thatched roof through which the rain penetrated, dropping upon the desks and leaving a pool upon the floor. The room measured $30\frac{1}{2}$ feet by $14\frac{1}{2}$ feet, and was $7\frac{1}{2}$ feet high, and the number of pupils on roll was seventy. When he visited the school, only twenty boys and twelve girls were present, but the air was so foul that he was obliged to keep the door open whilst he examined the children. No Latin was taught, and the reading and spelling were good, but the arithmetic was taught in an old-fashioned way. "But the characteristic feature of the school was one which I had least expected to find in such a place. The small and wretched room was filled in every available corner by stuffed beasts and birds; geological diagrams hung upon the walls: shelves were loaded and drawers filled with collections of fossils and minerals. In answer to my look of surprise, the master explained that he was an ardent naturalist; he had collected all these things himself, and used them in his teaching, giving a lesson to the whole school four afternoons in every week."

Bryce remarked that such a master would not be found in a Government school. If he had been found there, he would certainly have taught the three R's better and would have had a more suitable schoolroom. "But his time would have been too completely absorbed in bringing the children up to the 'Standards' of the Revised Code, to let him stray into the regions of natural history, which he taught so excellently well, and to the so great profit of the neighbourhood."

The Commissioners found the condition of the private schools to be generally unsatisfactory, but Fitch reported: "I have wholly failed to discover any example of the typical Yorkshire boarding school with which Dickens' *Nicholas Nickleby* has made us familiar. I have seen schools in which board and education were furnished for 20 l., and even 18 l. per annum, but have been unable to find evidence of bad feeding or physical neglect".

The proprietary schools were singled out for praise. Many of them had been founded under the influence of the reforms carried out by Dr Arnold and other public school headmasters. Amongst them were schools which sprang from the educational zeal displayed by the religious denominations, *e.g.* Woodhouse Grove, near Bradford, founded by the Wesleyans, the Congregational school of Silcoates, near Wakefield, the Friends' schools of Ackworth, and Bootham, York, and the Jews' College, at Finsbury. Others had been established by the Church, *e.g.* the Anglican schools founded by Canon Woodard at Lancing and Hurstpierpoint, and some, like Epsom, which received the sons of doctors, catered for certain professions. Many proprietary schools had become endowed and were administered by public boards of governors. They rivalled the older public schools in preparing their boys for university entrance, the professions, and the Services, *e.g.* Marlborough, Bradfield, and Cheltenham Colleges.

Although the Commission noted the reports on the schools of Scotland, America, and the Continent, it was thought that whilst much useful information could be gained from other countries, English secondary education had its roots in English institutions of the past and was suited to our character and temperament. The

Commissioners believed that the deficiencies revealed by the investigation could only be remedied by the establishment of a national system of secondary education and this might be based on the existing endowed schools.

They were greatly concerned about the inadequate provision for the secondary education of girls, and were much impressed by the evidence presented by Miss Buss and Miss Beale, the pioneers of secondary schools for girls. There were only thirteen secondary schools for girls in this country, and most of these offered a training inferior to that given by boys' schools.

The Commission recommended a complete overhaul of English secondary education. The primary need was a thorough revision of the constitutions and the governing bodies of the endowed schools, but in undertaking this, each school ought to be considered in relation to other schools in its area. Where necessary, new endowed schools would be established and all the schools would be placed under permanent supervision. This would involve the creation of new administrative machinery. It was thought that an enlarged and reconstituted Charity Commission, presided over by a Minister of Education, would form an effective central authority. The Charity Commission would visit schools, make schemes for their organisation and submit them for the approval of Parliament. It would appoint inspectors, audit school accounts, and use the money derived from useless and obsolete charities for educational purposes.

The problem of the local administration of education was difficult because no local authorities which could deal with it were in existence. The School Boards were not created until 1870, and they were only concerned with elementary schools. It was proposed that the country should be divided into provinces corresponding to the divisions of the Registrar-General, and an Official District Commissioner should be appointed by the Charity Commission for each area. He would be one of the trustees for every educational endowment and would inspect each secondary school in the district at least once in three years. Six or eight unpaid District Commissioners appointed by the Crown from the locality would assist him. The schemes for the reorganisation of the governing bodies of schools should aim at the inclusion of representatives of parents, public bodies, and universities, in addition to members co-opted from the original governors. The powers and duties of the governors and the headmaster were carefully defined.

The response of the Government was most disappointing. An Endowed Schools Act was passed in 1869 which set up an Endowed Schools Commission, to which was assigned the duty of drawing up new schemes of government. It was appointed for three years only, but at the end of this time it was continued for another year, and in 1874 its powers were merged with those of the Charity Commission. This body carried on with the revision of schemes of government until its work was given to the Board of Education and has now been completed by the Minister of Education. Progress was slow, but the framing of new constitutions for the schools affected their curricula and teaching methods. One important aspect of this work was the application of many endowments not specifically designed for boys' schools to the establishment of secondary schools for girls. Thus a scheme for Bradford Grammar School created two first-class schools, one for boys and the other for girls.

Many reasons can be advanced to explain the failure of the Government to carry out in full the recommendations of the Taunton Commission. One was the preoccupation of the Government with plans for filling the gaps in elementary education. Another was the problem of finding local authorities for secondary education and the prevalent distrust of Government intervention. Possibly the most important was the widespread apathy of the general public. The Taunton Commission was in advance of public opinion, and it was not until there was a recognition of the value of secondary education and a demand for it that further progress could be made.

Secondary Education for Girls

The most noticeable accomplishment was in the provision of secondary education for girls. Miss Buss, at the North London Collegiate School (founded 1850), and Miss Beale, Principal of the Ladies' College, Cheltenham (1858), inaugurated the movement for the secondary education of girls. The Girls' Public Day School Company, founded in 1872, took the North London Collegiate School as a model, and by the end of the century had built thirty-three schools, which provided secondary education for more than 7,100 girls.

Thring of Uppingham

As regards public school education, the latter part of the nineteenth century is memorable for the example set by another distinguished headmaster whom some would assess as having an even greater influence than Dr Arnold. This was Edward Thring, who, in 1853, entered upon what he described as his life's work at Uppingham. At the time of his appointment it was a small school which had been founded in 1584. His aim was to transform it into a large public school which would show in practice his own ideals of public school education. Thring believed in small classes as against the large classes to be found in the schools of the period. He thought that there should be no more than thirty boys in a form and that the ideal public boarding school should be organised into ten or eleven houses, each containing not more than thirty boys. This would give a school of less than 400 pupils, which he thought was the largest number that would enable a headmaster to know each boy personally. There is no doubt that if he had been alive to-day, he would have regarded the comprehensive school of 2,000 pupils as a monstrosity in which the headmaster would be a mere administrator.

Thring had been a scholar at Eton and he retained a vivid memory of the long dormitory there which was something to be avoided. The ideal was for each boy to have a separate cubicle and study. This was only possible if generous funds were available, but he found that his governors had other views. They were responsible for a similar school at Oakham and were opposed to any developments which would restrict its expansion. He resolved to put all the money he could spare into the rebuilding of Uppingham. His staff loyally supported him and offered their own savings for the reconstruction of the school. Like Arnold he had a firm belief in the value of the school chapel, and this was the first new building he decided to erect. He made immense efforts to raise money through subscriptions, and the chapel was finally completed in 1865 at a cost of £10,000. The governors gave little support to his efforts and he was running increasingly into debt when he started to rebuild the schoolroom.

At the critical moment the Taunton Commission claimed that Uppingham came under their jurisdiction. Thring was convinced that any Government intervention in the affairs of the public schools would threaten their freedom and independence. The only effective way of meeting the threat was by combined action, and his first step was to consult the heads of other public schools. The result was the formation of the Headmaster's Conference in 1869. The first members were Uppingham, Repton, Sherborne, Tonbridge,

Liverpool College, Bury St Edmunds, Richmond (Yorks.), Bromsgrove, Oakham, the King's School, Canterbury, Felsted, Lancing,
and Norwich.   At a later date the older public schools joined and
it became necessary to draw up conditions of membership.

A member school had to be satisfactory from an educational
point of view and must send an adequate number of boys to the
universities.   The maximum number of members was fixed at 150,
but in 1937 it was increased and the rules amended to admit direct
grant schools and even schools maintained by L.E.A.s, provided
that the necessary degree of autonomy was accorded to the school
and the headmaster.   The importance of this step appeared in 1942
when the President of the Board of Education defined a public
school as one which is a member of the Governing Bodies' Association or the Headmasters' Conference.   The former body was of
recent growth, being instituted in 1941 to discuss questions of
policy which were outside the reference of the H.M.C.   There is
only a slight difference in the membership of the two bodies.

Thring anticipated a later headmaster, Sanderson of Oundle,
in his belief that although in a large school boys will have a variety
of interests, tastes, and abilities, each one can do something well
if that something can be discovered by his teachers.   Hence he
insisted that the school should provide a variety of studies and
occupations.   He sincerely believed in the value of games and physical education, and in 1859 he opened the first gymnasium in England.   Uppingham had its own swimming-bath, school garden, and
workshops for wood and metal.   Although he was not a musician,
Thring was aware of the value of music and, assisted by one of his
masters, he developed a strong musical tradition in the school.

In 1875 a crisis occurred in the fortunes of the school with the
outbreak of an epidemic of enteric fever.   The school was evacuated to Aberystwyth.   It returned to Uppingham in 1878, where
Thring remained as headmaster until his sudden death in 1887.   In
addition to being an outstanding teacher he was interested in the
theory and technique of teaching, and his book, *The Theory and
Practice of Teaching*, 1883, was for many years the acknowledged
textbook for intending schoolmasters.

Welsh Intermediate Education

An event occurred in Wales in 1889 which had important repercussions on English education.   Secondary education there had
followed lines similar to those in England.   The eighteenth century

showed a deterioration corresponding to that in this country, but the awakening started in 1848 when Sir Thomas Phillips founded the Collegiate School at Llandovery, which was followed by the opening of girls' schools at Llandaff and Denbigh in 1853. Progress was slow until 1868, when the Reform Act created a demand for special consideration of Welsh education. The general election of 1880 at last convinced the Government that something ought to be done, and a Departmental Committee to investigate Welsh secondary education was formed under the chairmanship of Lord Aberdare to survey the supply of intermediate and higher education in Wales and recommend steps for its development.

The report of the Aberdare Committee revealed a state of affairs similar to those found in England by the Taunton Commission, and the immediate result was the establishment of university colleges at Cardiff and Bangor. The action in regard to intermediate education (that is education intermediate between elementary and university education) was delayed until 1889, when the Welsh Intermediate Education Act was passed. This created joint education committees as local authorities for every county and county borough in Wales. Each local authority was required to submit a scheme for secondary and technical education in its area and was given the power of levying a rate not exceeding ½d. in the £ if approved by the County Council. The treasury would make an equal grant on condition of an annual inspection of schools. A later development was the formation of the Central Welsh Board for Intermediate Education in 1896. The Act of 1889 influenced English education because it provided a pattern of local control of secondary education by the county and county borough councils.

The Administrative Muddle

Meanwhile, in England, educational administration had fallen into what has been described as an "administrative muddle". The English character and temperament was largely responsible for this. Until the present century the average Englishman has always been disinclined to look far ahead and to organise carefully planned systems, but has preferred to meet each new problem as it occurs. This was especially true of English education. The reader should by now have some idea of the multiplicity of agencies which contributed to our educational development, and will have realised the strength of the opposition to State intervention. The Bryce Commission, which now has to be considered, put this point clearly.

"There is one feature in this growing concern of the State with education which must not be here overlooked. The growth has not been either continuous or coherent, *i.e.* it does not represent a series of logical or even connected sequences. Each one of the agencies . . . was called into being, not merely independently of the others, but with little or no regard to their existence. Each has remained in its working isolated and unconnected with the rest. The problems which secondary education presents have been approached from different sides, at different times, and with different views and aims."

There were five central authorities concerned in one way or another with the schools.

(1) The Education Department was responsible for elementary education, but it had no jurisdiction over endowed elementary schools which possessed an income from endowments of over £100 per annum. The latter were the concern of the Charity Commission. The Education Department had some say in the conduct of secondary education. It was responsible for the supervision of the higher grade schools which shared in the elementary grant but provided what was in reality a secondary education. The Department also issued regulations for teacher training, both in training colleges and university day training departments, thus having a share in higher education.

(2) The Charity Commission was the central authority for secondary education, but it was mentioned above that it had some concern with elementary. Some secondary schools were outside its jurisdiction, *e.g.* the great public schools, proprietary schools, and schools founded less than fifty years before the Endowed Schools Act of 1869.

(3) The Science and Art Department was established in 1852. Its work will be considered in more detail in a later chapter. For the present it should be noted that it instituted a number of examinations and paid grants to schools which presented successful candidates. These schools might be endowed grammar schools, higher grade schools, technical institutions, evening classes, or colleges. Thus the Yorkshire College of Science received aid from the Science and Art Department. The schools which received grants from the Department were known as Organised Schools of Science.

(4) The Board of Agriculture had no jurisdiction over elementary schools, but it could inspect and aid with grants endowed grammar schools, evening classes, and university colleges in which education connected with agriculture was provided.

(5) The Admiralty and War Office organised their own schools for the education of serving members of the Forces and their children. They held examinations and awarded certificates. Each of the above departments issued its own regulations, often with no regard to what other departments were doing. Hence the prevalence of overlapping and contradictions.

In the local administration of education five distinct bodies were concerned.

(1) The School Boards, 2,568 in number, were elected to take charge of elementary education in those areas where there was no adequate provision by the voluntary bodies. They were also responsible for higher grade schools, higher tops of elementary schools, and evening classes. In so far, they had a share in secondary education.

(2) School Attendance Committees had been authorised by Lord Sandon's Act of 1876 and given powers to make school attendance compulsory in areas where School Boards had not been formed.

(3) Boards of Managers controlled voluntary elementary schools. They numbered 14,238 and each body corresponded directly with the Education Department.

(4) Secondary schools were administered by Boards of Governors; and in the proprietary schools affairs were managed by committees.

(5) Lastly, but destined to be the most important, were the County Councils and the County Borough Councils. These were the most recent arrivals on the educational scene. The Technical Instruction Act of 1889 had given power to these councils to levy a rate not exceeding 1d. in the £ for aiding or supplying technical education. In the following year, Parliament passed the Local Taxation (Customs and Excise) Act. Its aim was to recompense publicans for the loss of their licences in areas in which there was an excess of public houses. Many members of the House of Commons opposed the granting of money to publicans. For once, at least, the Chancellor of the Exchequer possessed a surplus which was not earmarked for any special purpose. He decided to hand it

over to the County and County Borough Councils, and one purpose for which the money could be employed was the encouragement of technical instruction. In 1893-4, nearly half a million pounds was made available for education, and much of it was used to rescue endowed grammar schools from their financial difficulties. The experience gained by the Councils was to stand them in good stead in later years. The fund was popularly known as the "Whisky Money".

The administrative muddle did not escape notice, and in 1893 two quite dissimilar bodies drew the attention of the Government to it. Resolutions were approved by the Bradford Independent Labour Party and by a conference on secondary education called by the Vice-Chancellor of Oxford. The result was that in 1894 a Royal Commission on secondary education was constituted. Its Chairman was Mr (later Viscount) Bryce. The Bryce Commission was instructed to carry out its investigations as quickly as possible, and it issued its report in 1895.

Bryce Commission

The Bryce Commission was, in some respects, the most important Royal Commission on education. Like the Taunton Commission, many of the recommendations made were in advance of the time and were not carried out in the form originally desired. There is some truth in the assertion that they were not completely put into operation until the Education Act of 1944. For the first time women were members of a Royal Commission, and although the Commission was primarily concerned with secondary schools, it felt that it could not do justice to its terms of reference if it reviewed secondary education in isolation. It therefore paid attention to both elementary and technical education.

The Report of the Bryce Commission opened with a survey of the progress which had been made since the Taunton Commission reported in 1868. It drew attention to the recommendations which had partially been carried into effect, e.g. the provision of new schemes of government for secondary schools and the institution of the Charity Commission as the central authority for secondary education, but it deplored that nothing had been done to create local authorities, to set up a central council for education, or to draw up a register of teachers. The Endowed Schools Act established only "a fragment of the system they had elaborated with so much foresight and patient statesmanship".

Four other agencies were mentioned which had contributed to progress.

(1) The School Boards were doing for primary education what it was hoped would be accomplished for secondary education. The growth of the higher grade schools was noted and the Report described them as "really secondary in their character" and that they had "stepped into the educational void" by supplying what approximated to the third grade secondary schools recommended by the Taunton Commission.

(2) The growth of the Science and Art Department and the grants it made towards educational work in those studies which had enabled a number of secondary schools to continue.

(3) A new feature was the creation of university colleges for higher education which were open to both men and women and five colleges for women only. The provision of University Extension courses was closely related to this growth of higher education which brought it within the reach of adults who otherwise would have been unable to obtain such instruction.

(4) Reference was also made to the "Whisky Money" which under the administration of the County and Borough Councils had given encouragement to technical and secondary education.

In addition, the Report mentioned the successful working of the Welsh Intermediate Education Act which furnished suggestions for the reform of secondary education in this country. Before 1868 the teaching profession in England had been unorganised, but because of ties of common interest, various associations had been formed. Amongst them were the Headmasters' Conference, the National Union of Teachers (started in 1870), the Association of Headmistresses (1874), the Association of Assistant Mistresses (1885), the Incorporated Association of Headmasters (1890), the Association of Assistant Masters (1892), and other similar organisations.

The growth of proprietary schools, the improved provision for the secondary education of girls, and the increased interest of the general public in education were also noted. All these developments had led to the present administrative problem of "the dispersed and unconnected forces, needless competition between the different agencies, and a frequent overlapping of effort, with much consequent waste of money, of time, of labour". The aim of the

Among them (handwritten)

Commission was to find out how far it was possible to organise a national system of secondary education, but this was no easy task.

The record of the Education Department since the Revised Code had given rise to serious misgivings. The Bishop of London thought that a Minister of Education would be the nominee of a political party and would change with every successive Government. It was also feared that technical and scientific education might put literary subjects into the background. A great change had occurred since 1869. Then, the sciences were struggling for recognition, but now it seemed we were heading for a one-sided education. "The importance of preserving all grammar schools which are, or can be made, efficient depends largely on the general ground that such schools represent especially the tradition of literary education. There is little danger at the present day that we shall fail to recognise the necessity of improving and extending scientific and technical instruction. It is less certain that we may not run some risk of a lop-sided development in education, in which the teaching of science, theoretical or applied, may so predominate as to entail comparative neglect of studies which are of less obvious and immediate utility, though not of less moment for the formation of mind and character."

justified fears (handwritten marginal note)

Finally, the fear was expressed that a State system of secondary education would be managed by the permanent officials of the Civil Service and result in bureaucracy. The Commission realised that something had to be done and decided that the establishment of a central authority to supervise elementary, secondary, and technical education was the lesser evil. At its head there should be a Minister of Education responsible to Parliament. How could the domination of party politics be prevented?

The Minister should be assisted by an Educational Council which should include members appointed by the Crown, representatives of the two older Universities and of the London and Victoria Universities, and of the teaching profession. The term of office of the Council would be six years, and to ensure continuity of experience and permanence of policy one third of the members should retire every two years. The relations between the Council and the Minister were the subject of some discussion. The Commission suggested that a good deal of educational policy was concerned with professional matters which were outside party politics, *e.g.* curriculum problems, inspection and examination of schools, the training of teachers, and the preparation of a register of teachers.

The Commission recommended the creation of local authorities for secondary education. Some members thought that the local authorities should be in charge of all types of education, but the majority took it for granted that the School Boards would be continued for elementary education. There was no doubt about the choice of local authorities. The Welsh Intermediate Act had worked efficiently, and in England the County and County Borough Councils had acquired considerable experience in administering the "Whisky Money". Hence, the recommendation was approved that the new local authorities for secondary education should be the County Councils, the County Borough Councils, and the Councils of towns with a population of over 50,000. A special scheme would have to be prepared for London.

The local authorities would carry out the following functions.

(1) An adequate provision of secondary schools in their areas, which in many districts would involve the building of new schools.

(2) The supervision of endowed schools, with power to make changes where desirable.

(3) It would be their duty to survey the whole field of secondary education in their areas with the object of bringing proprietary and private schools into the general system. This would entail the inspection of schools, the preparation of a list of efficient secondary schools, and the provision of scholarships to enable children of merit to pass from elementary to secondary schools.

(4) To administer moneys obtained from the rates or paid over by the Exchequer.

The members of the Commission found that no accurate definition of elementary, secondary, or technical education existed. Thus, when Sir George Kekewich was examined as a witness, he admitted that he was unable to draw the line at which elementary education ended and secondary education began. Moreover, technical education was regarded as something different in kind from secondary education. The Report contained an important statement on the latter point, which is generally believed to have been compiled by Mr (later Sir) M. E. Sadler.

"Secondary education is the education of the boy and girl not simply as a human being who needs to be instructed in certain rudiments of knowledge, but it is a process of intellectual training and personal discipline conducted with special regard to the profession or trade to be followed . . . All secondary schools . . . in so far as they qualify men for doing something in life, partake more or less in the character of institutes that educate craftsmen. Every profession, even that of winning scholarships, is a craft, and all crafts are arts . . . No definition of technical instruction is possible that does not bring it under the head of secondary education, nor can secondary education be so defined as absolutely to exclude from it the idea of technical instruction. Technical education is secondary, *i.e.* it comes after the education which has awakened the mind by teaching the child the rudiments, or, as it were, the alphabet, of all knowledge, and the better the whole of this alphabet has been mastered, the better and easier will later learning be. And secondary education is technical, *i.e.* it teaches the boy so to apply the principles he is learning, and so to learn the principles by applying them, or so to use the instruments he is being made to know, as to perform or produce something, interpret a literature or a science, make a picture or a book, practise a plastic or manual art, convince a jury or persuade a senate, translate or annotate an author, dye wool, weave cloth, design or construct a machine, navigate a ship, or command an army. Secondary education, therefore, as inclusive of technical, may be described as education conducted in view of the special life that has to be lived with the express purpose of forming a person fit to live it."

The Government decided to tackle the problem of local authorities first, and in 1896 a Bill, prepared by Sir John Gorst, assisted by Sir George Kekewich and Mr Sadler, was presented to Parliament. It proposed to go a step further than the Bryce Commission and to abolish the School Boards and constitute the County and County Borough Councils as local authorities for all types of school in their districts. It also suggested the giving of financial assistance to the voluntary schools, which were finding it increasingly difficult to make ends meet. The Bill was fiercely opposed by the representatives of the School Boards, by the Nonconformists, who objected to rate aid for elementary voluntary schools, and by the majority of the Liberal opposition. The Prime Minister decided to drop the Bill and to proceed with legislation for the creation of a central authority for education.

Board of Education Act

This was accomplished by the Board of Education Act, 1899, which set up a Board of Education to "superintend matters relating to education in England and Wales". It was to take the place of the Education Department, the Science and Art Department, and the Charity Commission in so far as it was concerned with education. The head of the Board was a President appointed by the Crown. It also consisted of the Lord President of the Council, unless, as happened in 1899, he was, in the person of the Duke of Devonshire, identical with the President of the Board; the Principal Secretaries of State; the First Commissioner of the Treasury; and the Chancellor of the Exchequer. Sir John Gorst, the Vice-President of the Education Department, was to remain as Vice-President of the Board until he retired in 1902. The President of the Board was assisted by a Consultative Committee of eighteen members, including women. It had a six year term of office, and its functions were to advise the Board on matters referred to it by the President and to prepare a register of teachers.

The Act only partially carried out the recommendations of the Bryce Commission. The Duke of Devonshire admitted that the Board only existed on paper. In its long history, it never once met. Its work was performed by the President, the Permanent Secretary, and the staff of secretaries and senior officials. The powers of the Board were vague in the extreme. What, for instance, did the term "superintend" mean? The Board, through its power of curtailing or discontinuing the Government grant, could always make its wishes obeyed, but it rarely proceeded to this extreme. It relied more on giving advice and encouragment than the power of the purse. The President was not a Minister of Education. He held but a junior office which often became the stepping stone to a higher appointment. Only four Presidents can be considered as really outstanding men: Mr H. A. L. Fisher, Sir Charles Trevelyan, Lord Eustace Percy, and Mr R. A. Butler.

The Consultative Committee was a mere shadow of the Educational Council proposed by the Bryce Commission. It could only deal with problems referred to it; it could only speak when spoken to. Nevertheless, it performed valuable work in the preparation of reports, e.g. the Hadow Reports on the Adolescent, the Primary School, and the Infant and Nursery School.

The establishment of a register of teachers was delayed until 1902, when the Board unwisely issued a register divided into two columns, one for elementary, the other for secondary school teachers. Quite rightly this procedure was severely criticised by the National Union of Teachers, with the result that the register was withdrawn. In 1907 the Teachers' Registration Council was formed, and it issued a list of teachers in alphabetical order. Registration was voluntary, and those teachers whose names were included in the register were entitled to use the letters M.R.S.T. (Member of the Royal Society of Teachers). It was hoped that registration would help in raising the status and dignity of the profession. Unfortunately, neither the Board nor the local authorities used the register to any extent in selecting candidates for promotion. with the consequence that many teachers were reluctant to pay the small fee demanded for registration. The Ministry of Education abandoned registration in 1948, but those teachers who had previously registered can still use the title of M.R.S.T.

SUGGESTIONS FOR FURTHER READING

S. J. Curtis, *History of Education in Great Britain,* sixth edition, U.T.P., 1965. Chapter V.

H. C. Barnard, *A Short History of English Education from 1760 to 1944,* University of London Press. Chapters XV, XVIII, XXII, XXIII to p. 244.

CHAPTER VI

THOUGHT ON EDUCATION, 1800-1850

At the end of the eighteenth century many different factors were playing their part in breaking down the somewhat complacent, pseudo-Lockian attitude of the intelligentsia. The general spirit was conservative, because the impact of the French Revolution was vivid in men's minds, and the results of the Revolutionary Wars were still undecided. Although some of the pioneers in the education of the poor were regarded askance as putative Jacobins, one of the main arguments put forward in favour of extended education was that, in leading men to Godliness, it would also reduce the danger of discontent and rioting. The Sunday School movement led by Robert Raikes, the Schools of Industry, developed by the indefatigable Mrs Sarah Trimmer, and the two great new societies for school foundation, were all expressions of this belief in education. The handicapped as well as the poor were remembered by the pioneers. Thus there were at least three schools for the blind in this country by the turn of the century.

Grammar school education had reached a low ebb for a variety of reasons—the inadequacy of endowments, the narrow curriculum, and the loss of prestige during the century when it was fashionable to advocate Locke's home education. A few public schools, however, grew strong and flourishing under able headmasters who revived traditional classicism at its best. Vicesimus Knox, Head of Tonbridge School from 1778 to 1812, was one of the leaders of this movement. His treatise *Liberal Education* emphasises the place of the classics, but expresses an enlightened attitude to other subjects. Samuel Butler took over the Headship of Shrewsbury School in 1798 when there was but one pupil on the roll, and during his thirty-eight years there he built up a great school. He demanded high academic standards and gained them by a careful attention to individual progress, a searching examination system, and the encouragement of self-reliance—and even a measure of self-government. Nevertheless, the classics remained the basic curriculum although history and geography were not omitted, Butler himself being something of a geographer.

By the turn of the century there was a multitude of private schools in existence, serving the middle classes as well as the upper, and catering for girls as well as boys. On the whole, these schools reflected realist, utilitarian trends of thought and offered a wider curriculum, which usually included French, "accompts", and a smattering of modern geography and science. Moreover, there was often a dancing master available, and there are records of dancing displays and of balls held jointly by neighbouring boys' and girls' schools. A further notable point is that many of these new schools were located *outside* the big towns and often at some distance from them. When such a school was advertised in newspapers, the healthy site was usually emphasised. It is tempting to read Locke into all these developments, but epidemics, road transport development, and mere fashion probably account for most of the features described above.

No doubt a great many well-to-do families employed men tutors to teach their children at home, but by this time a new kind of underpaid hireling had appeared on the scene—the governess, who was usually "a lady in reduced circumstances". We learn of the trials and indignities suffered by some of these women from writers such as Mary Wollstoncraft, the rebel who resolved to break the bondage of womanhood and to achieve equality with man—only to meet an untimely death through her own womanhood. Except to point out that such were the circumstances from which stemmed interest in, and agitation for, the better education of girls, we are not concerned with the unsatisfactory aspects of home education, but rather with those examples which indicate advances in ideas and practice. An excellent example is the home education of the family of the English utilitarian, R. L. Edgeworth.

The Edgeworths and Practical Education

A large and long-lived family, the Edgeworths stretch over the years before and after the turn of the century, but as their spirit is rather "brave new world" than *fin de siècle*, it seems fitting that their ideas should be considered along with the views of early nineteenth-century thinkers. Paterfamilias himself was pure eighteenth century in his exuberance and his man-of-the-world-liness, but his oft-quoted discipleship of Rousseau should not damn Edgeworthian education as a mere eccentric experiment.

It is true that as young men, Edgeworth and his friend Thomas Day resolved to work on the production of Emiles and Sophies.

Day adopted two little girls and put them through an austere Emilian régime, thinking to make them into modest, stoical, and unselfish housewives, either fit to be his bride. One girl emerged satisfactorily from this commando course, having been sheltered from the wicked world—especially from feminine vanities and frivolities—and having endured the "hardening process" in a somewhat severe form—the pain of hot sealing-wax on her arm, the fear of a pistol at her back. Nevertheless, she lost her husband-to-be by failing to obey his instructions in the details of her dress.

Edgeworth showed an even stronger faith in the supposed methods of the Master by bringing up his own firstborn like Emile. He recalls in his *Memoirs*, "I was but twenty-three years old when I formed this resolution . . . I dressed my son without stockings, with his arms bare; in a jacket and trousers which were at that time novel and extraordinary. I succeeded in making him fearless of danger, and, what is more difficult, capable of bearing privation of every sort. He had all the virtues of a child bred in the hut of a savage, and all the knowledge of THINGS which could be well acquired at an early age by a boy bred in civilised society. Of books he had less knowledge at seven or eight years old than most children have at four or five. Of mechanics he had a clearer conception and in the application of what he knew, more invention than any child I had then seen".[1]

However, by the time Edgeworth published his first major treatise, *Practical Education*, in 1798, the experiment had ended in failure a quarter of a century earlier, and his ideas had matured during the upbringing of many children resulting from his four marriages. It is interesting, however, that the most talented and capable of his children was his second-born, Maria, also a child of his first—and least clever—wife, and probably a victim of her father's early enthusiasm.

Maria Edgeworth (1767-1849) was already an established authoress—a writer of novels and children's stories—by the time she collaborated with her father in the writing of *Practical Education*. There is no doubt that her contribution to the work was considerable. She had read widely and had taken part with vigour and enthusiasm in the household education organised and encouraged by Edgeworth and his intelligent second wife. *Practical Education* is a kind of report of their experiments and the conclusions arrived at. Maria later claimed that her father was the

[1] R. L. Edgeworth, *Memoirs*, Vol. I, pp. 172-3, London, 1820.

first to pursue and recommend the experimental method in education. Although the strictures of the treatise were undoubtedly
derived largely from family experiences, the size of the family and
the great width of its circle of relatives and acquaintances, ensured
that the ideas of most of the "progressives" of the time were
reflected in the text.

Thus, after a somewhat Lockian preface, the very first chapter
is devoted to the ideas of a son-in-law—an unorthodox medico—
on "Toys", but the spirit of the chapter sets the standard for those
which follow. Education should be useful; toys ought to be the
kind which satisfy the analytic and constructive tendencies of
children. Children need toys which exercise both senses and imagination, and, say the writers, "As long as a child has sense and
courage to destroy his toys, there is no great harm done".[1]
Mechanical toys, and complete models (such as furnished dolls'
houses) are useless to children, but wood blocks, pencils, card
games, draughts, tops, kites, hoops, battledores, and shuttlecocks
are all valuable for training in various skills—comparison, construction, concentration, and manual dexterity. Moreover, "a
rational toy shop should be provided with all manner of carpenter's
tools, with wood properly prepared and with screws, nails, glue
and emery paper".[2] Among the many other detailed practical
suggestions, not a few have an entirely modern ring—the playroom
should have simple furniture and contain nothing dangerous or
valuable; there should be visits to workshops and factories, there
should be material for carrying out simple scientific experiments—
the chemistry set, in fact.

In discussing the next topic, "Tasks", the writers reveal their
divergence from Rousseau. While urging that formal lessons are
often started too early so that "temper and understanding have
been injured by premature instruction",[3] they suggest that learning
to read should be made easier by the careful handling of vowel
sounds and symbols. The Edgeworth method was probably on the
"Look-and-Say" principle. "All people," it is stated, "before they
can read fluently, have acquired a knowledge of the general appearance of most of the words in the language". It is not without
significance that the Edgeworths are sceptical about "the fashion
of late to attempt teaching everything to children through play".
Play is certainly an indication of a child's interests, and may thus

---

[1] *Practical Education*, Vol. I, p. 3.
[2] *ibid.*, Vol. I, p. 22.   [3] *ibid.*, Vol. I, p. 39.

suggest what teaching would be successful, but knowledge itself cannot be achieved without effort and hard work.

The problem of gaining and utilising the attention of pupils then concerns the writers. This attention is one of the most necessary skills and must be developed gradually by ensuring that all instruction is clear to the child's mind. "A child will be better pleased if he acquires one distinct idea from a lesson than if he retain a confused notion of twenty different things".[1] The child's attention should be exercised only for short periods, and there should be plenty of physical exercise between his mental efforts. Different children have differing capacities of attention, so that it is necessary to study each child. "If he be incapacitated from fatigue, let him rest; if he is torpid, rouse him with a rattling peal of thunder . . . You must diminish fear before you can command attention in a timid child."[2]

The eternal question of family relations with servants is dealt with in the vein of the great educators. Children must be sheltered from those who might teach them lying, bad habits, and bad manners. Even friends and visitors may do great harm by "this farce of civility"[3] which requires that children should be flattered and spoilt. The moulding of the sentiments and the training of character is no less important than in older educational theories. Evenness of temper combined with obedience should be fostered by a combination of sympathy, firmness, and example.

Good discipline is achieved by habit training and adult firmness and consistency—almost a reflection of Locke. To train a timid child in truthfulness it is necessary to show him he has nothing to fear from speaking the truth. On the other hand, the deliberate liar must be made to see he can gain nothing by deceit. Corporal punishment should rarely be necessary, and any kind of punishment should always be given immediately after the offence, so that the punishment is associated in the offender's mind with that kind of behaviour. The dread of parental disapproval is one of the best deterrents. Restraint in the expression of feelings is as desirable to the Edgeworths as to Plato. Thus, although praise is useful as a stimulus it should be given very sparingly.

Another Platonic stricture is that children's books should be censored, and that over-emotional stories and novels should be banned. It must have been Father Edgeworth who wrote, "We

---

[1] *Practical Education*, Vol. I, p. 78.
[2] *ibid.*, Vol. I, pp. 92-3.
[3] *ibid.*, Vol. I, p. 137.

know from common experience the effects which are produced upon the female mind by novel reading".[1] Fairy tales fall into the same category, and even Rousseau's favourite, *Robinson Crusoe*, is deemed too stimulating for lively boys unless they were intended for the armed services. The best kind of literature for young people is "the history of realities written in an entertaining manner",[2] but the writers give a warning that "the child is always the best judge of what is suited to his present capacity".[3]

On the question of poetry the Edgeworths take a Lockian stand —that poetry is "an agreeable amusement", but should be permitted only *now and again* because the inventive and reasoning faculties "must be injured by the repetitions of vague and of exaggerated description with which most poetry abounds".[4] That training in reading and writing should be based on interest, that simple, natural, straightforward talking is the best foundation for written English, are both ideas familiar to the modern teacher. The provision of good and interesting books at appropriate ages and stages is yet another task of schools to-day.

Like Locke, the Edgeworths would have grammar taught incidentally, largely through conversation. "When children have thus by degrees and by short and clear conversations been initiated into general grammar and familiarised with technical terms, the first page of Lily will lose much of its horror",[5] they contend, so that Latin, still necessary in the professions, would be started easily and could be mastered by a regular course of daily ten-minute lessons.

History and geography should be learnt so long as the starting points are sought in the contemporary world. Mere listing of place-names and dates must be replaced by studies of maps and modern events. The Edgeworths were the first to recommend the use of pictures in teaching these subjects. They suggest that prints should be made available in public libraries, for parents and teachers to borrow. Moreover, their concept of a five-foot globe of inflated fabric has only recently been realised as a commercial proposition. Maria reports in a letter of 1803 that their friend, Dr Birkbeck, used such a globe of silk, "swelled out and lighted by a lamp withinside, so that when the room was darkened we could plainly see the map of the world painted on it".[6]

[1] *Practical Education*, Vol. I, p. 333.   [2] *ibid.*, Vol. I, p. 338.
[3] *ibid.*, Vol. I, p. 343.   [4] *ibid.*, Vol. I, p. 367.   [5] *ibid.*, Vol. II, p. 403.
[6] Hare, A. J. C., *Life and Letters of Maria Edgeworth*, Vol. I, p. 131, Arnold, 1894.

Mathematics, too, should start—as to-day—with the concrete. Play and manipulation with half-inch cubes would make children familiar with number combinations, and after six months of daily five-minute lessons—at four years of age—the writing and recognising of figures in their various combinations would be mastered. At six, an understanding of numbers greater than ten can be helped by the use of black and white pebbles. After this it is a matter of frequent—but brief—periods of practice, and a thorough learning of tables. Geometry should begin with wood figures, both plane and solid, and should follow naturally from the early play with toys.

Mr Edgeworth and some of his sons were so deeply interested in experimental science that he regards it as a subject particularly suitable for children. He would have it learnt through the experiences of everyday life—the meaning of "fulcrum" through poking the fire, the principles of the pump by examining the household pump. He invented an elaborate machine of pulleys, wheels, and screws by which many mechanical experiments could be demonstrated. He also designed a perspective machine which was later constructed by Dr Birkbeck. Maria describes in her letter how he also invented a machine for telegraphy, "his pretty, delicate little telly".[1]

The depth of this family interest—at least on the male side—is shown by the contribution of a chapter on chemistry by one of the brothers. Here again, the use of the immediate environment is suggested, especially the study of home activities such as butter and cheese making, baking, and brewing.

After describing so full a curriculum which would obviously involve "activity methods" the writers drop a small bombshell by remarking that their scheme is intended for children from birth to the age of nine, the age at which most boys then started school. Thus the boys would be reinforced against the evils and imperfections of schools—the over-stress on the classics, the neglect of moral training, and the lack of continuity caused by holidays. Like Locke, who also disliked schools, the Edgeworths saw this first period of education not as one of inculcating information, but as a time for acquiring habits of industry and intelligent observation.

On the education of girls, *Practical Education* is somewhat disappointing, although better opportunities for the development

[1] Hare, A. J. C., *Life and Letters of Maria Edgeworth*, Vol. I, p. 131.

of interests and understanding are advocated. Maria's letters suggest that the sisters shared many of their brothers' interests and activities, including play writing, production, and acting.

Although there might seem to be little of Locke's austerity and "awe" in this jolly household of a century later, the educational principles accepted by the Edgeworths have more in common with Locke's concepts of sense experience and the "conduct of the understanding", than with Rousseau's belief in saving time by losing it. The writers indicate this more clearly at the end of the book when they stress the need for plenty of occupations to prevent too much day-dreaming and imagination. That such young children should learn to think about their own sense experiences is also following Locke, not Rousseau. Prudence, judgment, resolution, and thrift, which the Edgeworths aimed to cultivate, are virtues approved by Locke, but certainly not acquired by Emile at the age of nine.

Thus, although the Edgeworths had many useful contributions to make to British ideas on bringing up children, it cannot be said that they developed a really new educational theory. Their ideas are well matched by their utilitarian outlook and their lively enquiring temperaments. The task of interpreting Rousseau adequately was left to the Swiss teacher Pestalozzi. Maria visited his school twice, but although her letters indicate most friendly relations, she makes little reference to Pestalozzian ideas.

Trends in Early Nineteenth-Century Thought on Education

Practical Education was the most outstanding treatise on education in circulation during the first half of the nineteenth century. That is not to say there were no other brilliant writers who discussed education, but the Edgeworths, in giving detailed attention to the growing child, his needs and potentialities over a wide range of experience, appear to be engrossed in the process of education itself, for its own sake. The writer most nearly achieving a similar attitude was Lant Carpenter, a Bristol schoolmaster who, in his Principles of Education (1820), made frequent references to Practical Education. A product of a dissenting academy and a Scottish university, Carpenter had a more academic and theoretical approach to his subject, based on a thorough study of the ideas of his predecessors, particularly Locke and Rousseau. His discussion of the place of perception in learning is so akin to Pestalozzi's theory, that it seems possible he had read some the latter's books.

Carpenter's earlier writings had been on the education of poor children, and he was a particularly successful founder of Sunday Schools in the Bristol area. His *Principles*, however, concerned "that series of impressions whether intentional or accidental by which the development and cultivation of the various faculties and affections are affected".[1] Being the headmaster and proprietor of a successful co-educational boarding school for middle-class children, he addressed himself to the parents of such children— "intelligent, reflecting parents, sensible of the momentous duty of their charge".[2]

Although a deeply religious man himself, Carpenter had a great deal in common with the radicals and utilitarians of his day in his opinions and attitudes. He allied himself with movements for freedom—anti-slavery, Parliamentary reform, Catholic emancipation, and the foundation of London University. He even advocated equality of educational opportunity for girls. His treatise on education reflects his humanity and liberality; it also reflects his freedom from obsession with the past. It is a scientific work pointing towards the future development of psychology in suggesting that education must be based on "an enlightened and extensive acquaintance with the principles of the human mind".[3]

Most of the other writings of the period on middle-class education were old-fashioned and stereotyped in content and moralising in tone. A number of them were written by women. The most interesting views on this topic—in an entirely different category from Carpenter's—are those of Dr Thomas Arnold of Rugby. Arnold's belief that any wider system of education should be based on Christian humanism, led him to discuss current problems of education frequently in his letters, sermons, and essays. "He is perfectly educated who is taught all the will of God concerning Him, and enabled through life to execute it",[4] he asserted in his criticism of contemporary religious instruction in schools. He did not consider that children—whether in elementary or public schools —were gaining a love of the good and a willingness to do it. In his opinion, school education was too short and too utilitarian, and he criticised in particular the growing fashion of keeping boys at home under very inadequate instruction until the age of eleven or twelve, and then sending them to commercial schools where the

[1] Carpenter, L., *Principles of Education*, p. 1, 1820.
[2] *ibid.*, Preface p. vi., 1820.
[3] *ibid.*, p. 8., 1820.
[4] Arnold, T., *Sermons XVI*, Vol. III.

results of this early neglect had to be remedied. "I believe it often happens that boys in the lowest form of a commercial school require absolutely to be taught to read," wrote Arnold. "But supposing a boy able to read and write, his education, properly so called, then commences. He receives instruction in arithmetic, history and geography; in English grammar, and in compositions. The rudiments of physical science, carried on to a greater or less degree of advancement, are also taught him; and with a view to his particular business in life, he learns land surveying if he is to be brought up to agricultural pursuits or bookkeeping if he is intended for trade . . . This, however, has nothing to do with the knowledge which the Reform Bill calls for. A man may be ever so good a chemist, or ever so good an engineer, and yet not at all the fitter to enjoy the elective franchise." [1]

Arnold emphasised the need for a liberal education to fit the pupil for "the calling of a citizen and a man".[2] He did not consider that boys could gain such an education if they left school at fourteen, as was the common custom, and he was convinced that boys attending non-public schools conducted by laymen were not likely to have the intellectual, moral, and religious training which was an integral part of liberal education.

Arnold's ideal teacher was a cleric of great intellectual gifts, but these comments are not aimed towards the abolition of lay teaching. Rather do they reflect on the existence of profit-earning schools, for Arnold was by no means averse to a measure of State education. He declared, "The interference of the Government seems to be indispensable in order to create a national and systematic course of proceeding, instead of the mere feeble efforts of individuals to provide for the middling classes something analagous to the advantages afforded to the richer classes by our great public schools and universities".[3]

Although they looked at education from the opposite viewpoint of scientist and humanist, Carpenter and Arnold had one thing in common. They were both practical schoolmasters who appreciated that the process of education had fundamental problems of its own. True education was not achieved by the accumulation of a modicum of factual knowledge and the acceptance of conventional standards of manners and piety. To these teachers their

[1] Arnold, T., *Letter on Education of the Middle Classes*, 1832.
[2] *ibid.*   [3] *ibid.*

work was the education of children, whether rich, poor, or "middling", clever, dull, or "middling". Other writers considered "The Poor", or "The Mind", and other grand generalisations. Most utilitarians, for instance, regarded education with the eyes of philosophers and political scientists. The main concern of men like Jeremy Bentham and James Mill was the extension of education—outwards to all people, downwards to infants, and upwards to adults. They worked for the organisation of practicable—therefore cheap—universal education, but they aimed at social reform. Mill also discussed education in his *Analysis of the Phenomena of the Human Mind* (1829), and in an article written for the *Encyclopedia Britannica*, but the former was primarily a philosophical treatise and the latter no more than an intellectual exercise.

Many other writers touched on education from the sociological angle. Robert Owen's *A New View of Society* (1815) and Matthew Davenport Hill's *Public Education* (1825), are perhaps the most significant apart from Bentham's *Chrestomathia* of 1816, and, of course, the publications of Lancaster and Bell early in the century. During the second quarter of the century the concentration of literary effort on similar topics is even more marked. Very few, apart from Dr Arnold, raised their voices or their pens on behalf of middle and upper class adolescents.

This growing concern for the schooling of small children, especially the "infant poor", may be related to events described in another chapter. It is also very closely related to the work of Robert Owen in Scotland and Pestalozzi in Switzerland. Although they held strong views on the social function of education, both of these pioneers sought to educate the individual human being fully and richly. This concept is so different from the "reading for Godliness" idea of the charity and monitorial schools, that the Infant School Society of 1824 and the Home and Colonial Infant School Society of 1836 were quite different from the two earlier Societies in their aims and purpose. Unfortunately, the leaders of these new movements were limited either in their own power of understanding or in their opportunities to put ideas into practice. A few of them were, however, influential in their own time, and if their contribution to education is to be evaluated fairly, it is first necessary to examine the work of Pestalozzi, who inspired the teachers of many countries by his teaching and writing.

Pestalozzi (1746-1827)

In the year 1800 the great Swiss educator Pestalozzi was already fifty-four years old, yet he had only just entered on that phase of his career during which he was to win worldwide fame as a teacher. During his student days in Geneva, he was a disciple of Rousseau, and his later interpretation of Rousseau's social theory in his educational writings and practice was a great and permanent contribution to the improvement and extension of education. *Emile* he accepted in its true light—a fable for the conveyance of new guiding principles.

Although, during his years of fame, his pupils were often from rich homes, Pestalozzi remained at heart a teacher of the poor. He had experienced many years of extreme poverty through his attempts to alleviate the condition of the poor, which, as the Swiss industrial revolution proceeded, had become deplorable. He had used all his possessions—and his wife's money—on a scheme for the education of poor children on his farm, aiming to develop a self-supporting community in which the members would learn not only their letters but also how to farm, make cloth, become self-respecting, and live as honest, friendly comrades. During the years of penury which followed his financial failure, he developed and consolidated his ideas on education and society, finally putting them out in the form of a novel, *Leonard and Gertrude*, which sold well and brought him recognition. When the Revolutionary Era brought strife to Switzerland in 1798, Pestalozzi took a Government appointment to establish a colony for destitute children in the village of Stanz. Here he lived in a one-roomed building with eighty children for nine months, giving them not only training in the primary skills, but also the firm but loving devotion of a parent in the building up of standards of cleanliness, honesty, and morality.

His health was impaired by this experience, and after a long period of recuperation, he accepted the humble post offered him as assistant to the cobbler who was in charge of an elementary school in the small town of Burgdorf. His methods of teaching small children won recognition very quickly, and he was allowed to develop an educational institution in the local castle. Pestalozzi always hoped to have rich and poor boys together in his schools, but as more and more visitors flocked in to see the schools, it became more and more difficult to achieve his most cherished wish. In 1801 he published one of his most significant books, *How Gertrude Teaches her Children*, which continued the story of

Leonard and Gertrude, emphasising the educative activities of the ordinary poor home, and the relationship of that home and its occupants to the community and the Church. During the same period he wrote several non-fictional books, including *The Mother's Book* and *An A.B.C. of Sense Perception*. The latter gives the clue to his basic teaching principles. Like Locke, he saw that early learning must be based on sense experience, and like Locke, he handed on his convictions to other great educators. Both Froebel and Herbart, as well as Maria Edgeworth, visited Burgdorf.

In 1805 a new school was set up at Yverdun, near Lake Geneva, a prosperous and long-lived school where Pestalozzi was able to create the family community in which he believed so fervently. Unfortunately, such an atmosphere can hardly be preserved in a large "show-place" staffed by teachers who, however worthy, were more ambitious, less devoted than their leader. Yverdun was the centre of the new education, a training college for groups of student-teachers, and a Mecca for all people interested in education. It played a significant part in shaping future experiment in child education, but it was never the ideal school of its master's noble conception.

Pestalozzi's true aim was to change the mean and scanty public education, familiar to Switzerland as to England, into a rich and full education of each human being. He became one of the first observational psychologists in giving his close attention to the development of children—starting with his own son—from birth onwards through all the amazing achievements of childhood. "It is life that educates", he always maintained, and so his search was, like that of Comenius, for ways of fostering natural learning processes. Much of the child's early learning is by direct sensual contact with his surroundings, so that the teacher—or the mother, like Gertrude—has but to encourage the exploration of the environment. Thus the child feels the shape and surface of the window-panes by touch; he learns to count and to see differences and similarities with the help of his mother.

Pestalozzi tried to develop school teaching methods and materials based on the grading of sense experiences, from simple to complex, so that there would develop in the pupil a capacity for intuitive response to sense stimuli—that is, a response which, through practice and guidance, has become discriminating and selective. Intellectual learning would follow much the same pattern in stages as the pupil became ready for it. The concept of

Anschauung led Pestalozzi to "break up" the material far too much, especially in language and arithmetic, so that his psychology might be called the reverse of the modern Gestalt. His disciples often carried this idea to absurd extremes in textbooks and teachers' guides, just as they substituted books on *Objects* for the kind of object lesson that Pestalozzi intended.

In his curriculum Pestalozzi included handwork—a great innovation—and geography based on walks of observation. His pupils had their own little gardens and had ample time for recreation and exercise. Above all they were confident in the concern and affection their headmaster had for them. Untidy, but unselfish, temperamental, but generous and sympathetic, he was known to his pupils, for the best of reasons, as "Father Pestalozzi".

Many Britons visited his schools—Robert Owen, Andrew Bell, Lord Brougham, Maria Edgeworth—but it was perhaps inevitable that Pestalozzi's motivating belief in the need for social regeneration through universal education should go unrecognised. Pestalozzi believed that education would make the citizen of the *Social Contract* who accepted his "burden of necessity" and his station in life. Like Rousseau, too, he believed that a better education was given in a humble family than in a rich one. Family duties and responsibilities developed moral qualities as well as useful skills. It was not these great concepts which came to England with his disciples however. The few short-lived Pestalozzian schools of England were established mainly through the work of Dr Charles Mayo and his sister, who followed the methods of teaching they had seen used in Switzerland.

The Mayos were well equipped to extend the understanding of Pestalozzi's principles in this country. The Reverend Charles Mayo, an Oxford don, obtained leave from his college in 1819 in order to visit Yverdun, where he spent nearly three years acting as English chaplain and studying the work of the school. In 1822 he started a Pestalozzian school at Epsom, and after four years moved it to Cheam, where it continued until his death in 1846. In a lecture on Pestalozzi given at the Royal Institution in 1826, Dr Mayo emphasised his two main principles of teaching, first, that learning starts with the child's own experience—both sensual and mental—and, second, that teaching needs to be graded in accordance with the developing intelligence of the child.

Dr Mayo engaged Charles Reiner, a former pupil of Pestalozzi, to teach mathematics, elementary science, and physical geography at Cheam. Miss Elizabeth Mayo, his sister, also taught there for eight years, and all three teachers wrote textbooks. Miss Mayo's books, *Lessons on Objects* (1830) and *Lessons on Shells*, were reprinted many times, and in 1855 she wrote in a preface, "At first the idea of using the material world as a means of education was novel and untried in England; but the plain sound sense of the plan soon convinced teachers that, in addition to reading, writing, and arithmetic, the objects and actions of everyday life should have a prominent part in everyday education". It seems clear from this that Miss Mayo expected her teacher readers to obtain real specimens for the lessons described, but unfortunately the "object" book became an all too common reading and rote-learning book in later elementary schools.

Miss Mayo was one of the first English women to be employed in teacher training. In 1834 she became supervisor of the teaching in the schools and college of the Home and Colonial Society. She inspected programmes of work, suggested material and methods for courses of lessons, observed and criticised lessons, and gave demonstration lessons. It is clear that the committee of the Society wished to introduce Pestalozzi's methods into elementary education, for in 1837 it published *Practical Remarks on Infant Education*, containing two articles by Dr Mayo and some practical comments by Miss Mayo. The Society also published several books of specimen lessons by Miss Mayo.

Apart from the Mayo's work, the half-century is singularly lacking in genuine and honest attempts to put Pestalozzi's ideas into practice, or to discuss them in writing. Even his biographer, George Biber, one of his teachers who settled in England, neither practised nor discussed these ideas except in a somewhat critical vein in his *Memoir of Henry Pestalozzi and his Plan of Education* (1831). There is some evidence, however, that even before Miss Mayo's students became teachers, Pestalozzian methods were being practised in a modest way by some of the teachers in many new infant schools which were founded in the third and fourth decades of the century. The true situation is clouded by jealousy and rivalry on the part of several pioneers in this field, each wishing to be regarded as the inventor of a new system of education. The clearest evidence of Pestalozzi's influence lies in two books. The first is D. G. Goyder's *Manual of the System of Instruction*, first published about 1825, in which is described the activities of the writer's infant school in Bristol. Goyder freely acknowledges the source of his ideas. The second publication is *Letters on Early Education* (1827) by Pestalozzi himself, written, originally, to J. P. Greaves, Secretary to the London Infant School Society. In view of this evidence, it is not unreasonable to conclude that the influence of Pestalozzi may be traced in the work of the best-known infant teacher of his day, Samuel Wilderspin.

Samuel Wilderspin (1792 c.-1866)

Although Robert Owen saw Pestalozzi at work at Yverdun, his visit occurred several years after his own pioneer schools had been established in Scotland. With a main general aim of social reform, he had evolved principles of education which might well serve us to-day. Character training, good manners, experience with material, the use of the mother tongue, freedom from punishments—all these are matters not unknown to modern teachers. These ideas were imported into England through the efforts of Brougham and his friends, who had one of Owen's teachers appointed head of a new infant school in Westminster.

It was here that the era's most prolific writer on education received his early inspiration to become a teacher. Samuel Wilderspin, a London youth, earning his living as a merchant's clerk, became acquainted with James Buchanan, the Scottish teacher of Westminster Infant School. Buchanan taught the young man enough to set his own ideas fermenting, and also recommended him for the mastership of a new school. Thus, in 1820, at twenty-two, Wilderspin found himself in charge of Spitalfields Infant School and in possession of a wealth of good advice, including injunctions from Owen and Buchanan to read the books of Pestalozzi. As, by this time, Pestalozzi's fame as an educator was well established, and as his main writings were translated, it seems somewhat unlikely that an unfledged teacher, with a whole school to manage, would fail to follow such advice. Wilderspin, however, was neither as selfless as Pestalozzi nor as generous as Buchanan, for he soon claimed that he had evolved an entirely new and original method of educating young children. At this distance in time, however, perhaps it is not unreasonable to assume that Wilderspin's principles reflect the influence of Owen, Buchanan, Brougham (who had visited Yverdun), and Pestalozzi.

Within two years of his appointment, Wilderspin brought about the foundation of the Infant School Society, which aimed to found schools for children of two to six years, and to influence the training of teachers for these schools. During the somewhat brief existence of the Society, Spitalfields was its model school, and Wilderspin travelled the country setting up schools at the request of local committees.

His first publication, in 1824, at the beginning of his campaign, *On the Importance of Educating the Infant Children of the Poor,* was mainly an account of the depravity of the poor and the degradation of their children. Several of his other books also contain blood-chilling descriptions of delinquency and infant exploitation, and there seems no doubt that Wilderspin was continuing the campaign for social reform and regeneration through education. He gave credit to the Sunday Schools, but asserted that they were inadequate and that the pupils were too old. Similarly, there was no provision for infant education in the schools of Bell and Lancaster. The instruction and discipline of children under seven was urgently needed.

In his next book, *Early Discipline, illustrated* (1832), Wilderspin hurled a shaft at the already obsolete "dame" school, describing how he had found one of these "admirable and efficient institutions" to consist of "an old woman and three children in a barn without a single lesson of any kind".[1] In the same work he echoes Robert Raikes's belief that education of young children would lead to the regeneration of their parents. Describing the infant school as a refuge from neglect and contamination, he writes, "Under the care and direction of a kind and judicious instructor, and in the company of those of his own age, the child is led on, delighted, to the acquirement of useful knowledge, and its heart imbued by the sympathetical influence of love, equally conducive to its own happiness and to that of others, and this not only during infancy but through the whole of its future life. Everything is contrived for the bodily comfort, the mental advancement, and the spiritual welfare of the children. Amusement, instruction and affection are found co-operating together and with what effect, those only can conceive who have seen for themselves".[2] After this promising Pestalozzian opening, Wilderspin proclaims the need of every man for complete mental and physical education, so that the condition of all classes, and hence the prosperity of the state, be improved. He writes, "Let, then, the mind be taught to think, and the

---

[1] Wilderspin, S., *Early Discipline, illustrated,* p. 2, 1832.
[2] *ibid.,* p. 104.

judgment be fitted for correct decision . . . the intelligent will not be the dupes of demagogues or incendiaries, and the thrifty will discover a higher tone of feeling than their improvident neighbours".[1]

Infant education started this process by giving moral training and moulding dispositions "at that very tender age when they alone can be moulded . . . intellectual progress is but an accessory attainment".[2] It is clear, however, that Wilderspin intends much more than mere instructing by precept. He contends, "Everyone involved in infant education should ask himself, 'What is the nature of the being whose cultivation I am to undertake?' Knowledge of human nature is essential".[3] Emphasising that the infant is a thinking and feeling being, he continues, "Matter acts upon matter, mind acts upon mind, spirit acts upon spirit—the teacher must employ the right means for the appropriate task".[4]

His intention was to "educate the whole being, all the powers of the child early".[5] He claimed that he, not Pestalozzi, had discovered a system whereby all human powers might be cultivated. He trained the body through games and exercises, moral feeling through precept and example, ear and voice through music, the senses and intellect through object and picture lessons and oral narrative. He used the Bible as a textbook—according to his own report. He also emphasised the use of his playground. Nevertheless, he used a modified monitorial system, and his classroom methods, although introducing picture cards and mounted specimens, appear to have been limited to the oral inculcation of facts about these objects. A question-and-answer routine enabled monitors to put groups of infants through their paces until they could reel off the correct answers without thinking about the meaning of the words. Yet Wilderspin condemned mere memory work.

In theory, his methods were devised for the development of observation, judgment, and the ability to make personal decisions and opinions. "Nothing should be submitted to the child which it is not fully competent to understand," he argues. "Firstly foster curiosity and enquiry which is natural to young children. Then direct curiosity to proper objects so that he learns to reason and judge. He will eventually arrive at truth." [6] Thus his pupils —very small children—were introduced to arithmetic and geometry, but it is doubtful whether the mere handling of an abacus

---

[1] *Early Discipline, illustrated*, p. 312.   [2] *ibid.*, p. 193.
[3] *ibid.*, p. 171.   [4] *ibid.*, p. 173.
[5] Wilderspin's *A Manual for the Religious and Moral Instruction of Young Children*, p. 2, 1845.   [6] *The Infant System*, p. 63.

(which he claimed to have invented) gave much understanding of number concepts. Although the children handled geometric shapes they achieved little more than a rote knowledge of the names of the shapes—"A pentagon, a pentagon, a five-sided figure".

The process of learning to read—from alphabet to syllable to word—was by no means novel, but the introduction of flash cards not only enlivened the lessons but also made it easy for the moni-world," he writes, "where the little children are left to themselves; Geography was learnt by the chanting of cape-and-bay facts, and by the description of natural phenomena by the teacher—with a wealth of exaggerated gesture.

These were attempts to inculcate facts through memory in a reasonably humane way. Moral teaching was carried on throughout. Even arithmetic had its dual aim:

"Two pints will make one quart,
Four quarts one gallon strong,
Some drink too little, some too much,
To drink too much is wrong." [1]

Through singing, particularly, the children were supposed to absorb good and noble ideas as well as further information about the world. Wilderspin rejected the lyrics of many famous songs and composed new lines. He took other well-known tunes and added words to them. To *Ye Banks and Braes*, the children sang a song about stealing; to *Sicilian Mariners* they sang: —

"Tempted child, if deeply tried,
Always in your God confide
Never do distrust His power
Fear not the dangerous hour." [2]

Wilderspin's advocacy of co-education appears to the modern mind dependent on faulty psychology, but it is a viewpoint, which, together with his condemnation of immobility and passivity in schools, marks him out as a leader in education. Although perhaps not a great or original thinker, it is clear that he makes strenuous efforts to bring about better teaching and better learning. "One of the principle ends . . . is to make the children happy", he maintains in his first publication. He pursued this end, not only by devising didactic material, but also by providing space and opportunity for free play. The playground should be one of the

---

[1] Wilderspin, *The Infant System*, p. 258.
[2] Wilderspin, *Stanzas for the Religious and Moral Instruction*, p. 40.

most important parts of the school. Not only should it be edged by flowers and shrubs—which, incidentally, would be useful for outdoor nature lessons—it should also contain swings and other games apparatus. "The playground may be compared to the world," he writes, "where the little children are left to themselves; there it may be seen what effects their education has produced." [1] Wilderspin is reminiscent of Locke in his emphasis on moral education, the early formation of good habits, and the child's physical welfare. Like Locke, he also deprecates corporal punishment and is sceptical of the value of excessive rewards and punishments of any kind. His ideal teacher is not quite Locke's "paragon", but is nevertheless a man of integrity and intelligence. In addition, the Pestalozzian qualities of kindness and patience are also desirable.

In his first publication, Wilderspin makes a comment that stamps him as an immature thinker in comparison with Locke and Pestalozzi. "Every man comes into the world without a single innate idea," he wrote, "and has nothing but what he acquires from others." He lacked Locke's understanding of the nature of experience, and he did not achieve, even in later years, Pestalozzi's broad conception of the development of the human spirit.

Apart from the apparent reluctance of infant school pioneers to recognise originality in others, the weakness of Pestalozzi's influence in England may have been due, in some measure, to the dissemination of the ideas of his fellow-countryman, Fellenberg. Many British visitors to Yverdun received invitations to visit Hofwyl, where Fellenberg's efficient organisation and methods in his institution, greatly impressed those who had been somewhat bewildered by the experiments and contradictions of Yverdun. Moreover, several books were published in England about Fellenberg's methods[2]— methods which promised to make poor children into well disciplined skilled workers.

Contemporary European Thought on Education

J. F. Herbart (1776-1834)

While the Edgeworths were writing *Practical Education*, a young German student, working as a tutor in a Swiss family, was

---

[1] Wilderspin, S., *On the Importance of Educating the Infant Poor.*
[2] *E.g.* J. Attersoll, *Reports on Fellenberg's Institution for the Poor*, 1820; *e.g.* B. F. Duppa, *The Education of the Peasantry in England and what it ought to be, with an account of the Establishment at Hofwyl*, 1834.

surprised to find himself developing a keenly critical interest in education. He really wanted to be a great philosopher, an ambition he held throughout life, but he was destined to become more celebrated as an original thinker on education. Visits to Pestalozzi's school during his stay in Switzerland may well have fired his imagination in the first place, for his first writings—during the next few years—were largely on education, and contained tributes to Pestalozzi. From 1802 he lectured in philosophy and pedagogy at the universities of Göttingen and Königsberg. He was a prolific writer on philosophy and education, but, being no more theorist, he achieved the foundation of a training college for teachers and insisted on teaching every day in the demonstration school.

We are not concerned with the philosophy that he hoped would establish a great new school of thought, but it must be recognised that it is the basis of those principles of psychology and method which were to become accepted throughout Europe and America for a long period extending into the twentieth century. Even as Pestalozzi may be regarded as the first persistent observational psychologist, so Herbart was the first of the mathematical psychologists, believing that it was possible not only to build up the human mind by means of deliberate teaching material and methods, but also to measure the qualities, content, and complex combinations of that mind.

Realist in outlook, believing, with Locke, that the human mind has no innate ideas or qualities, and that experience is the basis of all education and development, Herbart described the mind or soul of the new-born baby not as a *tabula rasa* but as an empty arena. From the first, each experience of the infant came into the arena as a *presentation* which might possibly become a permanent part of the child's knowledge and understanding of his environment. New presentations, however, did not come into the arena as separate pieces of furniture, they could only remain (and, therefore, could only become useful) if they were related or connected in some way to presentations already there. Thus, the mental equipment of a human being was, according to Herbart's theory, an interrelated collection of presentations, which he called the *apperception mass*. This very soon became a complex structure, for many presentations could become combined with others to form ideas and concepts. Moreover, the whole structure was subject to constant change and flux, for each new experience, in making its presentation to the apperception mass, would seek to attach itself to some related factor already merged in the mass. If no previous presentation of a related kind had been received, the new presentation would find no way into the apperception mass, and the experience from which the presentation came would be fruitless.

The educational implications of such a theory are manifold. Locke maintained that man's greatest power—reasoning—could not be used until a fund of experience and empirical conceptions had been gained. Herbart maintained that reasoning could only follow the development of an apperception mass built up by rich and varied experience. Such experience—to be carefully selected and organised by the Herbartian teacher—would result in a "many-sided interest" on the part of the pupil, for Herbart conceived of interest as increased by knowledge and experience.

Integrity in selecting experiences for pupils was an essential quality of the Herbartian teacher, because his task was to build up a mind not only many-sided (and therefore free from prejudice), but also constituted of good, noble, and worthy ideas, so closely knit and so unrelated to evil that wicked and harmful ideas would find no place for themselves in the "circle of thought". Herbart's aim was the making of moral man, a balanced, well-adjusted personality, positively engaged in the practical working out of five moral ideas—the ideas of inner freedom, perfection, benevolence, right, and equity. This was an impressive aim which overestimated the power that could or should be wielded by a teacher.

A further difficulty for the teacher was the need to organise experiences related to each other, to ensure that the presentations would be absorbed. The disciples of Herbart often went to extremes in attempts to correlate material used in the teaching of different subjects. Perhaps more valuable for general application was Herbart's method of organising individual pieces of learning. Divided by Herbart into four stages, the process, as modified by his disciples, eventually became "the five Herbartian steps" which might well be used in lesson preparation to-day. First, "Preparation" should revise knowledge with which the new is to be related; second, "Presentation" should give the pupils experience of the new material; third, "Association" should enable the pupils to analyse the new experience and compare and contrast it with the old; fourth, "Systematisation" should be a recapitulation and the formulating of a conclusion; fifth, "Application" should be the use of the new knowledge or practice of the new skill for some significant purpose.

In the late nineteenth and early twentieth century, British educational writings—as well as school organisation and method—reveal the survival of Herbartian principles. Partial correlation of the curriculum was common, full correlation rare. The use of the five steps as headings in class procedure was widespread, but it is doubtful whether many teachers understood the underlying theory.

Friedrich Froebel (1782-1852)

When a young German tutor took three boy pupils to Pestalozzi's new school at Yverdun in 1807, the life of that tutor became the life of another great educator. Up to that time, Froebel, a poor country boy, has been struggling to complete his university studies in science and philosophy—studies seriously hampered by lack of funds and inadequate school education. He described the inspiration he received from Pestalozzi as the setting on fire of his soul, and although he soon showed promise of becoming a brilliant scientist, he refused a university chair in mineralogy, and after fighting in the war with France, he opened a school in a Thüringian village in 1816. For the rest of his life he worked with children and for children; living as humbly as Pestalozzi and, like his master, always hampered by financial difficulties.

His first book, *The Education of Man*, was published in 1826, the year before Pestalozzi's death. It put forward a theory of education which deserves recognition as a masterpiece of penetrating, far-seeing thought. Moreover, it was new and original thought which profoundly influenced the future course of educational theory. As a scientist, impressed by the new ideas on evolution (fermenting long before Darwin's *Origin of the Species* in 1859), Froebel saw the human being as a biological organism for which education need provide only nourishment and freedom. The organism had innate capacities and characteristics which could be either fostered or stunted in the course of experience.

This biological concept was somewhat modified by an idea probably derived from the fashionable German philosophy of the day, the idea of the reconciliation of opposites. This emerged in Froebel's theory as a law of growth and education. The human organism developed itself by activity, by varied activities, by contrasting activities. The reconciling of these contrasts was part of developmental experience, therefore education should provide the challenge of such contrasts. The outstanding expression of this in the Froebelian theory, is the need to reconcile individual and group interests. The human organism needs experiences as an individual and also experiences as a part of a human group, therefore education should provide opportunities for both individual activities and group undertakings. The child needs to learn how to keep these two aspects of his life in harmony by reconciling the contradictions and antagonisms which might well render him insecure and unhappy. In fact, Froebel hoped to educate for integrated harmonious personality through natural individual development and natural group experience. Pestalozzi's humble family was the kind of group Froebel had in mind, and his school was to reflect the atmosphere and activities of good family life.

Froebel was concerned with education as a continuous process. For a long time he hoped to set up an educational centre composed of a range of schools, a technical college, a nursery school, and a school for mothers. Later, he decided that the immediate need was for better schools for young children, and thus, through his experimental work and pioneer efforts in the establishment of infant schools and enlightened infant teaching, he became best known as the founder of the Kinder Garten. It is worth remembering to-day, however, that the play activities—both individual and group—the constructional material, and the "expression work" of the infant and nursery school, have behind them principles which Froebel intended to apply at all stages of education.

As he was neither a qualified philosopher nor a university professor of pedagogy, Froebel gained little reputation as a philosopher in his own time. Naturalism had gained no headway in western Europe, and Froebel's Pantheistic attitude was not acceptable to many people. His interpretation of the Hegelian concept of Unity was that the whole material world is an expression of God's will—that God is in everything. As he saw human life as an evolutionary process, he believed that education should be an active, fermenting element in man's striving to reach higher and higher—to become better and better.

These ideas are behind Froebel's new and refreshing views on how young people can be prepared for the future—how education can help them to cope successfully with changes that can rarely be predicted. The old type of education he regarded as sadly inadequate because it aimed to inculcate the values, habits, and knowledge of the past, and to train children only in the narrow range of skills practised in the past. The human organism had far greater potentialities than merely those conventional abilities and capacities that traditional teaching aimed to develop, claimed Froebel. His idea of a well-educated person was a balanced individual with well-developed abilities and well-adjusted social relationships and who would have, in addition, abundant spontaneity—a zest for tackling new problems, facing new situations, and mastering new knowledge. Froebel's educational aim was a world of men looking to the future instead of to the past, an idea particularly acceptable to his greatest disciple of a later era, John Dewey.

When Froebelian ideas reached England in the second half of the century, they were limited to those principles of infant education which a few women pioneers were able to put into practice in their new infant schools. The play activities of children at last became a recognised part of the educational process—the expression of inner impulses, ideas, feelings, and purposes.

English Writings on Education

In order to illustrate the continuity and variety of ideas on education in the first half of the nineteenth century, a selection of the main English publications is given below.

1795   Vicesimus Knox: *Liberal Education.*
1797   Andrew Bell: *The Madras School.*
1797   Erasmus Darwin: *A Plan for the Conduct of Female Education in Boarding Schools.*
1798   R. L. and M. Edgeworth: *Practical Education.*
1799   Hannah More: *Strictures on the Modern System of Female Education.*
1800   Philip Redhead Yorke: *Elements of Civil Knowledge.*
1800   Sarah Trimmer: *The Charity School Spelling Book.*
1801   Eliza Andrews: *Thoughts on Education.*
1801   Elizabeth Hamilton: *Letters on the Elementary Principles of Education.*
1802   William Baron: *Essay on Education.*
1802   George Crabb: *The Order and Method of Instructing Children.*
1803   Joseph Lancaster: *Improvements in Education.*
1803   Miss Hatfield: *Letters on the Importance of the Female Sex with Observations on Manners and Education.*
1803-6 S. Trimmer: *The Guardian of Education.*
1806   Maria Benson: *Thoughts on Education.*

1809   R. L. Edgeworth: *Essays on Professional Education.*
1809   Sir Thomas Bernard: *The New School.*
1810   Thomas Broadhurst: *Advice to Young Ladies on the Improvement of the Mind.*
1812   Sir Thomas Bernard: *The Barrington School.*
1813   Robert Owen: *A New View of Society.*
1813   Andrew Bell: *Elements of Tuition.*
1815   Carpenter, Joyce, and Shepherd: *Systematic Education.*
1816   Jeremy Bentham: *Chrestomathia.*
1816-24 James Mill: *Education* (a pamphlet, first published as an article in the *Encyclopaedia Britannica* in 1816. It was reprinted in the 4th, 5th, and 6th editions).
1817   R. L. Edgeworth: *School Lessons.*
1817   Helen Maria Williams: *A Summary Method of Teaching Children to read.*
1818   Miss R. C. Dalloway: *Observations on the Most Important Subjects in Education.*
1820   S. Butler: *A Letter to Henry Brougham on Certain Changes in the Education Bill.*
1820   Lant Carpenter: *Principles of Education.*
1820   P. H. Pullen: *The Mother's Book, Pestalozzi's Plan of Awakening the Understanding of Children.*
1821   Elizabeth Appleton: *Early Education.*
1822   Matthew Davenport Hill: *Plans for the Government and Liberal Instruction of Boys in Large Numbers.*
1823   Samuel Wilderspin: *On the Importance of Educating the Infant Poor.*
1825   William Wilson: *The System of Infants' Schools.*
1825   G. W. Goyder: *Manual of the System of Instruction.*
1825   Samuel Wilderspin: *Infant Education or Remarks on the Importance of Educating the Infant Poor.*
1825   Matthew Davenport Hill: *Public Education.*
1827   Pestalozzi: *Letters on Early Education.*
1827   William Newnham: *The Principles of Physical, Intellectual, Moral and Religious Education.*
1829   James Mill: *Analysis of the Phenomena of the Human Mind.*
1830   E. G. Biber: *Christian Education.*
1832   Samuel Wilderspin: *Early Discipline, illustrated.*
1834   B. F. Duppa: *The Education of the Peasantry in England.*

1835   Charles Reiner: *Lessons on Number and Lessons on Form Education* (a pamphlet).

1837   Home and Colonial Society: *Practical Remarks on Infant Education.*

1837   Central Society for Education: *Results of Statistical Enquiries.*

1837 c. Henry Dunn: *Popular Education or the Normal School Manual.*

1837   B. F. Duppa: *Schools for the Industrious Classes.*

1837   William Whewell: *On the Principles of English University Education.*

1838   Isaac Taylor: *Home Education.*

1838   H. Dunn: *National Education or the Question of Questions.*

1839   Kay-Shuttleworth: *Recent Measures for the Promotion of Education.*

1840   F. D. Maurice (Ed.): *Educational Magazine. Vol. I.*

1840   Samuel Wilderspin: *A System for the Education of the Young.*

1841   Kay-Shuttleworth: *Report of the Poor Law Commissioners on the Training of Pauper Children.*

1842   Mrs. L. M. Barwell: *Letters from Hofwyl by a Parent.*

1843   John Fenn: *The School Master's Legacy and Family Monitor.*

1845   Wilderspin and Terrington: *A Manual for the Religious and Moral Instruction of Young Children in Nursery and Infant Schools.*

1847   *The School in Relation to the State, the Church and the Congregation.*

1848   Crosby Hall: *Lectures on Education.*

1850   Joseph Kay: *The Social Condition and Education of the People in England and Europe.*

1852   Samuel Wilderspin: *The Infant System.*

1852   J. Wilkinson: *Popular Education.*

SUGGESTIONS FOR FURTHER READING

Curtis and Boultwood, *A Short History of Educational Ideas*, 4th edition, U.T.P., 1965. Chapters XIII, XIV, XV.

J. W. Adamson, *English Education, 1789-1902*, C.U.P., 1930.

B. Simon, *Studies in the History of Education, 1780-1870*, Lawrence and Wishart, 1960.

CHAPTER VII

ENGLISH THOUGHT ON EDUCATION, 1850-1900

Charles Dickens is said to have been an avid reader of Froebel. From his many references to the plight of school-age children in his own time, it is very probable that the English novelist admired and understood the work of both Pestalozzi and Froebel. Critical of current methods—whether the cruelty of the Squeerses or the oyster-prizing tactics of the Mrs Pipchins—Dickens put forward many a plea for the type of sympathetic teacher capable of cultivating the imagination of his pupils. The purpose of education was not merely to inculcate knowledge, but rather "to encourage a child's mind to expand itself like a young flower".

Wordsworth's *Prelude*, composed at the turn of the century but not published until 1850, brought a similar message to a smaller circle of readers. In Victorian England, these messages were slow in making their impact felt, and the leading educationists of the period did not choose to stake their reputations on such principles. Yet there were a few practical educators—their names now hardly remembered—who were firm in their discipleship of Pestalozzi and Froebel, and who were responsible for the survival and dissemination of their ideas. The results of their work have been profound enough to earn for them a place in the story of education—a place by no means subsidiary to that usually given to the greater names of the period. It is proposed to consider their ideas as one of the three main trends in Victorian thought on education. The other two schools of thought, with their famous protagonists, were concerned only incidentally with the developmental needs of small children. Their dominating themes were, on the one hand, a defence of "liberal" education based on the classics, and, on the other, a demand for the recognition of scientific study as an essential part of education.

The Classical Humanists

Chronologically, the movement for the revision of traditional education came first. Opinion was divided on the nature and extent of this revision. Some schoolmasters, such as George Moberley, head of Winchester from 1835 to 1866, adhered rigidly to the old classical method and material, but aimed to make teaching more efficient. Many others adhered rigidly to the old method and material without thinking very much about it. The innovators were those who believed that while the current practice and content of classical education held much that was sterile, obsolete, and irrelevant, it was, nevertheless, possible to recapture the original spirit of liberal education, to widen and revitalise the whole concept of classical studies so that they would indeed lead towards that "intelligent excellence"[1] which was the whole aim and purpose of education. It is clear that the resurgence of the classical ideal owed much to its preservation by men like Vicesimus Knox and Thomas Arnold during a period when it was not particularly fashionable in intellectual circles. It is equally clear that vigour and definition were given to this resurgence by Cardinal Newman's lectures of 1852. The matter of these lectures concerns University education, and so is not within the scope of this book, except in so far as it indicates the continuity and development of the classical ideal. The lectures have been reprinted many times since their first publication in 1859, and have a permanent place in British literature on education.

The influence of Newman's ideas was widespread. It was certainly a factor in initiating the reforms which took place in Oxford and Cambridge soon afterwards. The pursuit of knowledge for its own sake became a widely-accepted ideal of university education, and this had repercussions on the various kinds of secondary schools in its opposition to vocational, utilitarian studies and activities. To Newman, true education was the cultivation of "the force, the steadiness, the comprehensiveness, the versatility of intellect" which gives man command over his own powers, a capacity to make intuitive judgments, and an attitude of good sense, reasonableness, self-control, and straightforwardness. Such an education would prepare human beings for any kind of worthwhile occupation, whether in the sphere of scholarship, or of business, or of politics.

The great value of the major studies—grammar followed by mathematics—should be the training they give in order and method and their revelation of "rule and exception, of richness and harmony". The intellect should become a precise and critical instrument through the practice of accuracy and exactness. Only through

---

[1] Newman, *On the Scope and Nature of University Education*, p. 113, Everyman edition, Dent.

such exercise could the highest and widest levels of intellectual achievement be reached. Moreover, this exercise should be gained in a wide field of human knowledge and experience. Education is not mere book-learning; knowledge is not merely a set of subjects. "Knowledge forms one whole because its subject-matter is one," asserts Newman, "for the universe in its length and breadth is so intimately knit together that we cannot separate off portion from portion, and operation from operation, except by a mental abstraction."[1]

In this way Newman rationalises the inclusion of science in his concept of liberal education. "Sciences are the result of that mental abstraction", he explains, but for him they are merely "logical records" and not avenues of intensive investigation or research. In fact, Newman's university is a place where teaching and learning go on through cross-fertilisation of brilliant intellects, and through the insemination and nurture of ideas in the younger members. The greatest acquisition of the university student should be "a philosophical habit" based on an apprehension of the principles of knowledge, not a specialist qualification in a narrow field of skills and ideas. For research activities—no doubt necessary and useful—separate non-university institutions should exist.

Living, as he did, at the height of Victorian prosperity, Newman could hardly dispute the importance of "useful" studies and activities. He described men of special vocational skills—antiquarians, naturalists, lawyers, statisticians—as "most useful in their own place", but he pointed out that the possession of such skills did not necessarily give the breadth of mental culture which characterises liberal education. It is significant that the criticism here implied is not of specialist training in itself, but of the *way* in which it was acquired. No doubt Newman would have advocated a liberal education *before* specialisation. That culture might be gained equally well through a more philosophical and imaginative approach to special studies was not implied in any of Newman's writings.

Lest it might appear, however, that Newman would have approved of the General Studies courses of some modern universities, it must be emphasised that he rejected the idea of requiring students to pass examinations in a wide range of subjects. At least, he denied that this, in itself, would ensure the gaining of a liberal

[1] *On the Scope and Nature of University Education*, p. 11, Everyman edition, Dent.

education. A primary condition for the true educative process, was, in his opinion, the living together made possible and necessary in a residential university based on a tutorial system. Indeed, he points out that under such conditions, students "are sure to learn one from another, even if there is no-one to teach them".[1]

Although Newman's arresting and convincing arguments did little to stem the development of useful and specialist education, they provoked discussion among those concerned with the education of boys and young men, and stimulated interest in the reform and improvement of higher education. Their impact in the older universities has already been mentioned; their influence on the grammar schools was equally significant. In 1867, eight years after the publication of Newman's lectures, a group of university and public school teachers published *Essays on a Liberal Education*. The editor, F. W. Farrar, was a master at Harrow, four of his colleagues were university dons, the other three, masters at Harrow and Rugby and Eton.

Although ostensibly supporting the retention of the classical bias in secondary education, the writers make many devastatingly critical comments on contemporary classical education. In a long essay on the history of classical education, Professor Parker, of Oxford, reviews the development of thought on education, and asks, "Are the classics read to learn Greek and Latin, or are Greek and Latin learnt to read the classics?"[2] He points out, "the great English schools do not yet teach English". He is clearly critical of the contemporary system when he suggests there ought to be "as of old, a ladder by which a boy of rare intellectual power may climb from his parish school to a University education".[3] He advocates the liberal education of girls and the modernising of public school education.

In his essay on the theory of classical education, Henry Sidgwick[4], of Cambridge, urges strongly the direct teaching of English. He repudiates arguments that a knowledge of Latin helps in the reading of English, although he expresses appreciation of Joseph Payne's pamphlet on this subject. He comments scathingly on Thring's enthusiasm for classical writers as models of perfection. In a footnote he comments, "It is curious in contemplating English school life as a whole, to reflect how thoroughly we believe

[1] *On the Scope and Nature of University Education*, p. 138-9.
[2] *Essays on a Liberal Education*, p. 73, Macmillan, 1867.
[3] *ibid.*, p. 78.
[4] Professor of Moral Philosophy.

in natural exercises for the body and artificial exercises for the mind".[1] Science provides more natural exercises for the young, he claims; the external world excites curiosity and exercises the senses as well as the brain. Moreover, although "a knowledge of the processes and results of physical science does not by itself constitute culture", it is an essential part of the experiences that lead to its acquisition.

In his essay on liberal education in universities, Professor Seeley, of University College, London, criticises the method and quality of the teaching at Oxford and Cambridge as compared with the German system. He takes a line different from Newman's in that he blames the collegiate and tutorial system for mediocre teaching and the decline of real learning. The place of original enquiry and deep learning is inside the university, complementary to teaching and preliminary study. He advocates "the professional system" instead of the tutorial, because it involves teaching more deeply, and with greater concentration, than can be achieved by the college tutor, who has the task of guiding the student through the whole wide realms of his university studies.

E. E. Bowen, of Harrow, writes on teaching by means of grammar, in terms by no means favourable to classics teaching in general. "In every other fruitful enquiry," he comments, "we ascend from phenomena to principles. In classical study alone, we profess to learn principles first and then advance to facts . . . It is a truly a painful sight to see a boy sit down to master a set of clumsy rules, of which he will never use the half, and never understand the quarter . . . His time, his temper, his docility, his confidence in his teacher, his desire to improve—all these are sacrificed".[2] Bowen's remedy is to encourage reading for meaning first, with plenty of explanation and discussion in English; abstract rules may be found gradually from concrete illustrations. "The office of a teacher is to educate his pupils," he wrote, "to cause their minds to grow and work . . . to convince boys that intellectual growth is noble". Bowen suggests this could be done by teaching classics "so as to include more that is of rational interest and less that is of pedantic routine".[3]

Editor Farrar himself contributes an essay on Greek and Latin verse composition as a general branch of education. He denies that style in English expression is dependent on such exercises, and he condemns current practice by asserting, "All which has been

[1] *Essays on a Liberal Education*, p. 138.   [2] *ibid.*, p. 184-5.   [3] *ibid.*, p. 203-4.

discovered and all that has been written on education since the days of Ascham and of Milton has been discovered and written quite in vain". Instead of this "unfortunate relic of training" he would have "the knowledge of *things* and not of *words*; of the truths which great men have to tell us, and not of the tricks or individualities of their style".[1]

J. M. Wilson, science master at Rugby, writes on teaching natural science in schools. His vigour and style puts many a scientist of the period to shame, and his enthusiasm for teaching boys glows like a torch in the nebulous world of adult theory. "Most boys show a degree of interest in their scientific work which is unmistakeably greater than in any other study," he claims. "I am no advocate of a theory of education in which boys should learn nothing but what they show a taste for . . . The thing that is valuable in all education is effort; and it is an advantage which science possesses that the interest that boys take in it induces them to make efforts in its study." [2]

Wilson is keenly critical of the state of higher scientific studies in his own time. "At Cambridge a man may get the highest honours in mathematics and natural philosophy," he comments, "and have never seen a crystal, a lens, an air pump or a thermometer".[3] It is therefore hardly to be wondered at, he continues, if men like Dr Moberley condemn science as worthless in education. Yet the advance of science depends on the training of more and better scientists. Science must become an intellectual training—the development of observation, the practice of thinking, and the exercise of judgment. It must be realised that "the methods of science have affected all other studies" and all aspects of human life, so it is now "absolutely necessary that it shall be no longer excluded from liberal education".[4]

Wilson insists that science should be a compulsory subject in the public and grammar schools, at least for the middle forms. At the top of the school boys should be given the choice of continuing their scientific studies even at the expense of "some small portion of their classical work". It is interesting to find that he is content with two hours a week for science in each form. His idea of the content of a science course is also noteworthy—astronomy, geology, physical geography, and botany for the younger boys, and later, physics and chemistry. His ideas on methods of teaching

---

[1] *Essays on a Liberal Education*, p. 229.
[2] *ibid.*, p. 244.   [3] *ibid.*, p. 254.   [4] *ibid.*, p. 255.

are entirely relevant to our own times. Lecturing, even when illustrated, is almost useless; "the training consists of *doing*". To instruct in the content of the textbook is easier, to organise investigations for the pupils themselves is better.

The seventh essay—on the teaching of English—is written by J. W. Hales, a Cambridge tutor. The main interest of his comments is that they emphasise the most extraordinary neglect of the mother tongue at the higher levels of education. "While in French schools French is taught; in German schools, German; why is English excluded from English schools?" he demands. While he is scathing about the tyranny of Latin and impatient with prevalent arguments that English is not teachable, he is almost tentative in his suggestion that classics learning might begin somewhat later so that English could be taught, at any rate, in the lower school. He asks only that the boy should be made aware that language is logical and that "he should be made thoroughly familiar with the sentence". In fact, Hales speaks with some envy of "schools of a much lower social order"—the National and British schools—where sentence analysis was practised until the adoption of the Revised Code.

The essay on education of the reasoning faculties is by W. Johnson, a master at Eton. Although its psychology may be faulty, it relates educational theory to the teaching situation. It is, in fact, another plea for science and scientific method, for the writer proposes to encourage inductive reasoning, to "create an inquisitiveness".[1] He urges teachers "to encourage any gleam of a talent for observation, to encourage in particular the interest of the collector . . . to propound little puzzles in pneumatics and the like . . . to display a little apparatus of scientific instruments and toys".[2] The Romans taught geography and science, he points out, and as recently as the early nineteenth century it was customary to encourage children in observation of the environment. In his own days, however, "laborious games absorb much of the time which, in the days of Miss Edgeworth and Mr. Joyce, would have been spent in training the eye to observe things passing in field and hedge-row".[3]

Johnson also refers to the work of Dawes, of King's Somborne, whose school of nearly twenty years earlier was "the hope and delight of all who wished to make peasants think".[4] The pamphlet

---

[1] *Essays on a Liberal Education*, p. 318.
[2] *ibid.*, p. 318-19.   [3] *ibid.*, p. 321-2.   [4] *ibid.*, p. 322.

about this school was "obeyed faithfully" in an Eton classroom, at the cost of all Johnson's leisure, which was eaten up in the preparation of experiments.

But Johnson's topic is not the teaching of science, it is the training of reasoning. Therefore, he proceeds to point out how fleeting is the impression made on the young mind by even the most brilliant lecture-demonstrations—as, for instance, Faraday's. Facts and terminology can be learnt "through a long course of forgettings and remindings",[1] but neither of these methods gives any real training in reasoning. From this point, the focus of the argument moves to the teaching of classics. Examining critically the methods and principles accepted in his day, Johnson emphasises that "irrational imitation and phrase-mongery"[2] result. If it is necessary to learn style by imitation, let it be imitation of good modern writers who say something interesting to boys.

An important task of the classics master is, "to form in a boy's mind the habit of weighing and scrutinising general statements and abstract terms".[3] The traditional method of teaching—composition, construing, and parsing—has a disciplinary value; it ought to be adopted to modern material and ideas, so that the pupils will feel they are doing something useful and relevant to their future lives. As the same discipline could be exercised in the study of the French language, it would be reasonable to substitute French for Latin in the public schools.

The concluding chapter is on the social results of classical education. Lord Houghton, the writer, repeats the suggestion that French may perhaps be more relevant than two dead languages. Yet in the past the products of classicism "touched the rough manners of their age with a jovial grace and a genial delicacy, and they applied their wealth to the acquisition of those fine specimens of Greek and Roman Sculpture . . . the production of those sumptuous works of antique topography . . . the foundation of the British Museum, the introduction of the Italian Opera and the establishment of the Academy of British Artists".[4] This argument is continued in a vein partly ironic and partly nostalgic. The old classicism was wide and generous—it excluded no branch of scholarship. It bred complacency in the upper classes and imitation in those beneath, but it was a culture.

---

[1] *Essays on a Liberal Education*, p. 327.
[2] *ibid.*, p. 327.   [3] *ibid.*, p. 345.   [4] *ibid.*, p. 372-3.

Houghton believes classical education to be suffering from the national fixatives on the English gentleman ideal—"he is exhibited to us as an ideal of humanity which it is almost sinful to desire to improve or transcend".[1] If this unrealistic attitude persists, classical education will not deserve to survive. Its disciples need to modernise it, to broaden it into a liberal education fit for the modern world. Surely the little gentleman ought to "be furnished with all that constitutes the elementary education of the people in the most perfect form that pedagogic skill and science can supply?"[2] Surely, he should be able to speak with foreigners in the language of diplomacy, and to appreciate modern science and history. The advantages of the classical tradition can be secured if only the English habit of compromise be exercised between "The just exigencies of our age and the honourable traditions of past generations".[3]

The book, *Essays on a Liberal Education*, has been discussed at some length because it provides valuable evidence on real problems motivating writers and thinkers of the period. The quality of the essays, even when one cannot agree with the arguments, suggest that the state of public school teaching was not as poor as Lowe implied when he said that public schools ought to be subject to inspection.

Moreover, after surveying the essays, the attitude of the most eminent man of our group of classical humanists may be more keenly appreciated. Matthew Arnold was writing on education about the same time. Indeed, his publication of 1864, *A French Eton*, may well have suggested some of their main points to the writers of the essays—for instance, the need for science and English grammar in the curriculum.

Matthew Arnold (1822-88), son of the great headmaster who had already introduced a liberal curriculum at Rugby, had an Oxford degree in classics and a very brief experience of teaching at his old school. He appears to have had no intention of making a career in the field of education, but, finding a private secretaryship—even though to the Lord President of the Privy Council—not remunerative enough to enable him to support a wife, he sought his employer's advice and was rewarded by appointment as an Inspector of Schools, a post which he retained until his retirement.

Unfailingly kindly and charming though he was in the performance of his duties, they were never more than duties which

[1] *Essays on a Liberal Education*, p. 378.   [2] *ibid.*, p. 379.   [3] *ibid.*, p. 384.

earned him a living. Perhaps the circumstances of his appointment explain why he failed to draw inspiration from his daily
chores, and why his thinking about education was not particularly
related to his work—except when he was released from routine in
order to investigate education in other countries. He made three
visits to the Continent for this purpose. His first, to France,
Holland, and Switzerland, resulted in two publications, *The
Popular Education of France* (1861) and *A French Eton* (1864).
His second trip, in 1865, was to France, Germany, Switzerland,
and Italy, and his third, in 1885, to Germany, Switzerland, and
France. He also made a lecture tour in U.S.A.

His dominating interest and great talent was in literature and
poetry. He held the Oxford Professorship of Poetry for ten years,
although he did not take up residence in Oxford. He disliked the
title of Professor, but he aspired to recognition as a man of letters.
His plea for the revival of classical principles in poetry is reflected
in his championship of classical education—not the narrow
grammar grind, but the liberal education discussed by Farrar and
his colleagues. From his travels abroad he came to appreciate that
in French schools and German universities, very high standards
had been proven possible in spite of the inclusion of "modern
studies" and "useful knowledge" in the curriculum.[1] He came
to believe in the value of modern languages—as did his father.
Foreign systems showed him that his father's idea of national
middle-class liberal education was worthy of repetition. Having
observed the advantages and disadvantages of State education, he
gave his support to the campaign for a national system. He hoped
that it would involve the compulsory training of teachers to a high
level, as in Germany, but he also hoped teachers would not become
subject to State control as in France. In Arnold's view, a national
scheme would provide French teaching, and the teaching of Latin
as a modern language even in the elementary school. It is hardly
surprising that he maintained his opposition to the Revised Code
even though he belonged to the machinery that was to administer it.

Written in the same year as *Essays on a Liberal Education*,
Arnold's philosophical satire, *Culture and Anarchy*, contains much
that is relevant to his theory of education. He defines culture as
"a pursuit of our total perfection by means of getting to know, on
all the matters which most concern us, the best which has been

[1] Reported in *Schools and Universities on the Continent*, 1868.

thought and said in the world".[1] The value of culture is not in the mere acquisition of knowledge, but in its application to living in a changing world. There is no virtue in persisting in old habits or preserving old beliefs and methods, as a matter of course, without thinking, weighing up, and deciding anew.

Arnold denies that the classical education of Victorian England gave this culture. Like Lord Houghton, he deplores that it is associated with class distinction. Most of the public school class Arnold designates as the Barbarians because of their slavish devotion to physical activities—games and sports—and because their Latin and Greek fails to stir their intelligence and mental initiative. Another group of society he calls the Philistines because they hold false values—materialistic and utilitarian. Apart from the boys who are pushed into the public schools, middle-class boys receive a commercial or vocational training from adolescence onwards, and they become—Philistines. Arnold disliked intensely the private secondary schools set up by individuals or groups for training in some narrow field of skills or beliefs. The rest of society is the Populace . . . the working class, "now issuing from its hiding place to assert an Englishman's heaven-born privilege of doing as he likes".[2] For them, the limitation of education to the three R's of the Revised Code would not ensure culture.

Yet education itself could bring true culture, and therefore unity, to all people of the community. Arnold sees great forces of regeneration in a national system which would transcend the faults and follies of contemporary education. "Sweetness and light" would be achieved through a true education, through the appreciation of past nobility, present beauty and wonder, and future promise. The Barbarians must have a wider curriculum and more intelligent teaching. The Philistines must share the blessings of a liberal classical education, and not be at the mercy of pedagogues and scientists who despise Latin and Greek. The Populace must have literature, "the greatest power available in education".[3]

During his life Matthew Arnold wrote many more essays bearing on the same question, but enough has been said here to indicate that he was a true disciple of liberal classicism; although, far from being a pioneer or unique in his opinions, he was essentially a son of his father, who thought very much the same as the writers of *Essays on a Liberal Education*. His own contribution was his

[1] *Culture and Anarchy*, Preface, p. x.
[2] *ibid.*, Introduction, p. xv.
[3] *Reports on Elementary Schools*, p. 142, H.M.S.O., 1908. Report of 1871.

particular gift of expression which enabled him to reach a wider public in the dissemination of these ideas.

Before passing on, however, it is relevant to mention that for a much narrower circulation, Arnold wrote a great deal directly on education in the form of official reports. These are valuable, enlightening, and full of humour and humanity. He deplored children's "scantiness of vocabulary", he approved, in principle the introduction of geography and nature study into elementary schools, he complained of unintelligent, mechanical application of pedagogic theories. "The doctrine of Pestalozzi . . . may be excellent," he wrote, "and none can say that it has not found ardent friends to accept it and employ it; and the result is that one sees a teacher holding up an apple to a gallery of little children and saying, 'An apple has a stalk, peel, pulp, core, pips, and juice; it is odorous and opaque, and is used for making a pleasant drink called cider'. In virtue of like theories new methods of spelling, new methods of learning to read are called for. Some of them are ingenious. We must always remember, however, that their apparent conformity to some general doctrine, apparently true, is no guarantee of their soundness." [1]

To a man of Arnold's intelligence, temperament, and convictions, the creative throes of English national education were often unedifying and frustrating. Early in his career he inspected mainly the schools of Nonconformist bodies because he was not eligible to perform this work in Catholic or Church of England schools. He liked the practice in his schools so little that he became prejudiced against denominational education. Later he chafed at the limitations imposed on schools and teachers by the Revised Code; he criticised the Code continuously. Thus it was, no doubt, frustration and disappointment that shaped his own views on the content and method of primary education. He rarely saw any adequate interpretation of fashionable new theories, and he felt that only freedom for the humanistic teaching he himself had enjoyed, could give to State education the character and quality it deserved.

Examinations and payment by results deprived children of liberal education, and teachers of their rightful freedom. Yet he would have insisted on the teaching of formal grammar to young children, and the teaching of history to students in training, because, to him, these were the essentials without which culture could not be gained. He had no enthusiasm for practical and physical

[1] Report for 1878.

activities, although he accepted them as desirable in moderation. His hope for the improvement of teaching was that teachers would turn more and more to continued study, taking advantage of the opportunities offered by London University. Arnold helped to make that university into a teaching institution, for since its foundation it had functioned mainly as an examining body. The first necessity, to teach even science well, was a liberal education. "To have the power of using these data of natural science, a man must, in general, have first been in some measure *moralised*; and for moralising him it will be found not easy, I think, to dispense with those old agents, letters, poetry, religion. So let not our teachers be led to imagine, whatever they may hear or see of the call for natural science, that their literary cultivation is unimportant. The fruitful sense of natural science itself depends, in a very great degree, on having effected in the whole man, by means of letters, a rise in what the political economists call the Standard of life." [1]

Utilitarians and Scientists

The writers chosen to represent schools of thought opposed to classical humanism are John Stuart Mill, Thomas Henry Huxley, and Herbert Spencer. J. S. Mill (1806-73) was the son of James Mill, whose pamphlet of 1812, *Schools for All and not Schools for Churchmen Only*, had proved to be untimely yet prophetic. James Mill had supported Bentham's scheme for a Chrestomathic school—really a State secondary school for the middle classes—but he was not greatly motivated by the spirit of social reform, so strong in many of his contemporaries. His interest was purely intellectual, and his theory that the process of education could be guided by a science of psychology was original and sound, owing little to the expression of similar ideas by Continental thinkers.

Himself the son of a Scots cobbler, James Mill did not expose his own son to the kind of education he advocated for the nation. He taught the boy himself, starting him on Greek at three and Latin at eight, or so J. S. Mill affirms in his *Autobiography*. By the time ordinary upper-class boys were entering public school, this boy had reached a standard beyond that of many university students in classics, mathematics, and philosophy. Unexpected though it may be to find a disciple of Locke and Hartley laying such emphasis on the classics, the explanation lies in James Mill's belief that

[1] Report for 1876.

the virtues of Greek philosophy—intelligence, temperance, justice, and magnanimity—were those most likely to achieve his educational aim, which was to render the pupil happy both as an individual and as a member of society. Although in favour of the extension of education in all ways—schools for all, more universities, the diffusion of useful knowledge—the elder Mill deemed such measures of little value unless this harmony of development, this cultivation of discernment could be ensured. "Mere knowledge is not enough" was his belief when he set out to produce a well-educated man.

Although his ignorance of the real needs of childhood resulted in a revulsion of feeling on the part of his son, the training the boy received was no doubt a major factor in the development of his liberalism and open-mindedness. J. S. Mill continued the cult of utilitarianism—in fact, he devised the name—but his education and his natural intellectual capacity widened his horizons, so that his interpretation of utilitarianism was not that of his father or Bentham. It will be seen that he has much in common with the essayists of *Liberal Education*. The differences are largely a matter of emphasis.

His theory of morals, for instance, was avowedly utilitarian, accepting the "Greatest Happiness Principle" that right actions are those which promote happiness—that is, the absence of pain, the feeling of pleasure. Wrong actions are those which bring pain and prevent the enjoyment of pleasure. But Mill expresses an almost idealist belief when he qualifies this definition by adding that some kinds of pleasure rank higher than others, and that, therefore, in estimating the goodness and rightness of action or policy, the quality of the satisfaction to be gained must be weighed up at the same time as the quantity. This abstract concept might seem irrelevant to education, but it helps to explain Mill's view of the content of education. Similarly, his own training in collecting and weighing evidence before accepting anything as true—James Mill's interpretation of Locke's *Conduct of the Understanding*—is reflected in J. S. Mill's view on methods of education. His early writings, which were mainly on philosophy and logic, put forward his theory that all reasoning is fundamentally inductive.

J. S. Mill was not a teacher; he was not a university professor. He earned his living as an official of the East India Company. His writings, however, gained him high repute as a scholar, critic, and original thinker, and in 1867 he was elected Rector of St

Andrew's University. His inaugural address contains many of his
ideas on education, but he had already referred to problems of
education in earlier essays, particularly in his *Essay on Liberty*
(1869), in which he expressed concern at the threat to individual freedom implied by the growth of State control of education. He believed
that citizens should be required to have their children educated,
and even that poor parents should be able to obtain grants towards
school fees from public funds, but he was dismayed by contemporary disputes about the content and method of State education
—"a mere battlefield for sects and parties, causing the time and
labour which should have been spent in educating to be wasted in
quarrelling about education". He feared that State education, if
fully established, would become "a mere contrivance for moulding
people to be exactly like one another". He felt that a limited
measure of State education might be useful if it had a standard-
ising function—to provide good examples, to promote experiment,
and to stimulate competitive effort on the part of non-State schools.

It is perhaps not without significance that Mill gave his inaugural
address at St Andrew's in the year of the publication of Farrar's
Essays on a Liberal Education. The address dealt with many of
the same points, and as Mill was not a university man himself, it is
remarkable there were not more differences of opinion. He certainly
differed from Newman in his Philistine view of the function of a
university. He ignored the possible value of university life itself,
with its intellectual ferments and the interplay of personalities.
His concept was of a kind of Solomon's House for the collection
and dissemination of knowledge. It may be remembered, however,
that at least one of the classical essayists suggested that English
universities might do well to provide rather more professional
knowledge and rather less tutorial benignity.

He agreed with the general view of the classicists that university
education should be liberal and cultural, that vocational and technical specialisms should be studied in separate institutions. Profiting,
perhaps from his reading of Auguste Comte, the French sociologist,
Mill defined the function of universities as that of handing on
existent knowledge and culture adequately enough to enable the
next generation to go further forward. He differed from the classicists in taking no part in the campaign for the retention of the
classical bias in education. He was prepared to defend classical
education, especially against the attacks of extremists such as
Herbert Spencer who would have science dominating the school

curriculum as well as higher education. Mill was essentially a moderate who asked, "Can anything deserve the name of a good education, which does not include literature and science too?"[1]

He differed from the classicists in believing that any one subject could form the basis of higher education so long as wide and intelligent studies in other fields were required at the same time. His general principle of specialisation within a wide field of liberal studies gains much support at the present time. He differed from Bentham and his father in recognising the value of art and poetry in human experience. He was certainly in advance of his time in advocating the intellectual and political equality of women with men.

The claims of science in education were put more forcibly by the scientists themselves. The classical opposition had become, if not stronger, at least more vociferous, since the days of Edgeworth and the popular science lectures of Birkbeck, Davy, and their kind. The same work was being carried on by eminent scientists such as Faraday, who often demonstrated to schoolboy audiences, but there was considerable hostility and criticism to their work on the part of the classicists—as, for instance, Matthew Arnold's references to "Mr Bottles" and "Professor Silverpump" in his essays, *Friendship's Garland.*

Professor T. H. Huxley (1823-95) took up the cudgels on behalf of scientific education in no half-hearted manner. Although he was rather more biased toward science than Mill, he was considerably less extreme than Spencer in his claims for that subject. He came to the science of biology through work undertaken as a hobby during his early career as an assistant surgeon on an Admiralty vessel surveying Australian waters. He collected marine animals and later gave papers on his work to the Royal Society and Linnaean Society. Henceforward, his career lay in science. He became Professor of Natural History at the Royal School of Mines, and later held examinership and professorships in the University of London, the Royal Institution, and the Royal College of Surgeons. He held periods of office as president of all the great scientific societies. His researches and scientific publications were considerable, but he still had time to take an active part in current controversies and in community service. His educational appointments came in later life—Rector of the University of Aberdeen and member of the London School Board—but by that time he had

[1] *Inaugural Address.*

already given many years of thought and effort to the educational questions of the time.

It can hardly have been coincidental that in 1868, when discussion of liberal education was at its height, Huxley addressed the South London Working Men's College on *A Liberal Education and Where to Find it.* "Education is the instruction of the intellect in the laws of Nature," he said "under which I include not merely things and their forces, but men and their ways, and the fashioning of the affections and of the will into an earnest and loving desire to move in harmony with those laws".[1] Like Mill and Lowe he had no quarrel with the classics in education so long as they were taught well—he confesses that he would have welcomed the opportunity to take up the classics in his own schooldays. Like the best of the classicists he deplored the aridity of prevalent teaching methods which aimed at useless mechanical skills and unintelligent rote learning rather than an appreciation of the best ideas of the past. Huxley told his audience of working men that liberal education begins in childhood by a training that gives self-control of body and mind, the body doing "all the work that, as a mechanism, it is capable of", and the intellect acting as "a clear, cold, logic engine with all the parts of equal strength, and in smooth working order; ready, like a steam engine, to be turned to any kind of work, and spin the gossamers as well as forge the anchors of the mind".[2]

Huxley's suggestions for a school curriculum included biology, English language and literature, modern history and geography, with special reference to Britain, and the study of the world's great literature in translations. In addition, he advocated studies in sociology, politics, and morals. Such a balanced diet would surely produce the free man, "one who, no stunted ascetic, is full of life and fire, but whose passions are trained to come to heel by a vigorous will, the servant of a tender conscience, who has learned to love all beauty, whether of Nature or of art, to hate all vileness, and to respect others as himself".[3]

Huxley commented, somewhat reproachfully, that his investigation of English education had revealed no evidence that true liberal education was being attempted or achieved. It was not to be achieved in his time, but his enthusiasm, moderation, and integrity did much to persuade teachers and administrators that "a

---

[1] Huxley, T. H., *Collected Essays*, p. 83, Macmillan, 1895.
[2] *ibid.*, p. 86.   [3] *ibid.*, p. 86.

knowledge of the great and fundamental truths of Nature, and the laws of her operation" was at least as important to a responsible citizen as a store of quotations in Latin and Greek.

Huxley's varied official appointments and duties brought him into contact with influential people active in many spheres of education. He worked with equal interest for all stages of education —he planned a religious instruction syllabus for London schools, he acted as a Governor of Eton, and he looked forward to the day when it would be as easy to pass upwards from the Board school to the university as it was to proceed from the public school. The Education Act which made this possible was passed only seven years after Huxley's death.

The most extreme advocate of scientific education was Herbert Spencer (1820-1903), a schoolmaster's son who became a railway engineer at eighteen. His boyhood interest had been in science and nature study, but although he later wrote at considerable length on several branches of science, he was at no time engaged in practical scientific study in the same way as professional scientists like Huxley. Nevertheless, he became widely recognised as a scientific thinker, and in private life enjoyed developing his own inventions. From his middle twenties onwards he earned his living in literary work, at first as sub-editor of *The Economist* and later as an independent writer.

By the time he published his famous treatise, *Education, Intellectual, Moral and Physical*, in 1861, he had already written a great deal on science, psychology, and sociology. His critical attitude towards other thinkers, such as Auguste Comte, pioneer sociologist, showed a curious lack of humility and magnanimity. It is obvious that Spencer must have gained ideas and hints from many earlier writers, but he rarely refers to them. Yet his views carried conviction to all parts of the world. His *Education*, for instance, was translated into thirteen foreign languages before the end of the century, and it enjoyed a wide circulation in U.S.A.

Spencer's provocative tone was not universally appreciated, however. That gentle scholar, R. H. Quick, the first to recognise Spencer as an educational thinker in his *Essays on Educational Reformers* of 1866, complained, "It is perhaps to be regretted that Mr Spencer has not kept the tone of one who investigates the truth in a subject of great difficulty, but lays about him right and left, after the manner of a spirited controversialist . . . It has the disadvantage of arousing the antagonism of those whom he would most wish to influence. When the man who has no practical acquaintance with education lays down the law *ex cathedra*, garnished with sarcasms at all that is now going on, the schoolmaster, offended by the assumed tone of authority, sets himself to show where these theories would not work instead of examining what basis of truth there is in them . . . I shall proceed to examine Mr Spencer's proposals with all the impartiality I am master of".[1]

In *Education*, Spencer first asks the question, "What knowledge is of most worth?", and answers it by contending that although many subjects could be taught to children, science stands out as having far greater value than any other subject. It can give an appreciation of the laws of health, through hygiene and physiology, it can lead towards efficiency in earning a living, through physics and other sciences, and it can give preparation for parenthood through psychology and education—education thus being given the status of a science.

In addition, the future citizen needs to be initiated into the duties and knowledge of citizenship—and this through a study of the social sciences which would give an intelligent attitude towards elections. There is a familiar ring to Spencer's argument that a knowledge of science is essential to national safety. For individual satisfaction, he recommends training in the appreciation of art— a *scientific* training giving the ability to recognise artists' errors in lighting or perspective.

Spencer's second main purpose for science in education is the part it plays in mental training and development. He regards Latin and Greek as providing an intellectual discipline far less valuable than that of science. In the matter of memory alone, the rote-learning of language study is vastly inferior to the memory the pupil retains of his direct contacts with Nature. But observation and experiment give more than memorised fact; they stimulate reasoning and judgment, they develop initiative to go on finding out things for oneself, and they lead to the understanding of laws of Nature and society.

The second of the four lengthy chapters of *Education* deals with methods of intellectual education, following the argument that the methods of science point the way. Spencer deigns to accept the main principle of Pestalozzi, that education should follow the natural development of the child, that sense experience comes first,

---

[1] Quick, R. H., *Essays on Educational Reformers*, p. 440, Longmans Green, 1904 edition.

and that learning depends on the clarity of the impressions gained through experience. He refers to "the well-conceived but ill-conducted system of object lessons",[1] and although he also criticises some of Pestalozzi's own methods, he warns the reader to distinguish between "the fundamental principles of the Pestalozzian system, and the set of expedients devised for its practice".[2]

This chapter contains the famous maxims: from the simple to the complex; from the indefinite to the definite; from the concrete to the abstract; from the empirical to the rational. He suggests, for instance, that the grammar of a language should not be studied first, but last, and that in science, principles and laws should grow up slowly from experiment and observation. It will be remembered that the *Liberal Education* essayists echoed these points a few years later. Spencer also expresses belief in the race-recapitulation theory by suggesting that subjects should be introduced in the same order in which knowledge was acquired by the human race.

"As a final test by which to judge any plan of culture," he writes, "should come the question—Does it create a pleasurable excitement in the pupils? . . . The repugnances to this and that study which vex the ordinary teacher, are not innate, but result from his unwise system".[3] This throws on the teacher the responsibility for generating interest and enthusiasm in his pupils. He suggests that a growing recognition of drawing in schools is a sign that teachers "are at length adopting the course which Nature has perpetually been pressing on their notice".[4]

The third chapter is devoted to moral education. Here Spencer follows Locke and Rousseau in his reliance on the natural discipline of consequences. Attitudes are formed through the sentiments and feelings, he argues, so that it is useless to teach moral maxims or to attempt the inculcation of morals through intelligence. The suffering of small hurts and disappointments through personal failings—disobedience, unpunctuality, and suchlike—is one kind of punishment; consciousness of withdrawal of parental approval or esteem is another kind of punishment. Moral excellence should not be expected of children. Morality grows, even as body and mind grow. Part of the process of growth is learning, by practice, to be independent, self-controlled, and able to make judgments.

Spencer suggests that this process of moral development is usually hindered by fortuitous and haphazard treatment by adults.

---

[1] *Education*, p. 56, Williams and Norgate, 1893.
[2] *ibid.*, p. 64.   [3] *ibid.*, p. 70.   [4] *ibid.*, p. 79.

The remedy would appear to be a deliberate campaign on the part of the teacher. "You must more or less modify your method to suit the disposition of each child," he writes, "and must be prepared to make further modifications as each child's disposition enters a new phase".[1]

The last section of the book deals with physical education, which Spencer regarded as fundamental and yet shamefully neglected. The country gentleman pays great attention to the diet of his horses, but does not consider whether the food he provides for his own children is "adapted to the constitutional needs of growing boys and girls".[2] Yet, as it is now known that human beings are subject to the same organic laws as animals, it is time we made use of the principles discovered by the new "Science of Life" and applied them to the guidance of human development.

In his enthusiasm for the new theories of evolution, Spencer ventures on unsafe ground in discussing questions of heredity. Nevertheless, most of his suggestions are sound, although, to one who knows his Locke, not strikingly original. He advocates exercise, correct diet, sensible clothing, and freedom from the mental strain of excessive study. It is interesting to find, however, that although he does not mention Locke by name, he expresses disagreement with the "hardening" theory. "The common notion about 'hardening' is a grievous delusion," he writes. "Not a few children are 'hardened' out of the world, and those who survive, permanently suffer either in growth or constitution."[3] He would have been horrified at the inadequacy of the modern child's clothing, but he would have enjoyed watching modern girls at play.

Spencer dilates at length on the evils of "the forcing system".[4] He describes the miseries of students in training colleges instituted "for the purpose of supplying schools with well-disciplined teachers".[5] In one college, eleven and a half hours a day were given to study and one and a quarter hours to optional physical exercise, he states, and the students suffered frequently from headache, indigestion, diarrhoea, and breakdowns. Spencer blames the shortness of the course and the severe examination system, but he deplores that "a prevailing tendency to an unduly urgent system of culture"[6] had caused the development of such a system. "The physical underlies the mental," he concludes, "the mental must not be developed at the expense of the physical".[7]

[1] *Education*, p. 128.   [2] *ibid.*, p. 131.   [3] *ibid.*, p. 147.
[4] *ibid.*, p. 168.   [5] *ibid.*, p. 160.   [6] *ibid.*, p. 161.   [7] *ibid.*, p. 171.

The four sections of *Education* were originally written as separate articles for a journal. Thus there is no attempt to pull the arguments together in the form of a summary or conclusion. The effects of this—together with the style—is to emphasise in the reader's mind the author's preoccupation with the task of relating the life of the individual human being to the new scientific knowledge so rapidly becoming available in his own day. Although interested in Comte's sociology, he is not primarily concerned with social groups. He certainly shared J. S. Mill's dislike of growing State control, whether in education or in other aspects of life.

His criticism of classical education, as it was in his day, was justified. His anxiety about physical education was understandable in view of his own struggle with ill-health. His opinion of the educational value of literature, history, and the arts is perhaps a sign of lack of liberality in his own education. His essays provide little guidance for the practical teacher, but they provoke a strong mental reaction in the reader. To-day we do not need to be made aware of the demands of science. In Victorian days, however, the smooth, patronising, almost impartial, comments of Farrar's essayists were not forceful enough to change the old order. Only the drive of a Huxley and the sting of a Spencer could make Britain science-conscious.

Poets and Pedagogues

Early in this chapter it was suggested that during the second half of the nineteenth century, the cause of "child-centred education" was kept alive, and was, in fact, much stronger than is usually recognised. The poetry of Wordsworth was mentioned as a possible influence, but it would be unwise to attempt to assess its extent. Both J. S. Mill and Matthew Arnold were profoundly influenced by Wordsworth, and perhaps the ideas which inspired them are among those which some modern theorists on education find relevant and significant. It is enough to say that Wordsworth's message —his feeling for the relationship between Nature and the human spirit—may well have been interpreted by the "Pestalozzi-Froebelians" of the period.

The influence of Charles Kingsley (1819-85) was much more direct and certain. Although he achieved a classical first at Cambridge, and later became Professor of Modern History at that university, Kingsley was a naturalist by inclination. Some of his best-known books for children are really simple scientific treatises.

Moreover, in his youth he had connections with St Mark's Training College, Chelsea, and so had an insight into aspects of education often unknown to the "subject" protagonists. Kingsley was a fine writer of lyrical verse, but he also wielded his pen powerfully on behalf of the underdogs of his day. He was outspoken in his condemnation of a society which permitted dire poverty and misery to exist and increase in its midst. He described not only the exploitation of child labour, but also the filthy, insanitary conditions of lower-class life—conditions from which came the cholera epidemic of the mid-fifties.

Although a cleric himself—he became Canon of Westminster—he was critical of the religious prejudices of the day. Thus he stood firm as the opponent of conservatism and traditional privilege in those spheres of human affairs most closely related to education. In 1869, he became President of the Education Section of the Social Science Congress, to which he gave an address emphasising "the duty of the State to educate all alike in those duties which are common to them as citizens, that is, in all secular matters and in all matters also which concern their duties to each other as defined by law".

An equally great literary figure, John Ruskin (1819-1900), also gave valuable service to the cause of education. He was a prolific writer, and although he produced no treatise on education, he referred to it in almost every one of his books, pamphlets, and letters. As a creative artist, whose career was sixty years long, he is not always consistent in his view on education, and his meaning is sometimes obscured by the use of satire and paradox. He was critical of practically all prevalent methods of education, regarding them as superficial and lacking in worthy aims. At all levels he saw it valued only for its usefulness either for earning a living or for obtaining a place in society. The real purpose of education was neither of these. Education, he maintained, is an end in itself, to foster the abilities and virtues revealing themselves from infancy onwards. Physical health and beauty, and spiritual quality, could be achieved through education. Sentiments and attitudes could be developed, not through instruction, but through the atmosphere surrounding children—the excellence of teachers, the nobility of the great figures in history, the inspiration of poetry and music, the wonders of science and nature. This was yet another interpretation of "liberal education", Ruskin stressing not the subjects themselves, but the flowering of the human spirit under the right cultivation.

Yet he was completely realist in his attitude towards vocational education. The regeneration of society from the evils of the Industrial Revolution could only be achieved through the recapture of pride in manual skills. Ruskin would have every boy taught a trade, and all practical workers encouraged to develop their craftsmanship and to maintain its dignity. He advocated the setting up of State training schools for this vocational education. Thus he was in favour of a certain measure of State education—the State should ensure that free education should be enjoyed by all.

He saw the school as a place of beauty in a beautiful place. Preferably in extensive grounds, the building should be architecturally fine, and planned for the health of the inhabitants. The classrooms should be hung with fine pictures. Physical and moral health should be the basic aim of all schools, but apart from this, they should vary according to the needs of their pupils. Ruskin envisaged a flexible, many-sided system of education. His suggestions for State schools are contained in *Unto this Last* (1862), and his views on the value of literature in education in *Sesame and Lilies* (1864). In *Time & Tide* (1867) there are several discussions of educational questions, including his extremely original version of a tripartite system. This latter is composed of schools in cities, in the country, and by the sea, each kind peopled by children who are likely to spend their lives in similar environments. Town children were to learn mathematics and the arts, country children biology and practical farming, and seaside children physical geography, astronomy, and marine biology.

Many of Ruskin's ideas became fact within a relatively short space of time—school playgrounds and medical services, art and craft work in schools, the elevation of literature and history, the inclusion of nature study, and the study of better ways of teaching children. Fortunately for women, his well-intentioned but patronising and limited suggestions about girls' education have not been considered the strongest points of his contribution to education.

At this point, it is relevant to pick up the threads of the story of the women disciples of Pestalozzi and Froebel. By 1850, the methods advocated by Pestalozzi were well established in training colleges, which were now quite numerous. It is true that the interpretation of Pestalozzi's ideas was often out-of-date and stereotyped, but there were many devoted teachers working sincerely to foster the happy development of their pupils.

In 1854, with the strong support of Charles Dickens, the kindergarten movement was started in England by Baroness Von Marenholtz Bülow, newly arrived from Germany. Several years later she published in Berlin an interpretation of Froebelian theory, a work which appeared in England as *The Child and Child Nature* in 1879. The translator, Miss A. M. Christie, suggests that its object is "to promote a more thorough and universal understanding of the theories and philosophy on which Froebel's educational system is based".[1]

The first kindergarten was opened in Bloomsbury by Madame Ronge and Madame Kraus Boelte. Visitors, including an inspector of the National Society, were vastly impressed, and similar schools soon achieved success in other parts of the country. Within twenty years there were Kindergarten Associations in London, Manchester, Bedford, and Dublin. In 1874, the Froebel Society was founded. Thus there now existed a group of schools, which, because they were private schools, were patronised by the monied classes. This explains why kindergartens also became associated with the new Girls' Public Day Schools, and why a special system of teacher-training was established by the Joint Board of Froebel Associations.

Two more ladies from the Continent, Adèle Von Portugall and Eleanore Heerwart, were pioneer workers in Manchester, and they also contributed writings. Madame Michaelis, who came to England in 1874 from kindergarten work in Switzerland and Italy, was a prime mover in the foundation of the Society, and later in the foundation of a training college at Notting Hill. It is not without significance that her first engagement in England was to lecture to the School Board Teachers in Croydon.

In 1880, Emily Shireff published an excellent book, *The Kindergarten. Principles of Froebel's System and their bearing on the Education of Women, also Remarks on the Higher Education of Women.*[2] In 1889, Mary J. Lyschinska, a Superintendent under the School Board for London, published *The Kindergarten Principle, Its Educational Value and Chief Applications.*[3] The same Miss Christie who translated *The Child and Child Nature* was responsible for the foundation, in 1883, of the Art for Schools Association, which was patronised by Lord Leighton, William Morris, Robert Browning, Matthew Arnold, Bishop Temple, and Mr Mundella.

---

[1] Bülow, *The Child and Child Nature*, p. 111, Swan Sonnenschein.
[2] Sonnenschein and Allen.   [3] Wm. Isbister Ltd.

This brought to many schools, both voluntary and board, the kind of wall decoration favoured by Ruskin.

Enough has been said to show that the women pioneers of the period were not only numerous and enterprising, but also eager to extend the advantages of new ideas and methods to all kinds of schools. The Froebelian organisations were not intentionally based on class distinctions. The leaders were always ready to work on behalf of the teachers and pupils of the National schools. Notable among the men who helped in this work were T. G. Rooper and W. H. Herford.

The former, an Inspector of Schools from 1877, introduced kindergarten methods into infant schools, encouraged the making of school gardens, and urged the development of craft work and manual training.[1] Rooper also organised classes for pupil teachers, worked for the Parents' National Educational Union, and supported the foundation of a University College at Southampton. He was particularly interested in the teaching of geography through local study and practical work, and through the correlation with history. After his death a geography prize was established at Bradford Grammar School as memorial.

W. H. Herford, translator and editor of Froebel's *Education of Man*,[2] was admirably assessed by Michael Sadler: "He planted new ideas among us. He set up a new and more exacting standard of the teacher's skill and duty . . . But he also wrote what seems to me by far the best presentment of the educational doctrine of Froebel . . . And beyond this, in his little book, *The School: An Essay towards Humane Education*, he gave us one of the five masterpieces of English educational writing in the nineteenth century. In that book, as in his work as a teacher, it was the spirit of Pestalozzi which shone out again. For, much as Herford honoured Froebel, there was a different note in his voice when he spoke of some 'golden word of our master's master, Pestalozzi'".[3]

Herford had intended to become a Unitarian minister, but early studies in Germany and a period spent as tutor to Byron's son in Switzerland, gave him opportunities to learn about the work of the two great educators. His first small private school in Lancaster, run on Pestalozzian lines, survived only eleven years, but he found that no other vocation was fully satisfying, and eventually, in 1873,

[1] Particularly "Sloyd", the Scandinavian method then becoming known in England.   See Rooper, T. G., *Home and School Life*, A. Brown and Sons.
[2] Herford, W. H., *The Students' Froebel*, Pitman, 1893, 2 volumes.
[3] Introduction, p. x, of *The Students' Froebel*, Edition of 1916.

opened Lady-Barn House at Fallowfield, Manchester, a venture which was successful. Herford gave invaluable support to the cause of women's education, and he was particularly successful in his own teaching of girls.

Apart from the Froebelians, there were a number of contributors to pedagogical literature in the last quarter of the nineteenth century. Among the more eminent names are those of Edward Thring, Joseph Payne, and Joshua Fitch. Thring was headmaster of Uppingham School from 1853 to 1886, during which time he established a system radically different from that of the average public school. His main principle was the need to adjust school education to develop the capacities of each individual boy. "Nothing is too good to give to boys," he said, thus confessing his acceptance of the new doctrines, which placed first the wellbeing of the pupil. He wrote *Theory and Practice of Teaching* in the series of pedagogical works published by the Cambridge University Press towards the end of the century.

Joseph Payne was a successful master of private schools for thirty years before devoting himself to lecturing and writing on principles and methods of education. He was a pioneer on modern ideas of teacher-training in that he believed it necessary to help teachers to gain a deeper intellectual understanding of aims and principles. He was among the first to suggest that education be regarded as a science, and teaching methods be related to the methods of science.[1] In 1872, Payne became the first Professor of Education of the College of Preceptors, and thus the first professor of that subject in England. He was a highly successful lecturer to teachers and, like Herford, was a warm advocate of higher education for women. His lectures and essays were collected and published in 1883 as *The Works of Joseph Payne*. His guiding principle was that all teaching is self-teaching, and he advised his students to seek ways of generating this attitude in their pupils.

Sir Joshua Fitch started his career as a schoolmaster and, at twenty-eight, rose to be Principal of Borough Road Training College, where his work won the approval of Matthew Arnold. In 1863, he became an Inspector of Schools, and during thirty years of service, he filled many important offices, wrote many excellent reports, and played a large part in the direction of national education. His name is associated with reports on endowed schools, with the inquiries that preceded the 1870 Act,

[1] Payne, J., *The Science and Art of Teaching*, Longmans.

and with the courses of lectures on teaching held at the College of Preceptors and at Cambridge.[1] He published in 1881 his *Lectures on Teaching*, a comprehensive work, full of practical and commonsensical suggestions which are by no means irrelevant to modern teaching situations.

Foreign Influences and End-of-Century Tendencies

No contemporary foreign educator influenced late nineteenth-century English education in the same way as the giants of an earlier epoch. Nevertheless, German influence was strong, not only through the German ladies who settled here, but also through the various missions, official and unofficial, undertaken to study German education. Arnold, Fitch, Payne, Herford, all found their German observations stimulating. Herford also found inspiration in Switzerland, where the son of Fellenburg was maintaining Pestalozzian traditions. France and U.S.A. also supplied ideas and arguments to the many English visitors who sought ways of improving our own schools.

It is somewhat surprising that the names of Herbart and his disciples are so rarely mentioned by the returned pilgrims. The Herbartian movement was delayed until the turn of the century.[2] Moreover, although Rooper discussed "Sloyd" in his *Home and School Life*, the principles of Uno Cygnaeus,[3] the Finnish Froebelian, were not widely accepted in England until the twentieth century. John Dewey's experiment in Chicago did not take place until the last few years of the century, and thus he was almost unknown in this country until some time afterwards. On the other hand, the work of T. A. Ribot, the French psychologist, made a profound impression on Margaret McMillan, who was working on behalf of Bradford children when the new century dawned. She claims that Ribot contributed much to the development of beliefs which were to motivate her in her amazing work of the next thirty years. Her greatest inspiration came from Edouard Séguin, a French pioneer in the education of mentally defective children. But although he worked and wrote for many years in U.S.A., Miss McMillan found it impossible to buy a copy of his book in England in 1896.[4]

[1] Organised by the Cambridge Training Syndicate.
[2] John Adams published *The Herbartian Psychology* in 1897.
[3] 1810-88. N.B.—The first English teacher went to the Sloyd Training School in Sweden in 1884.
[4] McMillan, M., *The Nursery School*, p. 13, Dent, 1919.

A chronological list of the main publications on education of the half century reveals several interesting tendencies and a major omission. This latter is the failure of new scientific and socio-logical ideas to make any real impact on the theories and opinions of educators. Thus, although Charles Darwin's *Origin of the Species* was published in 1859, no discussion of its implications in education appeared before the end of the century. Spencer and Huxley stimulated the study of science, but gave considerably less attention to evolution in their educational theory than Froebel had given many years earlier.

Darwin's work had made available for the educator—whether scientist or not—a comprehensible theory of life, a theory that involved not only the possibility of inevitable change but also the possibility of inescapable heredity. In their unawareness of these bogeys, English writers were behind those of several other countries, but the new century soon found them arguing about heredity.[1] The question of education for a changing world remained for Dewey to expound in a later generation.

Other Works Representative of the Period

1855   Faraday, Whewell, *et. al.*: *Lectures on Education.* J. Parker.

1858   D. Benham: *Comenius's School of Infancy.* London.

1865   E. Sewell: *Principles of Education.* Longmans.

1866   E. Davies: *Higher Education of Women.* Strahan.

1867   S. S. Laurie: *On Primary Instruction in Relation to Education.* Blackwood.

        E. Thring: *Education and School.* Macmillan.

1868   T. Markby: *Practical Essays on Education.* Strahan.

1870   Dorothea Beale: *Reports on the Education of Girls.* Nutt.

        H. Campbell: *Compulsory Education.* Murray.

        N. Arnott: *Fundamental Principles of National Education.* Longmans.

1873   J. Morley: *Struggle for National Education.* Chapman.

1875   J. M. Leitch: *Practical Educationalists.* Macmillan.

1874   C. Kingsley: *Health and Education.* Macmillan.

1879   G. Coombe (ed. W. Jolly): *Education.* Macmillan.

        A. Bain: *Education as a Science.* Kegan Paul.

1880   R. H. Quick: *Locke on Education.* C.U.P.

[1] *E.g.* Hayward, F. H., *Education and the Heredity Spectre*, Watts 1908.

1881   T. Fowler (ed.): *Locke's "Conduct of the Understanding"*.
        Clarendon.
1882   Sir H. Craik: *The State and its Relation to Education*.
        Macmillan.
        S. S. Laurie: *John Amos Comenius*. C.U.P.
1883   H. W. Eve and A. Sidgwick: *The Practice of Education*.
        C.U.P.
        F. W. Farrar and R. B. Poole: *General Aims of the Teacher
        and Form Management*. C.U.P.
        D. Kay: *Education and Educators*. Kegan Paul, Trench.
1885   Cotterill: *Suggested Reforms in Public Schools*. Black-
        wood.
        F. W. Hackwood: *Notes of Lessons on Moral Subjects*.
        Nelson.
1887   Sophie Bryant: *Educational Ends*. Longmans.
        F. Froebel (trans. Heilmann): *The Education of Man*.
        Arnold.
        J. M. Wilson: *Addresses on Morality in Public Schools*.
        Macmillan.
1888   S. S. Laurie: *Occasional Addresses on Educational Sub-
        jects*. C.U.P.
        Sir P. Magnus: *Industrial Education*. Kegan Paul, Trench.
        A. Sidgwick: *On Stimulus*. C.U.P.
1889   J. J. Findlay: *Teaching as a Career for University Men*.
        Rivington.
        J. Landon: *School Management*. Kegan Paul, Trench.
1890   M. J. Lyschinska and T. G. Montefiore: *The Ethical
        Teachings of Froebel*. Trench, Trubner.
1891   "The Thirteen": *Thirteen Essays on Education*. Percival.
        E. Paget: *The Spirit of Discipline*. Longmans.
1892   A. H. D. Acland and H. L. Smith (ed.): *Studies in Second-
        ary Education*. Percival.
        T. Davidson: *Aristotle (First of Great Educators Series)*.
        Heinemann.
        J. F. Herbart (trans. Felkin): *The Science of Education*.
        Swan Sonnenschein.
        O. Solomon: *Theory of Educational Sloyd*. Philip.
        A. E. Shirreff: *Moral Training: Froebel and Herbert
        Spencer*. Philip.
1893   T. H. Huxley: *Science and Education*. Macmillan.
        E. Lyttelton: *Mothers and Sons*. Macmillan.

1893   A. E. West: *Alcuin* (*Third of Great Educators Series*). Heinemann.
1894   W. Jolly: *Ruskin On Education*. Geo. Allen.
1895   Dewey and M'Lellan: *Psychology of Number*. Arnold.
       E. E. Morris: *Milton's Tractate of Education*. Macmillan.
1896   M. W. Keatinge: *The Great Didactic of Comenius*. Black.
       Grace Toplis: *Leaves from the Note-Books of Frances M. Buss*. Macmillan.

SUGGESTIONS FOR FURTHER READING

Curtis and Boultwood, *A Short History of Educational Ideas*, 4th edition, U.T.P., 1965. Chapter XVI.

F. A. Cavanagh, *James and John Stuart Mill on Education*, C.U.P., 1931.

W. F. Connell, *The Educational Thought and Influence of Matthew Arnold*, Routledge and Kegan Paul, 1950.

A. V. Judges (Ed.), *Pioneers of English Education*, Faber and Faber, 1952.

J. Manning, *Dickens on Education*, O.U.P., 1960.

CHAPTER VIII

EDUCATION UNDER STATE SUPERVISION, 1902-1944

The Board of Education Act had established a central authority for education, but the Government was faced by two extremely difficult problems. In the first place it had become an urgent matter to decide upon some form of assistance to the voluntary schools. These were now mainly Church of England or Roman Catholic, since the majority of the schools which had been founded under the supervision of other religious bodies had been handed over to the School Boards. Secondly, the recommendations of the Bryce Commission about the establishment of local authorities for education had not been carried out and the Government, mindful of the abortive Bill of 1896, was not anxious to renew this experience unless events forced it to do so.

The financial position of the voluntary schools had been rapidly deteriorating in spite of the help given by Lord Sandon's Act of 1876 and the more recent Voluntary Schools Act of 1897, which had freed the schools from the payment of rates, abolished the 17s. 6d. limit for grant, and had made available an additional aid grant of 5s. per head to be paid through the Association of Voluntary Schools.

As Payment by Results gradually disappeared, the curriculum of the elementary schools had expanded. Not only were academic subjects such as history, geography, and elementary science finding a place, but practical activities such as handicrafts, domestic science, physical exercises, and games were being developed. At the same time more progressive ideas about the layout of school buildings were being adopted by the larger School Boards. The one long room containing several classes divided by curtains or a flimsy partition was becoming a thing of the past, and, in the newer buildings, was replaced by schools with a central assembly hall into which the different classrooms opened. Improvements had also taken place in methods of heating and lighting. All these changes were making education a much more costly business. At the time of the Revised Code it was assumed that the cost of educating an elementary school child would not exceed thirty shillings a year. Mr Forster in 1870 had accepted this figure, and he believed that a rate of 3d. in the pound would be quite sufficient to supplement the Government grant in paying for the education of a child in a Board school.

This assumption was indeed an optimistic one. As early as 1880 the cost per head in a voluntary school had risen to £1 14s. 10¼d., and in 1893 it reached £1 17s. 6¼d., of which 18s. 1½d. came from the Government grant, 2s. 4½d. from school fees, and 6s. 8½d. from voluntary contributions. The remainder came from interest on endowments and a fee grant which was paid to those schools which had abolished the payment of school pence. In contrast, the average cost per child in a Board school was £2 8s. 1½d. (in London it had reached £3 5s. 8¼d., of which the ratepayers contributed £2 16s. 11¾d.). The School Boards could meet the rising cost of schooling by raising the education rate, but this was denied to the voluntary schools. Hence, although the numbers on roll were greater than those in the Board schools, their only remedy was to stimulate the flow of voluntary contributions, but there was a limit to what might be expected in this way.

The Government knew full well that any measure which sanctioned the application of the rates to the upkeep of voluntary schools would be strongly opposed by the Liberals, who would be supported by the Nonconformists who objected to paying an education rate for schools in which religious teaching of which they disapproved was given. The curious feature of their opposition was that they did not object to the payment of taxes, part of which was assigned to the Government grant paid to voluntary and Board schools alike. Possibly, taxation by the Government seemed to be more remote than contributions made through the local rates. The Government realised that if the voluntary schools were unable to continue, the country would be faced with the provision of an enormous number of school places resulting in an overwhelming drain on the national exchequer. Naturally, the Government favoured a policy of delay, but the leaders of the Anglican and Roman Churches were constantly pressing for something to be done.

The logical solution seemed to lie in a comprehensive overhaul of English elementary education which would involve the abolition of the School Boards and their substitution by the local authorities recommended by the Bryce Commission. In addition, economic considerations counted. This country was being out-distanced in trade and industry by foreign competitors, especially the United

States and Germany. There was a very strong case for the provision of more efficient education—elementary, secondary, and technical. As Sir M. E. Sadler remarked, the position of England as a first-class power depended on sea power and school power.

Whilst the Government was making up its mind, its hand was forced by a series of events which originated in the intrigues of a somewhat junior civil servant. The story is briefly this. The previous Liberal Government had become alarmed about the rapidity with which this country had been losing markets overseas and falling behind her competitors in industrial output. In 1894, Mr Acland, Vice-President of the Education Department, was successful in obtaining Treasury sanction for the appointment of an official charged with the duty of keeping the Government informed about educational developments in other countries. The result was the establishment of the Office of Special Inquiries and Reports in the following year, and M. E. Sadler, who was previously mentioned in the account given of the Bryce Commission, was appointed Director of the new department.

Sadler's post demanded that he should be closely in touch with developments abroad, and this required visits to other countries to obtain first-hand information about what was being done in the educational field. As Sadler expressed it later, the function of his department was, in fact, the intelligence department of the Board of Education. When the scope of the Office expanded, there arose a need for an Assistant-Director who could take charge when Sadler was away from England. Robert L. Morant was appointed with the concurrence of Sadler.

Career of Morant

Morant's previous career reads like a romantic story. Born in 1863, he was educated at Winchester College and Oxford University. Originally he had intended to take Holy Orders, but his views changed, and in 1888 he became tutor to the children of the Siamese ambassador and then to the Crown Prince. During his stay in Siam he took in hand the reorganisation of its education, and so great was his influence that he was often called "the uncrowned king of Siam". In 1893 the French attempt to control the country aroused such indignation that Morant, in company with other Europeans, had to leave. On his return to England he was without a permanent post, and when he saw the advertisement of the post under Sadler he immediately applied for it.

At first Sadler held him in high esteem, but as soon as his position was consolidated, Morant began to show his hand. During his stay in Siam, amongst other things, he had become acquainted with Eastern intrigue. On his return to England he found that much had occurred with which he was unfamiliar. His first task was to bring himself up to date by studying the reports of the Cross and the Bryce Commissions. He realised the state of chaos into which educational administration had fallen, and he was convinced that the only way out of the muddle was to adopt the recommendations of the Bryce Commission with regard to local education authorities. The logical conclusion, at which the Commission had hesitated, was to give these authorities full control of both elementary and secondary education in their areas.

The existence of the School Boards stood in the way of this ideal, and Morant saw that the obvious solution was to get rid of them. He knew that this would not be an easy task. The problem was complicated by the rise of the higher grade schools in which both Sadler and Sir George Kekewich, the Secretary of the Education Department, had great faith. Could he, by discrediting the higher grade schools, bring about the downfall of the School Boards? Morant's "midnight reading" of the reports of the Royal Commissions provided the ammunition he needed. It was a dangerous thing for a comparatively junior member of the Civil Service to attempt to change the national policy in education. His chief weapon was his conviction that in supporting the higher grade schools by the use of public money voted for elementary education but employed to finance what was in reality secondary education, the School Boards had been acting illegally over a number of years.

Events played into Morant's hands. A dispute arose between the London School Board and the London Technical Education Committee, which had claimed responsibility for secondary education and was supported by the London County Council. Morant knew that Sir John Gorst, Vice-President of the Education Department, favoured the County Council. Morant, in a report on Swiss education which he had written in 1898, added a footnote in which he drew attention to the anomalous position of the higher grade schools. This had passed the scrutiny of Sadler and Kekewich. Morant contrived that Dr Garnett, who was defending the County Council, should see this footnote. Immediately Garnett challenged the legality of the London School Board's action with regard to higher grade schools.

The Government Auditor, Mr T. B. Cockerton, immediately saw the point, and surcharged the School Board with the amount which had been spent on the higher grade schools. The dispute was brought before the Queen's Bench Division of the High Court, and Mr Cockerton won his case. In an appeal, the court upheld the previous decision and declared that funds expended by the School Board for evening classes had also been used illegally. This presented the Government with an awkward problem, and in 1901 a special Act was passed by Parliament to legalise the position of the School Boards until a comprehensive survey of the educational system could be made and an appropriate measure enacted to deal with it.

Sir John Gorst had always considered that Kekewich and Sadler had been responsible for the abortive Bill of 1896. As a consequence he took Morant on to his staff, and when the time came for drafting the new Education Bill Morant was brought into contact with Mr A. J. Balfour, who was greatly impressed by his ability. Morant was given a large share in the drafting of the Bill.

When Mr Balfour succeeded Lord Salisbury as Prime Minister in 1902, several important changes were made in the Cabinet and Civil Service. Lord Londonderry succeeded the Duke of Devonshire as President of the Board of Education, and Sir John Gorst became due for retirement. Kekewich was also due to retire in 1903, but Morant knew that he might expect opposition from that quarter. Accordingly, he persuaded Lord Londonderry to appoint a competent person who thoroughly understood the education situation to take the place of Kekewich. Obviously, the choice fell upon Morant who became Acting-Secretary, and after the retirement of Kekewich in the following year, Permanent Secretary of the Board of Education.

The Education Bill recommended the abolition of the School Boards and their substitution by the County and County Borough Councils as the new education authorities. The Webbs, in Fabian Pamphlet No. 106, *The Education Muddle and the Way Out*, strongly supported the measure. Naturally, it was opposed by the School Boards. In justice to them, it should be said that the London School Board and the Boards of the large cities had done splendid work, but in many rural districts, the smaller ones, to put the matter kindly, left much to be desired in their administration.

The general feeling was that education ought to be considered from a wider point of view than was possible for *ad hoc* bodies which were not sufficiently in touch with other local government agencies. Mr Joseph Chamberlain resented the change, but, fortunately for the success of the Bill, he was incapacitated as the result of a street accident.

The chief opposition to the Bill centred round the proposal to secure rate aid for the voluntary schools. The Nonconformists were bitter in their denunciations and they were supported by the Liberals, who, having been out of office since 1895, saw a chance of supplanting the Government. One of their most prominent leaders was Mr Lloyd George, but as the debate continued it came to have less to do with educational principles and developed into a strenuous attempt to oust the Government. Although the Bill, with certain amendments, became law, the different factions of the Liberals became united in opposition.

Education Act of 1902

After an interval of more than fifty years it is possible to attempt a dispassionate appraisal of the Education Act of 1902. For the first time in our history elementary and higher education were dealt with together. The Education Act of 1870 was concerned with elementary education only. The Act of 1902 empowered the new education authorities (L.E.A.s) to provide for both types of education. This was an advance on the recommendations of the Bryce Commission. The L.E.A.s were given power to provide for education "other than elementary". This elastic term covered not only secondary schools but technical schools and institutions, training colleges for teachers, and even adult education. Thus L.E.A.s were able to give assistance to such bodies as the Workers' Educational Association (W.E.A.).

These new powers forced L.E.A.s to consider relations between the elementary and secondary schools in their areas. Before 1902 secondary education was mainly the privilege of children whose parents could afford to pay school fees. Now the view was gaining ground that secondary schools ought to be open to elementary school pupils who showed they could benefit from secondary education. This was a step towards the view that secondary education was a stage which should be available to every boy and girl.

The Education Act of 1902 provided the basic idea for the local administration of education for over forty years, and although considerable modifications were introduced in 1944, the general framework has continued to exist. It would be too much to claim that the Act established a national system of education, but it is just to say that it provided the basis on which such a system could be built.

The Act effected considerable economies in administration. Instead of 2,559 School Boards and 788 School Attendance Committees, there were now 330 L.E.A.s. As the County and County Borough Councils were concerned with education "other than elementary", Part II of the Act constituted them as authorities responsible for both types of education in their areas, and they were generally known as Part II authorities. In addition, Part III of the Act gave authority for elementary education only to municipal boroughs with a population of over 10,000 and urban districts with a population of over 20,000. They could, however, assist secondary schools. These Part III L.E.A.s were formed partly to placate the displaced School Boards but mainly to encourage local interest and initiative in education, a point which had been strongly stressed by the Bryce Commission. The Board schools which passed under the control of the councils were renamed provided schools because their buildings were provided and maintained by the L.E.A. They were often called council schools. The voluntary schools were now called non-provided schools because their buildings were provided by other authorities, mainly by religious bodies.

An important result of the establishment of the L.E.A.s was that education became one of the local services for which the councils were responsible. Other services administered by the local authorities included the highways, water-supply, sanitation, parks and recreation grounds, the local police force, fire prevention, public libraries, etc. This meant that education became recognised as a social service provided by the local authority and not something which was the responsibility of a body which stood outside the main system of local government. Each L.E.A. was instructed to appoint an education committee to which it could delegate its powers under the Act except those of levying a rate or borrowing money. This ensured that local finances remained under public control. The majority of the members of the education committee were to be appointed by the council, but others who had special knowledge of the district and of education could be added. In a few instances the whole of the council functioned as the education committee.

Non-provided schools now received rate aid. They usually had a body of six managers, four known as foundation managers, who were appointed by the religious body to whom the building belonged, and two who represented the L.E.A. The secular instruction was the responsibility of the L.E.A., but the foundation managers were responsible for seeing that religious instruction according to the trust deed of the school was given. The head teacher and staff were appointed by the managers, but the L.E.A. had the right of veto if a person selected was not satisfactory as regards his educational qualifications. Likewise, the managers could dismiss a teacher if the religious instruction he gave was below standard. The same right was given to the L.E.A. in the case of a teacher who was not competent in his teaching of the secular subjects. The managers provided the building, kept it in repair, and had to carry out reasonable alterations and improvements as required by the L.E.A., with the exception of damage due to fair wear and tear for which the authority was responsible. The teachers were paid by the L.E.A., who also provided furniture, books, and teaching apparatus.

Elementary education was limited to pupils under the age of sixteen except where no suitable higher education was available within a reasonable distance from the home of the pupil. Evening continuation schools came under the category of higher education. Part II L.E.A.s were given power to take over or assist secondary schools. Most higher grade schools became secondary schools, and the L.E.A.s could build additional secondary schools where they were needed. This gradually led to the provision of an adequate number of secondary schools to which children were admitted on payment of moderate fees. An Act of 1903 gave special treatment to the London district.

The abolition of the system of Payment by Results had brought about changes in Government grants. The Act of 1902 introduced a complicated formula for the calculation of grants. The object was to lighten the burden on the rates in poorer districts where the yield from the local rates was much less than in more prosperous areas. The attempt was not completely successful, and additional legislation became necessary to help the poorer authorities.

The Liberal opposition did not vanish when the Act became law. Encouraged by Dr Clifford and Mr Lloyd George, many Dissenters refused to pay the education rate. They were known as

Passive Resisters, and because of their refusal distraint was made on their belongings. In Wales, many districts refused to operate the Act. Mr Balfour took prompt action. In 1904 the Government passed the Education (Local Authorities Default) Act. If a L.E.A. refused to make adequate grants to its non-provided schools, the Board of Education was given power to deduct an equivalent sum from the Government grant and pay it direct to the managers of the schools. This was only applied to two authorities, because public opinion was strongly opposed to making children victims of a political and denominational quarrel.

When the Liberal Party came into power as the result of the General Election of 1906, efforts were made to repeal the Education Act. One attempt to abolish the Dual System by handing over the non-provided schools to the L.E.A.s was so drastically amended by the House of Lords that the Government had to admit defeat. Another attempt in 1908 was foiled by the united opposition of Anglicans and Roman Catholics who threatened in turn a campaign of passive resistance. A final attempt in the same year failed because the teachers joined in the opposition on the ground that the children should not suffer because of the wrangles of political parties. The Education Act had come to stay. By this time it was operating so successfully that no valid reason could be advanced for its repeal. Much of the credit for this belongs to Morant, who was determined to show that the Act was working so effectively that a return to the School Boards would be a disastrous step.

One of Morant's first tasks was the reorganisation of the Board of Education into three branches—Elementary, Secondary, and Technical. The Inspectorate was reorganised on a similar principle. The number of H.M.I.s was increased, especially in regard to women inspectors for girls' schools. His next step was to draw up a definite policy for elementary and secondary education. He knew that Sadler was unlikely to agree with his proposals, and therefore it would be necessary to get rid of him. By means which it is not necessary to describe in detail, he forced Sadler to offer his resignation. It was a great loss to English education that two such eminent men were unable to agree, but, unfortunately, Morant was the type of person who was unable to work in a partnership.

The Act of 1902 had instructed L.E.A.s to survey the educational needs of their areas and make plans for the extension and co-ordination of the different types of education in them. After his resignation, Sadler was employed by a number of authorities to conduct these surveys. He did this work so thoroughly that Morant, in the Report of the Board of Education for 1904-5, could not refrain from paying a tribute to Sadler's scholarship and insight. Sadler had been appointed to the Chair in the History and Administration of Education at the University of Manchester, which was afterwards followed by his acceptance of the office of Vice-Chancellor of the University of Leeds.

At this time, the essential distinction between elementary and secondary education had not been defined. The passage in the Report of the Bryce Commission (written by Sadler) had shown that there was no real difference between secondary and technical education. Morant thought along different lines. His knowledge of secondary schools was mainly derived from Winchester and the larger endowed grammar schools. Moreover, he was so prejudiced in regard to the higher grade schools that he did not perceive that they had pointed the way to a new kind of secondary education which was not bound by the classical and academic traditions of the older schools. Hence, in the *Regulations for Secondary Schools*, 1904, the secondary school was defined as one "which offers to each of its scholars up to and beyond the age of 16 a general education, physical, mental and moral, given through a complete graded course of instruction, of wider scope and more advanced degree than that given in elementary schools".

When the proposed course of instruction is studied, it is clear that Morant's conception of secondary schools differed considerably from that recommended by the Bryce Commission. He failed to take into account two important factors. The majority of secondary school pupils left at or before the age of sixteen, and only a minority proceeded to the universities. In spite of this, the course proposed was biased in favour of the few who would enter a university. The Regulations insisted on a course of at least four years in certain groups of subjects. These were: (1) English language and literature, history, and geography for at least 4½ hours a week; (2) at least one language other than English studied for a minimum of 3½ hours a week (six hours if two languages were taught); (3) mathematics and science, both theoretical and practical, for 7½ hours a week; and (4) drawing. Then followed the significant paragraph. "Where two languages other than English are taken, and Latin is not one of them, the Board will require to be satisfied that the omission of Latin is for the advantage of the school."

In justice to Morant it should be said that he was carrying out one of the opinions of the Bryce Commission. Its report had pointed out that at the time of the Taunton Commission, the claims of science for inclusion in the curriculum were only beginning to make themselves heard. Now matters had changed to such a degree that there was a real danger that scientific and technical studies might lessen the attention given to literary studies. The experience of recent years seems to show that there was some substance in this view. The weakness of Morant's policy was that he only envisaged one form of secondary education: that which was academic in character and prepared pupils for university entrance. This was supported in later years when the School and Higher School Certificate examinations were first introduced. The development of the secondary modern and technical schools has shown that secondary education can be of different varieties, but this was not to come for more than a quarter of a century.

When Morant came to deal with elementary education the story is quite different. He had little experience of elementary schools, and his outlook was not affected by pre-conceived ideas. Hence there was a freshness about the *Code for Elementary Schools*, 1904, which was missing in the Secondary Regulations and which was a complete contrast to the narrow vision of the Revised Code. In the introduction Morant wrote: "The purpose of the public elementary school is to form and strengthen the character and to develop the intelligence of the children entrusted to it, and to make the best use of the school years available, in assisting both girls and boys, according to their different needs, to fit themselves, practically as well as intellectually, for the work of life".

A similar spirit appeared in the *Suggestions for the Use of Teachers and Others concerned in the work of Elementary Schools*, 1905. The Preface declared: "The only uniformity of practice that the Board of Education desires to see in the teaching of public elementary schools is that each teacher shall think for himself, and work out for himself such methods of teaching as may use his powers to the best advantage and be best suited to the particular needs and conditions of the school . . . Teachers who use the book should therefore treat it as an aid to reviewing their aims and practice, and as a challenge to independent thought on such matters". When first published, the *Suggestions* was but a pamphlet, but later editions in 1908 and 1918 incorporated much of the experience of teachers and inspectors. A new edition was published in 1926, and this was again enlarged and revised in 1937. Since the last war the book has been reprinted.

Morant's reforms in teacher training are considered in a later chapter of this book. His attitude to technical education is important. As the reader will have seen, he was not sympathetic to technical instruction. *The Regulations for Evening Schools, Technical Institutions, and Schools of Art and Art Classes*, 1903-4, were mainly concerned with evening continuation schools. There was but meagre provision for day classes organised for pupils between fourteen and sixteen years of age. To enter a technical college, a student had to be over sixteen and to have spent at least three years in a secondary school. In 1905 the Board began the experiment of giving grants to day technical classes for ex-elementary school pupils. In the Report of 1908-9, the Board recognised these as junior day technical classes. The further development of the junior technical schools did not take place until after Morant had left the Board. When, in 1944, Mr Chuter Ede, then Parliamentary Secretary to the Board of Education, was asked the reason for the tardy development of our technical education, he replied: "Then we had the misfortune that, when the Act of 1902 was passed, its administration was left to one of the greatest autocrats who ever dwelt in the Civil Service—the late Sir Robert Morant, of whom it is said, 'He was not unprincipled but he was unscrupulous'".

The remainder of Morant's "reign" is important for the development of certain trends which were implicit in the Act of 1902. For many years teachers in poor districts of our great cities had come across numerous children who were handicapped because of lack of sufficient nourishing food. Some school log books record instances of teachers paying for food and hot drinks for these unfortunate pupils. In some places, voluntary bodies, such as the Salvation Army, provided meals for under-nourished children at the price of one penny per head. In the new Parliament which assembled in 1906, for the first time, the Labour Party was represented by forty members. One of their number proposed a private member's Bill which received Government support. The Education (Provision of Meals) Act, 1906, gave authority to L.E.A.s to provide premises and facilities to assist the work of the voluntary associations. If their funds were insufficient the L.E.A.s, with the approval of the Board of Education, were able to levy a rate not exceeding one halfpenny in the pound to defray expenses.

In the following year the extremely important Education (Administrative Provisions) Act was passed. In the nineteenth century some secondary schools employed their own medical officer to look after the health of the pupils, but nothing was available for elementary school children until the closing years of the century. In 1890 the London School Board appointed a part-time medical officer to examine mentally defective children. The appointment was made a full-time one in 1902, and the chief medical officer was given three assistants. In the following year an oculist was added to the staff, together with six trained nurses to inspect children notified by the head teachers. The Bradford School Board, however, was the pioneer in the school medical service. In 1893 it undertook the medical inspection of the children under its jurisdiction. An Act of 1893 permitted School Boards to instruct blind and deaf children in special schools or classes, and this was extended to mentally defective and epileptic children in 1899.

So far there had been no widespread demand for medical inspection, until the reports of medical officers who had examined recruits for the Boer War were published. Thousands of young men had been rejected as medically unfit for service. This led to the appointment of the Committee on Physical Deterioration in 1904.

Morant had always been a believer in the importance of good health amongst school children and in the nation at large. He had added organised games to the tables of physical exercises for elementary schools in 1906. Thus he welcomed the initiation of medical inspection. The Act did not provide a complete medical service. That developed gradually, and at first inspection was confined to elementary schools and it was not obligatory for parents to carry out the recommendations of the medical officers. A Medical Department of the Board of Education was created, and Dr (later Sir) George Newman was appointed Chief Medical Officer of the Board. This was a most fortunate appointment, and it has been claimed that Sir George and his colleagues saved more lives than had been lost during the First World War. The annual reports issued by Sir George were an important factor in making the nation health minded. One can estimate the progress made by comparing the situation revealed in the report of 1908-9 with that of 1917.

The Act of 1907 was also responsible for the initiation of what was known as the Free Place System. *The Regulations for Secondary Schools* of that year authorised the payment of a grant of £5 per head for each pupil between the ages of twelve and eighteen. In order to earn the grant a school had to conform to certain requirements. The school could not restrict admission to pupils who belonged to a particular religious denomination, and the governing body had to be reconstituted to include a number of representative governors, some of whom represented the L.E.A. The third condition was the most important. At least 25 per cent. of the intake each year should be pupils from elementary schools.

Before this date, secondary schools had been receiving small numbers of children from elementary schools, but the numbers admitted varied from district to district. The advent of the Free Place System involved some kind of test to ascertain whether those who wished to be admitted could benefit from this type of education. This was the beginning of what has been called the scholarship ladder to the university. As the secondary school course was organised to extend over four years, this fact fixed the age of entry for scholarship children somewhere between eleven and twelve years of age. This age is now generally described as eleven plus. The growth in the number of scholarships granted was remarkable. It rose from 47,200 to 60,000 in 1913, and to 143,000 by 1927. The Act also gave power to L.E.A.s to acquire land for building new secondary schools, with the result that many county and municipal secondary schools came into being.

In 1911 the resignation of Sir Robert Morant occurred under circumstances which have never been clearly explained. Briefly, these were as follows. At the request of Morant, a confidential memorandum was prepared by the Chief Inspector, Mr E. G. A. Holmes. It was concerned with the local inspectors appointed by certain L.E.A.s. The mystery is how such a private document got into the hands of people outside the Board of Education. Many local inspectors were elementary school teachers whose earlier experience had been gained during the period of the Revised Code and their outlook on education tended to be narrow and formal.

One paragraph of the report ran as follows. "Apart from the fact that the elementary teachers are, as a rule, uncultured and imperfectly educated, and that many, if not most, of them are creatures of tradition and routine, there are special reasons why the bulk of the local inspectors in this country should be unequal to

the discharge of their responsible duties . . . Having regard to all
these facts, we cannot wonder that local inspection as at present
conducted in the large towns is on the whole a hindrance rather
than an aid to educational progress, and we can only hope that the
local Chief Inspectors, who are the fountain heads of a vicious
officialdom, will be gradually pensioned off, and if local inspection
is to be continued in their areas, their places will be filled by men
of real culture and enlightenment."

At the time this confidential document became public, Mr
Holmes had reached the age of retirement, so that he had nothing
to do with the circumstances by which members of the Opposition
gained knowledge of its contents. Sir Samuel Hoare seized the
opportunity of attacking the Liberal Government. To Dr Clifford
it presented a chance of getting even with his old opponent, Sir
Robert Morant, and the N.U.T. claimed that a slur had been cast
upon the teaching profession. As a result of the acrimonious
debate which followed in Parliament, Mr Walter Runciman, President of the Board of Education, felt called upon to resign. Morant
also felt obliged to follow the same course. Mr Lloyd George, who
had so strenuously opposed the Education Act of 1902, felt that
the country could ill afford to lose the services of so able an administrator as Morant. He was, therefore, asked to accept the post of
Chairman of the Insurance Commission, and when, in 1919, the
Ministry of Health was established, he became Permanent Secretary, and was thus able to continue his educational work in a sphere
which had always interested him.

In the few years which elapsed before the outbreak of the First
World War there were signs of significant changes in the field of
education. It was felt that the methods and curriculum of the
elementary school were not suitable for the older scholars who
would shortly be leaving school to take up jobs in industry and
commerce. When the higher grade schools disappeared a few
higher elementary schools were started, but they were not encouraged by the Board of Education. The initiative of certain L.E.A.s,
especially those of London and Manchester, brought into existence
the central school. This appeared in London in 1911, and the
remaining higher elementary schools were absorbed into the system.
Manchester followed suit the following year, and within a short
time schools of this type were established in other parts of the
country.

At first the Board of Education watched the experiment with caution, and it was not until the Education Act of 1918 that these schools received full official recognition. Contemporary opinion did not realise that they heralded a new type of post-primary education. The central school offered a four-year course from the age of eleven plus to fifteen plus, and a limited number of bursaries were made available for parents who could not afford to keep their children at school beyond the age of thirteen or fourteen. The curriculum was given a definite practical bias, either industrial or commercial, but it was not purely vocational. Some schools made the mistake of aping the grammar schools and prepared their pupils for the same academic examinations, thus missing the real purpose of the new departure. Pupils were admitted on the results of the eleven plus examination. Those who were slightly below the standard for grammar school entry were given the opportunity of going to a selective central school. Later, non-selective central schools developed. All pupils in the area who had reached the age of eleven and had not been admitted to a grammar school, were drafted into this type of school. Such schools were often known as senior schools and were the forerunners of the secondary modern schools of to-day.

The two sisters, Rachel and Margaret McMillan, are associated with the development of the nursery school. In 1907 the Board asked the Consultative Committee to consider the problem of the education of children under the age of five, but after studying developments in France, Germany, and Switzerland, it suggested that the time was not yet ripe for lowering the statutory age of admission. Margaret McMillan had been a member of the Bradford School Board, which, as the reader will doubtless recollect, was a pioneer in the provision of school medical services. Ill-health forced her to leave the north and the sisters came to London, where they opened a school clinic at Bow in 1908. This was moved to Deptford in 1911, and it was here that they opened their first open-air nursery school. The experiment was warmly encouraged by Sir Robert Morant.

When hostilities began, their work was hampered by financial difficulties and the problem of obtaining staff. The L.C.C. was interested in the experiment and gave them a site for an enlarged school in the early part of 1914. The hard work and continuing disappointments absorbed the time and strength of the sisters and resulted in the illness and death of Rachel in 1917. She lived long enough to see her principles approved by Mr Fisher, the new President of the Board, who opened the enlarged premises a few months after her death. The sisters had received no assistance from public funds until after the outbreak of war when they received the sum of 7d. per day for minding each child belonging to munition workers. Once again the significance of the pioneer effort was not fully realised until after the war.

In 1913 the Board raised the status of day technical classes to that of junior technical schools. Even then they had to wait for many years before they were recognised as secondary schools. These schools aimed at the preparation for artisan or other industrial work or for domestic employment. The normal entrance age was thirteen, and a grant of £5 per head per annum was authorised. The pupils were selected from elementary schools, but although the schools were fee paying institutions, free places were awarded on the results of an entrance test. Some L.E.A.s preferred a more definite vocational training and experimented with day trade schools. In the same year junior art departments were recognised.

The Government was considering a plan which would include all types of secondary schools, the central, the technical and trade schools, and day and evening continuation schools. It was also intended to give Part III authorities control over higher as well as elementary education in their areas. All these intentions had to be postponed because of the outbreak of war in 1914.

At the beginning of the war many schools were requisitioned as billets for the new armies which were being raised. In 1917 conscription was introduced, and the loss of teaching strength became a serious problem which increased as the war continued. In addition, a number of teachers in girls' schools joined the women's auxiliary services. Classes became larger, and many boys' schools had to be staffed largely with women. Efforts were made to fill the gaps, and married women, retired teachers, and any who had sufficient educational qualifications were urged to give their services. Naturally, the standards of attainment were lowered, but the main objective, that of keeping the schools open, was achieved.

Because many schools were needed by the military authorities, and others were used as military hospitals or for accommodating refugees, L.E.A.s were forced to use Sunday Schools, places of worship, and public halls. Some training colleges had to seek temporary premises. In some areas a double shift system had to be adopted, but all was not loss. The Board of Education Report for

1914-15 stated: "By curtailing instruction it concentrates the efforts of teachers and scholars on essential matters. Further, the half-day out of school has sometimes been used to excellent purposes for games and physical exercises, swimming, open-air work, excursions, visits to museums and galleries, needlework parties, and the like. In a large town, where both open-air exhibitions and visits to galleries have been particularly well organised, the Inspector mentions that one headmaster in a school favourably situated is so convinced of the advantage of open-air work that he would not object to continuing the half-time plan when the war is over. The effect on the health of the children has also been good".

War conditions produced other changes. Many fathers were absent on war service and a large number of mothers were employed in munition factories. This resulted in inadequate family supervision of the younger members of the family with a consequent increase in juvenile delinquency and hooliganism. In 1917 L.E.A.s were encouraged by the Board of Education to open play centres for children and a grant of 50 per cent. of the cost was offered. The school meals service was extended to cover the holidays and the restriction of the halfpenny rate was abolished. This was continued after the fighting had ceased, and the wisdom of this decision was fully justified during the period of mass unemployment which followed the peace.

Education Act of 1918

In 1916 the Ministry of Reconstruction was constituted to plan the transition to peace conditions, and education received a good deal of attention in the deliberations of the Ministry. Mr Lloyd George decided to secure the services of a well-known scholar, and he offered the appointment of President of the Board of Education to Mr H. A. L. Fisher, a distinguished Oxford historian who was Vice-Chancellor of the University of Sheffield. The Education Act of 1918, generally known as the Fisher Act, fully justified the Prime Minister's choice.

At first, Mr Fisher contemplated an increase in the powers of the Board of Education so that reluctant local authorities could be forced to put the Act into operation, and he also suggested merging some of the Part III L.E.A.s in the county authorities. These proposals roused such opposition that he decided to abandon them and to concentrate on the new schemes he had in mind. Thus the framework of the Act of 1902 remained, but more power

was given to the L.E.A.s. Many clauses of the Act were permissive
and not mandatory, *i.e.* it was left to each L.E.A. to make its own
decision, and those who wished to put these clauses into operation
would be recompensed by adequate grants. This was really a
weakness in the Act. Another weakness was that because of the
dislocation following the war, *e.g.* shortage of school buildings and
in the supply of teachers, some of the chief provisions of the Act
were not to be put into force immediately.

The Act took cognisance of the new ideas and experiments of
the previous decade and adopted as its keynote the statement that
"children and young persons shall not be debarred from receiving
the benefits of any form of education by which they are capable
of profiting through inability to pay fees". Certain features of the
Act were permanent. For instance, the school leaving age was
fixed, without exemptions, at fourteen, and L.E.A.s were empowered to raise it to fifteen, though few of them did so. Another
clause abolished the half-time system from July 1922. This system
was a legacy from Sir James Graham's Factory Act of 1844. The
half-timers had decreased in numbers, but about 70,000, mostly
children employed in agriculture, still remained.

Another clause of the Act restricted the employment of children. No child under the age of twelve could be employed, and
those who were older were restricted to a maximum of two hours
on Sundays. During the week, no child was to be employed during
school hours, before 6 a.m., or later than 8 p.m. L.E.A.s, by means
of a by-law, could permit the employment of children over twelve
on a school-day for one hour before 9 a.m., but the same child
could not be employed for more than an hour after the afternoon
school. This was a concession to permit local tradesmen such as
newsagents to use children for delivering newspapers. Employment in mines, factories, and in street trading was rigidly banned
for children of school age. A L.E.A. could issue a licence per-
mitting children to take part in pantomime performances, but they
were carefully watched by the school medical officers to see that
this work did not affect their health. Medical inspection and treatment were extended to pupils in maintained secondary schools, but
remained optional for aided schools. L.E.A.s were empowered
to pay maintenance grants to pupils who held scholarships for
secondary education.

The grant procedure of the Act of 1902 was not working as
well as it had been hoped. Educational expenditure, two of the

main items of which were the cost of teachers' salaries and the building of new schools, was throwing an increasingly heavy burden on the rates. The Fisher Act introduced a percentage instead of a block grant. "The percentage plan is that the State and the locality contribute half each to the net expenditure of the L.E.A. on higher education. When income (chiefly in the shape of fees) has been deducted from the total cost, the Board of Education give a grant of 50 per cent. of what remains. This is called the Deficiency Grant. The expenditure on which the Deficiency Grant is paid must be 'recognised' by the Board."[1] This system did not apply in the same way to elementary education, since the State was already paying more than half the cost. A much more complicated percentage formula was devised for calculating the elementary grant. The Act also abolished all fees in elementary schools.

Mr Fisher proposed to give grants to nursery schools on the condition that they would be open to inspection. This was a permissive clause, and authorities who had not realised the value of the open-air nursery school were slow to take advantage of the permission. Even progressive authorities who began to build nursery schools slackened their efforts as soon as economy cuts came into force. Thus, in 1939 there were only 114 nursery schools, more than half of which had been built by private initiative.

Another change which was destined to last for only a few years was the establishment of day continuation schools. Mr Fisher would have liked to have raised the school leaving age to fifteen, but as he knew the time was not yet ripe for this, he adopted the alternative of part-time education up to the age of eighteen. Pupils who left the elementary school at fourteen would be required to attend a continuation school for 320 hours in each year, the distribution of the time being left to the L.E.A. In country districts it was more convenient to arrange for attendance in blocks of several weeks, but in urban areas attendances consisted of one whole or two half-days per week throughout the school year. The arrangements were to be completed in two stages. The first made it obligatory for ex-elementary school pupils to attend until the age of sixteen. After seven years from the appointed day the obligation was to be extended to eighteen.

[1] Ward. H. *The Educational System of England and Wales and its Recent History*, p. 61, C.U.P., 1939.

Mr Fisher realised that the success of the scheme depended upon the whole-hearted co-operation of employers. He visited the most important industrial areas to interview employers and managers to convince them of the value of the scheme. Most enlightened employers welcomed it. Indeed, some industrial concerns had started their own continuation schools many years before the Act was passed, *e.g.* Rowntrees at York. There were, however, some employers who were not willing to be convinced and were only too ready to throw overboard their responsibilities as soon as the opportunity presented itself.

This was not long in coming. In 1921 the economic state of the country caused the Government considerable alarm, and the Board of Education left L.E.A.s to decide whether they would run continuation schools on a compulsory or voluntary basis. London and many other other authorities continued the obligation. Later in the same year the Government set up a Committee on National Expenditure under the chairmanship of Sir Eric Geddes. The so-called "Geddes' Axe" put an end to further educational developments for the time being. The Committee recommended the reduction of education grants by one-third, and at the same time teachers' salaries were reduced and their pensions placed upon a contributory basis. Economic restrictions slowed down the building of new schools and gradually led to the abandonment of continuation schools. By 1939 Rugby was the only local authority which kept in being its continuation school.

It appears that the Government had become alarmed at the increase in the unemployment figures, and its fears were expressed by somewhat hastily considered cuts. In 1924 the Labour Party came into power for a short time and was able to soften the austerity which had been imposed. In the meantime, the Act of 1918 was consolidated with those parts of the existing law on education which had not been superseded. The consolidated law was brought into force by the Education Act of 1921.

Burnham Scales

Mr Fisher was much concerned about the supply of teachers for the post-war period, and he concluded that the way to speed up the number of entrants to the profession was to make it financially more attractive. In the latter nineteenth century the salaries of teachers were fixed by agreement with the managers of local schools or with individual School Boards. After 1902 the L.E.A.s fixed the salaries for their own areas with the result that the more wealthy authorities were able to attract the best teachers. There is no doubt that most teachers were grossly underpaid, and their financial difficulties were increased by the rising cost of living during the war. Temporary help was given through war bonuses and a supplementary grant, but Mr Fisher realised that the problem would have to be tackled on a national basis. After protracted negotiations a committee on which L.E.A.s and the N.U.T. were equally represented was set up in 1919 under the chairmanship of Lord Burnham. As a result of the work of the Burnham Committee, in 1921 the Board approved three standard scales to meet conditions in different parts of the country and a special scale for teachers in the London district. Two other Burnham Committees dealt with the salaries of teachers in grammar schools and technical institutions respectively.

Parallel with the increase of salaries fresh arrangements about teachers' superannuation were made. As early as 1846 Sir James Kay-Shuttleworth had instituted a scheme for elementary school teachers, but this was abandoned when the Revised Code was adopted. The Elementary Teachers' Superannuation Act of 1898 enabled teachers to secure an annuity through the payment of voluntary contributions, but the amount of the pension had now become hopelessly inadequate. Mr Fisher introduced a superannuation scheme which took into account the increased cost of living. The Superannuation Act of 1918 included all teachers in both elementary and secondary schools. At first the scheme was non-contributory, but the financial difficulty which arose in 1922 necessitated an amendment by which all teachers paid 5 per cent. of their salaries towards superannuation. To obtain full benefits the teacher must have reached the age of sixty and have spent thirty years in approved service. The scheme provided for a lump sum on retirement and an annual pension, both calculated on the recognised service of the teacher or half of the average salary of his last five years, whichever was less. Other Acts in 1925 and 1937 corrected certain anomalies of the scheme.

For some time the Labour Party had considered that the extension of secondary education to those who could profit by it was only a half-way measure. Various members of the Party had advocated secondary education for all children, and had envisaged it as including not only the existing secondary schools but also all types of post-primary education. This view was supported by many educationists who were outside the Party. Dr Tawney, in a publication entitled *Secondary Education for All* (Allen and Unwin, 1922), stated the views of the Labour Party.

He wrote: "The Labour Party is convinced that the only policy which is at once educationally sound and suited to a democratic community is one under which primary education and secondary education are organised as two stages in a single continuous process; secondary education being the education of the adolescent and primary education being education preparatory thereto. Its objective, therefore, is both the improvement of primary education and the development of public secondary education to such a point that all normal children, irrespective of the income, class or occupation of their parents, may be transferred at the age of 'eleven plus' from the primary or preparatory school to one type or another of secondary school, and remain in the latter until sixteen. It holds that all immediate reforms should be carried out with that general objective in view, in such a way as to contribute to its attainment. It recognises that the more secondary education is developed, the more essential will it be that there should be the widest possible variety of type among secondary schools. It therefore looks forward to the time when Central Schools and Junior Technical Schools will be transformed into one part of a system of free and universal education".

The Education of the Adolescent

One of the first acts of Sir Charles Trevelyan, the new President of the Board of Education, was to ask the Consultative Committee to consider the points which had been raised. Labour was succeeded by a Conservative Government in the autumn of 1924, but the President of the Board, Lord Eustace Percy, did not change the educational policy but decided to wait until the report of the Consultative Committee, which met under the chairmanship of Sir Henry Hadow, was published. This report on the *Education of the Adolescent*, generally known as the *Hadow Report*, was issued in October 1926. The Hadow Report is one of the milestones in the development of English education in the present century. Two distinct lines of thought influenced its recommendations. On the one hand it was progressive, but on the other, it looked back to the past, and was, perhaps, unconsciously affected by the prestige of the secondary grammar school.

The Report clearly indicated in the introduction the policy it recommended. "We desire to abolish the word 'elementary' and to alter and extend the sense of the word 'secondary'. The word 'elementary' has now become misleading . . . We propose to substitute the term 'primary', but to restrict the use of that term to the period of education which ends at the age of eleven or twelve. To the period of education which follows upon it we would give the name 'secondary', and we would make this name embrace all forms of post-primary education, whether it be given in the schools which are now called 'secondary', or in central schools, or in the senior departments of the schools now termed 'elementary'. If the term 'secondary' is thus given a wider sense, some new term will be needed to denote the schools which now have the monopoly of the name 'secondary'; and we suggest that they shall now be called by the name of grammar schools. If such schools are to be re-named, we should propose that the term 'central school' (which is neither clear nor particularly apt) should simultaneously disappear, and the term 'modern school' should take its place in the future. In such a scheme there will be two main kinds of education—primary and secondary; and the latter of these two kinds will fall into two main groups—that of the grammar school type, and that of the modern school."

It should be noted that no recommendation was made concerning the junior technical school. The Committee was influenced by the tradition of the last two decades, and whilst it was declared that these schools were "doing most valuable work and should be developed so far as is possible in accordance with the needs and requirements of certain local industries", no recommendation was made that they should be regarded as secondary schools.

One difficulty which had to be considered was that whilst in the grammar school pupils remained until the age of sixteen, the leaving age in other post-primary schools was fourteen. It was hoped that legislation to raise the leaving age to fifteen would soon be effected. Thus it was assumed that the education of the non-academically minded pupil could be undertaken in less time than the academic type of pupil in the grammar school. At the same time, the Report advocated that the curriculum of the modern school would be so arranged in the first two years as to facilitate transfer from one type of school to another. In the later years of the modern school course a practical and realistic bias should be introduced. Thus the modern school would be a poor relation from the start, although the Committee had stated that it should be regarded as a different but not an inferior kind of secondary school. Parents tended to draw the obvious conclusion from these recommendations.

Why should the age of transfer to secondary education be eleven plus? Was it possible in many cases to decide whether a child was more suitable for a grammar or a modern school at such an early age? Many psychologists had their doubts. The real reason was an administrative one. So long as the school leaving age was fourteen the transfer had to be before twelve in order to obtain at least a three year course in the modern school. In Scotland the age of transfer was twelve, and the public schools received their entrants at thirteen.

The Report did not emphasise the administrative reason, but put forward a pseudo-psychological argument. "There is a tide which begins to rise in the veins of youth at the age of eleven or twelve. It is called by the name of adolescence." The most realistic approach would have been the formation of an intermediate type of school for pupils between the ages of eleven and thirteen in which the emergence of their special abilities and interests could be studied and a more dependable decision could be made about the pupil's future. This would have involved raising the leaving age to sixteen and was not thought to be practical at that time. Thus the Hadow Report fixed the age of transfer at eleven plus and envisaged two kinds of secondary education, grammar and modern.

The Board of Education accepted the Report with caution. It was realised that raising the school leaving age would mean the immediate provision of at least 350,000 places in the schools and would entail a large increase in the number of teachers, and this would take several years. The Board thought that the first step would be the reorganisation of existing schools into primary and senior departments, replacing condemned schools on the "Black List" by new ones, and reducing the size of classes. This would take some years to accomplish. Guidance about reorganisation was given in a pamphlet entitled *The New Prospect in Education*.

The Hadow Committee realised some of the difficulties which had to be overcome. The Dual system was one obstacle. The managers of voluntary schools lacked the resources for a reorganisation of their schools. Certain measures were suggested which found a place in the Education Act of 1936. The existence of Part III authorities was the most serious problem. In each county there would be two authorities responsible for secondary schools. The County Council would be responsible for grammar schools, but the Part III L.E.A.s would also be concerned with many of the modern schools. This would result in the responsibility for a large number of secondary schools being divided between two authorities who might have quite different schemes.

The Report discussed several solutions, including the merging of Part III authorities with the county, but it favoured the view of developing more co-operation between both types of L.E.A. so that before the Part III authorities decided upon their schemes for reorganisation they should consult the county authority. The Report stressed that because of the smaller financial resources of the Part III L.E.A.s the county would be able to give advantages in the way of scholarships and amenities in the schools themselves. The fact that some of the Part III authorities were more progressive than certain of the counties was ignored.

The Labour Party returned to power in 1929 and Sir Charles Trevelyan went ahead with the work of reorganisation. He introduced a Bill to raise the school leaving age to fifteen and to pay maintenance grants to parents to enable them to keep their children at school for a further year. The Government seemed to ignore the facts that there was neither sufficient accommodation for the increased numbers nor the necessary number of teachers to cope with them. Another difficulty arose. The managers of voluntary schools, while ready to carry out reorganisation, objected that their funds were inadequate for the task. They would require more assistance from the State. An amendment was proposed to give power to L.E.A.s to assist voluntary schools to reorganise. The Bill was rejected by the House of Lords, and before an amended version could be presented the country was affected by one of the most serious financial crises in our history. The Government resigned and was succeeded by a National Government.

The new Government was obliged to take drastic measures to curtail expenditure. As far as education was concerned, the Government accepted a reduction of 15 per cent. (later reduced to 10 per cent.) in teachers' salaries and withdrew an Exchequer grant which had been made for three years to assist the building operations made necessary by the Hadow Report. New buildings were only permitted in most urgent cases, such as schools on new housing estates. Perhaps the most important change was the substitution of the Special for the Free Place system. After a child had been selected because of his attainment in the Special Place examination, the parent's income was considered. Those with an income below a certain figure could obtain a free place for their child, but all others were required to pay fees calculated on a sliding scale based on income and the number of children in the family. After 1933 the worst features of the slump disappeared and L.E.A.s were able to continue their building programmes, but at a more cautious pace. By the end of 1938 about 64 per cent. of the children over the age of eleven were in senior classes and the number of over-sized classes had been reduced. Reorganisation was more rapid in urban than in rural areas.

The Consultative Committee issued two more Hadow Reports; one on the primary school in 1931, and another on the infant and nursery school in 1933. It would have been more logical to have started with the infant school, but the order of issue was determined by administrative needs. Unfortunately, it resulted in the concentration of interest on the education of the adolescent, whilst that of the younger children tended to take second place. The primary school was becoming regarded as merely a feeder for the secondary school, but the publication of the Report of 1931 helped to correct this point of view. One could claim that the Report on the primary school was even more influential than the one on the adolescent. It focused attention upon the child rather than upon the instruction given in the school, and in reading it one can see the influence of recent psychological studies and the teaching of Professor Dewey, whose views, however, were accepted with a certain amount of caution.

Thus the Report stressed the delight that young children find in physical movement, the exercise of their senses, and the performance of tasks within their capacity. Some of the remarks made about the purpose and function of the primary school are now accepted as maxims that few would dispute, e.g. "the curriculum is to be thought of in terms of activity and experience rather than of knowledge to be acquired and facts to be stored" (p. 153). "The schools whose first intention was to teach children how to read have thus been compelled to broaden their aims until it might now be said that they have to teach children how to live" (ibid.). "Junior children . . . were little workmen, looking out for jobs to do, and largely incapable of finding them for themselves" (p. 57).

The Report gave attention to the project method advocated by Dewey and Kilpatrick in America, but it pointed out that it was not an entirely new method for it had been used by enlightened teachers of the past. The example of William Cobbett was cited, who, because of his dislike of the bookish curriculum of the schools, had taught his own children on lines which were similar to the project. The reader may remember how Dawes organised the instruction at his school at King's Somborne. The Report preferred to use the term "centre of interest", and the teacher was warned to avoid overworking the method in his enthusiasm for a new approach. Before adopting it the teacher should be sure that he really understood the method and had faith in it. It was pointed out that the project is more valuable with younger than with older children. When the child has reached the secondary stage of his education he is not only able but is willing to study subjects in a more systematic way than is possible with a thorough-going project method.

The clean break at eleven plus was approved, and it was suggested that there are two distinct stages in primary education; before seven and from seven to eleven. Headships of primary schools should be open to both men and women, but it was advisable for the senior assistant to be of opposite sex to the head. The recommendations of the Report were made known to teachers through the visits of H.M.I.s and through conferences and short courses organised by the Board of Education. The result has been that the primary school to-day is a far brighter and happier place than its predecessor of the nineteenth century. At first, enthusiastic teachers tended to think of everything in terms of an "activity" method, but experience has shown them that the basic subjects cannot be neglected.

The Report on the infant and nursery school adopted a common-sense attitude. It emphasised that the best place for very young children is the home, but when this failed they could often obtain much benefit from attending a nursery school or a nursery class which was part of an existing infant school. A considerable amount of space was devoted to a criticism of the inadequate buildings and arrangements of many infant and nursery schools. Emphasis was placed on roomy classrooms which admitted the maximum of fresh air and sunlight. Rigid desks should be replaced by suitable chairs and collapsible tables; the walls should be painted in light pastel colours and sufficient space should be allowed for free movement. In spite of the recommendations there still remains much to be done. In country districts there are still numbers of "all age" schools, many buildings are out-of-date, and classroom accommodation, to say nothing of cloakrooms and lavatories, leaves much to be desired.

As the financial position of the country improved the Government felt it could rescind some of the restrictions imposed during the slump. In 1934 the cut in teachers' salaries was restored. It was now considered that the raising of the school age was a practicable proposition. The Education Act of 1936 gave notice that the leaving age would be fifteen after 1 September 1939. In deference to representations made by employers the Board stated that pupils over fourteen could be exempted provided they entered employment which was judged by the L.E.A. to be beneficial. The problem of reorganising non-provided schools was tackled. The Act approved of grants to managers ranging to 75 per cent. of the cost of new buildings for senior pupils. A time limit was fixed within which managers could secure the increased grant. At the end of 1939, 519 agreements had been entered upon, but only thirty-seven had been acted upon when the Second World War started. The Act of 1944 honoured this agreement even when no building operations had begun. The outbreak of war put an end to further developments, but on the whole this had a beneficial side because it enabled the Government to consider the educational future in a more complete and thorough fashion.

Spens Report

The Consultative Committee issued yet another report at the very end of 1938 which formed a completion to the series of Hadow Reports. It met under the chairmanship of Sir Will Spens, Master of Corpus Christi College, Cambridge. The secretary of the Committee was Dr R. F. Young, who was responsible for the opening chapter of the Report which was a most valuable sketch of the development of secondary education in this country.

Although the Report was mainly concerned with the grammar and technical schools, it also realised that the modern schools envisaged by *The Education of the Adolescent* were part of the secondary system which ought to be regarded as a whole. In fact, the Committee insisted that the education given in modern schools, although differing in kind, should not be looked upon as being in any way inferior to that provided in the traditional secondary schools. There should be, therefore, parity between all types of school within the secondary system. The Hadow Report had not recognised the junior technical as a secondary school. This omission was now to be rectified. The Spens Report envisaged a tripartite organisation of secondary schools into grammar, modern, and technical. Some, but not all, of the existing junior technical schools could be absorbed into the new class of technical high schools. The latter should have parity with the grammar schools. Their pupils would be selected at the same age as the grammar school pupils, and a five year course from eleven plus to sixteen plus would be provided. The group of junior technical schools, which were mainly in the London area and which had previously been known as trade schools, were not included in the recommendation of the Committee.

In their treatment of the grammar school, the members of the Committee were inconsistent. They began by drawing attention to the curriculum of the grammar school which was planned for pupils who intended to enter a university, whereas only a small proportion of them actually did so, the majority leaving school at sixteen. The grammar school course ought to be modified in order to give attention to the earlier leavers, whilst the more specialised work necessary for university entrance would be given in the upper forms of the school, especially in the sixth form.

Having said so much, the Committee then decided that there was no reason to recommend any revolutionary change in the school curriculum, and then proceeded to make suggestions which, if taken at their face value, would inevitably do so. Thus it was recommended that the curriculum would gain in value if it were centred round some core or branch of study. Throughout the centuries the core had been provided by the Classics, but in a modern age it was thought that studies ought to be centred round the English subjects. In addition, it was considered that in country grammar schools, "a rural background and colour should be given to the teaching, especially in general science". On the other hand, some training of direct vocational value might be given in town schools, even to those who would be leaving at the age of sixteen. The pendulum had indeed swung to an opposite direction since the days of Morant. The Committee's recommendations about secondary school examinations will be considered in the following chapter.

The new technical high school should provide a course of studies parallel to those of the grammar school, and should be housed in the premises of technical colleges. The headmaster would become the head of a department, and the scheme would enable the school to be brought into close touch with local industries. Moreover, the presence of adult students would provide a valuable stimulus for the juniors. This arrangement would also make available the teaching staff and equipment of the parent institution. Some of these recommendations found their way into the statutory system of 1944, but the last suggestion, together with the change of the age of transfer at eleven plus, were not accepted.

The Report discussed a suggestion which is still a matter of controversy, namely, the creation of multilateral schools. It was thought that this type of school had the advantage of combining in the same school pupils of differing interests and abilities and would facilitate transfer of a pupil from an academic to a less academic course without a change of school. After consideration the Committee decided: "With some reluctance we have come to the conclusion that we could not advocate the adoption of multi-lateralism as a general policy" (p. 291). On the other hand, the Committee did not wish to exclude experiments. Thus in a rural area a small grammar school might be combined with a modern school to form what is now known as a bilateral school. In such a case the advantages might outweigh the disadvantages, especially if the right kind of head was in charge of the school.

The reasons advanced for rejecting the multilateral idea were given as follows: —

(1) To secure a satisfactory number of pupils for each stream, the school would have to be very large. The Report mentioned the figure of 800 or more, and stated that the Committee agreed that most pupils would benefit by being in a smaller school.

(2) The sixth form had a most valuable influence on a school. If the majority of the pupils left before the age of sixteen, the sixth form would be small in number and thus exercise a less direct influence on the school.

(3) It would not be an easy matter to choose a head teacher who would be fitted to control and inspire to an equal extent the different streams in the school, and the substitution of the influence of heads of "sides" for that of a headmaster or headmistress would not be as adequate. In addition, there was always the risk that the grammar school stream would unduly influence the modern stream.

SUGGESTIONS FOR FURTHER READING

The text of the Education Act of 1902 should be carefully studied because it gives the principles which, with modifications, have governed the local administration of education to the present day. The important element was the substitution of L.E.A.s for the School Boards. In assessing the personality, character, and contribution of Sir Robert Morant, the reader might begin with G. A. N. Lowndes, *The Silent Social Revolution*, Chaps. IV and V, O.U.P., reprint, 1941. B. M. Allen, in *Sir Robert Morant, a great Public Servant*, Macmillan, 1934, endeavours to give a fair appraisal of Morant's work, but he does not disguise his admiration of Morant as an administrator. On the opposite side one should read Michael Sadler, *Michael Ernest Sadler*, Constable, 1949, and Lynda Grier, *Achievement in Education, the Work of Michael Ernest Sadler, 1895-1935*, Constable, 1952. J. Graves, in *Policy and Progress in Secondary Education*, Nelson, 1943, gives a useful account of the progress in the field of secondary education up to the early years of the Second World War. The work of the McMillan sisters is described in Margaret McMillan, *The Nursery School*, Dent, revised edition, 1930, and by Albert Mansbridge, *Margaret McMillan, Prophet and Pioneer*, Dent, 1932.

P. I. Kitchen, *From Learning to Earning*, Faber and Faber, 1944, is a most interesting description of the continuation school at Rugby. H. A. L. Fisher left an account of his career in *An Unfinished Autobiography*, O.U.P., reprint, 1941. For details about the recommendations made in the reports of the Consultative Committee of the Board of Education, the reader should consult the three Hadow and the Spens Reports.

CHAPTER IX

THE NATIONAL SYSTEM OF EDUCATION

World War II

For some months before the actual outbreak of war the Government had been preparing plans to evacuate children and expectant mothers from London and those large cities which were considered to be specially vulnerable to air attack. They were to be sent to reception areas in districts where air raids were thought to be less likely. Nobody knew how hostilities would start, but the general expectation was that they would begin with air attacks of great severity. When war was declared the evacuation plans were put into immediate operation, and the first four days of September 1939 were taken up with the movement of the evacuees to the safety areas. It has been said that the Government ought to have rehearsed the evacuation plans, but for security and military reasons this was not possible. As the schools knew the position of their respective reception areas, one would have thought that head teachers would have been encouraged to visit them beforehand, but for some reason this rarely happened. The evacuation was a complex operation, which was administered by the Ministries of Health, Transport, and Home Security and the Board of Education.

On the whole the operation worked smoothly and efficiently. Very few schools failed to arrive at their right destinations, and those who were mislaid were quickly discovered and sent to their correct areas. A number of initial blunders, however, nearly wrecked the scheme. In the first place the Government insisted that evacuation should be voluntary. Hence it was of the utmost importance to obtain the co-operation of the parents. The authorities in London refused to guarantee that parties of school children would arrive at a particular destination. Many parents were unwilling to let their children leave for an unknown destination, and their feelings were quite understandable.

The more serious problems only appeared when the children arrived in the reception areas. Billets had to be found for them, but insufficient care was taken to ensure that they would find themselves in households where they could feel at home. Instances

were reported of slum children being sent to large houses occupied
by wealthy people in which the standards of behaviour and living
and outlook on life were entirely strange. On the other hand, pupils
accustomed to a more comfortable kind of life found themselves
in country cottages where the conditions were definitely primitive.
No doubt the change in their environment was beneficial to many
pupils, but there were cases in which mistakes caused a great deal
of misunderstanding and irritation. Fortunately, the expected air
attacks failed to develop, and this gave an opportunity for the
sorting out process. No praise can be too great for the teachers,
inspectors, education officers, and voluntary welfare workers who
did a magnificent job and brought order into what might soon have
developed into chaos.

After the children had been placed in suitable homes it was
necessary to make arrangements for their schooling. These varied
from district to district. Sometimes there was a hall or a Sunday
School which could be utilised, and this often meant that children
would be taught in buildings widely separated. In other areas the
newcomers shared the existing school accommodation and this
entailed the adoption of a double shift. Gradually these difficulties were solved. There were, however, compensations in spite of
the shortage of teaching apparatus in the temporary schools.
Teachers were forced to improvise, and they were astonished to
discover that they were able to dispense with aids which they once
thought were essential. When the weather was kind, a good deal
of work could be done in the open-air, and practical pursuits and
physical activities became a very important feature of school life.
There is little doubt that most of the children received benefit from
the fresh air and more healthy conditions of life.

The absence of the expected air raids led the authorities to give
permission to parents to visit their children. This soon proved to
be a mistake, for the visits unsettled the children and many began
to agitate for a return to their homes. Thousands left the reception
areas, but when the Blitz started in earnest in the autumn of 1940
a large number of them came back. All schools were closed in the
danger areas, and it was not until the raids slackened and adequate
shelter was provided that they were permitted to open again.
Meanwhile, thousands of children had lost precious months of
schooling.

One result was the bringing together of town and country. This
had its bad as well as its good results, and it was the former which

received most publicity. There were many stories passed from mouth to mouth, some of which found their way into the Press, about the shocking conditions which prevailed in the homes of many city pupils. Most of these were exaggerated, but some were literally true. Social workers had known for many years that filthy and verminous children existed in numbers, and that there were many homes in which the living conditions were unbelievably bad and in which there was little sense of decency or discipline. The general public, however, was not well informed about such defects, and when it began to learn from the newspapers and letters from friends in the country about the low standards of life and behaviour common to a large section of the community, a strong feeling developed that this state of affairs ought to be remedied as soon as possible. There arose a demand for an early overhaul of our educational system.

The first active move came from the religious bodies. The Anglican Archbishops, the Roman Catholic Archbishop of Westminster, and the Moderator of the Free Church Federal Council united in 1940 in presenting a memorial entitled, *A Christian Basis for Peace*. In the following year, the Archbishop of Canterbury, Dr W. Temple, headed a deputation of Anglicans and Free Churchmen to visit the President of the Board of Education and place before him their views on the organisation of religious education. Discussions started on the topic of educational reconstruction in groups of widely different interests. The revelations consequent on evacuation had so shocked the public conscience that there was a universal demand for a complete reform of the social services, and it was thought that it ought to begin with education.

The Government was well informed about these feelings, but it was loth to proceed with legislation until it had collected the opinions of those whose knowledge and experience it was desirable to have. A memorandum on post-war education was prepared. This was the "Green Book" of 1941, a confidential document intended for select individuals whose views were worthy of consideration, but in the words of Lester Smith, "it was distributed in such a blaze of secrecy that it achieved an unusual degree of publicity". The publication of the "Green Book" stimulated discussion in civil life, in H.M. Forces, and through discussion groups and the B.B.C., with the result that every aspect of reconstruction was carefully examined. The Board received an enormous amount of information from various official and voluntary bodies.

Education Act of 1944

The new President of the Board, Mr R. A. Butler, felt he was in a position to take the next step, which was the issue in July 1943 of the *White Paper* on *Educational Reconstruction*. The suggestions of the White Paper were, on the whole, acceptable, and this encouraged Mr Butler to proceed with drafting an Education Bill. This was introduced in the Commons in December 1943 and received the Royal Assent on 4 August 1944. Mr Butler realised that such a comprehensive overhaul could not take place immediately. Hence he designed it to come into force in stages, but unfortunately some of the dates decided upon had to be postponed.

Most major Acts of Parliament are divided into parts. The Act of 1944 contains five parts, of which the first and the last came into force as soon as the Royal Assent was received. The intention was to bring the second and fourth parts into operation on 1 April 1945, but because of difficulties which arose the section concerned with the raising of the school leaving age to fifteen was postponed for two years. Part III was to come into force at a date fixed by an Order in Council. This part became operative in September 1947, but for reasons mentioned later some clauses of the Act have still to be put into force.

Examining the Act clause by clause is a dull business, but fortunately it is not necessary for the teacher to know every detail, since he can always refer to the Act or consult one of the many excellent books which have been written on the subject. The following exposition is confined to the consideration of the main principles of the Act, starting with the changes that have taken place in the central administration of education.

The reader may remember that the recommendations of the Bryce Commission were only partly fulfilled in the Board of Education Act of 1899. It is justifiable to regard this part of the Act as completing the intentions of the Bryce Commission in regard to the central administration. The Board of Education has been replaced by a Ministry, and the functions of the Minister have been explicitly defined. He is required to take the initiative in promoting the education of the people of England and Wales and to see that the national policy in education is carried out by the local authorities. He has the power of requiring a reluctant authority to co-operate with the Ministry, and other sections of the Act extend his responsibilities. Thus he can intervene if he is convinced that any

L.E.A. or managers or governors of a school are acting unreasonably. He has also the power of issuing Statutory Regulations and Orders (S.R. & O.), which are concerned with the administration of the Act.

Two Advisory Councils for England and Wales, respectively, replace the Consultative Committee of the Board of Education. They are charged with the duty of advising the Minister, as they think fit, on matters connected with educational theory and practice without waiting until the Minister requests them to do so. This was the intention of the Bryce Commission when recommending the establishment of an educational council. The Minister appoints the chairman and the members of each of the Councils and an officer of the Ministry to act as secretary. Each Council includes men and women and also persons who have experience of education outside the statutory system. Details about terms of service, retirement of members, and procedure have been issued by the Ministry (S.R. & O. 152, 1945). Mr Butler's appointment of Sir Fred Clarke as Chairman of the Advisory Council for England was received with great satisfaction.

When the Education Bill was debated in Parliament, some Members feared that the additional powers given to the Minister could lead to an educational dictatorship, but in practice their apprehension was groundless. The Minister is responsible to Parliament and is required to submit an annual report giving an account of the way in which he has exercised his powers and duties. Any statutory order or regulation he issues must be laid before Parliament for a period of forty days, during which a Member of either House can raise an objection, which if sustained will annul the regulation. In his annual report, the Minister has to include an account of the composition and proceedings of the Advisory Councils and any M.P. can question the actions of the Minister and his officers. Every citizen has the right of criticising the actions of the Minister in a public meeting or through a letter to the Press, and can write to his M.P. to draw his attention to any matter which he feels should be discussed. All these checks secure that the powers of the Minister shall not be exercised in an arbitrary fashion. Those who read a daily newspaper or *The Times Educational Supplement* will have noticed that in every week of the sitting of Parliament the Minister has to deal with questions raised by Members.

An important change has been made in the system of local administration created by the Act of 1902. The Part II L.E.A.s have been retained, but the Part III authorities no longer exist. Thus the number of L.E.A.s has been reduced to 146. Some County Councils or County Boroughs were considered to be too small and financially unable to carry out the responsibilities placed upon them. In these cases the Minister can constitute a joint education board, and this has already been done in the joint board set up by the Soke of Peterborough and the City of Peterborough. There may in the future be other changes of a similar character.

The Act laid down the principle which should guide the aim of education. "The statutory system of public education shall be organised in three progressive stages to be known as primary education, secondary education, and further education; and it shall be the duty of the local education authority for every area, so far as their powers extend, to contribute towards the spiritual, moral, mental, and physical development of the community by securing that efficient education throughout those stages shall be available to meet the needs of the population of their area" (Section 7). This implies that every child shall pass from the primary to the secondary stage and that education ought not to cease when the child has left school. To complete Hadow reorganisation it was declared that primary and secondary education should be provided in separate schools. At the time of writing this has not been possible everywhere, so that some all-age schools dealing with pupils from five to fifteen years still exist, but these are rapidly diminishing in number.

The abolition of Part III authorities raised a storm of protest when the White Paper suggested it. No individual or group of individuals will passively accept "liquidation", as we saw in the case of the School Boards in 1902. The Part III authorities strenuously defended themselves and were able to show that many of them were at least as efficient and progressive as some of the smaller county authorities. Their arguments impressed the Government. An Explanatory Memorandum to the Education Bill was published which proposed a compromise. County authorities were given the power of delegating certain of their functions in primary, secondary, and further education to Divisional Executives. This was not obligatory, and some counties, or parts of them, could continue under the administration of the county. Altogether, 171 D.E.s were constituted, but this number has since been reduced. In some county areas they have been abolished and in others two or more of them have been grouped together under one divisional education officer.

In one respect the D.E.s have less power and responsibility than the Part III authorities. They cannot levy a rate nor negotiate a loan. On the other hand, their duties have been extended to cover all three stages of education, and they prepare and submit their own annual estimates of expenditure to the county authority. Opinion has been divided about the merits of divisional administration. It was thought that the Government would abolish D.E.s, but in the recent proposals for the reform of Local Government this idea seems to have been dropped. D.E.s vary in composition in different parts of the country. They have both executive and advisory functions, the extent of which depend on the amount of delegation the county authority is willing to grant. As a rule they include three types of member: representatives of the county council; representatives of smaller local authorities, e.g. a municipal borough or an urban or rural district; and members who represent certain interests and institutions such as religious bodies, a university, the teaching profession, and industry and commerce. Other people on account of their special knowledge and experience in the educational field may be added.

The White Paper also mentioned another type of authority, the Excepted District, which is similar to a D.E., but the borough or urban district council is the executive authority and can, in consultation with the county, prepare its own scheme for the development of primary and secondary education. Originally the condition for recognition as an E.D. was that the area should either have had a minimum population of 60,000 according to the 1931 census, or a public elementary school roll of not less than 7,000 on 31 March 1939. The second condition was to include some areas which had developed rapidly since 1931. At first only thirty-nine areas, mostly around London, could claim E.D. status. Pressure exerted by Part III authorities resulted in a modification. An area could claim E.D. status if its population, according to the estimate of the Registrar-General, was greater than 60,000 on 30 June 1939. This added eight more in the London area and one, Worthing, outside the London district. There was also a provision to meet exceptional circumstances, but only seven out of sixty-seven applications were granted. Some areas previously qualified withdrew their claims, and this left the number of E.D.s at forty-four. It is likely that in the near future other claims for recognition may be made.

All L.E.A.s were required to survey their districts and submit to the Ministry development plans showing their proposals for primary and secondary education by 1 April 1946, but some authorities found the time allowed insufficient and were granted an extension. Before submitting the plans the governors and managers of voluntary schools were to be consulted, and when the Ministry had approved a plan and issued a local education order, two months were allowed for considering objections.

The Dual System, with some important modifications, has been retained. The non-provided schools have reverted to their original title of voluntary, and fall into three categories. The smallest consists of the special agreement schools sanctioned by the Act of 1936. Agreements made under this Act but not yet carried out may be revived, but all such schools are secondary. Two new classes of voluntary schools have come into existence. Where the governors or managers of a voluntary school are able and willing to provide 50 per cent. of the cost of alterations and additions required to bring the school up to the standard of the building regulations demanded by the Ministry, the school can be recognised as aided. The governors or managers retain the right of appointing the teaching staff and of deciding the type of religious instruction to be given in the school. The foundation governors or managers of an aided school constitute two-thirds of the total number, but if they are unable or unwilling to shoulder the financial burden, the school becomes controlled. In this case the L.E.A. assumes full financial responsibility for the school. The foundation governors or managers are one-third of the total number and the religious teaching must be based on an agreed syllabus. The desire of parents for denominational teaching for their children has been met. This can be given by reserved teachers for not more than two periods a week. The provided schools of the 1902 Act are now known as county schools.

This compromise arrangement concerning voluntary schools resulted from the consultations with the different religious bodies. It signified the recognition by the State of their contributions to national education in the past and those which they still can make. The burden undertaken by the voluntary schools has become heavier in the post-war years, and many schools which accepted aided status have now been obliged to become controlled. The number of Anglican schools and departments fell from 9,204 in January 1947 to 8,210 in 1957. Some of the smaller schools had been closed, so that the number which remained was made up of 3,527 aided and special agreement schools, 4,412 controlled schools, and 271 whose status was still to be determined. The present tendency seems to be that the number of aided schools will continue to grow smaller.

A problem which has to be solved is occasioned by the increase in the birth-rate; the so-called "bulge". It was thought that the "bulge" would be temporary, but it is now realised that for some years to come the birth-rate will remain at a level higher than that of pre-war years. Taking into account the movement of population over a wide area, these two factors mean that school governors and managers will have to face demands greater than they anticipated when they accepted aided status. To give an example, a secondary school, known to the writer and now in course of construction, was originally designed for 500 boys and girls with a cost to the Church of £28,000. Increased population in the area has necessitated an enlargement to 680 places, so that the share of the Church will be at least £51,000. Delays in building operations which have produced an increase of $8\frac{3}{4}$ per cent. in costs since 1944 and the rise in the rate of interest on building loans have combined to make the situation desperate. In 1956 the Church Assembly approved the Church Schools (Assistance by Church Commissioners) Measure which made available the sum of £1 million by way of grants or loans extending over twenty-five years. This much needed help, however, will not be sufficient, and in November 1958 the Assembly approved a statement to be sent to the Minister asking for the grant to aided schools to be raised to 75 per cent. to enable the Church to play its full part within the statutory system of education. Other religious bodies, such as the Roman Catholic Church, are faced with a like situation.[1]

The 1944 Act produced a striking innovation by making religious education and worship obligatory in all schools. Parents still have the right of withdrawal, and no teacher is compelled to give religious instruction. Every schoolday must begin with a corporate act of worship which usually takes place in the assembly hall. In small schools which have no assembly hall the worship may be held in the classrooms. The worship in county schools may not be distinctive of any particular denomination and the religious instruction is based on the agreed syllabus which has been adopted by the local authority. The agreed syllabus is so-called because its contents have been agreed by panels representing the Church of

[1] The Ministry has now agreed (1959).

England, the Free Churches, the teachers' associations, and the L.E.A. Some L.E.A.s have preferred to adopt a syllabus drawn up by some other authority.

The earliest agreed syllabus, the Cambridgeshire, was produced in 1926, and it was so successful that it has been followed by other syllabuses. The first were little more than outlines, but it was soon realised that teachers would be glad of more detailed guidance with regard to method, illustration, and background information. Hence the older agreed syllabuses were revised and enlarged, and in place of being mere Scripture syllabuses they attempted to present the Christian religion as a way of life. Most dioceses of the Anglican Church have their own syllabuses of Church teaching which are used in conjunction with part or the whole of an agreed syllabus.

The Act no longer restricts religious instruction to the beginning or end of the school session. In county schools the work is inspected by H.M.I.s, but in voluntary schools the denominational instruction is inspected under arrangements made by the governors or managers. All these changes are the result of the development of friendly relations between the religious bodies, and would not have been possible in the earlier years of this century. One difficulty was that of securing the services of teachers who wished to give religious instruction and who possessed the necessary knowledge and training. The Ministry, the university departments of education, and the training colleges have, in various ways, done much to provide them. The Institute of Christian Education provides single lectures and courses and publishes each term a journal entitled *Religion in Education*, which contains articles and reviews of books which are of assistance to teachers. University Institutes of Education organise special study courses on the agreed syllabuses and some offer a course which leads to a certificate in religious education. The Archbishop of Canterbury's examination for the Lambeth Diploma in Theology is specially suitable for graduates in secondary schools, and is open to baptised Christians of any denomination. It demands a standard equivalent to that of an honours degree in Theology at the older universities. All these measures should bring about a higher standard of religious education.

The recognition of the principle of secondary education for all children, involved the abolition of fees in maintained secondary schools from 1 April 1945. It should be noted that the Act is completely silent about recommending any particular organisation for secondary education, whether tripartite or other forms. It stated the fundamental principle, sometimes called the "three A.s", that the education given at any stage must be in accordance with "the age, ability, and aptitude of the pupil", and laid an obligation on the parents to see that such education is secured for their children. If they do not wish their children to attend a school in the statutory system, they are quite free to send them to a fee-paying school outside the system, to provide a private tutor or governess for them, or, if they have the time, the knowledge, and the qualification, they can undertake the education of their own children.

It is now possible for parents to obtain the benefits of a boarding school education for their children. Some L.E.A.s have experimented by placing pupils in independent boarding schools, whilst others have encouraged either the building of maintained boarding schools, e.g. Middlesex, or the development of existing boarding sides of grammar schools, e.g. the West Riding of Yorkshire. Nursery schools and classes are compulsory wherever they are considered to be necessary, and the continuation schools of the Fisher Act were to be revived under the name of County Colleges. The latter were scheduled to open by 1950, but problems of the supply of buildings and qualified teachers, the critical financial situation of the country in the post-war years, and the increase in the birth-rate have caused the postponement of this section of the Act. Only Rugby, which still maintained the continuation school, was ready to switch over immediately to the county college. For similar reasons the raising of the school leaving age to fifteen was delayed for two years, and the next step of making it sixteen has been postponed indefinitely.

Direct-grant schools were permitted to retain fees. These schools originated in 1926 when grant-aided schools not maintained by local authorities were given the option of receiving a capitation grant for pupils over the age of eleven direct from the Board of Education instead of through the local authorities. In 1942 there were 232 such schools with 85,681 pupils. They were required to accept a minimum percentage of their intake from free or special place pupils. The remainder paid fees on a sliding scale based on the income of the parents. After the abolition of secondary school fees the direct-grant schools were asked to re-submit their claims. In some cases the direct grant was withdrawn, and a number of schools which had adequate endowments and who feared a loss of their freedom decided to become independent. Many of them found it difficult to make ends meet, and when the direct-grant list was reopened in 1956, they once more submitted their claims. The Labour Party has always opposed the retention of direct-grant schools on the ground that they confer privileges upon certain sections of the community.

The Act also required L.E.A.s to establish and develop social and games facilities such as playing-fields, camps, swimming-baths, gymnasia, and other kinds of recreation. They can also provide books and clothes for children, but the cost can be recovered from parents who can afford to pay. The school medical services and treatment have been extended to all schools, and since 1948 they have been the charge of the Ministry of Health. The supply of milk to children and the provision of school meals have also been extended. Those who can afford the cost are required to pay a small sum for the meals, but it was intended that they should be provided free of charge as soon as there was a sufficient number of canteens. The charge for meals has slowly risen with increase in the cost of living, but all pupils who take them receive a nourishing meal at a price well below that demanded by private catering establishments. The result has been a greater demand from pupils, and in most schools the opportunity for training in table manners and the necessities of a civilised life has been utilised.

The grant regulations were overhauled in order to equalise the rate burden in poorer areas. In 1947 the school meals grant was amended and now applies to all maintained, voluntary, direct-grant, and independent schools. The sections of the Act which apply to independent schools are summarised in Chapter XIII. Until 1958 the grants were on a percentage basis, but the Government has decided to replace this by a general block grant to local authorities. This decision has produced a good deal of controversy, but it remains to be seen how the grant will be administered before an opinion can be given.

A general survey of the Act of 1944 justifies the statement that it probably constitutes the most important single advance ever made in the history of English education. Naturally, when the Act was put into operation, certain flaws were discovered, and these had to be corrected by amending Acts in 1946, 1948, and 1953. These Education (Miscellaneous Provisions) Acts, however, did not affect the main structure of the principal Act. The Government has also proposed an overhaul of local government. At first it seemed that the existence of Divisional Executives would come to an end. A considerable amount of criticism was directed at the administrative efficiency of these bodies, but it seems as though D.E.s will be retained. There may be some change in their grouping, some of which has already occurred, and that the status of Excepted District may be conferred on some D.E.s. Some counties have discontinued D.E.s and others have been amalgamated in order to cut administrative costs, *e.g.* Lancashire and the West Riding.

Selection for Secondary Education

For some years a controversy has been continuing about the selection for and the organisation of secondary education. The first point of criticism has been directed at the clean break at eleven plus. Psychologists, teachers, and parents have had much to say on this matter. The reader may remember that the Hadow Report on the Adolescent, the Spens and the Norwood Reports supported this policy. At first the psychologists pointed out that eleven plus was rather an early age to discover the abilities and aptitudes of many children. One should take into account that the Scottish Advisory Council advocated a transfer to secondary education at twelve plus, and the public schools have for years admitted their entrants at thirteen. It has also been urged that the selection test for the grammar school makes the career of the pupil dependent on variable conditions which prevailed at the time he sat for the selection test. In reply it can be said that most authorities review the situation at thirteen plus. One would like to see much more two-way traffic at this age, and this might reduce the number of grammar school pupils who leave as soon as they have attained the age of fifteen. It is common knowledge that the age of eleven plus was adopted when the school leaving age was fourteen so that the pupil might have at least a three-year secondary school course.

Another criticism which carries considerable weight is that a pupil's career is to a greater or lesser extent affected by the district in which he lives. Some areas are more generously supplied with grammar and technical schools than others. Thus, in one district a pupil who would be considered suitable for grammar school education might be denied the opportunity in another in which there were less grammar school places available.

Perhaps the most frequent objection to the selection test has been based upon the alleged effect it has upon both parents and candidates. Once again the issue has tended to become a political rather than an educational one. On the whole the Conservatives have supported both the transfer at eleven plus and the tripartite organisation of secondary grammar, technical, and modern schools. The Socialists are whole-heartedly in favour of a multilateral or comprehensive secondary school.[1] Many parents regard the modern school as a poor relation of the grammar school, and have not realised that the type of training it provides is more suitable for a large number than the more specialised linguistic and scientific studies of the grammar school. The modern school is a comparatively new-comer in the educational field, and, therefore, lacks the tradition of the grammar school. Also, many secondary modern schools have to make use of older and unsuitable buildings which were originally occupied by elementary school pupils.

These considerations influence parents in the direction of regarding the modern school as providing an education which is greatly inferior to that of the grammar school. They are desperately anxious for their children to obtain a grammar school place, and believe that those who have not been successful in the selection test will suffer financially and socially after leaving school. The education given in a modern school is different from but not inferior to that given in the grammar school, and it provides a training which is more suitable for the majority of pupils who have neither the taste nor the will and ability to profit from the more academic atmosphere of the latter. Nevertheless, until secondary modern schools in their buildings, staffing, and amenities can approximate to those offered by the grammar schools, this feeling will persist. There are many modern schools which are pointing the way to a new conception of the training suitable for the majority of eleven-plus pupils. In spite of this, numerous parents try to push their children by all means in their power and pass on their anxiety to the children. In some cases this has reacted unfavourably upon the children and has produced in them a nervous tension, but experience seems to show that these are in the minority and have been exaggerated for political reasons.

Most local authorities are aware of these problems and have experimented in different ways to find a solution; *e.g.* by giving more weight to tests of general intelligence, opinions of head teachers, and junior school reports. Some have gone so far as

[1] The terms multilateral and comprehensive were generally used as synonyms until they were defined by the Ministry in Circular 144 (Organisation of Secondary Education), 16 June 1947. A multilateral school differs from a comprehensive by being organised in three streams. A bilateral school contains two streams, grammar and technical, or modern and technical, or grammar and modern.

virtually to abandon the selection test at eleven plus. The comprehensive school may or may not be the answer, and at the present
time one would be rash to make a permanent decision before a
wider body of experience is available. It is certainly a step in the
right direction to experiment, but it is unwise for any local authority
to force either a tripartite or a comprehensive organisation upon an
area which is strongly opposed to it or before the evidence for each
type of secondary education has been thoroughly sifted.

Some additional points have emerged during the last few years.
At first it was generally assumed that a comprehensive school must
be a huge establishment containing from 2,000 to 3,000 pupils.
Now it is recognised that a school of 800, or perhaps less, can be
organised on a comprehensive basis. Secondly, evidence has been
coming into this country from the United States where the comprehensive plan was at first welcomed in many areas as a solution of
the problem of class distinction. It seems that the desired result
has not always been obtained, but in some schools class distinction has actually been heightened when the more and the less
academic types of pupil have been educated under the same roof
instead of being separated by distance in space. Still more recently,
reports have come in that Americans are not by any means satisfied
with the results achieved in their schools. Some of the criticism
has been directed at the standards reached in schools which are run
in accordance with the views of Dewey and his disciples, but other
points of criticism seem to point to defects in the organisation of
American education.

The Ministry of Education in 1958 announced in a White Paper,
Secondary Education for All: A New Drive, an ambitious five-year,
£400 million plan for the improvement of English education. The
text of the White Paper shows that the Ministry has given careful
thought to the problems of grammar school selection and the organisation of secondary education in England and Wales. It does not
propose the abolition of the tripartite organisation, but it seeks to
remove parental anxieties about the effects of the eleven-plus selection test upon the children. The principle to be followed is to
ensure that "every child shall be able to travel along the educational
road as far as his ability and perseverance will take him". This is
in accordance with the spirit of the Act of 1944.

The means to this end will be a vigorous attempt to raise the
standards of secondary modern schools. This will involve an intense
drive for building new schools. The remaining all-age schools will

be abandoned as quickly as possible and efforts will be made to reduce the size of classes in both primary and secondary schools. Attention will also be given to those grammar schools of ancient tradition which are housed in out-of-date buildings. The needs of the voluntary schools will be studied sympathetically, and it is recognised that they will require further assistance if they are to play their full part in the education of the country.

There is no intention at present of adopting a compulsory raising of the school leaving age, but the Ministry calls attention to the fact that modern school pupils are tending, in increasing numbers, to remain at school longer than the statutory age of fifteen. Ten years ago the number of pupils remaining after fifteen was about 12,000: now it has increased to 38,000. One reason for this has been the provision by many modern schools of courses leading to the ordinary level of the G.C.E. examination. The Ministry hopes to develop such courses with a view to encouraging still more children to remain at school until after fifteen. Their future opportunities, if they take the extended courses, should be much greater than if they spent the rest of their school days at the bottom of their form in the grammar school. Opinions will differ whether this constitutes a departure from the original purpose of the modern school.

The new programme will naturally be expensive. It is planned to begin in 1960, and at the end of the five-year period this country will be spending more than £1,000 million a year on education as compared with the present approximate figure of £720 million. The Ministry hopes that the test at eleven plus will cease to be regarded as a remnant of the old scholarship examination, but will become an honest attempt to group pupils into courses which are suited to their interests and abilities. There will be no pressure exerted on L.E.A.s to adopt any rigid plan for organising secondary education in their areas. Experiments with comprehensive schools will continue. In fact, the Ministry feels that there is a need for such schools in sparsely populated rural districts and in urban areas with a dense population in which no schools with an established tradition exist. Hence it will not approve the closing of grammar schools to make room for comprehensive schools, nor does it think it a good thing that such schools should contain anything from 2,000 to 3,000 pupils.

To return to the Education Act of 1944; it is one thing to place an Act upon the statute book, but quite another to ensure that it works smoothly and in the way that was originally intended. One should remember that, like the Acts of 1902 and 1918, it was adopted before the conclusion of a major war in which this country was engaged. It is always difficult for any Government to forecast accurately the conditions that will obtain in the post-war period. In the present instance the rise in the birth-rate and the fixing of the school leaving age at fifteen added nearly a million children to the school population. There was a serious shortage of teachers, many schools had been destroyed or damaged, and the cost of materials and labour were soaring. Both political parties were resolved that a serious breakdown must be avoided.

Since it was not possible to build new schools on a lavish scale, the Minister of Education, Miss Ellen Wilkinson, devoted her energies to supplying prefabricated classrooms and suitable furniture as an emergency measure. The result was the HORSA hut and SFORSA furniture.[1] Even in places where it was necessary to build permanent schools to replace those destroyed by enemy action or to accommodate children on new housing estates, the shortage of materials and their cost proved a major difficulty. The regulations prescribing Standards for School Premises (S.R. & O. 345, 24 March 1945) envisaged a level which was far too costly. Because of the urgent need for economy, the regulations were modified and experiments were made with less expensive methods of construction. As the economic and financial position of the country worsened, a strict watch had to be maintained on all educational expenditure, but now there seems to be a reasonable expectation that matters will improve and that gradually our out-of-date and inadequate buildings will be slowly replaced by more suitable ones. The recent announcements of the Ministry of Education seem to confirm this. The other major problem, that of the recruitment and supply of teachers, is the subject of another chapter.

Secondary School Examinations

Before concluding this chapter it is necessary to say something about examinations in the secondary school. The Taunton Commission favoured external examinations for the secondary schools. One witness before the Commission declared: "The studies of the classroom must be those wherein progress can be definitely

---

[1] HORSA—Hutting Operation for the Raising of the School Age. SFORSA —School Furniture Operation for the Raising of the School Age.

measured by examination. For examination is to the student what the target is to the rifleman; there can be no definite aim, no real training without it". Some attempt had already been made to provide external examinations for secondary school pupils. The College of Preceptors began their school examinations in 1853, and the Oxford and Cambridge Local Examinations started in 1857. Inspectors advised pupil-teachers to sit for the London Matriculation. Only selected pupils, however, were entered as candidates and their parents paid the examination fees. The writer passed all three grades of the College of Preceptors and then obtained first class honours in the Oxford Senior Local. Only about a third of his form sat for these examinations. The idea of entering a whole form at one time had not yet been entertained.

It was not long before the different professional bodies instituted their own examinations, and thus the multiplicity of examinations in any one school began. In 1911 the Consultative Committee of the Board of Education was asked to investigate the multiplicity of examinations with a view to simplifying matters. Their recommendations were not put into force because of the outbreak of war, but in 1917 they were accepted. The universities were recognised as the responsible bodies for conducting the examinations, and to co-ordinate the work of the seven (later eight) examining bodies, an advisory committee consisting of representatives of the universities, the L.E.A.s, and the teaching profession was set up. This was known as the Secondary School Examination Council. The recognised examining bodies were the universities of London, Durham, and Bristol; the Joint Matriculation Board of the Northern Universities; the Central Welsh Board; the Oxford and Cambridge Schools Examination Board; the Oxford Delegacy for Local Examinations; and the Cambridge Local Examination Syndicate.

Two standard examinations were recognised. The first was the School Certificate, taken at the age of about sixteen and which was the test of a four-year course of general education, and the second, the Higher School Certificate, which was taken two years later and was intended for pupils who remained in the VIth Form to specialise in an advanced course in arts or science for which the Board of Education gave a special grant. In both, pupils in order to gain the certificate were required to pass in certain groups of subjects, but in the School Certificate, drawing, music, handicrafts, and housecraft (for girls) were included. The form and not the pupil was the unit for examination. Although the examinations were external, representatives of the teachers were brought into touch with the examining bodies and schools were allowed to submit alternative syllabuses. Heads of schools sent in an estimate of the merits of the candidates they entered, so that some degree of internal control was admitted.

The Board of Education emphasised that it should "be a cardinal principle that the examination should follow the curriculum and not determine it". This precept was largely ignored and the work of the secondary school became geared to examination requirements. Another mistake was that of allowing the School Certificate to serve a dual purpose, that of a school leaving examination and that of qualifying for matriculation exemption for university entrance. In the same way the Higher School Certificate became an entrance examination for a university honours course. The inevitable consequence was that employers regarded exemption from matriculation as being superior to the ordinary certificate.

The Spens Report deprecated this and showed that the effort to obtain matriculation exemption caused undue strain to less academically minded pupils. They often had to abandon such subjects as scripture, art, music, and handicrafts when they entered the Vth Form because only art or music qualified as subjects for exemption from matriculation. Hence the Report considered that the School Certificate should be a school leaving test only. The outbreak of the Second World War prevented the recommendation of the Spens Report from being adopted immediately. In 1941 the President of the Board of Education reconstituted the Secondary School Examination Council, under the chairmanship of Sir Cyril Norwood, to consider necessary changes in the secondary school curriculum and the form which the examinations should take.

The Norwood Committee reported in 1943 and suggested drastic changes. It recommended that the School Certificate should be an internal examination conducted by the individual schools, based on their syllabuses with papers drawn up by the staffs of the schools. As the change was so fundamental, a transitional period of seven years was suggested. In place of the Higher School Certificate, it recommended a school leaving examination held twice a year for pupils of eighteen and over. The examination would serve the twofold purpose of a university entrance test and of meeting the requirements of the different professional bodies.

The recommendations of the Norwood Report met with a considerable amount of criticism, so that the Minister felt justified in referring the whole matter again to the Secondary School Examination Council which published its findings in 1947. A single examination known as the General Certificate of Education would take the place of the previous School and Higher School Certificate examinations. It would be available at three levels, Ordinary, Advanced, and Scholarship, and the minimum age of entry would be sixteen. No marks of distinction would be awarded. The grouping of subjects would be abolished; candidates would be able to choose their examination subjects and the Certificate issued would only show the subjects in which they had passed successfully. The aim of the examination should be that of serving the needs of pupils who wished to carry their education to a higher level at a university or a technical or teacher-training college, or to secure exemption from the preliminary requirements of the different professional bodies. The Ministry emphasised that the new examination had in view the future studies of the candidates, and was not like the School Certificate, an assessment of what the pupil had accomplished in the past.

The G.C.E. was criticised from two points of view. Many schoolmasters objected to the minimum age limit which would force the exceptionally brilliant pupil to mark time. Mr George Tomlinson, who succeeded Miss Ellen Wilkinson as Minister of Education, refused to alter the regulation, but in 1952 his successor, Miss Florence Horsbrugh, whilst retaining the age limit, recommended that the head of a school would be allowed to enter a pupil at an earlier age if he considered it was desirable in the pupil's own interest. She also met the criticism that the able candidate received no credit for a brilliant performance in the examination by restoring the mark of distinction at the Advanced Level. It was hoped that the examination would prevent pupils from specialising too early, but this has not always been fulfilled.

Secondary school examinations are closely bound up with scholarship awards to universities and other places of higher education. From quite early times the universities had offered scholarships to promising students. Unfortunately, most Oxford and Cambridge colleges were tied to particular schools or families, and it was not until 1852, when the State intervened through the Royal Commissions on the Universities of Oxford and Cambridge, that the colleges were able to throw their scholarships open. It was not until after the Education Act of 1902, however, that the award of scholarships to both ancient and modern universities materially increased. Powers were given to L.E.A.s to award scholarships tenable at universities to the most promising pupils in their schools. The Board of Education entered the field in 1911 and announced that it would give grants for a four-year course at universities and university colleges to students who wished to take up teaching as their profession.

In 1920 the Board offered 200 State Scholarships which carried payment of tuition fees and a maintenance allowance. In the years which followed the number of State Scholarships was increased and, at the same time, the amount of grant which was paid to the holders. As a consequence of the Second World War, many young people suffered as regards their future careers. To assist those who had been hindered, the Board launched its Further Education and Training Scheme (F.E. & T.), which was put into operation before hostilities ceased. About 85,000 awards were made, of which 45,000 were for university courses. With the organisation of National Service in 1947 the scheme was allowed to run down, and for practical purposes came to an end in 1951.

State and L.E.A. scholarships were originally awarded on the results of the Higher School Certificate examination. A Working Party on University Awards appointed by the Minister in 1948 made recommendations which changed this procedure. After this date, candidates whose performance at the Advanced and Scholarship levels of the G.C.E. showed promise of gaining a good honours degree would be eligible for State Scholarships. These would include candidates under the age of twenty who had left school early and entered industry (Technical State Scholarships), and more mature students over the age of twenty-five (State Scholarships for Mature Students).

Candidates who did not seem to possess exceptional ability but showed promise of being able to benefit from a university training were eligible for L.E.A. awards. In 1953 there were 9,928 L.E.A. awards, of which 9,000 were major awards for university courses or courses at senior technical colleges. The awards made by local authorities have been severely criticised on the grounds that there seemed to be no uniform standard adopted by L.E.A.s and that some are more generous in the amount of maintenance grant than others.

The Anderson Committee in its Report published in 1961 recommended the abolition of State Scholarships after 1962. They would be replaced by the open entry scholarships offered by the universities and the holder of an open scholarship would be able to keep up to £100 of the scholarship without deduction from the Government grant. The idea of the change was to stimulate competition for entrance scholarships to the civic universities. This recommendation was accepted by the Minister of Education.

The Beloe Report

In November 1958 a Committee was appointed by the Secondary Schools Examination Council and issued its Report in November 1960. Its title was *Secondary School Examinations other than the G.C.E.*, and the Chairman was Mr Robert Beloe, then Chief Education Officer for Surrey. The Beloe Report deals with the growth of external examinations other than the G.C.E. which are conducted by a variety of independent examining bodies. Most of the candidates come from secondary modern schools and the non-selective streams of other secondary schools. From the time of the Hadow Report on the Adolescent, the institution of a school leaving certificate for the modern school had been mooted, but on the whole the idea did not find favour with L.E.A.s. The Ministry, in Circulars 289 of July 1955 and 326 of July 1956, had discouraged external examinations other than the G.C.E. for secondary modern pupils.

In spite of the unfavourable attitude of the Ministry, such examinations grew in numbers and in popularity, and there was a danger that if they were allowed to develop free from control and without co-ordination they might cause serious harm to the schools. The Crowther Report had considered the problems involved and concluded that about one-third of modern school pupils over the age of fifteen would benefit from external examinations below the level of the G.C.E. It recognised the dangers of large-scale external examinations, and preferred that they should develop along regional or local lines. The Beloe Committee unanimously recognised the value of such examinations, but considered that their rapid growth necessitated some form of national control.

At present, they fall under four fairly well marked categories. (1) Local examinations conducted by groups of schools or by L.E.A.s. These are generally designed for pupils in the fourth year, *i.e.* age fifteen. (2) School examinations conducted by bodies with regional or national coverage. These may be for the fourth or fifth year and either "group" or "subject" examinations. The London-based bodies are the College of Preceptors, the Royal Society of Arts, and the London Chamber of Commerce. The City

and Guilds of London Institute have intimated that they will probably enter the field of school examinations. In the regions are
the East Midland Educational Union (Nottingham), the Northern
Counties Technical Examinations Council (Newcastle-upon-Tyne),
the Union of Lancashire and Cheshire Institutes (Manchester), and
the Union of Educational Institutes (Birmingham), which covers the
West Midlands and the south and south-west of England. All these
have had a long experience of external examinations. The oldest
is the College of Preceptors, which started their school examinations in 1850. In 1953 the College planned the Certificate Examination on a group basis and permits pupils in the fourth year and
even younger to sit. (3) Further education examinations originally
designed for students attending part-time further education courses.
(4) Specialist examinations conducted by bodies which generally
have a national coverage. They were instituted for pupils wishing
to follow vocational and professional courses.

The Committee pointed out that local examinations seldom lead
to certificates which have more than local currency, and most of
them are designed for fourth year pupils. Since the tendency is
for an increase in the number of pupils remaining at school after
the statutory leaving age, parents, pupils, and employers prefer
an examination taken in the fifth year. Hence local examinations
will probably lose their appeal, and further education examinations are unsuitable for school pupils. It was agreed that external
examinations should not be taken by pupils before the end of the
fifth-year course, and the experience gained in the operation of
the old School Certificate showed that all examinations should be
"subject" rather than "group" examinations. The more able
candidates should be able to obtain a credit award. It is essential that the examinations should conform to the needs and the
interests of pupils, but ought not to be a lower level version of
the G.C.E. Whilst the general responsibility for the examinations
should be undertaken by about twenty Regional Examining Boards,
their form and content should be in the hands of the teachers. In
addition to teachers, representatives of the L.E.A.s in each region,
one or more persons representing institutes for further education in
the region, and one or more from the Area Training Organisations
and from the employers of the region should be included in the
Governing Councils of the Regional Bodies.

The Committee advised the Minister to take the initiative and
accept the examination for the Certificate of Secondary Education

(C.S.E.). It suggested that the Minister should fix a date from which he would be prepared to entertain applications from intending examining bodies who would accept the criteria drawn up by the Committee. Candidates from maintained schools who entered for a recognised examination should have their fees paid by the L.E.A. The Minister has the power to reject the proposed C.S.E., but it would be almost impossible for him to make his prohibition effective. If examinations other than the G.C.E. were not recognised they would still continue to develop, but would be entirely uncontrolled.

The Beloe Report did not receive unanimous support. A considerable number of teachers and education authorities were critical of the suggested examination. The Minister was in a difficult position and he did not reply immediately. To accept would be to change the policy of the Ministry, and he wanted time to examine the arguments on both sides. Eventually, in July 1961, Sir David Eccles told the Commons that he reluctantly decided to approve the Report in principle, but he thought it necessary to set up within his department a research and development group to study the problems in greater detail. He requested the Secondary Schools Examination Council to work out the means through which the general principles of such examinations could be applied.

At the request of the Minister there was a reconstitution of the Council in October 1961 so as to include representative members from technical colleges and people with knowledge and experience of non-selective secondary schools. The Council published its Fifth Report at the end of August 1962. It accepted the recommendations of the Beloe Committee and gave guidance for the task of the Regional Examining Bodies. It is entitled—*Examinations in Secondary Schools—The Certificate of Secondary Education*. When the comments of the teachers and L.E.A.s were received and considered, arrangements were made for the first examinations to be held in the summer of 1965. As a consequence of a Cabinet change in the summer of 1962, Sir Edward Boyle was appointed Minister in the place of Sir David Eccles. The new Minister approved the Report. Teachers will be given a large amount of control in the C.S.E. examination.

Education Act 1959

By 1958 the changing situation in the country threatened to throw a heavy burden upon the Churches if they were to carry out their part in the new developments indicated by the White Paper—

Secondary Education for All. In particular, there had been considerable changes in the population distribution since 1944. New towns and large housing estates had come into existence in various parts of the country with the result that many children were unable to make use of the existing voluntary schools. The "bulge" in the birth-rate necessitated greatly increased accommodation but building costs had soared without any substantial increase in the endowments of voluntary schools. Such changes had not been envisaged when the 1944 Act was passed. Differences in the views of the religious bodies complicated matters. The Roman Catholics asked that all post-war building should attract an increased grant. The Free Churches were at first suspicious about any increase of grant to voluntary schools. The Church of England was not prepared to accept any changes which altered the principles of the 1944 Act.

Discussions between the Church of England, the L.E.A.s, the political parties, and the Free Churches resulted in an agreement based on the analogy with the Education Act of 1936. The latter empowered L.E.A.s to make grants towards voluntary schools for senior pupils and which would match voluntary primary schools. The Education Act of 1959 raised the grant from 50 to 75 per cent. for new aided secondary schools and enlargements to existing schools. This only applied to building approved after 15 June 1959. The Bill was welcomed by the Liberal and Labour parties and received the Royal Assent on 29 July 1959.

N.U.T. Investigation into the State of our Schools

For some time complaints had been made by different areas about conditions in certain schools which ought to have immediate attention. The National Union of Teachers undertook a survey of conditions in schools of England and Wales. The Report, entitled *The State of Our Schools,* was published in January 1963. It was concerned mainly with primary and secondary modern schools but a further report on other schools has been promised in the future. Questionnaires were sent to over 30,000 schools and answers were received from more than 20,000. The Press, television, and radio provide the general public with information about improvements in certain schools in some districts. The great value of this survey is that it acquaints the public with what remains to be done in the country as a whole.

It is not possible in a short space to give anything like a full account of the findings of the survey. One can select, however, some of the most vital defects in numbers of schools. Many classes were found to have larger numbers of pupils than the standard demanded by the Ministry. Some schools were housed in buildings erected in the Victorian era and which had only received minor improvements. There was also a grave shortage of specialist teachers in secondary schools. Overcrowding was more common in the south of England but the proportion of out-of-date buildings was greater in the north. Many defects were found in primary schools, aided or controlled. Thus many schools reported that they had no hot water supply and the condition of the toilets was most unsatisfactory. In a few cases, the teachers' toilets were lacking and the staff had to share with the pupils. Most toilets were outside the main building and in severe spells of frost such as were prevalent during the winters of 1962 and 1963, they were invariably frozen. Modern equipment was scarce and even in some of the larger schools there was no library nor satisfactory accommodation for handicrafts, physical education, and school meals. In many urban districts some secondary modern and grammar schools were so over-crowded that groups of pupils were accommodated in buildings at some distance from the main school. Pupils in making their way to such improvised buildings had to cross main thoroughfares and incur danger from the increasing build up of heavy motor traffic.

The object of the Report was not to condemn the policy of the Ministry but rather to stimulate improvements in school conditions. Sir Edward Boyle recognised this but he hoped that it would not turn the minds of the public away from the most serious difficulties that have to be faced, especially the acute shortage of teachers.

SUGGESTIONS FOR FURTHER READING

The reader is reminded that until he has seen the Act of 1944 in operation, a perusal of it will yield small profit. Before studying the text of the Act he is advised to read a good commentary on it, such as H. C. Dent, *The Education Act, 1944,* third edition, University of London Press, 1947. A concise survey of English education as it is at present is given in R. Armfelt, *The Structure of English Education,* Cohen and West, 1955.

Those who are interested in comprehensive schools should read R. Pedley, *Comprehensive Schools To-day,* Councils and Education Press, and *Comprehensive Education: A New Approach,* Gollancz, 1956.

CHAPTER X

TWENTIETH-CENTURY THOUGHT ON EDUCATION

With universal elementary education firmly established, with secondary education becoming available from 1902, and with higher education in various fields progressing apace, the new century promised fulfilment of the aspirations of the old, and, with a few notable exceptions, Edwardian educators were content to re-interpret the teaching of their predecessors. Later, the nation was shaken by two world wars, and the structure and functioning of society was profoundly modified by the progress of science and the impact of the outside world. The climate of thought on education has been affected—if not completely determined—by national vicissitudes and crises. Thus it is not proposed to attempt the tracing of lines of thought throughout the period, but to consider the leading educators in three chronological groups, because the main individual contributions reflect the needs and problems of the times in which they lived and worked.

The First Period: 1897-1919

The end of this phase corresponds with the end of the Great War and the passing of the Fisher Education Act. The two decades had seen new political movements, the new discontent of women, new threats to the British Empire, and new challenges to old standards of living and behaviour. The great names of this period represent different categories of endeavour and experiment. Margaret McMillan and Homer Lane worked on behalf of underprivileged children. Their contributions are perhaps the most significant and relevant of the period. John Adams and F. H. Hayward strove to direct the thinking of teachers towards worthy aims and purposes. Enterprising headmasters such as Sanderson and Badley succeeded in justifying their own theories in practice. Enlightened administrators such as Sadler and Fisher gave intellectual prestige to the concepts of national education as yet unrealised. In addition, two other factors were, on the whole, beneficial and stimulating to the work of English teachers—the increasing contributions of psychological science and the increasing interchange of ideas with foreign teachers and thinkers.

Margaret McMillan was a middle-aged woman at the dawn of the twentieth century, but she had not yet embarked on her greatest project. She lived until 1931, but her main work was accomplished during the first two decades. The story of her practical achievements is told elsewhere, but, as a student of education and a leader of thought on education, she deserves a place alongside the eminent professors, administrators, and headmasters of the day. It is sometimes forgotten that her approach to education was intellectual as well as practical, and that her convictions were derived from philosophy and psychology as well as from her social conscience and her political bias.

A Scots gentlewoman with a Continental "finish", Miss McMillan first earned her living as a governess, but later joined her sister Rachael in London; both sisters becoming infected with an enthusiasm for social work and an interest in the new Socialist movement. Margaret had a striking appearance and excellent voice, assets that gained her a course of stage training at the expense of a titled lady, but even while engaged in these duties, the girl was taking an active part in Socialist campaigns. She was also teaching music to groups of factory girls, and was continuing her already extensive reading of literature on education, philosophy, and sociology.

In 1893 she took up a Socialist appointment in Bradford, where she found problems so immediate as to constitute a personal challenge. Henceforward, she could never become a mere cog in a party machine.

Within a year she won a place on the Bradford School Board, and she had already started her campaign on behalf of the hordes of dirty, adenoidal, undernourished children of the town. From this time onwards she published writings on questions relating to education, not regular or prolific, but excellent in quality and relevance. Her knowledge of music and voice-production made her particularly conscious of the prevalence of faulty breathing habits among the children. She wrote a pamphlet on this topic for distribution to mothers. As she fought her way towards the establishment of school baths, school meals, and school clinics, she also pursued her studies of the latest theories and researches in education and in mental and physical welfare. In 1896—the year she tried to buy a copy of Séguin's book—she published a pamphlet, *Child Labour and the Half-Time System*, and a few years later she completed her first book, *Early Childhood*, which reveals not only the depth of her human sympathy but also the width of her intellectual horizons.

Miss McMillan's educational theory is no mere imitation of Plato, Locke, Rousseau, or Spencer. Her social theory is no milk-and-water version of Kingsley, Ruskin, or Marx, but she had weighed up the ideas of these experts—and of many more—before deciding that physical welfare is a fundamental necessity in any scheme of education. Only when the health of the child from birth has been recognised as a basic human responsibility and community concern, can the other aims of education be sought with any prospect of success. The human organism is a unity; the growth of feelings, sentiments, and emotions depends on physical well-being and freedom from hunger and pain. Miss McMillan's kinship with Froebel may be traced in her assumption that emotion plays its part in child-development from the beginning. She describes how sense impressions—through sight, sound, touch, and smell—cause feelings of wonder that she designates "involuntary culture". Natural play activities give much experience of this kind—experience which teachers might well aim to extend in school. There is a hint of Herbart in her contention that education aims to produce "the ethical man or woman", a process dependent on the early foundation of a healthy body and a rich emotional life. Her description of reasoning as a "going forward upborne by emotion", is a concept later expounded by A. N. Whitehead in his analysis of the learning process into the stages "romance", "precision", and "generalisation".

Miss McMillan elaborated her philosophy in a pamphlet, *The Ethical Aim of Education*, an essay which reveals her growing interest in the science of psychology and in the actual process and methods of education. She regards current teaching methods as "a sin against the power of the emotions as the sustainer of all vigorous mental and moral life". Her aim is to persuade teachers that they should study "spontaneous attention" in their pupils and should try "to build up the powers of voluntary attention from the involuntary". Many other educators were also pleading that teachers should provide lessons in which children could be genuinely interested.

Margaret McMillan returned to London in 1903 to join her sister in planning a health centre. Within two years she published her main book on educational theory, *Education Through the Imagination*. Herein is ample evidence of her wide knowledge of educational ideas. An acquaintance with the writings of Froebel,

Arnold, Ruskin, and Spencer is hardly surprising, but familiarity with the pedagogics of Herbart, Tolstoi, and John Dewey is not usual outside the ranks of the professors of education. Psychologists, such as Ribot of France, and Stanley Hall of U.S.A., contributed much to the development of her theory, a theory which was not confined to the part played by imagination in child development.

"The creative power of the mind" is, in her view, the quality which every human being should be enabled to develop and use in his personal life and work. The school methods and the factory system of her day achieved only the suppression of this power. The adjustment of school curricula and methods to the psychological needs of the pupil should result in the production of an individual who will earn a living not merely by mechanical skill, but also with an intelligent, enterprising, and interested attitude.

Miss McMillan assumes that human beings have innate tendencies and capacities; therefore, her theory requires the arrange·ment of contacts and experiences, both in play and in activities resembling play, so that each child may acquire and co-ordinate primary sensations. These eventually lead to the refinement of perception and the development of those feelings and emotions on which expressive and creative imagination depends. With, perhaps, the exception of Stanley Hall the American psychologist, Miss McMillan is the first to point out the problem of the day-dreaming child, who, she maintains, has been denied those experiences which would have captured his attention for more real and creative mental effort.

In examining the characteristics of child play, she again stresses the individual nature of development and points out a problem that has not yet been solved—how to ensure that each youngster is stretched to the utmost of his capacity. She is perturbed not only by the limitation of intellectual growth, but also because the child may express "only a fraction of his personality".[1]

The fault, however, lies not only in the teacher with poor methods and in the industrial system with its mechanisation of humanity, but also in the mere physical stresses of social conditions which produce widely and rapidly in the child population myopia, faulty breathing, malnutrition, and other weaknesses. These prevent full participation in experiences which develop the emotions

[1] McMillan, M., *Education Through the Imagination*, p. 11, Allen and Unwin 1905.

—music, movement, drawing, poetry, handicrafts, even science. Moreover, many children in school cannot respond emotionally to such stimuli because their home life has not given them the early experiences—toys, love, and beauty—which give the preliminary development of the feelings.

It is not without significance that Miss McMillan regards art as a basic activity in education at all stages, partly because it contributes so greatly to the development of imagination and partly, perhaps, because she was essentially artistic in temperament. As an ex-actress she considered the training of speech as of great importance not only for health and for social poise, but also for the development of reasoning.

During the ten years which followed the publication of *Education Through the Imagination*, the McMillan sisters achieved the foundation of clinics and remedial centres, night camps and camp schools for boys and girls in Deptford, and an open-air nursery school. The nursery school was eventually moved from the camp site to a new location. Because Margaret wrote a book on nursery schools and because she later effected the foundation of a nursery training college, her name has become associated with infant education rather than with a much wider theory—and achievement. Her aim was always the free and full development of the intellect and personality of the individual. She saw no way of achieving this aim until there were no "deprived" children in the community and until teachers were prepared to find out how to help their pupils. Therefore, she had to start her practical work at the beginning—child health and infant teaching.

In *The Nursery School* she expresses some scepticism of current trends in psychology, because it was developing as a separate science with "the aloofness that spells failure". She hopes that the open-air nursery school will "clear the decks not only for actions, but also for observation" so that a real knowledge of child development may be built up. "Already we see that after a few weeks of new feeding, and bathing, and nursing of poor children", she writes, "all the problems are changed. A good many of them, indeed, go out of existence in a hurry." [1]

Margaret McMillan was instrumental in bringing remedial and preventive medicine into the orbit of national education. She provided proof positive of the power of doctors, dentists, nurses, and even ordinary teachers, to so improve the physical well-being of

[1] McMillan, M., *The Nursery School*, p. 327, Dent, 1919.

young children that learning difficulties and behaviour problems would remedy themselves. Had she not won her way, little would have been achieved through the ideas and experiments of professional educators. These latter now included a group of university professors of education—a group small at the beginning of the century, but destined to grow considerably in size and in influence. The outstanding representative of this group is undoubtedly Sir John Adams.

John Adams (1857-1934), knighted in 1925 as a distinguished professor of education, has rarely received credit for the first great service he rendered to education.[1] His earliest important publication, *The Herbartian Psychology Applied to Education* in 1897, performed three significant functions. First, it raised pedagogic literature to the standard and status it had enjoyed only spasmodically in this country. The earnest Thring, the sensible Payne, and the well-balanced Fitch were practical and somewhat pedestrian in their writings, but Adams had almost as much style as an Arnold, almost as much force as a Spencer, considerably more wit than either, and, to cap it all, a full and scholarly knowledge of *new* theories, *new* thinkers, *new* experiments, and *new* writings.

The second function of Adams's book was to interpret Herbartian principles intelligibly but critically to English teachers, so that the wave of enthusiasm for Herbartianism which followed was not as extreme as the corresponding movement in America, and was, on the whole, beneficial to English education. The third function followed naturally in emphasising the importance to education of the new and growing science of psychology. While precursors such as Bain and Sully[2] had done much to justify educational psychology as a university study, Adams set the seal on its respectability and paved the way for the acceptance of the contributions of later psychologists, particularly that of McDougall[3] in 1908.

One of his main arguments for the study of psychology lies in the famous quotation, "Verbs of teaching govern two accusatives —the master taught John Latin . . . He must know Latin and he must know John. Not long ago it was considered enough for him to know Latin"[4]. Less often quoted is a significant comment on fashionable teaching methods of his time: "The mere fact that

[1] First Professor of Education, University of London, 1902. Director of the London Day Training College, 1902-1922.
[2] Bain, A., *Education as a Science*; Sully, J., *Studies of Childhood*.
[3] McDougall, W., *Introduction to Social Psychology*, Methuen, 1908.
[4] Adams, J., *The Herbartian Psychology*, p. 16, Heath, 1897.

Froebelianism has obtained such a hold upon our educational system proves that it possesses elements of first-rate importance to the teacher. But as a Psychology it is simply non-existent. It suggests the immense importance of knowing John; which is much. It leaves, to others, the task of supplying this knowledge".[1]

From Adams's remarks it becomes evident that the impact of Herbart's ideas on English educators was not direct and immediate. Although Herbart did no more than point the way towards a science of psychology, his theories were receiving serious consideration by psychologists at the end of the century.[2] Thus Adams was the first to show the relevance of Herbartian ideas to teaching—at least, in this country, for he makes it clear that he recognises the work done in the U.S.A. by William James, Charles De Garmo, W. T. Harris, and John Dewey.

Although some commentators have decided that John Adams belongs to the Great Open-Minded Professor group, we beg leave to suggest that the Realism of *The Herbartian Psychology* is a very fair indication of the trend of his convictions and interests. It is true that his best-known book, *The Evolution of Educational Theory* (1912) defines for the first time with scholarly impartiality the characteristics of Humanism, Naturalism, Idealism, and Materialism, but Adams was too good a philosopher to have no viewpoint of his own. He was also too good a teacher to be vastly impressed by purely theoretical arguments. With theories about the condition of the human soul at birth he has little patience. " 'All babies are born good', says Lord Palmerston, echoing the sentiment that with Rousseau passed for philosophy, and that Wordsworth worked up into poetry." [3] This is indeed irony in place of the reverence usually lavished on at least two of these great names. Contending that Herbart's concept of the emptiness of the soul at birth is useful, Adams nevertheless concludes: "We do not know whether all souls are equal at birth, and, after all, it does not matter; for by the time the pupil makes his appearance in school, his soul is different from the other souls in his class".[4]

Adams is equally scathing in his examination of arguments for the inclusion of subjects in the curriculum. Herbart's theory of development through many-sided interest is acceptable because it emphasises the value of the subject for its own sake. "So far

[1] Adams, J., *The Herbartian Psychology*, p. 43, Heath, 1897.
[2] Adams refers to articles by G. F. Stout, 1888-91.
[3] Adams, J., *The Herbartian Psychology*, p. 81.
[4] *ibid.*, p. 106.

from opposing culture", writes Adams, "the Herbartian theory is the strongest supporter of the fine arts and *belles-lettres*. The increase in intension and extension of interest is the gauge of the development of a soul. We must lose ourselves in our subjects, not seek to keep them outside of us".[1]

Moreover, Herbart's concept of apperception enables Adams to draw attention to the fallacies of accepted ideas on the place of sense impression in education. "The educator who seeks to cultivate observation by supplying materials to gape at", he contends, "does not know the rudiments of his art. True observation is the offspring of interest and knowledge . . . Children can observe only what their apperception masses are prepared to act upon; to all else they are literally blind, deaf, callous". On the question of interest itself, Adams takes a firm Herbartian stand, very similar to the attitude taken by John Dewey about the same time. "Teachers are fond of talking about creating interest", he writes, "but this labour at least is spared to them. They have not to create, but only to direct interest. The most careless and inattentive boy at school is not without interest, not even without attention. The trouble is that he is interested in the wrong things. It is no doubt humiliating for the schoolmaster to accept a place in the scale of interest much lower than that held by a healthy bluebottle . . . Let but the master appear in a night-cap of sufficient brilliancy, and the bluebuzzer will buzz in vain. The night-cap teaching must characterise the earliest stages of infant education".[2] During the next quarter of a century, Adams wrote several books of value to teachers and participated in the progressive movements of his day, but his *Herbartian Psychology* was never surpassed.

A year after the publication of *The Herbartian Psychology*, Miss Catherine Dodd, a trainer of teachers, published the first of her several Herbartian books, *Introduction to The Herbartian Principles of Teaching*. She had visited Professor Rein, of the University of Jena, and with his help, had seen Herbartian methods worked out in German schools. Miss Dodd introduced similar methods into English primary schools and trained students in these methods. At one time she lectured in education at Owen's College, Manchester, and at another she was Principal of Cherwell Hall Training College. Miss Dodd not only comments with skill and enthusiasm on the

[1] Adams, J., *The Herbartian Psychology*, p. 134, Heath, 1897.
[2] *ibid.*, p. 259-60.

ideas of Pestalozzi, she also indicates that Herbart's ideas were discussed in the lectures of Professor James Ward, of Cambridge. In her book, she gives examples of "associated studies" for the infant school, and "concentrated studies" for the primary school. She works out lessons for various subjects and stages, but to us they appear somewhat ambitious.

Outstanding among British Herbartians was **Frank H. Hayward,** a philosopher captivated by Adams's "scintillating" *Herbartian Psychology*. He pursued research on Herbart's ideas—for a time in Germany—and published during the early years of the century, *The Students' Herbart*, *The Critics of Herbartianism*, and *The Secret of Herbart*. Turning completely to education, he became a tutor at a Pupil-Teacher Centre and wrote *The Educational Ideas of Pestalozzi and Froebel* and *Education and the Heredity Spectre*. He soon started a long career as an Inspector of London schools, and he continued to interpret and apply Herbartian principles in print as well as in his daily work. In 1909 appeared *The Primary Curriculum*, which presented these principles attractively at a practical level. In his Introduction, Hayward shows the relationship between the ideas of Froebel and Herbart. He adds a bitter comment on the injustice of criticisms made by opponents of the Herbartian movement. He ruefully admits, " 'The Herbartians' appear to consist in England of four dangerous animals, Professor Adams, Dr Davidson,[1] Miss Dodd, and myself". Hayward is infuriated to find the concepts of the richer curriculum and "many-sided interest" scorned by critics clinging to the obsolete faculty-training doctrine. In concluding, he remarks: "At present, education is helplessly and ignominiously hung up because no one really knows whether 'formal training' or 'faculty training' is, or is not, the name of a colossal delusion".[2] He predicts that the development of the "open-air school"—then an entirely new idea—would enable these problems to be solved naturally. "Our moral and civic instruction will be far more successful in a school society where each member has rights and duties", he writes. "Maybe this book will be the last ever published in which the four-walled classroom and the old-fashioned time-table of separate subjects will be assumed".[3]

[1] Author of *A New Interpretation of Herbart's Psychology*, Blackwood, 1906.
[2] Hayward, F. H., *The Primary Curriculum*, p. 436, Ralph Holland & Co., 1909.
[3] *ibid.*, p. 438.

While leaders of the Herbartian movement may have been few in number, there is no doubt that in many schools there were attempts to make subject-matter more meaningful and less dependent on mere words.[1] The English Herbartians performed a great service in pointing out that the teaching of all subjects—including science, which had promised so much in Spencer's day—had become completely verbal and mechanical, dependent on the passivity of the pupil and his capacity for rote learning. In this country, Froebel had always been relegated to the infant school, and it was left to Herbart to persuade elementary and secondary school teachers that schooling could be pleasant and enjoyable. Herbart, in throwing on the teacher the onus of "man-making", challenged his enterprise and ingenuity in the "presentation" of materials and experiences in his lessons in ways that gained and retained the attention and interest of pupils. The idea that it was helpful to show the relatedness of subjects and subject-matter led to many experiments in co-ordination and correlation, especially between geography and history. Only rarely was the concentrated or completely correlated curriculum put into operation. The most valuable achievement of the Herbartians was rather the enlargement of the "circle of thought" associated with the recognition of the usefulness of teaching techniques and the value of practical activities, from acting to gardening, from singing to pond-fishing, from painting to woodwork.

No doubt the intellectual demands on both teachers and pupils were too great for ordinary mortals, but Herbartian concepts proved to be incentives for rarer spirits. H. G. Wells, for instance, wrote in *New Worlds for Old*: "The majority . . . still fail to grasp completely the Herbartian truth, the fact that every human soul moves within its circles of ideas, resisting enlargement, incapable indeed, if once it is adult, of any extensive enlargement, and that all effectual human progress can be achieved only through such enlargement. Only ideas cognate to the circle of ideas are assimilated or assimilable; ideas too alien, though you shout them in the ear, or thrust them in the face, remain foreign and incomprehensible".

Leaders in education were inspired to debate among themselves the question of moral education, which was, of course, Herbart's main and outstanding purpose—the education of the Moral Man.

[1] Hayward maintained that Professor J. J. Findlay's *Principles of Class Teaching* (Macmillan), was "almost the only attempt to nationalise Herbartianism among us by retaining its most valuable features and judiciously supplementing or correcting its defects".

Between 1907 and 1909 a wide and comprehensive investigation was made into moral education in schools not only at home but also in U.S.A., France, Germany, Switzerland, Belgium, Norway, Denmark, Canada, Australia, New Zealand, and Japan. Innumerable men and women contributed to the enquiry, either financially or with time and effort. Professor John Adams spoke at a Congress in 1908, and Dr Hayward gave evidence to the Executive Committee. A report of the findings in the United Kingdom was published in 1909 as Volume I of Moral Instruction and Training in Schools, edited by Michael Sadler, who was then Professor of Education at Manchester. Hayward contributes a chapter on "The Need for Improved Moral Instruction", and Adams on "Precept versus Example".

Hayward strove for his ideals of moral and cultural education for another thirty years. In 1919 he and Arnold Freeman published *The Spiritual Foundations of Reconstruction: A Plea for New Educational Methods*, calling for the development of a common tradition of culture. It is not without significance that Sir Fred Clarke took up the same point two decades later at a comparable time of national crisis. In opposition to the "self-activity", "do-as-you-please" ideas which were rapidly gaining ground, the authors advocated the deliberate cultivation of group sentiments by "celebrations", by better, more sincere religious teaching, and by the use of ceremonial and inspiring addresses. The school and its heritage, the nation and its heritage—these should arouse feelings of "admiration, hope, and love". The rational and practical examination of society and citizenship should be a complementary activity of the classroom. Two further suggestions—that "scientific charts of time, space, and history" should be in every school, and that representatives of all parties, sects, professions, and movements should give talks in schools—remind us of Herbartian emphasis on history and on many-sidedness.

Ideas on Education from Abroad: 1897-1918

While many British writers on education were propagating and reinterpreting the doctrines of the great foreign educators of the past, many British teachers were experimenting in the direct application of teaching principles derived from contemporary foreign pioneers in new methods. Salomon's "Sloyd" and Montesorri's "Occupations" are outstanding examples of these new methods.

"Sloyd" was first devised by a Finn, **Uno Cygnaeus,** about the middle of the nineteenth century and it came to Britain during the last few years of the century through the work of **Otto Salomon,** who provided short training courses for foreign teachers at his training college in Sweden. The idea of developing fine handicraft in schools was obviously acceptable to disciples of Ruskin and to the "progressive" educationists. Some schools introduced wood-sloyd before the turn of the century. At Herford's school, Lady-Barn House, girls as well as boys were engaged in it. During the first few years of the twentieth century the word was increasingly applied to school woodwork. Salomon was convinced of the value of "sloyd" training for the ordinary teacher; that is, not merely for the handicraft specialist. He insisted that each member of his groups should gain an intellectual understanding of the principles behind the practical work, and that, despite language difficulties, the student should participate in discussion. Thus the teachers who returned to practice the new methods were particularly fitted to teach other teachers and to justify the inclusion of such practical activities in the school curriculum.

Cygnaeus had been inspired by Froebel. Now Salomon, disciple of Cygnaeus, having established his master's principles, set out to revitalise the whole curriculum, condemning sedentary, verbal learning and aiming to work out intellectual principles for organised games, cookery, needlework, and gardening. Unfortunately, he died in 1907 before accomplishing his task, but the results of his work in wood-sloyd were long felt in Britain. The activity was given significance and status by an insistence on painstaking craftsmanship, involving not only the perfection of manual dexterity but also the exercise of mental faculties in the execution of the task. This involved the grading of skills and tasks so that a boy would set out to make an article within his capacity though requiring pains, judgment, perseverance, and, moreover, the mental planning of operations and the utilisation of critical faculties. The article was required to be useful to the boy when finished—and finished it had to be. In theory, the young workman would learn to be neat, clean, efficient with tools, accurate, and independent in the process of manufacturing. In theory, he had to aim at skill in making difficult articles without a pattern. In theory, he ought to have the rich experience of fashioning splendid things from primary materials —from the unsawn log. In theory, the whole of education, all subjects, could be built up on this basic, essential human activity.

When we read of Dewey's similar belief in woodwork, we are reminded of "sloyd". In practice, of course, the success or failure of any scheme depends on the skill, knowledge, and guiding ability of the teacher.

It was inevitable that the high aims of the pioneers should fall by the wayside, for few schools would reorganise their whole curriculum at the demands of a "sloyd" teacher, and few of the latter could ensure that every single pupil would struggle through, without disappointment or frustration, to the achievement of a perfectly-made article. The main value of the "sloyd" movement in England was to join in the attack on the academic, verbalised curriculum that Adams and the Herbartians had already launched, and that Montesorri was approaching from another viewpoint. Until 1918, however, handicraft remained a luxury, outside the ordinary curriculum of elementary schools. The staff of handicraft centres were usually instructors who were rarely trained teachers. The Act of 1918 required that practical work should be included in the elementary school curriculum.

Maria Montessori (1870-1952) did not start her main educational work with children until 1907, yet before the outbreak of the First World War she had many disciples in this country and her methods were being practised by hundreds of teachers who had been initiated into them by the great woman pioneer herself. By 1907, Montessori had already achieved what was unusual success in an unusual sphere for a woman—a position at the University of Rome as a doctor of medicine. Her participation in education began with her interest in the reconditioning of some of the city's tenement buildings. It was difficult to know how to preserve the new standards of sanitation and cleanliness, and it was decided to open an infant school on the premises, partly to care for tenants' children while the mothers were at work and partly to try to inculcate habits of cleanliness and respect for property. The first classroom was on the ground floor and opened on to a garden, which was eventually used as children's gardens. This was the first "Casa del Bambini", or children's house, and others were soon established in other parts of the building and in other tenement blocks.

When the philanthropic director of the company owning the tenements appointed Montessori to the headship of the first school, he knew she was fitted for the work by interest and experience. She had already worked in a psychiatric clinic and had directed a centre for mentally defective children. Moreover, she had gained qualifications in experimental psychology and anthropological pedagogy by a long course of study, and she was entirely competent to develop the new enterprise. Starting as a private, philanthropic venture, its value, from both social and educational viewpoints, became so evident that the example was followed not only by charitable organisations, such as the Humanitarian Society of Milan, but also by local authorities, such as the municipality of Naples. Two further developments followed rapidly—the setting up, on similar principles and methods, of schools for children over six, and the creation of institutes for the training of teachers in the new methods.

The publication of *The Montessori Method* in 1912[1] proved to be excellent propaganda for a new "movement" which took hold in U.S.A. and Britain. The introduction of short training courses —of about four months' duration—drew hundreds of teachers to sit at the feet of Montessori. Although at first the courses were held in Italy, Montessori now started her long career of missionary work in foreign lands, teaching abroad at first for the sake of education itself, and later because there was no freedom to teach at home. In the 'thirties the German Montessori Society was dissolved by the Hitler authorities and the Italian Montessori schemes were suspended under Mussolini. In Britain the "movement" itself has always flourished, although limited by its association with Catholicism. The spirit of Montessori transcends sectarian barriers, however, and her methods, although by no means adequate for the modern concept of education, have served our schools well in pointing the way to intellectual and social development through practical activities.

Montessori's approach to education is that of the scientist. She reverts to Rousseau's view of the teacher as an organiser of environment, a person deeply concerned with the intellectual and emotional experiences of pupils, yet not actively participating in the events and engagements. The teacher's task is to see that there exists within reach of the child a choice of occupations, and that when the choice has been made, there should be no interruptions. The teacher must also devise material likely to attract the pupil to occupy himself with it. Moreover, the material should not only have a didactic purpose (as, for instance, the manipulation of buttons and buttonholes, the discrimination between light and

---

[1] Followed in 1913 by Culverwell's *Montessori Principles and Practice*, G. Bell & Son.

heavy, long and short, the recognition of colour, etc.), but should also be self-corrective, that is, capable of correct solution by trial and error.

The fact that a great deal of such material already existed owing to the inventive ingenuity of Montessori and her colleagues, may possibly account for the acceptance of these ideas in our infant schools. Froebel's "gifts", the solid geometric shapes used in constructive play (and originally conceived as "symbols to unlock the child's soul") must have seemed rather dull and limited against the intriguing variety of frames and form-boards provided for the new methods. Although the latter are now regarded as old-fashioned, they had the great advantage of stimulating senses often neglected but still useful to man—touch, smell, hearing. Modern apparatus for teaching number and reading is partly derived from the Montessorian, and modern infant and nursery schools empha-sise, as did Montessori, the individual nature of these learning experiences. But they also retain the Froebelian belief in creative, expressive activities—free drawing and painting, imaginative story-telling—and a faith in the kind of group activities rejected by Montessori.

Montessori's idea of a group is of individuals of different ages, each proceeding with his own occupation at his own rate, free from pressure by the teacher, and free from the rivalry of others. The teacher is there to give help as individuals require it. The older children are also to give help to their younger fellows. There is co-operation in small household tasks, such as serving food and clearing the table, but there are no collective games or singing. There is provision for free play, and a careful supervision of health and physical growth. There are no rewards and punishments.

Of the extension of Montessorian principles to the secondary school, it need only be said that Montessorians continued to invent apparatus for the self-teaching of most ordinary subjects of the curriculum. In the case of number and grammar, for instance, the apparatus took the form of boxes divided into compartments con-taining number groups or parts of speech, tables, shapes, cards, and other devices for providing individual children with practical material leading to purposive manipulation and thinking. The moral and social virtues—community service, self-control, manners, and poise were taught by suggestion, by atmosphere, and by practice in school affairs.

Thus the Montessorians provided a very adequate reply to suggestions that Madame Montessori, because of her early absorption in the education of mentally sub-normal children, failed to provide fully for the capacities and potentialities of normal children. At this distance of time it can be appreciated that Montessori's example in providing for individual development through practical activities was followed by a number of enterprising innovators who would not call themselves Montessorians. It might even be suggested that modern secondary school subjects would be more significant to many young people if they could be approached by practical and individual methods.

Space will not permit discussion of all notable educators of the first part of the century, but an all too brief reference must be made to the work and ideas of **Homer Lane.** While Margaret McMillan's aim was to foster the emotional development of youngsters, Lane's task was to straighten out emotional development that had gone wrong—much as Miss McMillan's primary problems was to remedy physical ills and weaknesses. Lane contended that human beings need freedom for the growth of their own powers of control and judgment. He believed they also needed the kind of love that gave respect, appreciation, and approval.

Homer Tyrell Lane was an American who came to England in 1913 to initiate a new Home Office scheme for the treatment of young delinquents. Lane, who had achieved success in establishing and conducting the Ford Republic, a boys' home in U.S.A.,[1] was earnestly intent on proving that a much more free kind of residential community would be even more successful in the rehabilitation of young offenders. He had trained as a teacher at the Boston Sloyd Training School, but his main interest had become psychology and child development. He had seized every opportunity to study children through voluntary work in hospitals, playgrounds, evening classes, and even prisons.

The story of the rise and fall of the Little Commonwealth must be left for the reader to seek in Miss Bazeley's book,[2] but the ideas of Homer Lane must be set alongside Miss McMillan's for their freshness, originality, intellectual penetration, and depth of feeling and sympathy. The Little Commonwealth was a State reformatory, but it was also a group of families held together by bonds of

[1] This was not the only experiment of its kind in U.S.A. See W. R. George, *Citizens Made and Remade* and *The Junior Republic*.
[2] Bazeley, E. T., *Homer Lane and The Little Commonwealth*, Allen and Unwin, 1928.

affection and responsibility. Lane took young offenders—both boys and girls—from the Magistrates' Courts, and allowed them to adjust themselves to the social conventions established by the "citizens" already in the colony. All citizens were engaged in earning a living by performing farm and family duties, and each group of youngsters — each family — was responsible for the debts and expenses incurred by its members. The citizens evolved their own system of self-government, their own standards of cleanliness, behaviour, and virtue, and they actually reached the stage of demanding formal education.

Lane maintained that his function was to give opportunities for this kind of self-development, and to show nothing but love and respect towards each citizen, even in the face of hooliganism. The new venture aroused a great deal of public interest, and Lane frequently lectured on his work. In 1916 he gave several lectures at South Kensington, and one of these, describing the early days of the Commonwealth, was published in *Four Lectures on Childhood*, edited by H. H. Symonds. "My function has been to encourage all activity, bad as well as good", he said. When asked by the citizens to restrain an unruly group of new boys, he explained: "We came here to do as we liked, and so long as we liked to break windows, yell, take fruit, and live at the expense of others, we would do so. If at any time we felt like doing something else that was more fun, we would do so". Lane defined the duty of a parent as, "to encourage all experiments of the child and assist him in reaching such conclusions as he will adopt as his own, so that he may, by the process of elimination, discard futile and false ideals".

In a lecture of 1919, Lane said: "Shall we adopt a method of teaching the old Mosaic system of attempting to destroy evil as though it were a positive force, in order to make room for good, or shall we adapt ourselves to reality (which involves ignorance) and try to make good more attractive than evil? I feel that evil is merely ignorance, that it is not a positive thing, but only is some previous good that the universe has outgrown . . . We must hate ideas that are destructive but never people, then we realise the good that is always there in everyone . . . We only gain ground by living lovingly".

Homer Lane's own book, *Talks to Parents and Teachers*, was not published until 1928, but his lectures, and his work as a psychologist after the closing of the Commonwealth made known his ideas during the post-war years. He always emphasised that one had first to get rid of authority in dealing with delinquents, because that has been the only order previously known to them. He deemed it essential that each youngster should find his own order, through freedom to exercise his own responsibility. To-day, this belief is held not only by many workers dealing with delinquents but also by most enlightened teachers and parents.

The Fertile Ground

At this distance of time it is abundantly clear that the pioneers and prophets of the first part of the century were not merely one-track minds ploughing parallel, never-meeting furrows in the abstract meadows of educational theory. By this time the teaching profession was expanding rapidly, not only through the normal development of elementary education, but also by the influx of highly educated men and women to whom the firm establishment of secondary education meant the opening up of careers in which their abilities could be exploited. Never before in history had the theorists, the innovators, the experimenters gained so much intelligent attention from so many practising teachers. Not that the latter were more receptive than the disciples of the old leaders— they were probably more resistant to "sales-talk". It was inevitable, however, that among the more enterprising spirits were those who found justification for the new ideas in their own work and beliefs.

It is appropriate, therefore, to conclude this examination of educational ideas in the first two decades of the century by indicating briefly some of the evidence of the spread of new ideas and attitudes among teachers concerned with the everyday problems of ordinary schools and "normal" children. First, just before the Great War, came a disturbing book by Edmond Holmes, who had been H.M. Chief Inspector of Elementary Schools. *What Is and What Might Be* (Constable, 1911) was a condemnation of the methods of teaching then prevalent throughout the country. Holmes emphasised the stultifying effects on children of passivity and repression by contrasting such conditions with the freedom and activity found in Miss Finlay Johnson's village school in Sussex. An inspector campaigning for the abolition of obedience to authority as a guiding principle in life! This was indeed a challenge to all teachers, and it is safe to assume that any British teacher who ventured on "freedom", "activity", and "play" experiments at this time, had read this book and had been encouraged and invigorated by it. This was certainly true of two outstanding teacher-writers, Norman MacMunn and Caldwell Cook. It was also true of a teacher who has always been too busy to write, E. F. O'Neill.

MacMunn was an Oxford graduate and a teacher of modern languages at King Edward VI School, Stratford-on-Avon. His book, *A Path to Freedom in the School* (Bell, 1914), reveals him as an innovator in "activity methods" and self-government in his own sphere, but it also records his discipleship of Montessori and Homer Lane. In his Preface he writes: "As the doctrines of Rousseau were to the social revolution of yesterday, so, it seems to many of us, the doctrines of Montessori will be to the educational revolution of tomorrow. But just as the message of Rousseau was reinforced by the words and actions of other leaders of intellectual revolt, so we, our minds ripe for change, are finding other sources of inspiration in collateral movements for the emancipation of the young. Of these, none is more wonderful and more inspiring than the Little Commonwealth for young delinquents directed by Mr. Homer Lane".[1] Tributes are also paid to other "leaders of the movement for the emancipation of the child", Mr. Edmond Holmes, Professor Culverwell, and Professor John Adams.

MacMunn's principles—which he appears to have practised with some success—are based on individual work at individual rates, or "differentialism", as he called it. But his scheme is not merely a forerunner of the Dalton Plan, for he envisaged that although each pupil would work at his own task and solve his own problems, he would at the same time teach a fellow pupil and in return be taught by him. Each boy would be engrossed in something different from his colleague, and so each would have new things to teach the other. The teacher's problems of organisation—so that all the bits of learning are related, relevant, and progressive—are very obvious, but the scheme does cope with the problem of encouraging both individual and co-operative effort.

Although MacMunn is confident that such methods lead to greater intellectual effort and achievement, it is clear that, to him, their effects upon character and self-discipline far outweigh other considerations. One suspects that his concept of complete liberty in a controlled environment smacks more of Rousseau than of Montessori, but, of course, the psychology of his day, especially theories on the nature and function of play, also influenced his

[1] MacMunn, N., *A Path to Freedom in the School*, p. 7, Bell, 1914.

thinking. He describes the "natural" child as not liking to be helped, and as "struggling with infinite patience to reach a self-proposed goal".[1] In his emphasis on the youngster's need for "slight but constant difficulties" to overcome, he is saying very much what John Dewey had been saying for a number of years in U.S.A. Later, A. N. Whitehead was to make the same point in his *Aims of Education*.

MacMunn states the whole aim and purpose of his own teaching when he urges the right of children "to establish and maintain the principles of their own discipline".[2] He means intellectual discipline as well as any other kind. "Once our children are free", he contends, "their will is to gain power on the lines of the interest placed before them. Thus if we desire to make them tidy, we need and should say little about the negative untidiness, but let them see first, if necessary by games, and then by suggestion, that the effort to be tidy, like every other effort, can be a manifestation of natural activity".[3] This points the way to a moral education more effective than the old precepts and prohibitions.

Both Norman MacMunn and his contemporary, Caldwell Cook, put forward the ideal of a Commonwealth School, that is, a self-governing community following Lane's principles. MacMunn's own innovation was the idea of partnership. "Each boy will have a private tutor", he maintained, "in addition to a series of intellectual directors to feed the tutors with ever-new knowledge".[4] This book was reprinted several times in the years that followed. In 1926, Sir Percy Nunn wrote the preface to a new edition, now entitled *The Child's Path to Freedom*.

H. Caldwell Cook, in his *Play Way* (Heinemann, 1917), makes no mention of Homer Lane, nor, indeed, of any other living educator except Holmes and MacMunn—the latter only in a footnote because he disagreed with the use of partnership as a basic method, although he used it as subsidiary device. Cook is, in fact, by no means polite in his comments on pedagogy. It is probable that it was identified in his mind with psychology, for he writes: "As the artist creates in a flash that which critics take years to expound, so the playboy gaily produces innumerable works of self-expression, while his teachers are fumbling blindly in the murk of theoretical psychology. Education will always be the stodgy process it is to-day, until teachers throw the pedagogical professors overboard

[1] MacMunn, N., *A Path to Freedom in the School*, p. 21, Bell, 1914.
[2] *ibid.*, p. 8.　　　[3] *ibid.*, p. 58.　　　[4] *ibid.*, p. 149.

and turn their whole attention upon the boys. Pedagogy, forsooth! The very word reeks of humbug. Play, sir, is what you need for boys." [1]

Whatever the derivation of his idea, Cook's chapters hold a lasting magic for those who enjoy teaching and who are not partial to "sit-stillery". Much of his material was collected—and some published as articles—before the war, but in welding it together he was looking ahead to a Better World. "The Play Way is an endeavour to achieve right conduct in a true blend of the functioning of all man's powers. If it is true to say that we must not act without thinking, why is it not equally true to say we must not think without acting?" [2] He saw school education as a many-sided active life—he calls it "general education"—in which boys should learn how to *do* in order to learn, and how to learn in order to do.

Cook was a genius in the application of play methods to the teaching of English. He felt deeply that such methods could be applied throughout schools, not as diversions but as active ways of learning. His own pupils really did lap up poetry, pour out verse, act plays, make plays, speechify, and make models. They organised themselves with the greatest efficiency because they hated to miss a moment of the English lesson. It is true that they grew accustomed "to command without a trace of domineering and to obey without a taint of servility". [3] Cook gives us a view of educational fashion of his day by commenting that it was unnecessary to justify self-government, as it was "one of the cardinal tenets in most proposed reforms". [4] It is not unlikely that his condemnation of "spoon feeding and repression" stemmed from Edmond Holmes, for he writes: "Apart from a few foundations recognised as progressive or experimental, school as we know it to-day is a gigantic humbug" [5]—a sweeping generalisation for a young teacher to make. One significant plea he makes, however—that teachers should not wait until they get into ideal schools before trying to initiate reforms. The place for the reformer, however modest and limited his effort, is in the schools where most children are taught.

Cook pays indirect tribute to Homer Lane by referring to the Little Commonwealth and by calling his own ideal the Play School Commonwealth. He feels that much more of "subject" material

[1] Caldwell Cook, H., *The Play Way, An Essay in Educational Method*, Heinemann, p. 169, 1917.
[2] *ibid.*, p. 15.   [3] *ibid.*, p. 47.   [4] *ibid.*, p. 54.   [5] *ibid.*, p. 55.

could be made significant and relevant to citizenship and current events. He damns Civics as tame and inadequate, failing entirely to deal with social evils and political wire-pulling. His concept of school as "a little world in itself" may seem different from John Dewey's, but both men saw school as a place where youngsters should meet the problems of the contemporary world outside.

In 1914, when Cook was contributing his articles on his methods to *The New Age*, Edmond Holmes and seven others were setting up a new organisation called "The Conference of the New Ideals in Education". At its first meeting it discussed Montessori's methods. Four years later the Conference heard a young teacher, Edward F. O'Neill, speak on "Developments in Self-activity in an Elementary School". The following year, 1919, at Cambridge, the same young man addressed the same large body, introduced by Edmond Holmes himself, who had been immensely impressed and enthused by a visit to O'Neill's school. He had wrought wonders during his few months' leadership, and he continued this work at the same school—Prestolee, in Lancashire—for over thirty years. As the story can now be read[1], it must suffice to suggest that Mr O'Neill's great ideas, as well as his great gifts and insights, were developed during this period—the second decade of the century— which, in the light of history, is worthy of more attention than it has hitherto received. It seems very probable that a large number of ordinary teachers—and extraordinary ones—were intent upon the improvement of methods of teaching, or rather, of organising learning. The narrow idealistic classicism of the grammar school and the narrow realistic utilitarianism of the elementary school were still strong, but had already been undermined by the Edwardian Herbartians and their like. Curriculum widening, the rejection of the "transfer of training" theory, the aim of preparing the young for citizenship through education—all these prepared the way for the phase of a "freedom" cult largely derived from psychology. By 1919 we see these two "new" protagonists marshalling their forces for the struggle which later saw the rout of the Herbartians. For the Herbartians were "man-makers" and practically abolished Nature from their considerations. The New Realists and the Freudians took great account of natural factors in the development of individuals. Although differing widely in aims and methods, they stood together on the issue of "self-activity" as opposed to the class lesson system. The Herbartians almost took over the

---

[1] Holmes, E., *The Idiot Teacher*, Faber & Faber, 1952.

mantle of the old Idealism in transmitting "the vision of greatness" and inculcating moral standards. Their opponents flew the
flags of "new media", "self-discipline", and "indirect teaching of
morals" (the latter to Hayward's great disgust). Yet there was not
so much difference between the best of them. A school like
O'Neill's may have both individual work and "celebrations", self-
government and country dancing; the dedicated teacher can blend
methods to meet the needs of his pupils.

The widespread nature of the interest in practical experiment
in teaching method may be checked by reference to two books
published about 1920, but dealing with experiments proceeding
during the period under discussion. Alice Woods's *Educational
Experiments in England*[1] ranges widely over different types of
schools and different kinds of experiments—the Caldecott Community (a boarding school for the children of working people),
rural studies at Knaresborough, federal government in a northern
high school for girls, a monitorial system in a Midlands elementary
school, "moot" government at Letchworth, freedom at Thorp
Arch Industrial School, the scrapping of the time-table at O'Neill's
school, parent-teacher relations in York, Miss McMillan's open-air
school, Montessori methods at Kirkstall Road Infant Department,
Leeds, Selfridge's day continuation school, and many others.

The second book is *The New Era in Education*, a collection of
articles edited by Ernest Young. Twenty-seven experimental
schemes are included, and the editor asserts that a complete
account of current research would have resulted in a tome "too
big to handle and too expensive to purchase". Charlotte Mason's
"teach yourself" methods are described; Valentine Bell writes on
Local Survey in Lambeth by elementary schoolboys; two school
journeys (one by canal) are outlined; self-activity, independent
study, self-government, partnership, practical civics, scouting, and
the use of museums and libraries—all these topics, and many more,
are dealt with in relation to real schools, real pupils, and real
teachers; the latter including O'Neill and MacMunn.

In retrospect, the healthiest aspect of all this "new education"
is its wide extension into the national system of elementary and
secondary schools. This was the true reflection of the educational
thought of the era. The more celebrated examples of enterprising
schools were often either oddities or anachronisms. Some had
led the way long before the general advance, as in the case of

[1] Methuen, 1920.

Bedales and Oundle. The former was a private co-educational boarding school which, under the guidance of J. H. Badley, enjoyed an unusual measure of freedom and self-government throughout the period.[1] The latter was a public school developed from a declining grammar school by the vigour of F. W. Sanderson,[2] whose belief in workshop activities and science was not only a reflection of Ruskin and Cygnaeus, but also a portent of mid-century trends.

Other Works Representative of the Period

1897   P. A. Barnett: *Teaching and Organisation with Special Reference to Secondary Schools.* Longmans.

C. S. Bremner: *The Education of Girls and Women.* Swan Sonnenschein.

Sophie Bryant: *The Teaching of Morality in the Family and the School.* Swan Sonnenschein.

1898   C. Cookson (ed.): *Essays on Secondary Education.* Clarendon Press.

T. Davidson: *Rousseau and Education According to Nature.* Heinemann.

J. J. Findlay: *Principles of Class Teaching.* Macmillan.

H. Holman: *English National Education.* Blackie.

1899   Annette Churton: *Kant on Education.* Kegan Paul, Trench, Trubner.

J. Fotheringham: *Wordsworth's "Prelude" as a Study of Education.* H. Marshall.

J. Welton: *The Logical Bases of Education.* Macmillan.

1900   B. Bosanquet: *The Education of the Young in Plato's Republic.* C.U.P.

J. MacCunn: *The Making of Character.* U.L.P.

L. Tolstoi: *The Religious Education of the Young.* Free Age Press.

1901   P. A. Barnett: *Commonsense in Education.* Longmans.

K. Groos (trans. Eliz. Baldwin): *Play of Man.* Heinemann.

1902   H. T. Mark: *The Teacher and the Child.* Pilgrim Press.

T. G. Rooper: *Educational Studies and Addresses.* Blackie.

1903   T. C. Allbutt: *On Professional Education.* Macmillan.

Alice Woods (ed.): *Co-education.* Longmans.

[1] Badley, J. H., *Bedales: A Pioneer School.* Methuen, 1923.
[2] Wells, H. G., *The Story of a Great Schoolmaster* . . . [F. W. Sanderson]. Constable, 1924.

1904   Charlotte M. Mason: *Home and School Education*. Kegan Paul.

T. Raymont: *The Principles of Education*. Longmans.

1905   R. L. Leighton: *The Boy and His School*. Murray.

Sir Oliver Lodge: *School Teaching and School Reform*. Williams and Norgate.

1906   Sir N. Lockyer: *Education for National Progress*. Macmillan.

C. Lloyd Morgan: *Psychology for Teachers*. Arnold.

J. Welton: *Principles and Methods of Teaching*. U.T.P.

1907   Sara A. Burstall. *English High Schools for Girls*. Longmans.

F. H. Ellis: *Character Forming in School*. Longmans.

J. W. Harper: *Education and Social Life*. Pitman.

M. W. Keatinge: *Suggestion in Education*. A. C. Black.

F. H. Matthews: *The Principles of Intellectual Education*. C.U.P.

W. E. Urwick: *The Child's Mind. Its Growth and Training*. Arnold.

1908   F. F. Carlton: *Education and Industrial Evolution*. Macmillan.

J. S. Remington: *Education of Tomorrow*. Pitman.

1909   Millicent Mackenzie: *Hegel's Educational Theory and Practice*. Swan Sonnenschein.

Welton and Blandford: *Principles and Methods of Moral Training*. U.T.P.

1910   P. B. Ballard: *Handwork as an Educational Medium*. Geo. Allen.

E. T. Campagnac: *Poetry and Teaching*. Constable.

T. Mark: *The Unfolding of Personality as The Chief Aim in Education*. Unwin.

1911   E. G. A. Holmes: *What is and What Might Be*. Constable.

T. Raymont: *The Use of the Bible in the Education of the Young*. Longmans.

1912   G. Stanley Hall: *Aspects of Child Life and Education*. Ginn.

J. W. Slaughter: *The Adolescent*. Geo. Allen.

1913   B. Bosanquet: *The Value and Destiny of the Individual*. Macmillan.

1913   C. Grant and N. Hodgson: *The Case for Co-Education.* G. Richards.

   E. G. A. Holmes: *The Tragedy of Education.* Constable.

1914   H. Holman: *Séguin and his Physiological Method of Education.* Ginn.

   A. Darroch: *Education and the New Utilitarianism.* Longmans.

   J. Welton: *What Do We Mean By Education?* Macmillan.

   E. Lyttelton: *The Corner-Stone of Education.* Pitman.

1915   B. Dumville: *Teaching, Its Nature and Varieties.* U.T.P.

   A. S. Neill: *A Dominie's Log.* H. Jenkins.

   A. F. Shand: *The Foundations of Character.* Macmillan.

   W. G. Sleight: *Educational Values and Methods.* Clarendon.

1916   B. Branford: *Janus and Vesta.* Chatto and Windus.

   E. T. Campagnac: *Converging Paths.* C.U.P.

   M. W. Keatinge: *Studies in Education.* Black.

   W. H. S. Jones: *How We Learn. Primer of Scientific Method.* C.U.P.

1917   A. C. Benson: *Cambridge Essays on Education.* C.U.P.

   W. Boyd: *From Locke to Montessori.* Harrap.

   Margaret McMillan: *The Camp School.* Allen and Unwin.

   Maria Montessori: *The Advanced Montessori Method.* Heinemann.

   J. H. Simpson: *An Adventure in Education.* Black.

1918   Sir J. Adams: *The New Teaching.* Hodder and Stoughton.

   P. J. Hartog: *Examinations and their Relation to Culture and Efficiency.* Constable.

   K. Richmond: *Education for Liberty.* Collins.

SUGGESTIONS FOR FURTHER READING

Curtis and Boultwood, *A Short History of Educational Ideas,* **4th** edition, U.T.P., 1965. Chapters XVIII, XIX.

Sir J. Adams, *Modern Developments in Educational Practice,* U.L.P., 1922.

D'Arcy Cresswell, *Margaret McMillan, a Memoir,* Hutchinson, 1949.

E. M. Standing, *Maria Montessori. Her Life and Work,* Hollis and Carter, 1957.

CHAPTER XI

TWENTIETH-CENTURY THOUGHT ON EDUCATION
(continued)

The Fisher Act of 1918 promised the upward and outward expansion of school education, and although the high purpose of this Act was doomed to frustration, the spirit of the teaching profession remained alert and enterprising throughout the 'twenties, buoyed up by the anticipation of the imminent implementation of the Act. Experiment was in the air, and there are ample records of innumerable innovations in teaching and organisation. For a decade after the war the general attitude of teachers, trainers, professors, and administrators was one of open-mindedness. The schemes and experiments were almost all devoted to the kind of education defined by Adams as "paidocentric".

Yet, in spite of the richness of British writings on education, it is proposed to consider first in this section a foreign educator, John Dewey. Although, chronologically, he might appear to belong to the preceding period, in spirit as well as in fact he is best seen against a background of eager, interested, and co-operative teachers. Dewey was known to the intelligentsia of European education before the First World War,[1] but his teaching had but limited influence in this country until the post-war period—when many points of his doctrine had been rendered significant by the changes brought by the great upheaval.

John Dewey (1859-1952) was nearly sixty when the war ended, but his most famous book, *Democracy and Education*, had been published only two years earlier in the U.S.A. The experimental work which had formulated and fixed his theory of education was nearly twenty years behind him, but he was to remain a force in the world of education for a further thirty years. Dewey started life as an ordinary New England country boy who passed through his country's public school system to the university and acquitted himself so brilliantly that after a very short period of school teaching he was appointed to a university post. He had read philosophy, history, and psychology, and, as American universities reflected at that time the German pattern, it was almost inevitable that he

---

[1] In *The Primary Curriculum* (1909), F. H. Hayward writes: "Dr Dewey's *School and the Child* is fifty years in advance of present day educational thought in England; but the student may well study it for the vistas it opens up. Dr Dewey is one of the few educational writers who have something to say" (p. 410).

should become a professor of philosophy and education. With Dewey, education was no mere sideline. In both fields, his work was brilliant and significant.

During the last few years of the nineteenth century, Dewey developed the Laboratory School in connection with his department of the University of Chicago.[1] Admitting his debt to Froebel, Dewey insisted that the school should be conducted like a good kindergarten. He selected teachers who were trained in Froebelian methods—although the school catered for children up to thirteen. He stressed that he held to Froebel's aims; the school was to train children in co-operative and mutually helpful living; the learning activities were to arise from the impulsive attitudes of the pupils; the teacher was to notice how these individual tendencies became engaged in the process of living together, so that he (the teacher) could learn how to introduce into the school, at the child's level, the occupations and pursuits of the outside world.

The freedom of the teachers to experiment in the introduction of activities which might engage the interest of pupils, resulted in the gradual evolution of a new curriculum. This lengthy experiment enabled Dewey to make the claim which shook the educational world to its foundations—that the whole of school education could be based on cooking, textile making, and workshop activities. Dewey wrote several books during this period, the three most significant being *My Pedagogic Creed* (1897), *The School and Society* (1899), and *The Child and the Curriculum* (1902),[2] all of which give the layman a clear idea of Dewey's aims and methods and the reasons for his viewpoint—a viewpoint which remained practically unmodified through his long career.

From 1904 onwards he was Professor of Philosophy at Columbia University, New York, but his concern for, and participation in, educational experiment and discussion, continued so fully and fruitfully that he was recognised as a leader in Europe as well as America during the years preceding the First World War. After the war, he spent a considerable time teaching in the Far East, and was in world-wide demand as an adviser, lecturer, and leader. Perhaps the first of his books to reach any large number of English teachers was *How We Think* (1910), although his earlier *School*

[1] J. J. Findlay's *Principles of Class Teaching* (Macmillan, 1902) has thirteen references to this work as described in *The Elementary School Record* (Chicago University Press).

[2] English version, *The School and the Child* (Blackie, 1906) included *The Child and the Curriculum* and some essays from *The Elementary School Record*. Editor, Professor J. J. Findlay, of Manchester.

and Society was also published in this country. Of wider influence, however, were two of his wartime books, *Schools of Tomorrow* (with Evelyn Dewey) and *Democracy and Education*, published in 1915 and 1916 in U.S.A. and a little later in Britain. The first described his school experiments and the second was a timely and relevant argument that education ought to be more than mere instruction—that school is a place for living, working citizens, a place where youngsters gain worth-while experience both as individuals and as members of groups. Perhaps Homer Lane drew some of his own inspiration from such ideas.

Of Dewey's many other books on education, the student will find of particular interest *Experience and Education*, published in 1938. In it are found almost all the characteristics, the viewpoints, the attitudes, and the idiosyncracies that any commentator on Dewey would wish to emphasise. His debt to German philosophy, particularly Hegelian, is revealed in the preface beginning thus: "All social movements involve conflicts which are reflected intellectually in controversies . . . It is the business of an intelligent theory of education to ascertain the causes for the conflicts that exist, and then, instead of taking one side or the other, to indicate a plan of operations proceeding from a level deeper and more inclusive than is represented by the practices and ideas of the contending parties".

Dewey's attitude towards traditional principles and methods is then shown by his plea that mere compromise be avoided and that "a new order of ideas and activities" be developed, in spite of the great difficulties which always arise when tradition and custom are discarded. He points out that the pressure of such difficulties had led to "a return to what appear to be simpler and more fundamental ideas and practices of the past". In 1938, as to-day, many educators were seeking inspiration from ancient Greece. Dewey always maintains that the custom of inculcating knowledge and ideas of the past—usually through books—is both harmful and useless. The young are too immature, too inexperienced for the subject-matter and methods used; the subject-matter itself is too static, too much of the past, to be of use to those who will live on into the future.

Dewey also restates his attitude towards freedom and discipline. In a Dewey school, the cult of individuality would not mean licence; freedom of activity would not mean that nothing worth while would be learnt. The disciplining of the self through the experiences provided by the school is an essential part of the educative process. The achievement of enough experience to be able to proceed to the study of organised subject-matter is a very desirable part of the educative process. Furthermore, it matters very much what kind of experience each youngster obtains at the formative stages. Experience itself is not necessarily educative— it must be the right kind of experience for the young person at the stage at which he is. "Some experiences are mis-educative", writes Dewey,[1] having particularly in mind many of the experiences of traditional education. Thus the teacher's task is "to arrange for the kind of experiences which, while they do not repel the student, but rather engage his activities, are nevertheless, more immediately enjoyable since they promote having desirable future experiences".[2] This rejects a current idea that "new" methods such as Dewey's, tend to dispense with the teacher as the active, controlling spirit in the classroom.

The same point, in a wider context, is made in a discussion of education for democracy. It is for the adult community to decide to make the education of its children into the humane, kindly, and fruitful development that ought to proceed from a humane, kindly, and forward-looking democracy. Dewey has no hesitation in admitting that biological habit-formation must play its part in the evolution of the decent, tolerant, sympathetic, co-operative citizen of a democracy.

Thus, the Deweyan teacher has the great responsibility for helping the young to evaluate experience. "It is the business of the educator to see in what direction an experience is heading", writes Dewey. "There is no point in his being more mature if, instead of using his greater insight to help organise the condition of the experience of the immature, he throws away his insight . . . The educator is false to the understanding that he should have obtained from his own past." [3]

In addition, the teacher needs to observe the growth of attitudes and habitual tendencies in youngsters, so that any attitudes detrimental to continued growth may be remedied by the provision of new experiences. The teacher needs to understand individual pupils, and to be able to read their minds. The contacts and influences experienced by a child are all-important, whether human or physical, and whatever the home, the locality, and the abilities

---

[1] Dewey J., *Experience and Education*, p. 13, Macmillan, 12th Reprint, 1950.
[2] *ibid.*, p. 16.   [3] *ibid.*, p. 32.

of each child, he needs the help of his teachers to extract from these physical and social surroundings the kind of experiences that lead to growth and more growth. The teacher is a protector and a shield from harm, as is the parent, but he is also an engineer of situations in which takes place that "interaction" which is the essence of experience. He must also arrange that these experiences have continuity, that they expand, develop, progress, and grow.

Another of Dewey's main concepts emphasised in *Experience and Education* is that education must take into account that human life is lived in groups, and that an essential part of individual growth is the acceptance of social controls or, rather, intelligent participation in the formulation of desirable social controls. He cites as an example games and the team spirit, but he feels that children should learn many other things together. He appreciates the difficulty of developing a self-disciplined, active community from a group of individuals with varied backgrounds and previous experience, but he believes that careful planning can achieve it. Here, gently but firmly, he dissociates himself from the kind of American "progressivism" which was at that time motivating a large number of teachers. Dewey points out that while the willingness to give children freedom should be applauded, anti-social behaviour and backwardness in learning must be expected unless the educators' plan has provided opportunities to learn "one of the most important lessons of life, that of mutual accommodation and adaptation".[1] Although he often denied the existence of aims of education, Dewey here affirms, "The ideal aim of education is creation of power of self-control".[2]

Dewey urges that the learning process itself should be the active, outward reaching of the human organism that he discussed many years earlier in *How the Mind Works*. The school should provide stimuli to arouse the child's impulses so that he formulates his own genuine and personal purpose for entering upon some activity. He suggests that the formation of purposes needs three elements—observation, previous knowledge, and judgment. These elements are translated into a plan of action, a consideration of possible consequences, and a decision whether or not to carry out the plan. He suggests that the "progressive" schools often forget the elements of foresight and judgment, so that activities spring

---

[1] Dewey J., *Experience and Education*, p. 68, Macmillan, 12th Reprint, 1950.
[2] *ibid.*, p. 75.

from mere impulses and desires. It is clear that Dewey intends the teacher to share in the discussion and consideration of plans of action, and so help the development of intelligent foresight and judgment. Traditional education ignores personal impulses and provides no guidance in personal planning. But the traditional teacher is no more at fault than the supposedly enlightened teacher who provides a wealth of objects and materials in his classroom yet does not suggest how they might be used. "The suggestion upon which pupils act must in any case come from somewhere", writes Dewey. "It is impossible to understand why a suggestion from one who has a larger experience and a wider horizon should not be at least as valid as a suggestion arising from some more or less accidental source." [1] He does not mean that the teacher shall impose his suggestion on the pupils, but that he shall encourage discussion of one or more suggestions so that the whole group may reach a decision to embark on "a co-operative enterprise". Dewey describes the process as "reciprocal give-and-take, the teacher taking, but not being afraid also to give". [2]

In many other ways, Dewey emphasises that the Deweyan teacher is no mere bystander. He must certainly select and plan the experiences of pupils so that they have practice in tackling new and more complex problems which develop further their foresight and judgment. He must also see that the essential experience and knowledge acquired by the human race is mastered and made useful for the future. As an example, although the young cannot study science in an adult way, they need to be introduced to scientific subject-matter "and be initiated into its facts and laws through acquaintance with everyday social applications". [3] Although the teacher should not "start with knowledge already organised, and proceed to ladle it out in doses", [4] he should aim to foster in his pupils the growth and organisation of facts and ideas.

Finally, while always stressing the need for rich social experiences, Dewey again confounds his critics by repeating that learning and intellectual organisation is an individual business and that each youngster can only develop himself by constant practice in testing his own ideas or hypotheses in the pursuit of his individual aims and purposes.

Space will not permit discussion of Dewey's pragmatic philosophy, often known as Instrumentalism, but the influence of such

[1] Dewey J., *Experience and Education*, pp. 84-5, Macmillan, 12th Reprint, 1950.   [2] *ibid.*, p. 85.   [3] *ibid.*, p. 98.   [4] *ibid.*, p. 102.

philosophical ideas on British teachers was far more limited than the inspiration given by his practical suggestions for making school work more fruitful for the pupil and more relevant to the needs of a rapidly changing world. Dewey's own school organisation became known as "The Problem Method" because it was planned to give youngsters practice in pursuing intelligently activities they themselves felt to be worth while. Of course, they were usually tempted by subtle suggestion into such activities by the cunning of good teachers. Many attempts to follow similar schemes failed because this latter factor was ignored.

Dewey's disciples, particularly William Kilpatrick, worked out more fully in theory the concept of problem-solving under the term "Project Method", a form of Deweyism which became better known in this country and was put into practice widely during the inter-war period.[1] Some schools, such as Dartington Hall, were able to test the method fully and fairly—children might be found building their own boat, setting up their own stage, and carrying through their schemes to completion. But the general school system could not throw off entirely its traditions, and thus the resultant compromise, so distrusted by Dewey, led inevitably to a reaction against new-fangled notions.

The ideas of two other American educators obtained a firm, although limited, foothold in English schools during the same period. Helen Parkhurst's "Dalton Plan", and Carleton Washburne's "Winnetka Plan" had much in common with Dewey's scheme for individual growth, in that they abolished routine class learning and gave each pupil the opportunity to learn and progress at his own rate. The Dalton Plan in particular appealed to many English teachers, perhaps because they were able to gain some of its advantages by a modified form of individual assignment work, even if the schools themselves did not turn over to a "laboratory" system. Many schools had specialist rooms and laboratories, but only a few abolished class organisation and allowed pupils to work in subject laboratories by free choice—as did Miss Parkhurst and her colleagues.

English Writings on Education Between the Wars

Although Dewey's ideas can be traced in English experiment and theory of the second decade of the century, it is a little

---

[1] See Gull, Hilda K. F., *Projects in the Education of Young Children*, McDougall's, *circa*, 1926.

surprising that his name is only occasionally mentioned by writers of that period.[1] In the 1920's, however, Dewey on the one hand, and "new psychology" on the other, were acknowledged to be the stimuli producing a more widespread revolt against traditional methods, and in particular against the oral instruction of passive, regimented classes. Would-be reformers often appeared to recommend the throwing out of both bath-water and baby, while the kind of educational experiments which gained publicity were very frequently of a type which the layman would judge as "too extreme to be sound". Thus it was quite soon after the war that the Neills started Summerhill, and A. S. Neill began the series of readable, provoking books that made his school known to far more people than its visitors. Yet, writing in 1945, Neill said, "Summerhill is not mine; it belongs to a collective movement that embraces many —Freud, Reich, Homer Lane, Norman MacMunn, Caldwell Cook, Edmond Holmes, educationists in Europe and America of whom I have never heard".[2] But not John Dewey? It would be dangerous to generalise on one example, but it seems possible that the methods and motives of the psychologists were producing in England very much the same results as in America, except that the reaction against "progressive" education was not so violent here as in U.S., and, therefore, Dewey was not blamed so heartily or so wrongfully for the less acceptable results of what might be called the revolution in education.

Reaction was certainly not strong enough to bring the new movement to a standstill. Traditionalism in its old form suffered a real defeat, and those who could not accept the new realist and pragmatic concepts were faced with the task of keeping alive the flame of the old idealism until such a time as the torches could be re-lit. The spirit of Plato and the Arnolds was perpetuated by the few, among them Professor Campagnac[3] and Richard Winn Livingstone, the latter writing little specifically on education after his *Defence of Classical Education* of 1917 until his emergence as a leader of thought on education during the second war.

When, in 1938, Frank Hayward looked back over this period, critical of the cult of freedom and embittered by lack of public interest in more moderate and unsensational reforms in education,

[1] *E.g.* Norman MacMunn commends warmly Dewey's concept of discipline.
[2] Neill, A. S., *Hearts not Heads in the School*, p. 35, Herbert Jenkins Ltd, 1945.
[3] Campagnac, E. T. (Professor of Education, University of Liverpool), *Education in its Relation to the Common Purposes of Humanity*, Pitman, 1925.

he concluded that of all the publications on this topic only one was worthy of mention—Percy Nunn's *Education, Its Data and First Principles*. As this has remained one of the main textbooks in the study of education for nearly forty years, it may well prove to be a classic of the half-century. It was, no doubt, a stabilising influence during a period of change and uncertainty.

Sir Thomas Percy Nunn (1870-1944), the successor of Sir John Adams as Director of the London Day Training College, won his early reputation as a scientist and a philosopher. Adams's leaning towards a realist theory of education set the stage for Nunn's later work in this sphere, but in the days before the First World War, Nunn's writings in philosophy, though not prolific, won wide recognition among scholars. Passmore describes him as "the first in England to formulate the characteristic doctrines of the New Realism".[1] Bertrand Russell, who helped to make this movement intellectually reputable, thought so highly of Nunn that he asked him to read proofs of his own writings.

Nunn also won the respect of psychologists, who, at last free from the domination of philosophy, were forging a new science. McDougall, whose classic *Outline of Psychology* appeared in 1923, actually used terms coined by Nunn in the expression of his ideas on education, first published in 1920 under the title *Education, Its Data and First Principles*. The best example of this is the use of the Greek *hormé* to signify the outgoing striving of the human organism—individual effort, biological impulse, yet distinctively human endeavour to achieve self-realisation in and through the natural human milieu, society.

In his biological analogies, Nunn has much in common with Dewey. Both believed it to be the nature of the human organism to thrust out eagerly in self-development—an innate urge to perfect and improve the organism and its biological family. Both would agree that the problem of education is to foster this striving upward in the scale of evolution. Both would deplore an education which sought its goal through "self-expression" alone. They shared a liking for the theory that the development of the individual recapitulates the development of the race. They held firmly to a belief in empirical methods of learning, especially for children, and they were convinced that the highest kind of intellectual activity could

[1] Passmore, J., *A Hundred Years of Philosophy*, p. 259, Gerald Duckworth, 1957.

develop from the practical skills and knowledge of the good craftsman.

As Sir Percy's *Education* is readily available, it may be more useful to discuss here some later views expressed in one of the Harrow Lectures of 1930, entitled *The Significance of Science in Education*. He describes science as "one of the typical forms assumed by the creative activity of the human spirit during the long history of its development", and again as "man's age-long effort to enlarge his intellectual control over the universe disclosed to him in space and time". He likens science to poetry in being "a disinterested activity of the creative spirit", yet he regards it equally as "a sublimation of the practical knowledge of the craftsman who is wise in his work".

It is only to be expected that Nunn gives a high place in education not only to science, but to the methods of scientists—methods by which the whole realm of science was opened up. He discusses processes of learning—both long-term and short-term—in relation to three "stages" which have a remarkably close affinity with the stages discussed by his contemporary, A. N. Whitehead, in his own theory of rhythmic cycles of learning.[1]

First comes the Wonder stage, when the youngster enjoys intriguing experiments just "for fun"—perhaps with electricity in the atmosphere. Then follows the Utility stage, when the youngster finds that these curious happenings can be turned to good account to work dynamos, to give light, and to transmit messages. After this, the stage of System is reached, when the pupil is able to review and organise his new knowledge and to distil from it fundamental principles which have wider application. The suggestion that a new stage of Wonder is now reached—at a higher or more complex level—accords very closely with Whitehead's concept of the cyclic progress of learning. To-day, Whitehead's version—"Romance, Precision, Generalisation"—is more widely quoted, but in the inter-war period it was Nunn who influenced teachers and experimenters. In several subject-fields his theory served as a guide in the evolution of principles of teaching method. Thus James Fairgrieve's *Geography in School*,[2] still the best of its kind, owes much to the skilful use of Nunn's concepts.

---

[1] *The Rhythm of Education*—first published as a pamphlet by Christopher in 1922.

[2] Fairgrieve, J., *Geography in School*, U.L.P., 1926.

Nunn's complaint in 1930 was similar to that of Whitehead in 1932—that the commonest mistake in teaching is to assume that pupils are able to start at the system stage. Whereas Whitehead uses the phrase "inert ideas" to explain the result of such mistakes, Nunn makes a plea on behalf of the child. "For the average pupil during the greater part of his school life, the desire to understand how things are made and work, and of what use they are in the big world is by far the strongest motive to intellectual effort. The more we think about the problems of our trade, the more clearly it appears that the full value of the 'system stage' cannot be realised unless it is rigorously postponed to the later years—shall we say the post-certificate years?—of the school course".[1]

For the science teacher, Nunn has a particular word of warning which is still relevant to-day. He urges that science must be a creative activity, not a set of hidebound tenets. "Reality is a movement of certain invisible and intangible entities that lurk behind the veil of sensible phenomena", he points out in criticism of the kind of scientific attitude which defines "patterns which exclude the possibility that there is any place in life for freedom or spontaneity, or what we used to think of as action of mind".[2] His remedy is that more biology should be taught to restore the balance of interest and to "foster the conviction that life has its own irreducible categories with which those of physical science must somehow be reconciled".

To emphasise his anti-mechanistic viewpoint, he concludes: "I am content to believe that life may be wholly permeated by physical and chemical factors, provided that I am allowed also to believe that the autonomy of which my consciousness assures me and which I observe by sympathy in other creatures is not an illusion".[2]

Although, as a philosopher, Sir Percy could not agree with Dr Dewey, as an educator he was warm in his appreciation of the American's beneficial influence on the work of practising teachers. It was largely through the efforts of British professors of education —particularly Nunn and J. J. Findlay, of Manchester—that teachers and students were made intelligently aware of Dewey's ideas, and that Dewey himself was welcomed as a lecturer in this country.

At the same time, the eminent British philosopher **Alfred North Whitehead (1861-1947)**, on his retirement from London University,

---

[1] Nunn, T. P., *The Significance of Science in Education*, p. 125, Harrow, 1930.
[2] *ibid.*, 128.

took up a professorship of Harvard. This interchange of great minds is a notable event in an era which some modern writers have condemned as disillusioned and aimless.[1] Whitehead's ideas on education had matured during that fruitful second decade of the century, so that when he went to U.S.A., he took not only his genius in mathematics and philosophy, but also his version of the New Realists' contribution to educational theory. His *Aims of Education* is a collection of addresses given between 1912 and 1928, treating with clarity and wit a set of topics which never lose their fascination for the educator—a theory of learning, freedom and discipline, technical education, the classics in education, the content of a mathematics course, and the function of universities.

In his practical views on education, Whitehead has much in common with both Nunn and Dewey. With them, he repudiates "freedom" methods in their extreme form and the definition of education as a mere fostering of growth: "He (the teacher) is there to avoid the waste which in the lower stages of existence is nature's way of evolution".[2] With Nunn and Dewey he aims at intellectual excellence and insists that the way towards this starts with particular facts, "concrete and definite for individual apprehension", and not with "general statements which have no reference to individual and personal experiences".[3] He does not recognise a dichotomy between liberal and vocational education: "The antithesis between a technical and a liberal education is fallacious. There can be no adequate technical education which is not liberal, and no liberal education which is not technical; that is, no education which does not impart both technique and intellectual vision. In simpler language, education should turn out the pupil with something he knows well and something he can do well".[4] This is not merely a commonsense viewpoint; it stems from an examination of the weaknesses of Platonic culture. Fred Clarke, a decade later used the same motif in his social theory; to Nunn and Dewey it described the only kind of education worthy of the name.

One of the most quoted points of difference between Nunn and Dewey is, in fact, less a difference between the ideas of the two professors than a difference between two growing bodies of opinion among educationists and teachers. On the one hand is Nunn's

---

[1] See Lester Smith, W. O., *The Impact of Education on Society*, p. 26, Blackwell, 1949.
[2] Whitehead, A. N., *Aims of Education*, p. 62, Williams and Norgate, 1929.
[3] *ibid.*, p. 97. [4] *ibid.*, p. 74.

contention that the supreme educational ideal should be individuality; on the other hand is Dewey's emphasis on the need for social consciousness and efficiency. The two ideas are by no means incompatible, for Nunn indicates clearly that individuality can only flourish in society, and Dewey insists that an effective society can only be made by effective individuals.

The concensus of opinion in England throughout the period was on the side of individualism. Even when writers purported to consider the demands of society, they made little attempt to analyse its needs. In 1921, in discussing the school as a training ground, Nancy Catty maintained: "The community is best served by training every citizen to do the best and the most difficult work that he can accomplish".[1] In the same year, Maxwell Garnett, in a volume based largely on the psychology of William James, implied that education for citizenship involves the widening of individual opportunity within a highly selective national system.[2] In 1922, Professor Campagnac wrote: "The business of education is to give members of a visible state the freedom of the eternal society".[3] About the same time, Crichton Miller gave a reminder of the practical situation: "The possibility of individual achievement is indeed very closely bound up with the principle of group work; for it is often only by the division of labour that an end can be accomplished which satisfies the child's sense of achievement without overtaxing his powers".[4]

In 1924, Professor Millicent Mackenzie discussed, in *Freedom in Education*, ways in which the growing materialism of society could be resisted. Greatly influenced by Edmond Holmes and Rudolph Steiner, she regarded freedom as a spiritual value which would help the youngster to become "a self-controlled, self-governing agent in life".[5] She contended that traditional methods produce in children a docility which "permits the building of artificial personality under the influence of certain forms of religion, philosophy, or social theory".[6] Nevertheless, although she regarded psychology as a useful tool for the teacher, she did not wish to see

[1] Catty, N., *Modern Educational Theory and Its Applications*, p. 93, Sidgwick and Jackson, 1921.

[2] Maxwell Garnett, J. C., *Education and World Citizenship*, C.U.P., 1921.

[3] Campagnac, E. T., *Society and Solitude*, p. 25, C.U.P., 1922.

[4] Crichton Miller, H., *The New Psychology and the Teacher*, p. 231, Jarrolds, 1922.

[5] Mackenzie, M., *Freedom in Education*, p. 26, Hodder and Stoughton, 1924.

[6] *ibid.*, p. 35.

psycho-analysis and mental testing become unduly influential on educational theory.

Towards the end of the first post-war decade, the Headmaster of Harrow School, Dr Cyril Norwood, won aclaim for the wisdom and moderation of his views on education—views which affirmed the current belief in individualism. His book, *The English Tradition of Education*, was widely read, perhaps because it was—as we see in retrospect—little more than a wise and mild commentary on the *status quo*. The problems he sees are often the problems of to-day: "I dream of a time, not so far distant, when this education will extend to the age, not of fifteen but of sixteen, and of a time not so near, but still to be longed for, when all boys from sixteen to eighteen will be formed into groups for continued education, and the instincts which lead them to form gangs and to seek dubious adventures can be sublimated by right occupation and by responsibility into virtues of national value".[1] In realms of educational theory, however, it is clear that he has little faith in "social education" as such. "There are, in fact, no dodges, no methods by which, through education, the progress of events can be rapidly forced, if the foundations are to be secure. If the teachers are convinced, they will pass their convictions on to the children, and the education on which the cause of international peace can be most firmly based is certainly that which is not directed to this specific end, but founded on practical Christianity, culture, and character."[2]

On the other hand, a year later, when lecturing on *Unity and Purpose in Education*, Dr Norwood moves somewhat further from traditionalism in implying that there is no fixed content of education. "It ought to be our common aim", he asserts, "to make education responsive to the needs of our national life, and since these continually change and develop, so ought the content of our education to be continually changing and developing. I mean that we ought to be consciously striving to turn out servants of the community, and within that aim we ought to seek to develop individual character and individual gifts to the full, always with a social reference". It is clear from other comments that Dr Norwood envisages the achievement of a Platonic society in which the masses will be well enough educated to "contentedly accept the direction of those who know".[3]

[1] Norwood, C., *The English Tradition of Education*, p. 187, John Murray, 1929.
[2] *ibid.*, p. 297.   [3] Harrow Lecture, 1930.

Although English educational theory remained basically individualistic, the few years before the Second War saw the strengthening of the opposing viewpoint. In 1931, L. P. Jacks subtitled his new book, *A Plea for a New Spirit in Education*, and defined education as "a social enterprise demanding a general mobilisation of the energy, intelligence, idealism, and courage of the entire community".[1] He also defined it as "that which fits the whole man for his grand vocation as a member of society and a citizen of the world".[2] He preceded Fred Clarke in demanding that society itself be educative, that it provide "a type of education addressed to the whole man, to the whole woman, and not episodes but sustained. For what is the use of educating a child or an adult to the point of fitness and then turning them loose on the world to become unfit next week?"[3] He also emphasised, as Clarke did later, that "no sharp division can be made between leisure occupations and labour occupations. What is labour at one stage may become leisure at another".[4] In 1937, when he was Headmaster of Mill Hill School, Jacks published *Education as a Social Factor*, in which he developed further these ideas which mark a resurgence of idealism in English educational theory. Plato and Matthew Arnold return to the educational scene.

Support for the social viewpoint, and at the same time a reminder that children have their own rights, came from Professor John MacMurray, who, though not an educationist, exercised considerable influence as an eminent scholar deeply concerned with questions related to education. In 1935 he wrote: "Children must grow into wholeness, and the business of early education is to provide carefully and fully for this natural growth in the integration of the natural capacities. The early discipline of personality has to lay the foundation for the development of interdependence and co-operation in joy among all the elements of personality and between children. It is a training in rhythmic co-operation, in doing things that it is a joy to do together, not in learning things that may possibly come in useful later on".[5] While John Dewey might have replied that the experience of co-operation would come in useful later on, he would have had no quarrel with MacMurray's

---

[1] Jacks, L. P., *The Education of the Whole Man*, p. 27, U.L.P., 1931.
[2] *ibid*, p. 39.   [3] *ibid.*, p. 49.   [4] *ibid.*, p. 120.
[5] MacMurray, J., *Reason and Emotion*, p. 151, Faber, 1935.

assertion that "personality is something that only exists between people and which cannot exist in the individual in isolation".[1]

No discussion of these problems nor of this era is complete without a consideration of the views of the philosopher **Bertrand Russell (1872-)**, who has made invaluable contributions to twentieth-century thought on education. Because he has been an intellectual giant of the present post-war period, Russell's educational philosophy cannot be relegated to a past era. Because he is a great philosopher, his ideas on education cannot be dismissed as outmoded. Yet history will probably judge that he is the British representative *par excellence* of the movement which prevailed in education during the inter-war period throughout the democracies of the Western world. In philosophy, its followers may have belonged to a number of schools of thought—Russell himself changed the name of his own brand of philosophy from time to time—but if we use the term scientific humanism to cover these generally realist viewpoints, it describes reasonably well the attitude of Nunn, Whitehead, and Russell. The last named, more experienced in child education than Whitehead, and more experienced in philosophy than Nunn, had no little skill as a writer, and his books were widely read by intelligent laymen. The challenge of many of his arguments won him an *enfant-terrible* reputation, but, in perspective, his views—even "advanced" ideas on morals and discipline—fit very neatly into a Rousseau-Montessori pattern, completely opposed to the "freedom" cult of Freudian psychology.

Russell justifies Rousseau's "save time by losing it" theory by the findings of child-study. He urges the development of Montessorian methods of individual activity because he holds the growth of strong original personality to be an essential for human survival and progress. Part of education is to learn to discriminate between real moral behaviour and mere convention or expedient. But there is no suggestion that education should be without plan, without values, without standards. The production of expert scientists is as essential to twentieth-century civilisation as the making of philosophers was to Athens. The need to foster and preserve intellectual freedom through education is as great now as in Plato's time.

Russell's own education and upbringing played their part in the evolution of his educational principles with their exaggerations and near-eccentricities. Born into an aristocratic family governed

---

[1] MacMurray. J.. *Reason and Emotion*, p. 83. Faber, 1935.

by tradition and Victorian piety and austerity, he rejected the kind of education he himself received as a child, but he appears to have absorbed from the grandfather who brought him up, a brand of liberalism which envisaged that an intellectual élite would be able to bring about ordered progress throughout the world—a gradual cessation of war and an extension of democratic government.

After studying mathematics and philosophy at Cambridge, he chose the life of a scholar instead of a political career. His pacifism, already firmly fixed, caused him some personal isolation during the First World War, and afterwards he spent some time in travel, including a visit to the Far East. It was not until the middle 'twenties that he settled down to practical education—largely through the stimulus of parenthood—so that while his books sometimes betray the enthusiastic amateur in teaching, they never suggest immaturity or superficiality. Russell's main books specifically on education belong to the inter-war years—*On Education* (1926) and *Education and the Social Order* (1938). Several of his other books, however, contain significant discussions of education, particularly a post-war volume—*Authority and the Individual* (1949).

On Education is particularly relevant to present-day problems —problems of equal opportunity, problems of science in education, and problems of educational aims—and it also puts in focus some of the views for which Russell has been criticised. Thus, in later years, he often tilted at national education and advocated independent schools, but here he accepts the ideal of universal education. "Whatever I shall advocate will be capable of being universal." he writes, "though the individual should not meantime sacrifice his children to the badness of what is common".[1] He fears uniformity, he fears mediocrity, and eventually, of course, he fears abuse and exploitation.

Russell's hopes for progress in democratic education are expressed by a comparison of Locke and Rousseau, planning for aristocratic education, and Montessori and McMillan, working with children in slums. If such wonderful work can be done among deprived people, what could not be achieved in a society well fed, well housed, and made resistant to disease? He has no doubt that modern science could bring about such conditions of life—conditions which stress not so much an abundance of physical goods, but rather the removal of the great obstacles to mental

[1] Russell, B., *On Education*, p. 16, Allen and Unwin, 1926.

excellence—starvation, disease, fear, insecurity. "All this is of such immeasurable value to human life that we dare not oppose the sort of education which will tend to bring it about", he writes. "Without physics and physiology and psychology, we cannot build the new world. We can build it without Latin and Greek, without Dante and Shakespeare, without Bach and Mozart . . . Nevertheless, there is another side to the question. What will be the good of the conquest of leisure and health if no one remembers how to use them?" [1]

On the question of discipline, Russell feels deeply. He cannot conceive of education without discipline, and is relieved to find that Montessori schools have plenty of it: "The rules (*i.e.* the school rules) were like the rules of a game and were obeyed as a means of enjoyment".[2] He is bitterly opposed, however, to the discipline of the old regime, and he condemns Arnold of Rugby for his flogging of boys for the "moral evil" of idleness. "Probably many of Dr Arnold's pupils suffered from adenoids",[3] he comments.

Russell denies discipleship of Rousseau in pointing out that he erred in claiming children are born good, even as Arnold erred in associating himself with the opposite doctrine. Children are not naturally either good or bad says Russell. Their development, one way or the other, depends on mothers, on environment. Education is part of that environment, and should foster the development of the good traits of character which appear during the good preschool life—stability, courage, sensitiveness, and intelligence. Russell feels that formal education often diminishes or distorts this development—boredom instead of vitality, conformity instead of courage, conventionality instead of sensitivity, incuriosity instead of intelligence. "There is ground for sober optimism", writes Russell, "in the fact that most people's instincts are, at first, capable of being developed into good forms. A proper education would make it possible to live in accordance with instinct, but it would be a trained and cultivated instinct, not the crude, unformed impulse which is all that nature provides. The great cultivator of instinct is skill; skill which provides certain kinds of satisfaction but not others. Give a man the right kinds of skill and he will be virtuous; give him the wrong kinds, or none at all, and he will be wicked".[4]

---

[1] Russell, B., *On Education*, p. 27, Allen and Unwin, 1926.
[2] *ibid.*, p. 35.   [3] *ibid.*, p. 42.   [4] *ibid.*, p. 137.

Russell does not consider that skill in classical languages is an adequate training in virtue. "A classical education is almost entirely critical", he asserts, "a boy learns to avoid mistakes and to despise those who commit them. This tends to produce a kind of cold correctness in which originality is replaced by respect for authority. Correct Latin is fixed once for all—it is that of Virgil and Cicero. Correct science is continually changing, and an able youth may look forward to helping in this process. Consequently, the attitude produced by a scientific education is likely to be more constructive than that produced by the study of dead languages".[1] To further this argument, Russell points out the similarity in ideals of Plato's Republic and the Russian State of 1920. In fact, he attributes to science in education the same function that Dewey gives to social science—the generating of initiative, enterprise, constructiveness, and, above all, understanding and love for fellow human beings and, therefore, a resistance to forces leading to futile wars.

Soon after its first publication, *On Education* appeared in U.S.A. under the title *Education and The Good Life*. Russell's eminence as a philosopher has always earned him world-wide attention, but in this case his ideas were acceptable to a large section of American educationists, including the Neo-Realists led by F. S. Breed. They were also in line with the general attitude towards education—revolt against traditionalism, and acceptance of new methods, new subjects, new concepts of child-development. In this country, Russell was suspect because of his frank rejection of the old taboos of sex and religion. In U.S. he was no more extreme than Dewey and less so than the Freudians, but it is doubtful whether it was widely grasped that he (like Dewey) stressed, above all, the need for individual intellectual excellence.

The passing of the years brought no real change in Russell's theory of education. The same main points emerged in *Education and the Social Order*. He maintains that a good individual is not necessarily a good citizen. Even a good person needs to exercise will to become an effective member of the community. He must also, in a democratic society, be prepared to compromise in ways which may limit his own effectiveness, because his fellow citizens have equal rights. Russell believes that education could preserve the best of individual culture while at the same time producing

[1] Russell, B., *On Education*, pp. 142-3, Allen and Unwin, 1926.

citizens, but he warns that State education needs to be based on a broad view of citizen qualities. If only the more limited virtues are required—punctuality, honesty, routine, and discipline—then the new and hard-won freedom in education will be doomed because it produces other qualities.

Russell's concept of freedom in education gives little place to free and spontaneous learning of abstract knowledge. He agrees that children may enjoy acquiring concrete knowledge, but he suggests they must be induced to do what is not natural to them —to acquire abstract knowledge—"the knowledge that makes a civilised community possible".[1] Moreover, the education of children should implant in their minds the idea of "difficult success". It is significant that Dewey, too, in his own way, postulated that education as a mere fostering of natural growth was an inadequate preparation for life in a modern society.

Russell gives to the home a distinctive function in education. It preserves diversity between individuals; a diversity needed for co-operation so long as it is not too extreme. To the possessive emotions of parents, however, he attributes much of the instability and aggressiveness existent in our society.

He predicts that society itself will become more organic with the progress of science. "To educate rightly those who are going to be officials is therefore very important in a scientific state", he maintains. "The education of the bureaucrat will be an education for a special type of citizenship." [2] The education of these carefully selected, intelligent people should be broad—"the way to make men useful is to make them wise, and an essential part of wisdom is a comprehensive mind".[3] They should also have special training, of course, to become experts in different fields.

As a preparation for this new society, the education of young people should encourage individualism. If they experience too intense group pressures they may become timid and conventional. Unusual opinions should be encouraged, and conformity to adult standards not demanded, at least until adolescence. Compulsory learning of abstract subjects such as mathematics at too early an age, may result not only in dislike of knowledge, but also in docility and the belief that there are always definite answers. Moreover, too much study may cause emotional strain and fatigue. "By means of short hours, voluntary lessons, and good teaching",

---

[1] Russell, B., *Education and the Social Order*, p. 43, Allen and Unwin.
[2] *ibid.*, p. 86. [3] *ibid.*, p. 87.

Russell contends, "it is possible to cause about 70 per cent. to learn from love of knowledge".[1] It is such an attitude that will enable higher education to generate the spirit and impart the technique of enquiry.

For the teacher, especially at this higher stage, there are problems of avoiding the over-simplification and monotony that often come from deliberate planning. He must also learn to adapt himself more quickly to new needs. Russell has no patience with arguments about ultimate values, for they cannot be proven right or wrong. The teacher's task is to foster the development of the reason by practice on problems which lend themselves to logical reasoning. The practice of judgment is essential in order that propaganda may be resisted. "Communism should be debated on the wireless on alternate Mondays by the Soviet Ambassador and Winston Churchill, school children should be compelled to listen, and after the debate has lasted three months each school should take a free vote. On Tuesdays, India should be debated between Gandhi and the Viceroy; on Wednesday, Christianity between Stalin and the Archbishop of Canterbury. This would be a real preparation for taking part in a democracy, and would teach the difficult art of extracting the truth from an *ex parte* statement."

After the war, in 1949, Bertrand Russell published *Authority and the Individual*, a work of great significance and value to the educator. It is largely concerned with the changes that science has brought to human societies. They have become larger, but they can still cohere, partly through the bonds wrought by science and partly because universal education has made it possible to instil an artificial loyalty throughout a large population. This being so, the individual innovator, in any realm of knowledge, thought, or behaviour, has a role even more important than in the past. Formerly, the destiny of whole societies was profoundly influenced by visionaries: "Prophets, mystics, poets, scientific discoverers, solitary men whose thoughts and emotions were not subject to the domination of the herd".[2]

Such people are still needed to give value and quality to the struggle for survival. This is not merely a matter of evolution. With the help of science to create security and well-being, undesirable human traits such as greed and fear can be reduced to relative

[1] Russell, B., *Education and the Social Order*, p. 167, Allen and Unwin.
[2] Russell, B., *Authority and the Individual*, p. 113, Allen and Unwin, 1949.

unimportance in human affairs, but this will not automatically bring the millenium. "We shall not create a good world by trying to make men tame and timid, but by encouraging them to be bold, adventurous, and fearless, except in inflicting injuries upon their fellow men." [1] Russell suggests that practical measures should be taken to guard against the swamping of individuality in the over-large group. Within the large group, power should be delegated to "small groups in which the individual is not overwhelmed by large numbers".[2] A person will use initiative and accept responsibility if he is conscious of his capacity to bring about the desired result. This point is surely pertinent to current problems in politics, industry, and commerce. It is also pertinent to education, and might well be considered as the sizes of schools, colleges, and universities are increased to an extent hitherto unknown in this country.

The Second World War and After

In the middle 'thirties, there had been signs of a strengthening of a quasi-Deweyan social theory among English educators, and it continued to hold its own largely through the efforts of Professor Fred Clarke. The predominant educational theories and psychologies, however—all mainly individualistic—were doomed by the outbreak of war, for events seemed to prove that they were responsible for national unpreparedness and lack of cohesion. It mattered little that the real criminals had been the economic situation and the political mismanagement which had resulted in neglect of education.

The pre-war period was condemned as one of pandering to self-expression, of indulgence in haphazard experiments, and of the encouragement of spontaneous egoism in children. This phase of criticism continued after the war. Writing in 1946, Marjorie Reeves quotes Bertrand Russell's plea for "opportunities of growth and the removal of hampering influences", as an example of a prevalent distrust of training in moral and social habits. This is less than fair to Russell.[3] W. R. Niblett and Lester Smith, writing a few years later, maintain that *laisser-faire* was prevalent in education as well as in economics in the years before the war.[4] Now

---

[1] Russell, B., *Authority and the Individual*, p. 124, Allen and Unwin, 1949.
[2] *ibid.*, p. 98.
[3] Reeves, M., *Growing Up in a Modern Society*, p. 30, U.L.P., 1949.
[4] Niblett, W. R., *Essential Education*, p. 26, U.L.P., 1947. Lester Smith, W. O., *The Impact of Education on Society*, p. 29, Blackwell, 1949.

that we are further away from the war and have seen yet another swing of the educational pendulum, it is time to appreciate and commend the sterling work of psychologists—Susan Isaacs, Olive Wheeler, Burt and Vernon, and others—and the depth and vision of the few outstanding educational theorists. One thing is certain. It will not do to compare inter-war English education with that of U.S.A. The system was different, the scope for "free experiment" was different, the amount of education was different, and the dominant educational philosophy was different. If the characteristics of the younger generation turned out to be similar, then the reasons must be sought elsewhere. Neither Deweyism nor extreme "freedom" education was ever widely predominant in Britain. Fred Clarke almost succeeded in his campaign for a modified Deweyan social education during the war. The 1944 Education Act probably did as much to frustrate his design as it did to bring it to partial fruition, for by the time it was passed, a new conflict in educational philosophy had taken its toll.

Sir Fred Clarke (1880-1952) received his knighthood during the war as a recognition of his services to education, especially on committees, such as the McNair, actively engaged in the planning of post-war education. In 1944 he became the first Chairman of the English Advisory Council. He had occupied chairs of education in South Africa and Canada before succeeding Sir Percy Nunn as Director of the University of London Institute of Education in 1937. By this time, he was already deeply conscious of the contribution which might be made by sociology to educational thought, and in particular he was interested in the work of Karl Mannheim. Writing on "The Crisis of Freedom in Education" in 1939,[1] he contends that splendid as Nunn's concept of the fine, free individual may be, the very nature of English life, with its deep rooted but unexamined characteristics, has, in fact, produced a "peculiar combination of self-restraint and social and mental conformity". He thus implies that new methods of education had not spread widely, and "freedom" experiments, though no doubt producing happier schools, had not given freedom for the individual either widely through the nation or deeply in the person.

Real freedom involves the bearing of strains and tensions in the rough and tumble of contact, and even conflict, with the physical world and with fellow human beings. Clarke feels such

[1] Laborde. E. D. (Ed.), *Problems in Modern Education*, pp. 86-103, C.U.P.

freedom is, in any case, dangerous, and he allies himself with the comment of a German *emigré*, Adolph Löwe: "A large-scale society can stand the strain of freedom of action on the part of its members only if the individualisation of action on the part of its members is kept within definite limits. The individual must pay for this freedom by being turned, to a certain extent, into a type. The price of liberalism as a social principle is the sacrifice of self-indulgence".[1] This was the concept on which Clarke built his theory of education, his later writings being developments of this theme. After the war, neither he nor any other educational writer pointed out that the generation which led us into war was not brought up in the period of "individualism" and "natural learning"; the people who did most of the hard work and brave deeds of the war had been those very children whom critics of the 1940's regarded as "egoistic", "under-exposed", or "ultra docile".

Sir Fred, however, is not criticising the English nation itself. He believes it to have qualities of conventionalism and lack of thorough "individualisation" of which he heartily approves, for he refers to "English freedom" as the kind which is likely to be most fruitful and lasting because it rests on an agreed social discipline. To foster such a freedom he would have more attention given to institutions; first, the family, but also to industrial and economic institutions. This, written in 1938, is perhaps one of the first signs of the beginning of the phase of "educational planning"—at least in theory.

Although in his regular lectures Sir Fred was wont to expound many of Dewey's ideas in counterblast to Nunn's individualistic theory, he was neither a pragmatist nor a pedagogic disciple of Dewey. His chief inspiration in philosophy was the American idealist, Hocking, and his guides in educational planning were history, sociology, and religion. This is abundantly clear in *Education and Social Change*,[2] a small book, published in 1947, in which he advocates the unification of the school system as a step in the planning of a social order "much more thoroughly collectivist".

In 1941, he writes in the *Sociological Review* on "The Social Function of Secondary Education", forecasting the introduction of forms of state "educative control" at least up to the age of eighteen. He discusses the need for an "Educative Society" in which there is

---

[1] Löwe, A., *The Price of Liberty*, Hogarth Press, 1937.
[2] Sheldon Press.

no sudden passage from the shelter of school to the hard, uncaring outside world.   He is sceptical of the concept of the school as a microcosm of the world, and considers that the creation of a national Youth Service is far more likely to provide the experience and guidance that young people really need.   He urges the reform of secondary education, not only to give each child full opportunities for development free from class distinction and traditional inequalities, but also to ensure the abolition of the false antinomy between the vocational and the cultural.   He envisages, with Mannheim, a planned social and economic order under effective democratic control, an order in which each person masters some of the techniques needed in an industrial society.   Such skills may be gained partly in school, partly in part-time continued education through the co-operation of industry, and partly by adult education.   There should be the possibility of continuity.

With Whitehead, Sir Fred wants education to be "adventurous", to militate against the danger of mass-society and machine production.   The function of secondary education in a free society should be "to maintain and enhance social unity while providing for effective social differentiation and continuous readaptation. This, with the purpose not only of promoting economic well-being but also of rendering all forms of individual activity, economic and non-economic, both socially significant and culturally fruitful".

These ideas are more fully developed in *Freedom in the Educative Society*,[1] in which he discusses the problems of "planning for freedom" in an English society which he likens to the Platonic educative society.   To confirm his idealistic viewpoint, he extends Matthew Arnold's concept of culture into one that is relevant to life in a modern organised industrial society.   A true culture would emerge from the common life and experiences of a healthy society. A common purpose of that society would define itself, and this should be heeded both in school and outside.   The whole content of education should be relevant to it, and the teachers chosen should be its especially sensitive representatives.   That is, education cannot create a new society, it can only reflect the one in which it exists. There should be an increase in emphasis on specific functions and not on individuality, maintains Clarke, and training for playing a part in a society should have "citizen consciousness" behind it. Lest it appear that Clarke is dissolving the individual completely

[1] U.L.P., 1947.

in his social function, it should be mentioned that his theory envisages that the school should have a great measure of autonomy, and thus remain responsible for its own community and the development of the individuals in it. In fact, he maintains that although education should be to the type it should also make possible development "beyond the type". Of the relations between individual and society, he spoke frequently in terms of "the expanded self" and "a community of persuasion".

Sir Fred Clarke's version of a modern Republic has, no doubt, given both inspiration and food for thought to educators of the past twenty years, but in print he has had few disciples. The main after-effects of his work have been to stimulate and reinforce the claims of sociology to a place in the field of studies covered by education. The impact on educational thought has been comparable with the impact made by psychology thirty years ago. After the first ferment, psychology was packed off to learn its own business; now sociology has the task of discovering more about the functioning of society, and Sir Fred's theories about that functioning are awaiting re-evaluation.

Of longer duration has been a different manifestation of the idealist revival. Its most eminent apostle has been **Sir Richard Livingstone (1880-)**, a classical scholar whose career had already been long and distinguished before the outbreak of war. He was Vice-Chancellor of Queen's University, Belfast, from 1924 to 1933 and of Oxford University from 1944 to 1947. His series of contributions to contemporary educational thought started with *The Future in Education*[1] in 1941. This dealt mainly with adult education, but *Education for a World Adrift*,[1] in 1943, was an avowedly Platonic discussion of character training and education for citizenship. He is severely critical of Dewey's principles and of his influence on American education. He objects strongly to Dewey's view that secondary education should be general and cultural and that university and higher education should be specific. Livingstone considers that specialisation in English universities may lead to the production of "barbarian" graduates. He feels there is great danger of over-specialisation in English secondary schools. He makes no mention of the possible cultural value of depth of study if there is quality in the teaching. As to citizenship, Livingstone regards the residential public school as the only type of English school giving adequate social education. Living

[1] C.U.P.

as a member of a big School and a smaller House, a boy "imbibes instinctively the fundamental principles of good citizenship".[1]

Sir Richard confirmed his views in the Rede Lecture of 1944 on *Plato and Modern Education*. In 1947 he published *Some Tasks for Education*, and in 1952 *Education and the Spirit of the Age*. In this last, he comments: "The twentieth century is the child of liberalism—that is, of freedom and reason. Freedom is negative; it is a condition of the good life, but does not tell us what the good life is".[2] He deals with the inadequacies of a scientific education, but he also counters possible criticisms of a broad liberal education as superficial. "The remedy". he suggests, "is not to dole out snippets of history, literature, art, and science, but to develop a mind sensitive to values and aware of their infinite variety".[3]

Livingstone regrets "our loss of the wider and more philosophic Greek view". He deplores our tendency to emphasise not only science itself but also the use of scientific methods even in other fields. He would prefer history and literature to be concerned with the education of the sentiments, with the perception of values, and with the conveyance of "the vision of greatness". Criticism and analysis have come to play too great a part in the study of these subjects. "To the injunction 'Teach your pupil to think', I should like to add a further injunction, 'Teach your pupil to see and feel'. The soul has two eyes, and both need developing fully; if either is shortsighted, the vision is imperfect. There is the critical, analytical eye which measures and assesses and protects man from illusions and delusions. But there is also the eye which enables them to contemplate, enjoy, and adore." [4]

This last point may well be one which has the utmost significance for post-war idealist educators. Many of their fears for a "world adrift" are clear—the absence of standards, the falsity of values, apparent laxity of morals, maladjustment in vocation, in society, or in personality, lack of balance in education for earning a living, for living in society, and for personal satisfaction—all these human faults and failures have been observed in other ages. It is not surprising that in reaction to the preceding long phase of realism and individualism, many thinkers should turn elsewhere for solutions. Plato offered rule by "goodness, beauty, reason",

---

[1] Livingstone, R., *Education for a World Adrift*, p. 253, C.U.P., 1943.
[2] Livingstone, R., *Education and the Spirit of the Age*, p. 25, O.U.P., 1952.
[3] *ibid.*, p. 100.   [4] *ibid.*, p. 102.

and an education giving "an intellectual attitude to life" and "knowledge of the first rate". Plato offered "the training of character by discipline of the body, the will and the intelligence". Plato offered the hope of preserving the spiritual world—by education through "the vision of greatness"—from being sacrificed to science or economics or sociology. Plato offered the restoration of the common virtues of person and citizen by the old process of habituation. Plato offered a citizen education which would not rob the person of his individuality by mere "type production". But, above all, Plato offered harmony—"the real problem is to harmonise man".[1]

Livingstone, in asking that children be taught to feel, is posing the same problem as C. S. Lewis in his *Abolition of Man* (1946). Profoundly shocked by the critical and analytical nature of a school textbook on English, Lewis, although not himself an educationist, discusses brilliantly the folly of educating a generation of Men Without Chests, people without magnanimity—heart—feeling—the element that harmonises and balances the intellect and the appetites. His criticisms of education, which range from methods of teaching to the evils of educational planning, reveal his idealist philosophy and his faith in the universality of goodness and truth.

"The right defence against false sentiments is to inculcate just sentiments", writes Lewis. "By starving the sensibility of our pupils we only make them easier prey to the propagandist when he comes."[2] He is confident that training in habits of feeling and behaving is as effective as intellectual training. "I had sooner play cards against a man who was quite sceptical about ethics, but bred to believe that 'a gentleman does not cheat', than against an irreproachable moral philosopher who had been brought up among sharpers",[3] he asserts. Yet he is well aware of "the power of some men to make other men what they please", and he comments bitterly on the prospect of an era of man-moulding scientific techniques.

His concept of education is personal. "Where the old initiated, the new merely 'conditions'. The old dealt with its pupils as grown birds deal with young birds when they teach them to fly: the new deals with them more as the poultry-keeper deals with young birds—making them thus or thus for purposes of which the birds know nothing. In a word, the old was a kind of propagation

---

[1] The quotations in these paragraphs are from *Some Tasks for Education* and *Education for a World Adrift*.
[2] Lewis, C. S., *The Abolition of Man*, p. 14, Geoffrey Bles, 1946.
[3] *ibid.*, p. 20.

—men transmitting manhood to men; the new is merely propaganda."[1] His protest at the "treatment of mankind as mere 'specimens'" is one very closely related to the views of existentialist and personalist thinkers.

Livingstone and Lewis represent a school of educational thought which flourished at the turn of the half-century, and which has, as yet, encountered little opposition in print. The most widely discussed foreign publication on education was the report of the Harvard Committee in 1945.[2] The introduction, by Dr J. B. Conant, earned commendation, but stimulated argument. Eric James, writing in 1949 and 1951,[3] repudiated the idea of a common core of education for all people, and emphasised the need for the education of an élite. Sir Walter Moberly had already emphasised the need for "intensive education for a select few for leadership",[4] and the fear of a decline in the quality of education at the top has continued to influence the opinions of many critics of recent changes in the educational system. M. V. C. Jeffreys, in his inquiry into the aims of education which he calls *Glaucon*—after Socrates' stooge, as he reminds us—criticises the Harvard Report for its "lack of clear and firm belief about the nature and destiny of man".[5] His own views are nearer to Clarke's than are most others of his group, for, while reinterpreting many Platonic concepts, he also claims a place for the family in education. "The family, not the individual, is the real unit of society",[6] he writes.

Summary and Conclusion

During the inter-war years, the main characteristic of educational theory was a concern for the individual and his full development. At first, in high hopes of the implementation of the Fisher Act, writers and experimenters studied child development and the practical detail of teaching method. As time brought little change in the national system of education, the dissatisfaction of educators showed itself in pleas for recognition of the social function of education and demands for the unification and extension of the national system. During the war, these demands were partially met

[1] Lewis, C. S., *The Abolition of Man*, pp. 19-20, Geoffrey Bles, 1946.
[2] *General Education in a Free Society*, Harvard U.P., 1945.
[3] James, E., *An Essay on the Content of Education*, Harrap, 1949; *Education and Leadership*, Harrap, 1951.
[4] Presidential Address to the Classical Association of St Albans, 1944.
[5] Jeffreys, M. V. C., *Glaucon: An Inquiry into the Aims of Education*, p. 62, Pitman, 1950.
[6] *ibid.*, p. 59.

by the provisions of the Education Act of 1944. Later, the development of the Welfare State and the revival of industry brought security and well-being to a larger proportion of people than had ever before enjoyed them. Yet it seemed that the millenium had not been reached after all. Not only did the new situation bring new problems—shortage of suitable school buildings, shortage of teachers, disputes about selection for secondary education—but it failed to remedy those faults, in society and in individuals, which had previously been attributed to insecurity and to inequality of educational opportunity.

Present-day writers on education are deeply concerned about this. Some are openly critical and pessimistic, others criticise by implication, drawing contrasts between the evils of to-day and the "goods" of previous ages. They are eager to find remedies, but have few new solutions to offer. There is little of pragmatism in their outlook. They feel that the best preparation for the uncertainties of the future is a thorough—though enlightened—inculcation of the values and standards of the past.

Perhaps the greatest promise of re-orientation in contemporary educational theory is the existentialist view of human relationships. In the modern, massive, planned societies, the person can again be himself, respect his fellows, and love his God. The teacher and the learner again make real the abstract called education. "In learning from time to time what this human being needs and does not need at the moment, the educator is led to an ever deeper recognition of what the human being needs in order to grow. But he is also led to the recognition of what he, the 'educator', is able and what he is unable to give of what is needed—and what he can give now, and what not yet." [1]

Other Works Representative of the Period

1919   F. N. Freeman: *How Children Learn*. Harrap.

K. Richmond: *The Curriculum*. Constable.

1920   E. A. Craddock: *The Class-Room Republic*. Black.

W. G. Sleight: *The Organisation and Curricula of Schools*. Arnold.

1921   J. E. Adamson: *The Individual and the Environment*. Longmans.

A. S. Neill: *A Dominie in Doubt*. H. Jenkins.

G. Sampson: *English for the English*. C.U.P.

---

[1] Martin Buber, *Between Man and Man*, p. 101, Kegan Paul, 1947.

1922   Sir J. Adams: *Modern Developments in Educational Practice.* U.L.P.

Evelyn Dewey: *The Dalton Laboratory Plan.* Dent.

R. H. Tawney, (ed.): *Secondary Education for All.* Allen and Unwin.

1923   J. H. Bradley: *Bedales: A Pioneer School.* Methuen.

F. Clarke: *Essays in the Politics of Education.* Clarendon.

Mrs O'Brien Harris: *Towards Freedom: The Howard Plan of Individual Time-tables.* U.L.P.

1924   Sir W. H. Hadow: *Citizenship.* Clarendon.

A. J. Lynch: *Individual Work and the Dalton Plan.* Philip.

J. H. Whitehouse and G. P. Gooch: *Wider Aspects of Education.* C.U.P.

1925   P. B. Ballard: *The Changing School.* U.L.P.

J. J. Findlay: *The Aims and Organisation of Education.* U.L.P.

Charlotte M. Mason: *Towards a Philosophy of Education.* Kegan Paul.

1926   K. Lindsay: *Social Progress and Educational Waste.* Routledge.

J. Ward: *Psychology Applied to Education.* C.U.P.

1927   H. Bompas Smith: *The Nation's Schools: Their Task and Their Importance.* Longmans.

Mabel J. Reaney: *The Place of Play in Education.* Methuen.

1928   B. A. Howard: *The Mixed School.* U.L.P.

R. Steiner: *Education and Modern Spiritual Life.* Anthroposophical P.C.

1929   H. R. Hamley: *School Discipline.* Macmillan.

G. H. Thompson: *A Modern Philosophy of Education.* Allen and Unwin.

Olive A. Wheeler: *Youth: The Psychology of Adolescence and its Bearing on the Reorganisation of Adolescent Education.* U.L.P.

B. A. Yeaxlee: *Lifelong Education.* Cassell.

1930   R. Gurner: *Day Schools of England.* Dent.

Susan Isaacs: *Intellectual Development in Young Children.* Routledge.

Lord Eustace Percy: *Education at the Crossroads.* Evans.

1931   N. Davies: *Education for Life.* Williams and Norgate.

1931 R. Hitchcock: *Education or Catastrophe.* Sidgwick Jackson.

W. J. McCallister: *The Growth of Freedom in Education.* Constable.

1932 Susan Isaacs: *The Children We Teach.* U.L.P.

S. T. Millis: *Education for Trades and Industries.* Arnold.

Dora Russell: *In Defence of Children.* H. Hamilton.

1933 B. A. Abbot: *Education for Industry and Commerce.* O.U.P.

H. C. Morrison: *Basic Principles of Education.* Harrap.

1934 Nancy Catty: *Theory and Practice of Education.* Methuen.

L. B. Pekin: *Progressive Schools: Their Principles and Practice.* Hogarth Press.

W. Rawson: *A New World in the Making.* New Education Fellowship.

1935 F. C. Happold: *Citizens in the Making.*

E. A. Loftus: *Education and the Citizen.* Routledge.

A. A. Matthews: *Education for Life.* Nelson.

R. H. Nettleship: *The Theory of Education in Plato's Republic.* O.U.P.

T. Raymont: *Modern Education.* Longmans.

1936 H. R. Hamley: *The Education of the Backward Child.* Evans.

J. H. Simpson: *Sane Schooling.* Faber.

Olive A. Wheeler: *Creative Education and the Future.* U.L.P.

1937 Dorothy E. M. Gardner: *The Children's Play Centre.* Methuen.

Margaret Phillips: *The Education of the Emotions.* Allen and Unwin.

F. Smith and A. S. Harrison: *Principles of Class Teaching.* Macmillan.

1938 S. H. Bailey: *International Studies in Modern Education.* O.U.P.

G. J. Cons and Catherine Fletcher: *Actuality in School: An Experiment in Social Education.* Methuen.

E. E. Reynolds: *Freedom to Mature: A View of Education.* Macmillan.

Ella R. Boyce: *Play in the Infants School.* Methuen.

1939 J. Cohen and R. M. W. Travers (ed.): *Education for Democracy.* Macmillan.

1939   A. S. Neill: *The Problem Teacher*. Jenkins.
1940   W. P. Alexander: *The Educational Needs of Democracy*. U.L.P.
      P. E. Vernon: *The Measurement of Abilities*. U.L.P.
      T. C. Worsley: *Barbarians and Philistines*. Hale.
1941   H. Pinsend: *The Principles of Teaching Method*. Harrap.
      F. H. Spencer: *Education for the People*. Routledge.
      T. C. Worsley: *The End of the Old School Tie*. Seeker.
1942   E. Green: *Education for a New Society*. Routledge.
      D. Hughes: *The Public Schools and the Future*. C.U.P.
      W. O. Lester Smith: *To Whom do the Schools Belong?* Blackwell.
      H. G. Stead: *The Education of a Community*. U.L.P.
1943   F. C. Happold: *Towards a New Aristocracy*. Faber.
      J. C. Maxwell Garnett: *The World We Mean to Make*. Faber.
      W. K. Richmond: *Blueprint for a Common School*. Routledge.
      B. Stanley: *The Education of Junior Citizens*. U.L.P.
1944   F. M. Earle: *Reconstruction in the Secondary School*. U.L.P.
      Charlotte M. Fleming: *The Social Psychology of Education*. Routledge and Kegan Paul.
      P. I. Kitchen: *From Learning to Earning*. Faber.
      A. Victor Murray: *The School and the Church*. S.C.M.
1945   C. Black: *The Educational Reconstruction of Education*. Gollancz.
      J. H. Panton: *Modern Teaching Practice and Technique*. Longmans.
      Olive A. Wheeler: *The Adventure of Youth*, U.L.P.
1946   J. J. B. Dempster: *Education in the Secondary Modern School*. Pilot Press.
      B. A. Fletcher: *Education and Crisis*. U.L.P.
      A. T. Glover: *New Teachings for a New Age*. Nelson.
      M. L. Jacks: *Total Education: A Plea for Synthesis*. Kegan Paul, Trench, Trubner.
1947   W. B. Curry: *Education for Sanity*. Dent.
      D. Thompson and J. Reeves (ed.): *The Quality of Education*. F. Muller.
1948   R. W. Jepson: *Clear Thinking*. Longmans.
      J. Mander: *Old Bottles and New Wine*. Newnes.

1948   J. F. Wolfenden: *The Public Schools To-day.* U.L.P.

1949   R. Armfelt: *Education: New Hopes and Old Habits.* Cohen and West.

H. C. Dent: *Secondary Education for All.* Routledge and Kegan Paul.

Sir W. Moberly: *The Crisis in the University.* S.C.M.

J. W. Skinner: *School Stresses: The Grammar School Today and Tomorrow.* Epworth Press.

1950   Lord Hemingford: *Co-education.* Longmans.

M. L. Jacks: *Modern Trends in Education.* Melrose.

R. W. Rich: *The Teacher in a Planned Society.* U.L.P.

1951   C. H. Dobinson: *Technical Education for Adolescents.* Harrap.

G. Highet: *The Art of Teaching.* Methuen.

A. G. Hughes: *Education and the Democratic Ideal.* Longmans.

R. Morris: *The Quality of Learning.* Methuen.

1952   G. H. Bantock: *Freedom and Authority in Education.* Faber.

Nancy Catty: *Social Training from Childhood to Maturity.* Methuen.

H. C. Dent: *Change in English Education.* U.L.P.

1953   Agatha H. Bowley and M. Townroe: *The Spiritual Development of the Child.* Livingstone.

E. B. Castle: *People in School.* Heinemann.

H. C. A. Gaunt: *School. A Book for Parents.* H. Jenkins.

1954   J. J. B. Dempster: *Selection for Secondary Education.* Methuen.

G. Kendon: *Children of the New Estate.* Methuen.

W. R. Niblett: *Education and the Modern Mind.* Faber.

J. H. Simpson: *The School Master's Harvest.* Faber.

1955   Olive Banks: *Parity and Prestige in English Secondary Education.* Routledge and Kegan Paul.

M. V. C. Jeffreys: *Beyond Neutrality.* Pitman.

I. L. Kandel: *The New Era in Education.* Harrap.

P. F. R. Venables: *Technical Education.* Bell.

1956   F. C. Campbell: *Eleven Plus and All That.* Watts.

J. J. B. Dempster: *Purpose in the Modern School.* Methuen.

R. Pedley: *Comprehensive Education—A New Approach.* Gollancz.

1956   H. A. Reé: *The Essential Grammar School.* Methuen.
1957   Jean E. Floud, A. H. Halsey, and F. M. Martin: *Social Class and Educational Opportunity.* Heinemann.
       A. N. Gilkes: *Independent Education.* Gollancz.
       A. V. Judges (ed.): *Education and the Philosophic Mind.* Harrap.
       V. Ogilvie: *The English Public School.* Batsford.
1958   S. J. Curtis, *Introduction to the Philosophy of Education,* U.T.P.
       A. Montagu, *Education and Human Relations,* Calder.
       J. U. Nef: *Cultural Foundations of Industrial Civilisation.* C.U.P.
1959   A. V. Judges, *The Function of Teaching,* Faber.
       R. W. Livingstone, *The Rainbow Bridge,* Pall Mall.
       R. S. Peters, *Authority, Responsibility and Education,* Allen and Unwin.
       J. Wolfenden, *The Educated Man Today and Tomorrow,* S.C.M.
1960   W. R. Niblett, *Christian Education in a Secular Society,* O.U.P.
       K. H. R. Reese Edwards, *The Secondary Technical School,* U.L.P.
       F. M. Stevens, *The Living Tradition. Social and Educational Assumptions of the Grammar School,* Hutchinson.
1961   E. B. Castle, *Ancient Education and Today,* Penguin.
       B. A. Fletcher, *A Philosophy for the Teacher,* O.U.P.
       M. V. C. Jeffreys, *Revolution in Teacher Training,* Pitman.
       T. W. G. Miller, *Values in the Comprehensive School,* Oliver and Boyd.
1962   C. Brogan, *The Nature of Education,* Oldbourne.
       A. Arnold-Brown, *Unfolding Character—The Impact of Gordonstoun,* Routledge.
       A. S. Neill, *Summerhill. A Radical Approach to Education.*
       L. A. Reid, *Philosophy of Education,* Allen and Unwin.
1963   G. H. Bantock, *Education in an Industrial Society,* Faber.
       J. Huxley, *Education and the Humanist Revolution,* (Fawley Lecture), Southampton University.
       W. R. Niblett (Ed.), *Moral Education in a Changing Society,* Faber.

1963   R. Peers, *Fact and Possibility in English Education*, Routledge.

1964   M. Burn, *Mr. Lyward's Answer*, Hamish Hamilton.

F. T. Willey, *Education Today and Tomorrow*, Joseph.

T. H. B. Hollins (Ed.), *Aims in Education: the philosophic approach*, Manchester U.P.

1965   G. H. Bantock, *Education and Values: Essays in the theory of education*, Faber.

T. S. Eliot, *To Criticise the Critics and other writings*, Faber.

L. Elvin, *Education and Contemporary Society*, Watts.

SUGGESTIONS FOR FURTHER READING

Curtis and Boultwood, *A Short History of Educational Ideas*, 4th edition, U.T.P., 1965. Chapters XVII, XIX.

S. M. Robertson, *Craft and Contemporary Culture*, Harrap for U.N.E.S.C.O., 1961.

Lord James of Rusholme, *Education and Democratic Leadership*, O.U.P., 1961.

C. P. Snow, *The Two Cultures and the Scientific Revolution. Rede Lecture*, C.U.P., 1959, and *Recent Thoughts on the Two Cultures*, Birkbeck, 1962.

CHAPTER XII

TECHNICAL SCHOOLS AND COLLEGES AND THE YOUTH SERVICE

Before the third decade of the nineteenth century, technical education in its modern meaning was almost non-existent. During the Middle Ages and in the Tudor and Stuart periods, craftsmen gained their knowledge of the trades they pursued through the apprenticeship system. During the seventeenth and eighteenth centuries there were a few isolated attempts at giving a more formal type of instruction, *e.g.* the Mathematical School of Christ's Hospital, founded in 1673 to instruct forty boys in grammar, arithmetic, and navigation. Some of the charity schools of the S.P.C.K. endeavoured to give their pupils some elementary training in the trades they were going to follow after leaving school, and the industrial schools taught such useful occupations as gardening, carpentry, cobbling, and printing for boys, and spinning, knitting, sewing, and straw-plaiting for girls.

It was not until 1836, however, that the Government began to realise that technical instruction was essential if Britain was to keep the industrial and commercial supremacy she had gained during the Napoleonic wars. In that year a normal school of design was established for which the House of Commons voted a sum of £1,500. From 1841 onwards, annual grants were made in support of provincial schools of design. These were supervised by a public office which eventually became the Board of Trade. By 1852 there were seventeen provincial schools of design, situated in such important industrial centres as Manchester, Birmingham, Glasgow, Leeds, and Paisley.

The Great Exhibition of 1851 awoke the Government to the realisation, that although British industry and craftsmanship were still supreme, that place could only be maintained by the provision of better organised scientific and technical instruction, both in the schools and for older people after they had entered industry. In 1852 the normal school of design became the Department of Practical Art in the Board of Trade. The following year a Science Division was added, and the Department changed its name to the Science and Art Department of the Board of Trade and was housed at South Kensington. In 1856, when the Select Committee of the

Privy Council became the Education Department of the Committee of Council, the Science and Art Department came under its supervision. During this period the central colleges of technology at South Kensington were established. Thus the Royal College of Chemistry opened in 1845, and the Government School of Mines and Science applied to the Arts was established in 1851. The two were amalgamated for a period, but were separated in 1890 under the titles of the Royal College of Science and the Royal School of Mines. The Normal School of Design became the Royal College of Art in 1896.

One of the principal functions of the Science and Art Department was the encouragement of science and art teaching in the schools, and for this purpose it instituted examinations and made grants to those schools which presented successful candidates. The result was a definite increase in the number of science classes from 38 with 1,300 pupils in 1851 to 70 with 2,543 pupils in 1861. The supply of an adequate number of qualified teachers in science and the arts proved difficult. One would have thought that the obvious way of increasing the supply would be the establishment of a training college, but the senior officials of the Department thought a satisfactory way of solving the problem would be to institute a special qualifying examination without providing a means of ensuring that the candidates had adequate preparation for it. The consequence could have been easily foreseen: teachers crammed from their textbooks, and when they were appointed to a school they adopted the same procedure with their pupils in order to obtain the maximum grant possible. It has been asserted that some candidates were able to pass the examination in chemistry without having had any practical experience in a laboratory and, perhaps, without having seen or used a test-tube. It was also said that the highest number of certificates in agriculture went to young men who had never stirred beyond the precincts of Whitechapel. Many higher grade as well as endowed secondary schools presented candidates for the South Kensington examinations, and if the Department served no further purpose, by means of its grants it kept in being many grammar schools which otherwise would have been obliged to close their doors. One important effect, however, followed; science became assured of a permanent place in the school curriculum.

In spite of these measures, British industry began to lose ground when compared with its chief competitors, Germany and the United

States. This was apparent at the Paris Exhibition of 1867, and the Government adopted the traditional procedure which followed a difficult situation. In 1871 a Royal Commission under the chairmanship of the seventh Duke of Devonshire was appointed to inquire into our institutions for providing technical instruction. In its report of 1875 the Commission surveyed technological developments in other countries.

The Devonshire Commission stimulated the London City Livery Companies to appoint a committee in 1877 to draw up a national scheme of technical instruction. This led to the foundation of the City and Guilds of London Institute which encouraged the teaching of applied science in schools and evening classes, issued syllabuses, and conducted examinations in technical subjects. Grants were made to successful examination candidates, but, at first, were not paid to students who held responsible posts in industry which rendered them liable to income-tax. This unfortunate mistake was not rectified until 1897.

Three important events in the last quarter of the nineteenth century gave considerable impetus to the growth of technical education. The first was due to Quintin Hogg, the grandfather of Lord Hailsham (now Mr Quintin Hogg). When a young man he became deeply interested in the education of the poorer members of society and began teaching a ragged school in 1864. From this he passed to a boys' home in Drury Lane, and eventually, in 1878, he opened a Working Lads' Institute. This was so popular that it soon outgrew its premises, and in 1880 he acquired the building in Regent Street which was known as the Polytechnic. This had been a place of popular entertainment, but had fallen into financial difficulties. Hogg still retained the original title, and for some time ran his institute without the support of public money.

For some years the population of the City of London had been moving outwards from the centre, and it became desirable that the many educational endowments of the City parishes should be redistributed. This was effected in 1883 through the City Parochial Charities Act, which freed nearly £80,000 per annum for the benefit of more distant parts of London. The Polytechnic benefited by this redistribution, and a scheme was also prepared for the establishment of a number of institutions similar to the original Polytechnic. When the London County Council was brought into being by the Local Government Act of 1888, the polytechnics came under its supervision. They have a very wide range of activities. They not only retain their original functions of promoting social intercourse and healthy recreation, but they are educational centres of outstanding importance. They give secondary and technical education, provide day technical instruction for more advanced pupils and evening classes for apprentices and work-people in a wide range of technical and industrial subjects, but they also organise commercial and foreign language classes. Many of the more advanced students are prepared for the degrees of the University of London.

The other two events, the Technical Instruction Act of 1889 and the Local Taxation (Customs and Excise) Act of 1890, have already been mentioned on pp. 96-7. The "Whisky Money" which became available under the latter Act had grown to £859,011 by the turn of the century, and although the Act of 1890 was repealed by the Education Act of 1902, the money was still set aside for higher education. During these twelve years it had made possible the foundation of twelve polytechnics or technical institutes in London, thirteen in the provinces, and more than one hundred organised science schools.

Another important development of technical and further education sprang from the recommendations of the Cross Commission in regard to evening schools. Previously the evening schools had catered for older students who had not passed through the elementary school and who needed instruction in the basic subjects. The wider opportunities which now existed for obtaining elementary education were rendering such courses obsolete, and the Commission recommended that the schools should be reorganised as evening continuation schools. This was accepted by the Code of 1890 with the result that the evening schools widened their syllabuses and began to give instruction in languages, science, art, handicrafts, and domestic work. This side of education became so popular that a separate Code for evening continuation schools was issued in 1898. The upper age limit for students was abolished so that older students could attend and grants were awarded for attendance instead of examination results. Additional subjects were admitted, e.g. technical subjects, physical training, and commercial subjects such as shorthand, typing, and book-keeping. In spite of the fact that attendance at evening schools had nearly doubled by 1899, a good deal of the instruction remained at the elementary level.

Students were permitted to choose the subjects they wished to study, but often their choice involved them in difficulties. Thus a student might select mechanical engineering as his study, but he would soon discover that he also needed an adequate knowledge of mathematics, physics, and machine drawing. In addition, he would be handicapped if he did not possess a good knowledge of English. The group system was introduced to solve this problem. Experiments had been carried out at Manchester Technical School in 1890 and the course system was fully developed in St Helens and Halifax by 1901. During the next few years the group organisation was adopted by many towns in Lancashire, Yorkshire, and Cheshire. In 1907 the Board of Education urged L.E.A.s to adopt the group system.

The students fell into two categories—those who eventually hoped to enter a technical college and those who would not proceed further than the courses provided in the evening continuation school. The former class was considered the more important and the grouped courses were planned with a view to the student's present occupation or that which he desired to enter. As a rule there were five main groups: industrial, commercial, rural, domestic, and general. The majority of students was to be found in the first two groups, but eventually the general courses were found attractive and the domestic courses appealed to women. At Reading the L.E.A. and the University College organised a joint scheme for evening students.

One result of the Education Act of 1902 was that the L.E.A.s took control of most of the evening continuation schools whether they had previously been run by the School Boards, or technical instruction committees, or organised by private bodies. In this way technical and continuation education became associated. After 1926 the example of London was followed and the evening continuation schools were renamed Evening Institutes and classified into Junior and Senior Institutes. The former mainly catered for boys and girls between fourteen and seventeen years of age. The latter dealt with older students. In addition, advanced courses, usually planned for two years, were provided in the larger institutes, and they were able to give the students a greater freedom in the choice of subjects.

At the beginning of this century the view generally held in this country was that the technical school should concentrate on the theoretical study and the workshop on practice. Thus the Technical Instruction Act of 1889 had defined technical instruction as that given "in the principles of science and art applicable to industries and in the application of special branches of science and art to specific industries and employments". It was expressly stated that the instruction should not include the practice of any trade or industry. This was directly opposite to the view held on the Continent, where the importance of workshop apprenticeship was strongly emphasised.

Although in some industries the traditional view is still accepted, in others it began to break down after the First World War. The first to be affected was the building industry. Thus the instruction given in plumbing included the actual practice of the craft. This idea spread to other trades and industries so that it became common to find classes in carpentry and joinery, plastering, pattern making, acetylene welding, and other practical crafts in technical schools. This has given rise to the distinction between a Minor and a Major course. The former denotes a training in craftsmanship or in workshop operations, whilst the latter is mainly concerned with the principles which underlie those operations. Naturally there can be no hard and fast distinction between the two. It was found necessary to include certain theoretical subjects, such as arithmetic, physics, or chemistry in the Minor course, which in many cases was planned in view of a subsequent Major course.

In the early years of this century technical and scientific instruction was largely influenced by the examinations of the Science and Art Department and the City and Guilds of London Institute. This unduly narrowed the scope of the instruction and made it difficult to introduce subjects which did not appear in the examination syllabuses. Accordingly, in 1904 the Board of Education announced that it was prepared to give grants for subjects other than those approved by the Science and Art Department. This policy not only encouraged technical schools to introduce new subjects, but it attracted teachers who, because of their general education and industrial experience, were competent to plan their own courses of instruction. In 1911 the Board discontinued the lower-grade Science and Art examinations, and by 1918 the advanced examinations, together with the lower examinations of the City and Guilds of London Institute, were abolished. There was, however, a wide demand for tests which could be applied to students at different stages of their work, and it was felt that such examinations should have a national standing. Certain regional examining bodies, e.g. the Union of Lancashire and Cheshire Institutes, the Union of Educational Institutions, the East Midland Educational Union, and the Northern Counties Technical Examination Council, and it became the Board's policy to encourage their development.

It was still felt that this policy was not entirely what was required, because the unions did not cover the whole country and their certificates were on a regional and not a national basis. The answer was the institution of national certificates awarded on the results of three to five years systematic study. The first move came in 1921 when the Institute of Mechanical Engineers, in conjunction with the Board of Education, developed a scheme to issue national certificates and diplomas in mechanical engineering. The success of the scheme led to the introduction of similar schemes, e.g. Chemistry (1921), Electrical Engineering (1923), Naval Architecture (1926), Building (1929), Textiles (1934), Commerce (1939), Production Engineering (1941), Civil Engineering (1943), Applied Physics, Metallurgy (1945), and Applied Chemistry (1947).

The certificates are of two levels. The Ordinary National Certificate is awarded on the results of a senior part-time course of three years, and the Higher National Certificate on the results of an advanced part-time course to those who have already gained the first certificate and have covered another two years' work. Ordinary and Higher National Diplomas are available for full-time students in technical colleges. The introduction of the national certificates and diplomas has had a marked effect on the work done in senior technical institutes. The students gain a qualification approximate to a university degree in their subject, and the standards of teaching have risen considerably.

The development of the junior technical school has already been dealt with on p. 178, and in its relation to the Spens Report on p. 191. It was not until 1 April 1945 that these schools, together with junior commercial schools and junior art departments, became recognised as secondary technical schools. At that time there were slightly over 300 schools with about 65,000 pupils on roll, of whom more than two-thirds were fourteen years of age or over. There were few pupils over fifteen, and this is explained when one realises that the age of entry was twelve or thirteen. In 1957 there were only 290 such schools or departments containing about 94,500 pupils, but in addition there was a number of pupils in the technical streams of bilateral and multilateral schools.

The position of day courses in technical institutes and colleges has been more promising. The most rapid development has been in the number of part-time day release students. Before the Second

World War, only the most enlightened employers were willing to release their young workers to attend part-time day courses, but since then industrial firms have increasingly recognised their value. Thus, in 1938 only 42,000 employees were released for part-time training during the day. These numbered nearly 417,000 by 1957.

The value of technical and commercial education was brought to the notice of employers through the reports of inquiries conducted into this type of education, *e.g.* the Goodenough Committee on Education for Salesmanship, 1931, and the Clerk Committee on Education for the Engineering Group of Industries, 1929. It needed, however, the lessons learnt from the war to emphasise that an organised scheme of technical and technological education was essential for this country. One should note the distinction between "technical training", which is given in evening institutes, technical schools, and the smaller colleges, and "technological training", which denotes the advanced study and research undertaken by the universities and the senior technical colleges.

Percy Report

It had long been a matter of comment that there was too little co-ordination between different agencies whose function it was to provide technological training in the same region. This did not apply to London because the South Kensington group of science and technological colleges were included in the faculty organisation of the University of London. The Ministry of Education appointed in 1944 a special committee on Higher Technological Education. Its report, generally known from its chairman, Lord Eustace Percy, as the Percy Report, was issued in 1945.

The members of the Percy Committee fully understood the issues involved. The Second World War had demonstrated the necessity for more highly-trained scientists and technologists than those available to our enemies. There is no doubt that technology played a decisive part in the winning of the war, and it is no less important in these days of peace. For many years, our British industrialists had been slow to apply, in the fullest sense, scientific and technological knowledge. The crux of the matter was that this country, although a sufficient supply of trained craftsmen was available, lacked highly-trained technological personnel. There was an urgent need for scientists and technologists who not only possessed expert knowledge but could also apply the results of their researches to industry and had ability in organisation and administration. At the lower level the nation was more adequately supplied, but at the highest level there was an acute shortage.

It was essential to secure a much greater output from the universities and the senior technical institutions. It used to be assumed that the universities would produce scientists and technologists and the technical colleges would train technicians and skilled craftsmen. This idea had now broken down and it would be necessary for both types of institution to provide a training for its students which would fit them to take up senior posts in industry. Hence there would have to be much greater co-operation between the universities and the senior technical colleges than had so far been obtained. The Percy Report was largely concerned with the different branches of engineering, and it emphasised that the output of skilled engineers would have to be at least half as large again as the pre-war number. It was thought that the minimum should be about 3,000 annually, of which 45 per cent. should be supplied by the universities.

To bring this about, the Committee recommended that a small number of the larger technical colleges should be selected in which courses approximate to university degree courses should be developed. Such colleges should be given a large measure of self-government and responsibility, and the Government should assist them by means of capital grants similar to those given to universities, and the salaries paid to their staffs should be comparable to those paid in the universities. These colleges of technology should give an award approximately equivalent to a university first degree.

It was on this latter point that there appeared a divergence of views. All members of the Committee agreed that the selected colleges should conduct their own examinations but some national body should be appointed to guarantee a uniform standard. This requirement could be satisfied by the institution of a National Council working through an academic board. It was also agreed that this involved the creation of an external examining body and that the qualifications awarded should have the prestige of a university degree. The disagreement appeared when the Committee came to consider the title of the qualification.

Some members of the Committee were of the opinion that it should be a degree, and a B.Tech. was suggested. They also thought that advanced research should be recognised by the award of the degree of Tech.D. Others thought that industrial employers would pay more attention to the kind of training the applicant had undergone than to the type of paper qualification he possessed. They suggested a diploma instead of a degree. As opinion was equally divided on this question, the decision was left to Lord Eustace Percy. The Committee was fortunate in having him as Chairman, for not only was he acquainted with the situation in technical education, but he had been President of the Board of Education and, in addition, as Rector of the Newcastle Division of the University of Durham, he possessed an intimate knowledge of universities.

He was, therefore, an ideal arbitrator, and in a *Note to the Report* he outlined the difficulties that would arise if the larger technical colleges were authorised to grant degrees. This would mark the beginning of a whole series of claims. The university colleges, the Royal Colleges of Art and Music, and many other institutions for higher education would be justified in asking for the same treatment. The line would have to be drawn at some point, and he had no doubt where this should be. He wrote: "In all civilised countries the power to confer degrees is the distinguishing mark of a university. In this country the power can be exercised only if it is granted by an Act of Government, and Government has jealously restricted such grants. Government policy has been based on the principle that a university should be a fully self-governing community of teachers and students, working together in one place, with substantial endowments of its own, mature enough to set its own standards of teaching and strong enough to resist outside pressures, public or private, political or economic".

We shall see, however, that the demand for technological degrees persisted in a modified form in the claim for the establishment of a technological university. Lord Eustace Percy suggested that the selected colleges should receive the title of Royal College of Technology and should be empowered to grant at the graduate stage the Associateship of the Royal Colleges of Technology, and at the postgraduate stage, the Fellowship.

In addition to the Royal Colleges of Technology, a small number of National Schools of Technology, dealing with the needs of smaller but important industries, should be established within existing colleges. It was also recommended that Regional Advisory Councils and Academic Boards should be formed in England and Wales to work in co-operation with a National Council of Technology. The function of the regional councils would be that of promoting the co-ordination of technological education in the universities and the senior technical colleges of the region and industry should be fully represented on the regional organisation. Altogether eight regional councils were suggested. Consultation between central bodies in England and Wales and in Scotland should be arranged.

One important recommendation was about the development of sandwich courses. These are an alternative to full-time education in a senior technical college. The students who are admitted to the course, which lasts three, four, or five years, generally spend about six months full-time in the college and the remainder in industry. Some industries, mainly mechanical and electrical engineering, had already organised this form of training. It was suggested that other industries might develop similar schemes of training.

The Government was not slow in carrying out the recommendations of the Percy Committee. It is interesting to note that the Government accepted the Report in its entirety with only small differences in nomenclature. In 1946, ten Regional Advisory Councils were set up, followed by the establishment of a National Advisory Council of seventy-two members. This elaborate structure was strongly criticised by some eminent educationists. Thus, W. O. Lester Smith wrote: "Outlining its aims in a short circular, the Ministry demanded 'substantial progress' and in the course of a few weeks; and accompanying this document was a schedule showing England and Wales sliced into ten regions, in each of which conferences were hastily summoned of representatives, not only of universities, technical colleges, and local authorities, but of various bodies associated in any way with further education in its widest connotation. Advisory Councils, representative of the various interests, and Academic Boards were set up; and, later, as a coping stone to this regional mosaic, a National Council was constituted".[1] H. C. Dent characterised the National Council as "a cumbrous body",[2] and Sir P. F. R. Venables, after a critical examination of the regional councils, concluded that it was questionable whether they were worth the time and effort they consumed.[3]

It soon became evident that even with the greatly increased intake of students by the technological departments of the universities, the country would not have nearly enough technologists and

---

[1] *Education in Great Britain*, p. 159, O.U.P., 1949.
[2] *Growth in English Education*, p. 137, Routledge and Kegan Paul, 1954.
[3] *Technical Education*, pp. 135-41, Bell, 1955.

the Government looked to the senior technical colleges to supply the need. Hence the National Advisory Council recommended the establishment of an independent National Council for Technological Awards to create and administer the awards to successful students who had pursued approved courses in technology. It was thought that the standard of the work and the award should be equivalent to a first degree at a university. The Council would be assisted by two Boards of Studies, the first for engineering and the second for other technologies. In July 1955 the Government accepted the recommendation and appointed Lord Hives, Chairman of Rolls Royce Ltd, as Chairman of the new National Council.

Another development was the establishment from 1946 onwards of National Colleges to give advanced instruction in specialised technological subjects which could not easily be provided by the universities, or the local authorities. So far the following colleges have been established: Horology and Instrument Technology, Foundry Work, Rubber Technology, Heating and Ventilating, Leather, Food Technology, Aeronautics, and the Royal College of Art. The latter, which developed from the Normal School of Design and which was established in 1896, was completely reorganised as a National College in 1949. The National Colleges offer a full-time advanced course and also a longer sandwich course. Students who undertake the latter come from two sources: those who have been successful in a part-time course and have been awarded the Ordinary National Certificate, and those who have entered direct from school and have been successful in passing in five subjects in the G.C.E., of which at least two must be at the Advanced Level.

One industrial firm commented on the sandwich courses as follows: ". . . we recruit each year about eighty-ninety public and grammar school leavers who have had sixth form experience and preferably one or two subjects at Advanced Level in the G.C.E. These boys come to us for five years' training, during which we send them to a major college of technology, for six months in each of the four years of the course, for full-time study. The rest of the five year period is spent in gaining industrial training and experience. The object here, as for graduates, is to train for professional employment of the kind already indicated. This arrangement of education and training undoubtedly benefits some boys more than would a university course followed by industrial training. They mature and learn more professionally by the opportunity of industrial contact and training during their formative years. A very high regard in all departments of the Company is paid to men trained in this way. Their studies are just as extensive and advanced as those of the university graduates although perhaps less academic and more practical in approach. Difficult as it is to generalise, it appears that whilst they may not be so much at home in research or development activity as are graduates, they are just as well trained, some perhaps better, for design or executive work as in production. We regard both graduates and students as professional trainees, one group the complement of the other".[1]

In spite of all these developments, the Government still considered that the country was not obtaining the number of technologists and technicians it needed. It was felt that we were lagging behind the output of technologists of such countries as the U.S.S.R. and the United States, and that our own position was so critical as to call for urgent action. Accordingly, in February 1956 the Government issued a White Paper on Technical Education in which a five-year programme of development was outlined. It was pointed out that only about half of the students who completed advanced courses in technical colleges became technologists. The wastage could not be made up through part-time day release and evening classes, and the White Paper considered: "Advanced sandwich courses would therefore probably become the main avenue of progress towards the highest technological qualifications".

After a debate in the Commons, the Minister, in June 1956, proposed provisionally to designate eight colleges of advanced technology. These were the Royal Technical College at Salford, the Bradford Institute of Technology, the Loughborough College of Technology, the Birmingham College of Technology, the Cardiff College of Technology, and in London, the Battersea, Chelsea, and Northampton Polytechnics. Later, he hoped to designate two more colleges, one in the south-west at Bristol, the other in the north-east, the Rutherford Technical College, Newcastle, where no existing college was yet suitable for designation. This policy called for far-reaching changes in the colleges. In all the colleges, except one, a good deal of elementary work was being carried on, and this would have to be transferred elsewhere. Most of the colleges were

---

[1] Quoted from *Technical Education*, p. 10, a Report submitted to the West Riding Education Committee in Sept. 1955, and revised Jan. 1958, by A. B. Clegg, M.A., the Chief Education Officer, and J. M. Hogan, B.A., Assistant Education Officer.

inadequate as regards buildings and equipment, and only the colleges at Salford and Birmingham and the Battersea Polytechnic could reach these requirements in a reasonably short time. They were designated on 1 October 1956. Loughborough and the Chelsea Polytechnic were designated on 1 January 1957, and the remainder later in the same year. The colleges were required to give a sound education in science and technology and their applications, but at the same time they were to organise a scheme for liberal studies and the principles of industrial organisation. This was a wise precaution, because many educationists had feared that the drive for technological education might have the effect of relegating the humanities to the background at the very time when they were most necessary to young people.

Two more Colleges of Advanced Technology (C.A.T.s), have since been added to the list. The site of the Bristol College was considered to be unsatisfactory and now it is being developed on a new site. It was added to the list in September 1960. The tenth C.A.T. is the Brunel College in Middlesex. Brunel was thought to be up to the required standards in regard to work and the qualifications of the staff but the site was not suitable for a C.A.T. After some discussion, the Middlesex L.E.A. offered an alternative site and Brunel was designated in 1962. The Minister decided to make no further designations and changes in the status of existing colleges until the Report on Higher Education (Robbins Report) became available.

At the time of their designation, the C.A.T.s, with the exception of Loughborough, were financed and controlled by the L.E.A.s. Loughborough from 1952 had received direct grant from the Ministry and possessed an independent governing body. It was decided to bring the other colleges into line with Loughborough and the transfer took place at the commencement of the 1962-3 financial year. One important feature connected with the acquisition of a new status was the establishment of academic boards having functions similar to those of a university senate.

In January 1961, a White Paper, *Better Opportunities in Technical Education,* was published. Among other recommendations, attention was drawn to the importance of English and general studies in part-time courses. The result was that a report, *General Studies in Technical Colleges,* was issued in 1962. It dealt with the problems of introducing such studies in part-time courses. In the same year two important developments occurred; the introduction of courses leading to the Diploma in Management Studies, and the approval of three year sandwich courses for the Higher National Diploma in Business Studies.

Circular 305, June 1956, classified technical colleges under four categories. The first consists of the C.A.T.s which deal with technological studies of the highest level. Regional Colleges which at present number twenty-five, and which spend a considerable amount of their time in advanced work, fall into the second category. The third category consists of about 160 Area Colleges which deal largely with lower level studies but it should be noted that some in this group are developing an increasing proportion of advanced work. Finally there are the Local Colleges which at present train junior technicians and craftsmen but also provide a considerable amount of general education. This classification was not intended to be absolutely rigid. It is possible for a college to move from one category to another. Thus Local Colleges which begin to include some advanced courses may eventually become Area Colleges.

The Albemarle Report

The Report on the *Youth Service in England and Wales* was drawn up by a Committee with the Countess of Albemarle in the chair. The Committee was appointed in November 1958 and presented to Parliament in February 1960.

It is convenient at this point to summarise the development of the Youth Service. Like so many other important movements in this country it began with voluntary effort, *e.g.* the Y.M.C.A. (1844), the Y.W.C.A. (1835), and the Scout movement originated by Lord Baden-Powell (1908), and the Girl Guides, founded in 1910. Valuable work was also being done in youth clubs connected with the religious bodies. The State first began to be concerned with youth work when King George's Jubilee Trust was formed in 1935 to raise funds for purchasing playing-fields. The Government began to make grants for physical training and in 1937 the National Fitness Council was formed to administer the money. At the beginning of hostilities in 1939 it became the National Youth Committee. In June 1940, Circular 1516 (*The Challenge of Youth*) was issued and the Board of Education recognised the Youth Service as a part of further education. In 1942 the National Youth Committee was renamed the Youth Advisory Council and the appointment of youth leaders was considered in the McNair Report.

Finally, the Education Act of 1944 placed upon L.E.A.s the duty of the education of youth, and offered the county college as an ally of the Youth Service. Training courses for youth leaders were arranged and there seemed to be a promise of a bright future. In 1945, however, the Ministry decided to delay the putting into operation of the McNair recommendations as regards youth leaders. The final shock came with the post-war economic crisis, and the Ministry gave the priority to building new schools and the development of technical education. The recommendations of the Jackson Committee (1949) and the Fletcher Committee (1951) concerning the conditions of service of professional youth leaders were not put into effect. The consequence was that the Youth Service came to be regarded as a poor relation of the other educational services and this affected public interest in the movement.

The Albemarle Report did not attempt to gloss over the picture. It stated quite frankly that "the Youth Service is at present in a state of acute depression. All over the country and in every part of the service there are devoted workers. And in some areas the inspiration of exceptional individuals or organisations, or the encouragement of local education authorities, have kept spirits unusually high. But, in general, we believe it true to say that those who work in the Service feel themselves neglected and held in small regard, both in educational circles and by public opinion generally. We have been told time and time again that the Youth Service is 'dying on its feet' or 'out on a limb'. Indeed, it has more than once been suggested to us that the appointment of our own Committee was either 'a piece of whitewashing' or an attempt to find grounds for 'killing the Service' " (para. 2).

The Albemarle Committee did not accept the latter remarks, and stated its belief "that a properly nourished Youth Service is profoundly worth while". In support of this belief it urged a "new look" which should be governed by the characteristics of the post-war generation of young people. Hence Chapters 2 and 3 of the Report dealt with the problems of "Young People Today" and the justification for, and aims of, the Youth Service. These chapters are interesting because of their penetrating analysis of the social and psychological problems of young people.

The major recommendations of the Committee included the extension of the Service to all young folk between the ages of fourteen and twenty. The lower age limit was thought to be important because it established a link between those still at school and those who left at the age of fifteen. The Minister of Education was advised to draw up a ten-year development plan for the Youth Service, and for this period to form a small advisory committee of not more than twelve members under the title of the Youth Service Development Council. At least two of the members should be appointed because of their special knowledge of the problems of Wales. In step with this, L.E.A.s should form a sub-committee of the Education Committee which would be responsible for the Youth Service in their areas. The voluntary associations should be adequately represented on these committees, since it is important to develop the voluntary principle and raise the standards of the voluntary workers. Young people should have opportunities for participation as partners in the Service, which should provide them with opportunities for "association, training, and challenge" of the right kind.

The Ministry should strengthen its administrative arrangements and consider the design of generous and imaginative buildings for the Service. An emergency training scheme should be inaugurated to secure an increase in the number of full-time leaders by at least 600 by 1966. A committee should also be appointed to negotiate on such questions as salaries and the allocation of increased Ministry grants. As soon as possible an emergency training college offering a one-year course in youth leadership for men and women should be opened. The Area Training Authorities should be invited to assume responsibility for supervising all courses in their areas and for recommending successful students as qualified youth leaders. Existing full-time leaders who had served satisfactorily for a period of five years should be regarded as qualified, but a date should be fixed after which no entrants could be recognised because of experience alone. L.E.A.s should increase the number of part-time leaders whose salary should depend on the kind of work they were doing. They should also organise part-time training for part-time leaders, paid or voluntary, and make arrangements for providing paid instructors for youth clubs and similar groups. At the end of the first five years, when the Ministry grants ceased, the L.E.A.s should exercise in full their powers under the Education Act of 1944 in making capital grants to voluntary youth groups. Other financial arrangements were also suggested.

The Ministry grasped the urgency stressed by the Report, and early in the year a Youth and Adult Services and General Branch in the Ministry was created under an Under-Secretary with adequate staff. In March 1960 the Youth Service Development Council met under the chairmanship of the Minister. One result of the meeting was the publication in November of *Youth Service,* a monthly issue which included discussions and exchange of views by experienced workers in the field. A youth service building programme was issued which approved work to be started in the period 1960-2 up to the value of £3 million, and in August a £4 million programme for 1962-3 was announced.

The National College for the Training of Youth Leaders has opened in premises vacated by the City of Leicester Training College which aims at providing the 600 full-time leaders needed by 1966. Existing courses at the University College of Swansea and Westhill Training College, Birmingham, have been continued. New full-time courses have been approved, and the amount of Ministry grants to national voluntary youth organisations has been stepped up. Some new organisations received recognition for grants and money was made available for experiments to discover new ways of approach to young people. The Youth Service is now enjoying the "new look" recommended by the Albemarle Report.

SUGGESTIONS FOR FURTHER READING

A. Abbott, *Education for Industry and Commerce in England,* O.U.P., 1933, provides a full account of technical education in the pre-1939 period. Abbott was formerly Chief Inspector of Technical Schools.

Sir P. F. R. Venables, *Technical Education,* Bell, 1955. This is a useful and challenging work which contains chapters by specialist authors.

H. C. Dent, *The Educational System of England and Wales,* University of London Press, 1961, gives a full account of recent developments in English education up to the close of 1960.

CHAPTER XIII

THE INDEPENDENT SCHOOLS

If the reader turns back to Chapter IX he will see that it is entitled "The National System of Education". The national system includes two types of school; those which are maintained by the local education authorities through money received by Government grants and through the local rates, and those schools which are not assisted either by grants from the Ministry or the rates. The former group of schools constitute the statutory system of education; the latter, the independent schools. The Education Act of 1944 defined an independent school in Section 114 as "any school at which full-time education is provided for five or more pupils of compulsory school age (whether or not such education is also provided for pupils over that age), not being a school maintained by a local education authority or a school in respect of which grants are made by the Minister to the proprietor of the school".

There are several points about this definition which require an explanation. In the first place, the last part of the definition was carefully framed so as to exclude the voluntary schools associated with the religious bodies, the aided grammar schools, and the direct grant schools, all of which receive Government grants, and in the two former categories, in addition, are assisted by the rates. The next point to notice is that the independent schools are not excluded from the national system. In a complex community such as our own, one should not be surprised to find that the national system includes types of school which are vastly different in their origin and varied in their characteristics. Most people would consider this a strength rather than a weakness in our national life. The independent schools, then, although not included in the statutory system, are recognised under certain conditions by the State, and this constitutes one of their claims to be part of the national system. We shall see later that they have affiliations with schools in the statutory system in many other ways.

The independent schools can be divided into three main categories. First of all there are the private schools, which in the nineteenth century were often described officially as "private adventure schools". They are schools which are run for profit, either by individuals or by a company. The second class consists of the preparatory schools, which cater for younger children and prepare them for entry into the third category, the public schools. The reader is recommended to turn back to Chapter I to recall to his mind the different kinds of school which existed at the beginning of the nineteenth century. A start may be made by a consideration of the private schools.

During the last century private schools varied greatly in efficiency. The Newcastle Commission sharply criticised a large number of them. At that time there was no legal obstacle to prevent any individual from opening a school in his own house, even if he possessed no qualification nor experience in teaching. Some of the cases singled out by the Commissioners seem almost inconceivable to a modern reader. These schools were not open to inspection, unless they asked for it, and the inefficient ones were not likely to do this. The Report of the Newcastle Commission gives numerous instances of the terrible conditions which were encountered when the Commissioners visited the worst types of private school. They reported: "When other occupations fail for a time, a private school can be opened, with no capital beyond the cost of a ticket in the window. Any room, however small and close, serves for the purpose; the children sit on the floor, and bring what books they please; whilst the closeness of the room renders fuel superfluous, and even keeps the children quiet by its narcotic effects. If the fees do not pay the rent, the school is dispersed or taken by the next tenant". The mistresses were described as "generally advanced in life, and their school is usually their kitchen, sitting, and bedroom". The room "was often so small that the children stand in a semicircle round the teacher. Indeed, I have seen the children as closely packed as birds in a nest, and tumbling over each other like puppies in a kennel".

The mistresses and masters would not be tolerated for one moment at the present day. "None are too old, too poor, too ignorant, too feeble, too sickly, too unqualified in one or every way, to regard themselves, and to be regarded by others, as unfit for school-keeping—domestic servants out of place, discharged barmaids, vendors of toys or lollipops, keepers of small eating-houses, of mangles, or of small lodging houses, needlewomen who take on plain or slop work, milliners, consumptive patients in an advanced stage, cripples almost bedridden, persons of at least doubtful temperance, outdoor paupers, men and women of seventy and even eighty years of age, persons who spell badly (mostly women, I grieve to say), who can scarcely write and who cannot cipher at all."

Even as late as 1869, one school was decribed as being held "in a small low room, in a back court. There were forty-four boys of ages varying from four to fourteen. In the middle sat the master, a kindly man, but a hopeless cripple, whose lower limbs appeared to be paralysed, and who was unable to stand up. The boys formed a dense mass round him, swaying irregularly backwards and forwards, while he was feebly protesting against the noise. In a corner the wife was sitting minding the six or eight youngest children". One wonders what kind of education the pupils received.

It might have been thought that these revelations would have stirred the Commissioners to drastic action. They were so complacent, however, that they recommended that a private school should receive a grant if it was properly ventilated and drained and if the inspector gave a good report on it. Their idea was that this would get rid of the worst schools and that a better type of person would be encouraged to open schools. They also recommended the admission to the Teachers' Certificate Examination of those who had a good moral character and possessed at least three years' teaching experience. The Commissioners came straight to the point when they offered an explanation for the popularity of private schools. To send a child to one of these institutions was a mark of respectability; "the children were more respectable and the teachers more inclined to fall in with the wishes of the parents. The latter, in choosing such schools for their children, stand in an independent position, and are not accepting a favour from their social superiors". In fact, the motives of the parents could be summed up in the one word "snobbery".

As public attention was drawn to the inefficiency of so many private schools, the worst of them tended to disappear, but it was a very slow process. Even after the Education Act of 1902 it was only by a circuitous method that a really bad school could be closed. The means employed were to issue summonses against a number of parents because they failed in their duty of ensuring that their children were receiving adequate instruction in the three Rs (Lord Sandon's Act, 1876). Their defence would be that the children were attending the private school kept by Mrs X. The magistrate would reply that he had no knowledge that such a school existed, and the inspector would be requested to ascertain if it did. This meant a visit to the school. If denied admission, he could not truthfully say that the building was a school. On the other hand, if he was admitted and found that adequate instruction in the three Rs was not being given, the school would be condemned on that ground. The parents would be fined, but would take good care to withdraw their children from the school, and Mrs X would have to close down for lack of customers. It was only in extreme cases that this procedure was followed, and many schools which were far below the standard of those under the L.E.A. continued to function.

The Education Act of 1918 made it compulsory for the person responsible for a school not in receipt of grants from the Board of Education to furnish to the Board the name and address of the school with a short description of it. The consolidating Act of 1921 stated that it was not a defence in school attendance proceedings to say the child was attending a school which provided efficient elementary instruction unless the school in question was open to inspection by the Board or by the L.E.A., and that satisfactory attendance registers were kept. The Board had notified that it was ready to inspect any private school, if requested to do so, free of cost. Efficient private schools availed themselves of this offer, and proudly headed their prospectuses with the words: "Inspected by the Board of Education". The obligation to notify the name and address of the school to the Board was not strictly enforced, so that in 1944 it was not possible to say exactly how many private schools existed. It was generally assumed that they numbered more than 4,000, some quite good, others satisfactory, and others, again, inefficient. The majority of these had never been inspected.

The Government did not contemplate the closing of efficient private schools. The Act of 1944 directed the Minister of Education to appoint a Registrar of Independent Schools who should keep a register of them. Certain schools which were already recognised as efficient secondary schools, and some preparatory and private schools which had previously been inspected, were exempt from registration. A school found to be inefficient because of inadequate buildings, or an unqualified staff, or for some other grave reason, could be removed from the register. The proprietor was given the right of appeal to an Independent Schools' Tribunal consisting of a chairman appointed by the Lord Chancellor from the legal profession and two other members appointed by the Lord President of the Council from persons who possessed teaching or administrative experience. No officials, either of the Ministry or of a L.E.A., are eligible for appointment.

This section of the Act could not be brought into operation at once because of the shortage of H.M.I.s and difficulties as regards building materials and labour and the lack of teachers, which made it unreasonable that schools should be required to remedy their deficiencies within a fixed time. By March 1949 the situation had eased, and the inspection of independent schools began and continued at the rate of about 150 a month. By 1957, the Ministry had recognised 1,450 independent schools as efficient, and it was considered that this section of the Act could be put into force completely. In July of that year, proprietors were notified that they would be required to register their schools by 31 March 1958. The registration was provisional, and its continuance depended upon the kind of report rendered by the inspectors after their visit. During 1957, 145 schools were closed, of which 138 were of recent origin and which had become known to the Ministry for the first time. This is a comment on the strictness with which earlier regulations had been enforced.

It was expected that the number of private schools would rapidly decrease after 1944, but this did not happen. The reason was that many middle-class parents were faced with a difficult problem. Their children could not obtain entry to a grammar school unless they were qualified through the grammar school selection test at eleven plus. The only other way open to them was through a public or direct grant school, and these had a long waiting list. Competition was so keen that few children who failed to pass the grammar school entrance test would be considered. The result was that a number of private schools which offered an education similar to that given by the grammar school came into existence. The necessity of registration and inspection guaranteed their efficiency. Moreover, some primary schools, run by private teachers who were qualified, opened their doors to younger children whose parents were anxious for them to pass the selection test.

The preparatory schools aim at preparing their pupils for public school entrance. In the earlier part of the last century, very few schools of this type existed. It was the usual practice to plunge small boys at eight or nine years of age into the difficulties and dangers of a large public school. After 1850, however, the number of preparatory schools began to increase rapidly. Two of the main reasons for their development were the extension of the railways, which facilitated travel (most of the preparatory schools are boarding schools), and the increasing prestige of the public schools. At the present time there are nearly 500 preparatory schools distributed over the country, though the larger number is to be found in the south and the south-east of England. Some of the public schools and the larger independent and direct grant grammar schools have their own preparatory departments, but by far the greater number of the preparatory schools are privately owned.

The preparatory schools take their pupils at the age of eight to nine years and prepare them for the Common Entrance Examination to public schools. This was established in 1903. There are a few preparatory schools for girls, but the majority only admit boys. In July 1914, the Board of Education altered its definition of a secondary school so as to include preparatory schools, which were now considered to be an integral part of the public school system. The upper age limit for the preparatory schools is about 14, and pupils between $13\frac{1}{2}$ and that age who have been successful in the Common Entrance Examination can apply for entrance to the public schools. Obviously, the curriculum of the preparatory school is strongly influenced by the requirements of the public schools. Hence it includes classics, modern languages, mathematics, and elementary science, which are subjects not taught at that age in the primary schools of the statutory system.

The preparatory schools are very efficient establishments. Their very existence depends upon their success in getting their pupils accepted by the public schools, and they have had no difficulty in obtaining recognition from the State. Their fees are high, but they can offer many advantages to pupils whose parents can afford to pay them. The buildings are quite adequate, and many of the schools are situated in delightful surroundings outside large towns, in the country, or near the sea. Naturally, the equipment varies with the size of the school and the amount of capital possessed by the proprietor, but they usually have their own playing fields, gymnasia, swimming-baths, and art and craft rooms. In some cases the school possesses its own chapel.

The preparatory schools have their own professional organisation, the I.A.P.S. (Incorporated Association of Preparatory Schools), which is in close association with the Head Masters' Conference. The Association was founded in 1892 when some fifty headmasters of preparatory schools "met to discuss the size and weight of the cricket ball to be used by their boys". The Association was incorporated in 1923. In liaison with the Head Masters' Conference since 1906, a Joint Standing Committee has met at regular intervals to discuss matters of common interest.

Public Schools

The public schools during the nineteenth century have already been discussed in the first chapter of this book (pp. 16-18) and in Chapter V (pp. 80-4 and 91-3). It now remains to consider the development of public school education since the days of Thring of Uppingham. In the first place, it is important to understand what is meant by a public school, and as soon as this question is put a considerable difficulty is encountered in providing an accurate definition. The Clarendon Commission confined its attention to nine of the greater schools, but the ordinary man would add at least another twenty to this number. Amongst these would be certain large grammar schools, of which Manchester Grammar School is an example. There are also certain endowed schools, such as Uppingham and Oundle, made famous by their distinguished headmasters, and in addition some newer schools founded in the nineteenth and the present centuries. It is at once obvious that when we speak of the public schools we cannot regard them as merely members of a species which had a common origin and possess common characteristics. It is not too much to say that each school, like the individual angels of the medieval philosophers, constitutes a species itself.

When Mr R. A. Butler was asked in the House of Commons in 1942 to define a public school, he replied that it is a school which is "in membership of the Governing Bodies' Association or Headmasters' Conference" (see pp. 92-3). If this is accepted as a working definition, then all public schools need not be independent schools. One would have to include the direct grant schools and certain aided and even maintained secondary grammar schools, all of which receive Government grants and, in a few cases, grants from a L.E.A.

Very largely because of the work of Dr Arnold, Sir H. M. Butler of Harrow, Thring of Uppingham, and many others, the concluding years of the last century constituted a period in which the public schools enjoyed great prosperity and increased enormously in prestige. Even in the early years of this century, Sanderson of Oundle, whose work will be discussed later, demonstrated that a traditional public school could adapt itself to meet the most stringent requirements of modern times. In fact, the public schools reached such a position in public esteem that new schools such as Stowe and Canford in 1923, and Bryanston in 1928, were founded. In recent years, however, the public schools, popularly understood as comprising about twenty or thirty of the larger schools, have come in for increasingly bitter criticism. Unfortunately, the issue has been blurred, as in other educational discussions, by the intrusion of party politics. Most of the criticism has come from the left wing, and a good deal of it from those who have only known the outside of the schools they condemn or who judge them by their experiences of some forty years ago.

The main attack has followed the lines that the public schools constitute a "closed shop", open only to the sons of the well-to-do, and that they are one of the main causes of our class divisions. It seldom occurs to the supporters of this view that they may be putting the cart before the horse. In general, schools tend to reflect the existing divisions of society, but do not create them. On the other hand, there is more foundation to the criticism that having accepted the social distinctions which exist, the public schools may tend to perpetuate them. It is also asserted that the existence of the public schools is a negation of democracy. Much labour has been spent in compiling statistics to show that over three-quarters of the senior posts in central and local administration are held by men who have had a public school education. The same is said to be true of the Services, the Church, and the professions. This is probably correct if we consider conditions of forty or fifty years ago, but the public schools are meeting with increasing competition from the grammar schools of the statutory system. The inuendo is that some kind of nepotism exists, but the facts could have another interpretation, namely, that the kind of education provided by the public schools was highly efficient in producing the kind of leaders deemed to be necessary some years ago. One has to realise that great changes have occurred during the last few decades and that the public schools are also changing.

The idea that the public schools constitute a "closed shop" was much more true of the nineteenth century, but even at that period, Christ's Hospital took its entrants from those who had attended elementary schools, and quite a number of public schools had a system of open scholarships available to the sons of parents of moderate means. Although the public schools are not a part of the statutory system, they have so many links with it that one is justified in regarding them as part of the national system. During the present century the scholarships schemes of these schools have been placed on a wider basis. Thus, the late Bishop of Peterborough, Dr Spencer Leeson, when headmaster of Winchester, instituted a very generous system of scholarships at his school. Rendcombe College, in Gloucestershire, admits boys from primary and preparatory schools in almost equal numbers, and at Giggleswick, in the West Riding of Yorkshire, nearly a third of the intake comes from the locality of the school and is selected on the results of a scholarship test. The Royal Naval College, Dartmouth, takes pupils from all types of school.

It is not so widely known as it should be that in 1919 the H.M.C. offered to open their doors to ex-elementary schoolboys. Mr Fisher carefully considered the offer, expressed his thanks for the spirit which prompted it, but regretted that he could not at the time accept it because of the small demand for such places. The Board of Education promised that the offer would be kept in mind, and if the need arose in the future they would avail themselves of it.

Another link is that of inspection. The Board of Education Act, 1899, empowered the Board to "inspect any school supplying secondary education and desiring so to be inspected". The public schools were not at first eager to accept the proposal. Up to 1914, only nine had asked for inspection, but by 1921 nine more schools, including Harrow and Rugby, were added to that number. Eton and Shrewsbury were inspected in 1936, and Oundle in the following year. As a result of the Education Act of 1944, all the public schools are open to inspection.

The common ground between the public schools and the maintained secondary schools was extended in 1917 when the School and Higher School Certificate Examinations were instituted, and this link remains now that the G.C.E. has taken their place. Pupils from the public schools and the maintained grammar schools have entered for the same examinations and have competed for university open scholarships and for the award of State and L.E.A. scholarships. The governing bodies of the public schools, though keeping their independent status, admit representatives from the L.E.A.s on their boards of governors. Again, there is frequently competition in games and athletics between the local grammar schools and the public school in the same area.

The public schools have had a marked influence upon the development of other types of secondary school. Thus, nearly every grammar and secondary modern school has adopted the prefect system, which although not the invention of Dr Arnold of Rugby, owes its modern form to him. The House system is another example. In the residential public school each boarding house was a definite unit of the organisation. Grammar and modern schools have adopted the nomenclature, although their houses are a somewhat artificial unit serving as a link between the form and the school as a whole. Probably many members of a house have never realised the origin of the term. There is also a certain amount of two-way traffic between the two types of school in regard to staffing. The writer remembers when a few years ago he was appointed a governor of a secondary modern school, he found that the headmaster had been a housemaster in a public school. In a similar way, the societies which form an important item in the secondary schools of the statutory system, are an adaptation of the public school societies, though the latter developed from necessity rather than choice. The staff of the residential public schools, after the evening "prep" was concluded were faced with the problem of providing worthwhile activities for their pupils. Hence the formation of literary and debating societies, historical, geographical, and scientific societies, all of which, with many others, are now a commonplace in the schools of the statutory system.

Finally, the influence of the public schools on methods of teaching and on the curriculum is by no means negligible. One can cite the example of Sanderson's experiments at Oundle and the Direct Method of teaching both classics and modern languages which had been practised by Dr Rouse and his colleagues at the Perse School, Cambridge. In the same school, Mr Caldwell Cook did much to popularise both the Play Way Method in the education of younger pupils and initiated experiments in the writing of original verse. It was felt that the points of contact between the two systems ought to be extended and the place of the public schools in the national system clarified, and this was the problem which the Fleming Committee set out to tackle in 1942, and in the Report of 1944 a number of suggestions were made.

Fleming Report

The Fleming Report recommended that the Board of Education should compile a list of schools not maintained by local authorities and which were willing to play their part in association with the statutory system. They should be grouped into two categories, for which separate schemes—Scheme A or Scheme B—should apply. Both schemes would apply equally to boys' and girls' schools. Scheme A would be concerned with the direct grant schools, of which the majority were day schools. If they joined the scheme they would be required either to abolish tuition fees or to grade them according to a sliding scale based upon the income of the parents. Boarding charges should be graded in the same way in all schools participating in the scheme. The L.E.A. would be entitled to reserve a number of places, the exact number being a matter of agreement between the governors and the local authority. Tuition fees would be paid by the L.E.A., and also boarding fees, and the appropriate amount would be recoverable from the parents based on a graded scale. A minimum of one-third of the governing body would be nominated by the L.E.A. This scheme applied only to those schools which were not recognised as independent according to the definition of the Act of 1944.

The larger public boarding schools fell into Scheme B. The Board of Education would award bursaries to qualified pupils who had attended for at least two years at a grant-aided primary school. The bursaries would include tuition and boarding fees, and the amount given be dependent on the income of the parents, with total remission of fees where necessary. Schools which accepted this scheme would be required to accept a minimum of 25 per cent. of their annual admissions to pupils from primary schools. The scheme of admission should be reviewed at the end of each five-year period. L.E.A.s would be able to reserve places at particular schools for their pupils, and parents should make their applications for bursaries through the local authority. They would be entitled to apply to any school which accepted the scheme, and if they applied for more than one they should indicate the order of their preference. The candidates would be interviewed by a Regional Interviewing Board appointed by the Board of Education, and the recommendations would be sent to a Central Advisory Committee which would make the final recommendations to the Board of Education. The regional boards would consist of about four members, and should include the head of one of the public schools which had accepted the scheme, a head teacher of a primary school, and a representative of a local education authority.

The Fleming Committee now encountered a difficult problem—that of the age of transfer. The age at which a pupil was received by a secondary school was eleven plus, but most of the public schools took their pupils at thirteen. These entrants had previously attended a preparatory school and had been instructed in classics, modern languages, mathematics, and science. It was suggested either that the bursar should spend two years in a grammar school or he might be sent to one of the preparatory schools, provided that it was not a school which was solely run for profit.

The recommendations of the Fleming Committee were patently a compromise, and as a rule none of the parties to a compromise solution are whole-heartedly in its favour. It certainly did not satisfy the extremists who wished to destroy the public school system. On the other hand, the heads of some of the grammar schools were opposed. They complained that it would be unjust to the grammar schools to cream off their best pupils, intellectually, and also those who by their character and personality had become leaders in the school. This seems to be rather a selfish attitude. The good of individual pupils has a claim to consideration as being as important as that of the institution. It is not so much the individual in himself who counts, but the benefits he receives which can be used in the interests of the nation as a whole.

The results following the Report of the Fleming Committee fell greatly short of what the Committee had hoped. Some of the public schools were hesitant at committing themselves, very largely because they valued their independence and were suspicious of any move on the part of the State which might threaten it. At the same time the demand for public school places has been nothing like it was anticipated it would be. The Reports of the Ministry of Education give only slight evidence of progress. The Report of 1947 mentions the setting up of a Central Advisory Committee, presumably to carry out the functions recommended by the Fleming Committee. In the first year of the Committee's operation there were 594 places at its disposal, of which 358 were in the independent schools and 85 were applied for by local education authorities. In the following year 155 places were allotted, but the Report mentions this was insignificant when compared with the number of places given as a result of direct negotiations between the L.E.A.s and the schools themselves. Thus, 566 were at direct grant and 2,096 at independent schools. In 1949 there were 184, and in 1950 102 places were at the disposal of L.E.A.s The majority of places were the result of direct negotiation. It seems that the Advisory Committee did not fulfil the hopes of the Fleming Report, and it came to an end in 1951.

The Fleming Committee thought that there would be less difficulty in initiating their proposals in girls' public schools than in boys'. The reasons given were that a girl does not gain the same advantages and social privileges from attending a public school as does a boy; that there is a freer interchange of staff and pupils between day and boarding schools, and that the girls' schools, being of more recent origin than the boys' schools, did not possess the same strong classical tradition. Another factor which counted was that all secondary school mistresses had a single association (the Association of Head Mistresses, founded by Miss Buss and Miss Beale in 1874), whilst headmasters were divided between two bodies —the Headmasters' Conference and the Headmasters' Association. There was no Common Entrance Examination, the curriculum was more flexible and varied, and girls' schools had been accustomed to receiving their entrants at varying ages so that preparatory schools were not so essential as in the case of boys.

Generally speaking, there were few secondary schools for girls existing before the middle of the nineteenth century. The enthusiasm which sprang from Dr Arnold inspired a desire to create comparable schools for girls. The two most famous schools of this period were the North London Collegiate School, founded by Miss Buss in 1850, and the Cheltenham Ladies' College, founded by Miss Beale in 1853. It was, however, a handicap to such schools that university education was denied to women who needed such a qualification to teach in them. Hence the main efforts became directed to opening the universities to women students. The account of this struggle is given in the last chapter of this book.

The Fleming Report also included an interesting historical chapter on the development of secondary education in Wales, together with a review of the endowed schools which remained external to the county scheme set up by the Welsh Intermediate Education Act of 1889. The proportion of schools which were completely or mainly boarding was less than that in England. The problem of language was extremely important. Until the latter part of the nineteenth century the Government had adopted the unfortunate policy of forcing the use of the English language upon the Welsh schools. The reaction of Welsh nationalism to this policy is seen in the foundation of Llandovery School by Thomas Phillips in 1848. Its foundation deed explicitly stated that the school aimed at the study and cultivation of the Welsh language and literature. Later in the century the Government was more sensible in its attitude to teaching Welsh in the elementary schools, and in 1927 the Report of the Board of Education on *Welsh in Education and Life* showed a warm appreciation of the language, literature, and history of the Principality. Hence it was important in the application of Schemes A and B to Welsh schools to ensure that they would not be segregated from Welsh social life. They should also continue the pupil's bilingual instruction. As Sir Fred Clarke pointed out, our English system of education has largely been imposed from above. In distinction to this, education in Wales, whether elementary, secondary, or university, came as a result of a popular demand.

Sanderson of Oundle

It is perhaps fitting to conclude this chapter with a brief account of the work of F. W. Sanderson of Oundle, one of the outstanding public schoolmasters of the present century. He had been for some years a form-master at Dulwich before he was appointed to Oundle in 1892, and in the thirty years he held this post he completely changed the character of the school. Oundle originated in the bequest of Joan Wyatt in 1485, who left property for the maintenance of a master to teach grammar. In 1556, Sir William Laxton, Lord Mayor of London and Master of the Grocers' Company, gave considerable property into the charge of the Company to support a grammar school in his native town of Oundle. When the Company found that a grammar school already existed in the town, it decided to take over and develop the Wyatt foundation. The school had a somewhat chequered history. The Grocers' Company was not an ideal body for developing the fortunes of the school, which soon suffered from its proximity to Rugby and Uppingham.

When Sanderson took over he found that there was little to distinguish it from any other country grammar school of moderate size. It had a strong classical bias and sent its best pupils to the universities. The number of boys had fallen to less than 100. When Sanderson died suddenly in 1922, it had become one of the foremost schools in the country, containing more than 500 pupils and possessing a long waiting list for entry.

Sanderson had been appointed to Oundle to revive the school, and he started this process as soon as he took office. He was neither a psychologist nor a student of educational theory, but like many other famous headmasters he was essentially a practical teacher.

He understood boys and the things and activities which interest them. There were, however, certain defects in his understanding of educational aims. Thus he thoroughly disliked classroom studies. He often referred to classrooms as tool-sharpening rooms, necessary at a certain stage of the educational process, but always subsidiary. This attitude sprang from his lack of experience of the class teaching which had developed in English elementary and secondary schools.

He was also a scientist, and this led him to stress science as affording the best example of creative thought in the service of mankind. Even science, unless it was studied from the point of view of its service to humanity, was, in his eyes, of little value as a school subject. It was not so much the subject which mattered, but the spirit in which it was studied. He often said that the traditional spirit of school learning was individualistic, acquisitive, and possessive, whereas it ought to be social, co-operative, and creative, and for this other rooms than classrooms were needed. He realised that in order to carry out his ideas it would mean a great rebuilding programme. Thus the school became gradually equipped with laboratories, workshops for joinery and engineering, a machine shop and forge, a foundry, and an experimental farm. He also added art and music rooms, an observatory, a large library, and a museum. Thus Oundle School became one of the best-equipped educational institutions in the country.

Sanderson at first experienced intense opposition to his reforms from both boys and staff. In his enthusiasm he was in a hurry to get things done, and did not always introduce changes in the most diplomatic way. Moreover, he was at first a man of violent temper, but as he grew older he mellowed considerably. One historian of Oundle School has described the first eight years of his headmastership as the years of conflict. In the end his enthusiasm and his obvious sincerity enabled him to win over both boys and staff, and one of the monuments to his memory is the book *Sanderson of Oundle*, a personal tribute written by members of his staff. Like Thring of Uppingham, he believed that every boy had an interest in something and could do something. The problem for the schoolmaster was to discover what these things were. Hence his maxim was, "Education must be fitted to the boy, not the boy to Education".

He believed that schools should be in the closest and most intimate touch with the community. He wanted to break down the distinction between the life inside the school and life in the community outside it. "Adult life should not be a breaking away from school, but a continuation and a development of school." Like Dewey, he thought of the school as a community in miniature. Schools should exercise boys in the same kinds of activities and interests as they would be called upon to use after they had left school. Hence he did not fear the term "vocational", but saw vocation as the centre about which a boy's interests were moving, and wished to seize this natural interest and turn it to good account, to develop it in the right atmosphere into a right spirit of true work in the service of the community. Although Sanderson is not mentioned by name, one can see the impact of his ideas throughout the Hadow Report on the Education of the Adolescent.

He believed that the work carried out in the school should be real work. "Sanderson was always strongly in favour of the work done in the shops being 'real', something that boys would realise at once was of genuine value; models and toys and petty jobs were all useful enough in giving a certain manual dexterity, but genuine commercial work could be made much more truly educational. The whole process from drawing-office to the final erecting and testing, he held, should be followed, if possible, and a real insight gained into the reason for the design, into the properties of various materials used, and into the way in which each part fulfilled its purpose." [1] When the First World War broke out the workshops at Oundle were sufficiently well equipped to make a valuable contribution to the war effort. The boys helped in turning out the shells and other munitions so badly needed by our troops. Each form was sent in rotation into the workshops for a week, and the boys not only had the satisfaction of doing something they liked but the greater joy of knowing that what they were doing was hastening on final victory.

Sanderson also took great interest in the teaching of the Arts subjects. As in science, he demanded that they should be given full opportunity in creative work in history, geography, and English. This idea was at the base of his scheme for library study. For him the library was the workshop for the Arts subjects, and in it the boys should be trained in both individual and group work. They would learn how to make the best use of a library, how to use books for answering simple questions arising from their studies, and eventually to embark upon some elementary research work.

[1] *Sanderson of Oundle*, p. 357, Chatto and Windus, 1924.

Sanderson's projects were carried out in the environment of a large public school where money was no object, but his work has its lessons for other types of school. The grammar schools of to-day can learn much from the example of Oundle, and the secondary modern school may find an answer to many of its problems through a study of what Sanderson accomplished.

SUGGESTIONS FOR FURTHER READING

The student is advised to read carefully the Fleming Report, *The Public Schools and the National System*, H.M.S.O., 1944. *Sanderson of Oundle*, Chatto and Windus, 1924, is well worth reading, even though the first-hand account given by members of the staff is at times given to hero worship.

Other useful books on the public schools are:
D. Hughes, *The Public Schools and the Future*, C.U.P., 1942.
E. H. Partridge, *Freedom in Education*, Faber and Faber, 1943.
Spencer Leeson, *The Public Schools Question*, Longmans, 1948.
Sir J. F. Wolfenden, *The Public Schools To-day*, University of London Press, 1949.

CHAPTER XIV

ADULT EDUCATION

Adult education in the modern sense did not exist in this country until the early years of the last century. Its history falls into two well-marked periods, with 1850 as a convenient dividing point. In the earlier period there were three main factors which governed the development of adult education. It started with the efforts of the religious and philanthropic bodies to satisfy the desire of adults for education. Another factor was the result of the discoveries made in the physical sciences, and towards the middle of the period adult education was affected by social and political agitations which eventually found expression in the Chartist movement.

After 1850 the whole outlook was changed by developments in social and economic conditions. The universities started to take an interest in adult education, and the State, which became increasingly concerned with elementary education, was forced to take adult education into account. As more elementary schools became available and literacy became more general, the State began to regard the education of adults as an extension of primary education, but even now, in spite of increased assistance by way of grants, much adult education is carried out by voluntary effort.

Before 1800 there were three interesting isolated experiments in adult education. The Minutes of the S.P.C.K. for 8 March 1700 mention two individuals, John Pierson and John Reynolds, who undertook the instruction of a group of adults in reading and the Catechism, and in 1711 the Society recommended the establishment of evening schools for adults. This advice was carried out by Griffith Jones, who had about 1730 established a system of circulating schools in Wales in which both children and adults received instruction.

The second experiment was an offshoot of the Sunday School movement in Birmingham. The problem to be faced was how to retain young people who had become too old for that type of teaching, and in 1789 the Birmingham Sunday Society was formed to teach the three R's, and later, geography, bookkeeping, drawing, natural science, and other subjects were added. The instruction spread to week-day evenings. The students included some of the best artisans of the town, who became known as the "Cast-iron Philosophers".

Another example was the foundation of the first adult school at Nottingham in 1798 by William Singleton, a Methodist, and Samuel Fox, a Quaker. The importance of this school is that some fifty years later it became the stimulus to an adult school which opened in Birmingham. The early adult school movement started at Bristol in 1812, when William Smith, a doorkeeper of a Methodist chapel, assisted by a merchant, Stephen Prust, established an *Institution for Instructing Adult Persons to read the Holy Scriptures*. Dr Pole, a member of the Bristol Committee, wrote a *History of the Origin and Progress of Adult Schools* in 1814. He claimed that the first school exclusively for the instruction of adults was opened in North Wales by the Rev. Thomas Charles of Bala in 1811. Pole spoke of him "as the first Establisher and Father of Adult Schools".

Dr Pole was a member of the Society of Friends and an enthusiastic supporter of the British and Foreign Bible Society. He was an exceedingly able lecturer, and from 1802 delivered series of lectures in Bristol on such subjects as chemistry, the economy of nature, and mineralogy, all illustrated by his pencil sketches and models. William Smith attended them and was impressed by the statement that Bibles were useless to many poor folk who were not able to read. In partnership with Stephen Prust, he opened a small evening school in 1804. Such was the demand for instruction in reading and writing that within thirteen months there were nine schools for men and the same number for women. This development showed the necessity for some kind of organisation, and shortly after the formation of the Institution for Instructing Adult Persons, Dr Pole became a member of the Committee.

His *History* was excellent propaganda for the new movement, and as it circulated in all parts of England and Wales the growth of adult schools was phenomenal. By 1820 there were schools in most of the larger towns and also in rural districts. One of the most interesting was that of Severn Street, Birmingham, founded by Joseph Sturge in 1845. It started off badly, and Sturge, hearing of the success of Singleton and Fox at Nottingham, sent a deputation to learn the secret of their success. The result was that he made a number of important modifications at Severn Street, and thus the isolated experiment at Nottingham entered into the main stream of the adult school movement.

Another historian of adult education, J. W. Hudson, recorded that by 1850 the adult schools were in decline. The increasing number of elementary schools had lessened the need for teaching the three R's to adults, and political agitation had diverted the interest of the workers to other directions. Later in the century, the adult schools were to experience an astonishing revival. Factory owners began to encourage their employees to take an interest in the machines they operated and the processes in which they were engaged. This brought about a new type of adult education, and for its origin we have to go to Scotland. At this time there was no clear dividing line between non-vocational and technical education.

In 1755, John Anderson took up his duties as Professor of Oriental Languages in the University of Glasgow. He soon became interested in other subjects, and in 1757 was appointed to the Chair of Natural Philosophy, which in our day would cover physics and chemistry. Anderson had been associated for many years with James Watt, who introduced improvements in the steam engine. Anderson seems to have been interested in all branches of science, and if he had lived at the present time would have been a strong advocate for teaching general science in secondary schools. During his life at Glasgow, Anderson established a library and accumulated a unique collection of scientific apparatus. At his death in 1796 he left all these "to the Public for the good of Mankind and the Improvement of Science, in an Institution to be denominated 'Anderson's University'". In 1912 the Institution became the Royal Technical College, Glasgow. In 1799, Dr George Birkbeck was appointed Professor of Natural Philosophy and Chemistry in the Andersonian Institution.

Anderson had delivered a number of lectures upon experimental physics which were attended by some of the workmen who constructed his models and apparatus. Dr Birkbeck found that the workmen were interested in knowing more about the apparatus they were making. In spite of the prediction that "the mechanics would not come, that if they did come they would not listen, and that if they listened they would not understand", he resolved to invite them to his classes. The experiment was a great success, and after four years Dr Birkbeck was able to report: "For three successive seasons I had the gratification of lecturing to 500 mechanics. An audience more orderly, attentive, and apparently comprehending I never witnessed".

In 1804, Dr Birkbeck left Glasgow for London, but his place was taken by Dr Ure, who continued the classes. Dr Birkbeck practised as a physician in London, but he retained his interest in adult education and was influential in founding the London Mechanics' Institute in 1823. In the same year, the Glasgow Mechanics' Institution was founded by seceders from the Andersonian Institution. The next year the Manchester Mechanics' Institute started, and was followed by similar institutes in Huddersfield, Leeds, and other industrial towns. The first Union of Mechanics' and other Literary and Scientific Institutions was founded in the West Riding of Yorkshire, and the example spread to other parts of the country. J. W. Hudson, in the *History of Adult Education* (1851), records that the number of institutes in England had grown to 610, with a membership of more than 600,000.

The Mechanics' Institutes were an important step in the growth of scientific and technical education, and in a number of places they eventually became important technical institutes and colleges. The London Mechanics' Institute developed into Birkbeck College in 1907, and in 1920 was recognised as a school of the University of London for evening and part-time students. In the 1860s there was a general decline in the fortunes of the Mechanics' Institutes. The mechanics tended to drop out, and their place was taken by members of the middle classes. This, however, was not so marked in Yorkshire, where working-class members continued for a long time to be in the majority.

When the Mechanics' Institutes were developing, a factor of quite a different character was contributing to adult education. After the repressive legislation of the Napoleonic War period was repealed and the existence of trade unions became possible, working men began to support them, but when they found little improvement in their condition they turned their attention to parliamentary reform. It was not long before they discovered that the Reform Act of 1832 had merely transferred political power to the middle classes, and this caused them to look elsewhere for guidance. Robert Owen attracted attention, and his emphasis upon education as a means of social regeneration encouraged the formation of Owenite Societies which made adult education one of their chief aims.

A stronger motive, however, was provided by the political agitation associated with the Chartist movement. William Lovett was one of the most remarkable of the Chartist leaders. "Like his friends, Francis Place and Thomas Cooper, he was one of the workmen of whom it may be said that amid heart-breaking discouragement, poverty, and failing health, and political persecution, the hunger for knowledge 'haunted them like a passion'."[1] Lovett formulated an educational programme which was at least a couple of generations ahead of his time. He advocated an education provided free by the State and administered by locally-elected bodies. He did not live to see his proposals accepted, but they were carried out by others.

In 1842 the first People's College was opened in Sheffield by an Independent Minister, and it continued until 1879, when Firth College, which eventually became the University of Sheffield, was founded. The idea of People's Colleges spread to other cities, but of the number which were founded only two, the Working Men's College in London and the Vaughan Memorial College, Leicester, have retained their original name and purpose. The latter was founded by Canon Vaughan and is now associated with the University of Leicester.

The Sheffield People's College provided the inspiration which led F. D. Maurice and his friends to establish the London Working Men's College, Red Lion Square, in 1854. Maurice, when a professor at King's College, London, had already been a leader in the attempt to secure suitable training for private governesses. As a result of his efforts, Queen's College, Harley Street, was opened for women in 1848, with Maurice as its first principal. Miss Buss and Miss Beale were among the early students of this college. Maurice was a sincere Christian, but he also owed much to Chartist principles as enunciated by such as Lovett.

The London Working Men's College was open to any manual worker over the age of sixteen who could read and write and understood the first four rules of arithmetic. A Bible class was the first to be started, and this remained one of the best attended classes. Maurice had been asked to resign his Chair at King's because his religious views were considered by some to be unorthodox. His resignation gave him the opportunity of devoting himself to the adult education movement and to gather round him a band of colleagues who shared his ideals, such as Charles Kingsley, Dante Gabriel Rossetti, Lowes Dickenson, Tom Hughes, and John Ruskin. These men developed the tradition of liberal education,

---

[1] *Final Report of the Adult Education Committee*, Ministry of Reconstruction, p. 18, H.M.S.O., 1919.

but it was less the quality of the staff which brought about its success than the clear insight into the needs of the students which was the guiding principle behind the work of the college.

University Extension

The modern period in adult education was ushered in by the University Extension Movement. The idea seems to have originated with William Sewell, the founder of two public schools, St Columba's and Radley. Sir Michael Sadler claimed that the genesis of the idea was contained in a paper which Sewell submitted to the Vice-Chancellor of Oxford in 1850. He wanted the universities of Oxford and Cambridge to endow a system of local professoriates, each giving instruction under the authority of the two universities. The reply was that the scheme was financially impracticable, but Sewell suggested it could be financed partly from the University Press, partly by small fees contributed by the students, and partly through private endowments and benefactions. Sir Michael judged Sewell's plan as brilliant but premature, but when University Extension became a fact, the movement followed the broad lines envisaged by Sewell. His idea was that if the people could not be brought into the universities, the latter could carry university teaching to them.

The actual start of the movement sprang from a young Scot, James Stuart, who had been lecturing in the north of England at the invitation of the North of England Council for Promoting the Higher Education of Women. His lecture was followed by an invitation from the Rochdale Co-operative Society to lecture to its members, and whilst doing so an incident occurred which stimulated Stuart to practical action. He wrote: "One day I was in a hurry to get away as soon as the lecture was over, and I asked the hall-keeper to allow my diagrams to remain until my return next week. When I came back he said to me, 'It was one of the best things you ever did leaving up these diagrams. We had a meeting of our members last week, and a number of them who were attending your lectures were discussing your diagrams, and they have a number of questions they want to ask you, and they are coming to-night a little before the lecture begins'. About twenty or thirty intelligent artisans met me about half an hour before the lecture began, and I found it so useful a half-hour that during the remainder of the course I always had such a meeting". In 1871, Stuart persuaded several bodies for whom he had lectured to appeal to the authorities of

Cambridge University, asking them to organise lecture centres. They approved the idea, and the first university extension lecture courses were provided at Derby, Leicester, and Nottingham in 1873. In 1876 the University of London formed its University Extension Society, and Oxford made similar arrangements in 1878.

The university extension movement was a curious mixture of success and failure. From the standpoint of working-class education it was a disappointment. The universities were left to bear the whole burden of financing the lectures and courses. The only means of lightening the burden was to attract large audiences so that through fees and local subscriptions they could become largely self-supporting. To obtain larger audiences the lectures had to have a wide appeal, which sometimes led to superficiality. Too much reliance was placed on single lectures or short courses, with the consequence that the instruction ran the risk of becoming discontinuous and unsystematic. When university extension classes became eligible for grant under the Adult Education Regulations of the Board of Education, this handicap was removed.

The story of the early years of the movement has a similarity to that of the Mechanics' Institutes. The place of manual workers tended to be filled by members of the middle classes who desired to obtain the higher education which for various reasons had been denied to them. One important result of the movement was, as we shall see in the next chapter, that many of the modern provincial universities originated from university extension work. The establishment of departments for adult education by the universities has given a new lease of life to the movement.

Parallel with university extension, other types of adult education appeared or were revived. Thus the adult schools and colleges recovered much lost ground largely because of the efforts made by the Society of Friends. At the same time a number of non-Quaker adult schools were opened, and as the revival gained impetus the value of association became recognised. After 1874 a number of local unions were created, *e.g.* Midland, Leicestershire, Somerset, London, and Norfolk. The trend towards association gave rise in 1899 to a National Council of Adult School Associations, which in 1914 changed its name to that of the National Adult School Union. The revival was characterised by the same mixture of religious and philanthropic motives which created the early adult schools, and which now became expressed through the foundation of educational settlements and residential colleges. One may mention such residential colleges as Woodbrooke (1902), Fircroft (1909), the Co-operative College, Manchester (1919), Hillcroft College for Women at Surbiton (1920), the Catholic Workers' College at Oxford (1921), and the Avoncroft College for Agricultural Workers at Bromsgrove, Worcestershire (1925).

The pioneer of educational settlements was Toynbee Hall, opened in 1884 to commemorate the work of Arnold Toynbee in the East End of London. Toynbee was a friend of Canon Barnett, and gave up his vacations to deliver extension lectures in Barnett's district of Whitechapel. Canon Barnett founded the settlement after Toynbee's death. It performed a valuable function by bringing university men and women into close contact with the workers. Through living in working-class areas they acquired a first-hand knowledge of the conditions of life which prevailed and were able to share their knowledge and experience with the workers. The Society of Friends took a prominent part in settlement work, and T. E. Harvey, the M.P. for the northern universities, was for a considerable time Warden of Toynbee Hall. Other educational settlements were Swarthmore, Leeds (1909), St Mary's, York (1909), and the Homestead at Wakefield (1913). The settlements at Leeds and York were non-residential. The L.E.A.s also began to take an interest in the provision of residential colleges. Quite recently the West Riding acquired Grantley Hall, near Ripon, to provide week-end and longer courses in a variety of subjects. Some of the work was associated with education in H.M. Forces.

At the same time a demand for education arose within the working-class movement itself. One of the most significant developments was the foundation of Ruskin College, Oxford, in 1899 by three Americans, Mr and Mrs Vrooman and Professor Beard. The aim was to give "a training in subjects which are essential for working-class leadership, and which are not a direct avenue to anything beyond". Their idea was "to take men who have been merely condemning our institutions and teach them, instead, to transform these institutions, so that in place of talking against the world, they will begin methodically and scientifically to possess the world". The college received the support of the trade unions.

These aims, however, failed to satisfy the more radical members of the student body, especially those who had Marxist sympathies, and in 1909 a number seceded to form the Labour College. The latter has now been superseded by the National Council of Labour Colleges. They were denied Government grants because of the official insistence upon an unsectarian and non-political approach to studies. As a result, Ruskin College was reorganised in 1910 and its management put into the hands of the trade unions and the working-class societies which support it. Wales did not possess an adult residential college until Coleg Harlech was opened in 1927.

The W.E.A.

A further revival affected the Co-operative movement, which had suffered an eclipse during the Chartist agitation. A large part of the funds earmarked for education had been expended on explaining the principles of co-operation to members and urging the value of co-operation in trade and industry. The movement needed clear ideas about education and a central authority to give direction. During the present century the movement has given a more prominent place to educational activities in the stricter sense, the number of students has increased, and the quality of the work has risen. The spirit which motivated the movement has been recovered and has had an influence on one of the present-day bodies for providing adult education, namely, the Workers' Educational Association.

The W.E.A. originated in what Professor H. C. Dent has termed the "Triple Alliance" of the co-operative educational movement, university extension, and the trade unions. It is certainly the most important agency for adult education in the last half-century, not only on account of its numerical strength but also because it has modified our ideas about the nature and methods of adult education.

Its founder, Albert Mansbridge, was born in Gloucester in 1876, and after a brief period as a junior civil servant he became a clerk in the Co-operative Wholesale Society. As a young man he had gained experience of evening classes, university extension, and classes organised by the co-operative movement. He was also a devoted member of the Church of England, and became a licensed lay reader. His meeting with Charles Gore, later Bishop of Birmingham and then of Oxford, brought him into contact with the Community of the Resurrection which Gore had founded. In his spare time Mansbridge taught typewriting and social history in a London School Board evening school. He had, therefore, a wide experience of the different kinds of adult education available, and was not satisfied with any one of them. The chance to express his own ideas came in 1898 when he attended a Whit week-end

Co-operative Congress at Peterborough. His fellow members were impressed, and this led to an invitation to read a paper on Co-operation and Education in Citizenship at a co-operative conference connected with the Oxford University summer school in 1899.

The paper had a chilly reception, and one writer for the co-operative press sarcastically wrote: "The writer of the paper had aimed at the moon and hit a haystack". The hostile criticism did not daunt him, and in reply he sketched his idea of the triple alliance. A number of the workers gave him support, and encouraged by this Mansbridge and his wife became the first two members of the Association to Promote the Higher Education of Working Men. Simultaneously, he expressed his views in the University Extension Journal. In 1903 a provisional committee of the new movement met, and later in the same year the Association was publicly supported by most of the universities and labour organisations. The consequence was the formation of the first branch at Reading in 1904. After this the movement began to spread, and by 1906 there were eight branches covering the south, north, and the midlands.

The next step was a national conference of the Association in 1905 at Oxford under the presidency of the Dean of Christ Church. A resolution was accepted to ask the Board of Education to find out from L.E.A.s how far and under what conditions employers and employed in the different areas were willing to support legislation for compulsory attendance at evening schools. A deputation to the Board was received by Sir W. Anson and Sir Robert Morant. No immediate action followed, but the Board referred the question to its Consultative Committee, which reported in 1909. This was one of the first influences which led to Mr Fisher's scheme of continuation schools in the Education Act of 1918. William Temple, Bishop of Manchester and afterwards Archbishop of Canterbury, came to the conference on evening schools and was so impressed that he became the first President of the Association.

Criticism of the title of the Association led to the adoption of the name The Workers' Educational Association. Its aims were explained by Mr Childs, Principal of University College, Reading, and later the first Vice-Chancellor of the University of Reading. Sir Robert Morant followed the growth of the W.E.A. with much interest, and was instrumental in persuading New College, Oxford, to make a grant to cover the expenses of an experiment which led to the adoption of the tutorial class system. The story of the tutorial class has often been told, but space will only allow of an outline of this development.

It seems that in 1906 the University Extension Committee at Rochdale were very worried about the success of their lecture classes. If the methods of the lecturer were too academic, the audience dwindled, but if, on the other hand, the lectures were too popular, the large numbers in attendance made a serious discussion difficult. The committee decided to consult Mansbridge, who told them that if Rochdale guaranteed to produce thirty students ready to pledge themselves to attend the class for two years and do the written work required, he in turn would obtain for them the services of one of the most brilliant teachers and scholars in England. The Rochdale Committee agreed and secured R. H. Tawney as tutor. The problem of finance was solved by a grant of £300 by New College to the Oxford University Extension Delegacy.

At the same time a similar request came from Longton, in Staffordshire, where Mr Tawney was also appointed as tutor. Events so fell out that whilst Rochdale was the first to organise a tutorial class, the first to actually start was at Longton. The reason was that Longton had arranged for the class to meet on Fridays and Rochdale on Saturdays. Hence Tawney met his first class at Longton on Friday and went to take his Rochdale class the next day. Mr T. W. Price, in his story of the W.E.A., relates: "All shades of political opinion and religious belief were represented, and this gave piquancy to the discussion hour—which was an 'hour' in name only, for the discussion went on until the caretaker became restless, and then was continued in the street. At Rochdale, Mr Tawney would frequently arrange to have tea and spend the evening at the home of one of the students, and on these occasions other members of the class would crowd into the house to the limits of the accommodation—and even beyond—and the discussion would often go on until the early hours of the morning".

The tutorial class experiment was a great success. Within a short space of time, not only Oxford and Cambridge colleges but nearly every university and university college in the country was supporting tutorial classes. The problem of organisation was met by the creation of a permanent joint committee of the W.E.A. and the university in each university area. In some cases the L.E.A.s were invited to send representatives to the joint committee. A Central Joint Advisory Committee for Tutorial Classes was also formed.

The next problem was finance. Some L.E.A.s had already assisted the W.E.A. under the clause of the Act of 1902 which empowered them to aid education other than elementary, and the Board of Education had also given help under the Regulations for Technical Schools, Schools of Art, and other forms of Provision for Further Education in England and Wales, 1918. The final report of the Ministry of Reconstruction, 1919, recommended the the granting of public money. This advice was acknowledged by the issue of the Regulations for Adult Education, 1924, which enumerated the conditions under which the Board of Education would recognise adult classes and make grants to them. The Regulations have been expanded and modified several times after that date, especially after 1944. Some L.E.A.s accepted financial responsibility for W.E.A. classes, *e.g.* the West Riding of Yorkshire.

The W.E.A. had a remarkable growth. By 1948 there were nearly 900 branches federated into 21 districts. The number of branch members was about 39,000, and more than 103,000 men and women were attending the classes. These represented a fair cross-section of the community. The bulk of the students were manual workers and those engaged in nursing or home duties. Numbers fell during the Second World War, but began to rise again when peace came.

W.E.A. classes include university tutorial classes of three years duration, a small number of advanced tutorial classes, one-year classes, and terminal courses. From the start the W.E.A. insisted that the subjects studied should fall within the definition of liberal education and that technical instruction should be outside its province. Economics, history, and literature have been favourites, but in recent years there has been a demand for classes in international relations, philosophy, and psychology. Classes in biology and geology have been popular, and musical appreciation appeals to many students. The tutorial class meets twenty-four times each year, and the usual duration of a meeting is two hours. The first hour is devoted to lecture or teaching, but is less formal than the university lecture period. The second hour is given up to discussion in which students can ask questions and are encouraged to present their own points of view. Practical work is included for classes studying science. Students are expected to read widely, and a supply of book boxes is organised. There is also a central library for the use of students. All students accept the requirement that written work must be submitted at regular intervals.

At one time students were expected to write an essay each fortnight, but this demand proved to be unrealistic, and the usual practice is for three or four essays each session. The standard laid down was that the work should be equivalent to that required in a particular subject in a university honours course. This demand was nonsensical because the majority of students needed careful tuition in how and what to read. The writer has had a few students who have been accepted by residential colleges and even for an honours course at a university, but most have had to be coached to produce anything which even approaches university standards. It should be remembered that most students left school at fifteen, so that academic studies after a gap of three or four years or even longer present difficulties. The writer's own experience is that the tutorial class provides a splendid opportunity for those who abandoned their studies when they left school and after some years returned to them with minds stored with experience gained in industry or commerce.

This bears out the Report of 1928 (*Adult Education in Yorkshire*, Board of Education Pamphlet, 59). The Report drew attention to certain tendencies which in recent years have seriously been considered by responsible officers of the W.E.A. The first is concerned with standards of written work. A definite deterioration was noticed in comparison with the essays submitted in the earlier period. To quote the Report (p. 17): "Probably fewer students find the act of writing a serious difficulty, but on the other hand the essay revealing striking originality of thought couched in language unconsciously inspired by familiarity with the Authorised Version of the Bible is much rarer than it once was. The influence of journalism—not always of the best type—is more apparent. Nor is it at all evident that more time is devoted to reading, although books of the best kind are more accessible than formerly". One would be interested to know how far the introduction of television has hastened this decline.

The second tendency noted was the gradual change in the type of student. At first most were associated with the trade union organisation, but as the curriculum became wider other people were attracted so that the classes more and more represented a cross-section of the community. Quite a number of "black-coated" workers, professional people such as teachers and members of the middle classes enrolled. It is the same trend noticed in the Mechanics' Institutes and university extension movement of the nineteenth century. No doubt Mansbridge would have been opposed to it, but it is worth while considering whether the broader basis of the classes is a sign of strength rather than of weakness.

W.E.A. classes encountered many difficulties in the Second World War. Both students and tutors had to travel considerable distances under black-out conditions, and in some of the larger centres of industry teaching was interrupted by aerial bombardment. The writer remembers several occasions on which the class was carried on in the comparative safety of an air-raid shelter. Naturally, membership declined, though not as much as might have been expected. When the Government introduced "staggered hours of work", regularity of attendance suffered, but for the time being the grant regulations were relaxed.

Since the war the universities have reorganised their extra-mural work by the establishment of extra-mural departments under a Director of Extra-mural Studies, and some have formed a Department of Adult Education with a professor as academic head. Some universities have opened residential colleges which provide both shorter and longer courses for adults. Nottingham was a pioneer in this development. The work of these departments is usually organised through committees of which the Tutorial Class and Extension Committees are prominent. Services education is organised through a Services' Committee, but now that national service is coming to an end considerable changes may be expected. The practice of different universities varies in detail, but as a rule the committees work under the direction of an Extra-mural Board on which the university, the L.E.A.s, the W.E.A., and other bodies for the provision of adult education are represented. The full-time tutors are often represented on the Board and its committees.

It is now over fifty years since the W.E.A. was formed, and it has been felt that it is now time to take stock of the present situation and to forecast future tendencies and developments. This was undertaken by Professor Raybould, the Head of the Adult Education Department of the University of Leeds. (See *The W.E.A.: The Next Phase*, W.E.A., 1949; *The English Universities and Adult Education*, W.E.A., 1951; and *Trends in English Adult Education*, ed. S. G. Raybould, Heinemann, 1959.) In addition to a discussion of the trends already noted, Professor Raybould is concerned about the status of the W.E.A. in the future. At present it is a voluntary organisation which, however, receives considerable support from public funds. Most of our educational ventures started in a similar way and eventually came under the control of the State and the local authorities. Will this happen with the W.E.A.? Will its work be taken over by the local authorities and become part of their scheme for further education? If it still continues to exist, will it cease to be a responsible body and merely confine itself to student organisation? Some have thought that this is inevitable, but Professor Raybould does not agree.

He considers that it would be a great disaster for working-class education, and he refers to the example of the relations between the universities and the University Grants Committee as pointing to a means through which the voluntary nature of the W.E.A. could be maintained. He wrote: "If education of this kind is to be really vital, and if the students for whom it is intended are to have confidence in it, it must be carried on in an atmosphere of complete freedom, with nobody, student or tutor, feeling that he had better choose his words carefully lest he offend some local councillor or administrator, who, in pursuance of his official rights, responsibilities, or duties, may chance to visit the class".

Recent Developments

In the period between the two wars there were two interesting developments in adult education. The first was concerned with rural education, the formation of the Cambridgeshire Village Colleges through the initiative of Mr H. Morris, the Education Secretary to the County Council. The colleges constitute, at one and the same time, schools for children, and educational, social, and cultural centres for the adults of the district. The scheme was actively encouraged by the Carnegie United Kingdom Trustees. The first college to be opened was at Sawston, in 1928. Eleven other colleges were proposed, but their erection was set back by the economic crisis, and it was not until 1937 that the college at Bottisham was opened, and this was followed by Linton in 1938 and Impington in 1939. The outbreak of war put an end to further extension, but when the war ended further colleges were started.

The other development was concerned with the new housing estates built after the First World War, and was initiated by a conference held in 1929 at which the National Council of Social Service and other bodies were represented. The New Estates Community Committee (later the Community Centres and Associations Committee) was created to provide community centres to promote a healthy social life on the estates. In 1944 the Ministry

of Education issued a pamphlet entitled *Community Centres*, which
stated that the general responsibility for the development of community centres had now been taken over by the Ministry and the
L.E.A.s. In the pamphlet the Ministry of Education expressed
its opinion that all villages, especially those with a population
greater than 400, ought to be provided with a village hall.

In rural districts the Women's Institutes have proved to be an
important educational influence. The idea originated in Canada,
and was brought to this country by Mrs Arthur Watt shortly after
the outbreak of the 1914-18 War. Because of war conditions their
activities were largely practical, being connected with food production, jam making, and the bottling of fruit. Later they developed
cultural activities which now cover a wide field. Each county has
its federation of Women's Institutes, and these are united in the
National Federation. The latter issues a monthly magazine, *Home
and Country*, which includes a supplement dealing with the activities of the different county federations. In 1948 the National
Federation opened its own college, Denman College, near Abing-
don, Berks. The wide range of activities is illustrated by those
carried out in one month in the Lindsey (Lincolnshire) district.
They included talks on Lincolnshire crafts and industries, France,
America, drama, care of the feet, and plants and flowers; there were
demonstrations of plastic work, fabric printing, sweet making,
salads, smocking, skin curing, and dressmaking. Individual institutes organised flower shows, concerts, and various competitions.
Most Women's Institutes run a dramatic society, and there is keen
competition between institutes in play production.

In urban districts the corresponding organisation is the Townswomen's Guilds. The individual guilds are federated in the
National Union of Townswomen's Guilds. The members of the
guilds show a keen interest in social studies, civics, current affairs,
and in choral and dramatic work. There are also classes in light
handicrafts and homecrafts, which have had considerable appeal,
especially since the "do-it-yourself movement" has become
popular.

The voluntary agencies for the promotion of adult education are
so numerous at the present day that it is impossible to do more
than mention a few which place education in the forefront of their
aims. The Y.M.C.A. and the Y.W.C.A. have since their inception
played an important part in youth and adult education. The
former started from a meeting of a few young men for prayer and

Bible reading in 1844 in a bedroom on the premises of Hitchcock and Rogers, retail silk mercers, of Ludgate Hill. The leader of the group was George Williams (later Sir George), who was the son of a Somerset farmer. The success of this small group gave him the idea of extending the Young Men's Society to every drapery business in London. In those days the hours of business were much longer than at present, and often assistants began their day's work at seven in the morning and continued until quite late at night. Now the Early Closing Regulations have considerably curtailed working hours. These young people lived in lodgings or on the premises of the business house, and were mainly out of touch with the churches and other organisations which were concerned with their spiritual and intellectual welfare.

The new organisation was given the name of the Young Men's Christian Association, and its aims were to encourage comradeship, united prayer, and Bible study. Williams received enthusiastic support from Lord Shaftesbury. The Y.M.C.A. extended its work to men engaged in other trades, and the Great Exhibition of 1851 gave an opportunity for it to interest visitors from all parts of the world. The American Y.M.C.A. was founded in the same year. At the jubilee of the association in 1894, delegates attended from all countries of the world. The Y.W.C.A. was founded to carry out similar work amongst women. The Y.M.C.A. does not restrict itself to the large towns, but its influence extends to remote rural districts. Red Triangle Clubs have been formed in many out of the way villages, and the association has co-operated with L.E.A.s, university extension, and other organisations for providing adult education.

The Y.M.C.A. was a pioneer in providing educational and social facilities for members of H.M. Forces. Even before the 1914-18 War the Y.M.C.A. tent was a regular feature in the training camps for both Regulars and Territorials, and when war broke out the Y.M.C.A. stepped into the breach and developed educational facilities at a time when Forces education was suspended. This was done in co-operation with the universities, the W.E.A., and the L.E.A.s. Altogether, the Y.M.C.A. spent about £250,000 on the work. Exactly the same happened at the outbreak of the Second World War, when the Y.M.C.A., with other voluntary societies, filled the gap until the educational services were able to operate again.

There are numerous associations connected with the churches. Albert Mansbridge was instrumental in establishing the Church of England Tutorial Classes. These started in 1917 and were organised on a pattern similar to those of the W.E.A. Voluntary associations connected with the religious bodies include the Church of England Men's Society, the Mothers' Union, the Girls' Friendly Society, the Catholic Social Guild, the Brotherhood movement, and the Men's Fellowships connected with the Free Churches. Other voluntary bodies connected with adult education include the British Drama League, the Co-operative Guilds, the Welsh Eisteddfod, and the English Folk Dance and Song Society. There has also been a revival of university extension, and several universities have instituted a certificate which serves as an incentive for those taking the courses.

The Arts Council of Great Britain developed from the wartime organisation known as C.E.M.A. (Council for the Encouragement of Music and the Arts). It received the grant of a Royal Charter on 9 August 1946. From 1940 the Council received a Board of Education grant, but since 1946 its income has been derived directly from the Treasury, and the Chancellor of the Exchequer has been the responsible minister. The Charter stated the aims of the Arts Council as developing "a greater knowledge, understanding, and practice of the fine arts—and, in particular, to increase the accessibility of the fine arts to the public—to improve the standard of execution of the fine arts and to advise and co-operate with Government departments, local authorities, and other bodies on any matters concerned directly or indirectly with those objects". The Council constituted a number of regional offices and separate committees for Scotland and Wales. One of its important activities consisted in supplying art exhibitions, and this service developed considerably when valuable pictures concealed for safety during the war became again available to the public. Another of its functions has been the formation of arts clubs in different parts of the country. It also arranges exhibitions in the visual arts, assists symphony concerts in industrial areas, and sponsors a large number of dramatic ventures. To organise its work in the different branches of art, advisory panels for music, art, and drama have been formed.

Another important agency in adult education is the B.B.C. For many years it has organised broadcasts to schools in a great number of subjects. Some of the courses in music and foreign languages have appealed to adults as well as to children. In addition to pure entertainment it has always included in its programmes talks and series of lectures for its adult audience. Among these are symphony concerts, recitals, travel talks, and discussion of current affairs, and courses on musical appreciation. Towards the end of the Second World War the B.B.C. broadcast a number of talks on social, economic, and educational problems which reached a very wide audience, including both people at home and members of the Forces overseas. A demand arose for a more serious type of programme, and to meet it the B.B.C. added the Third Programme in order to cater for "the alert and receptive listener, who is willing first of all to make an effort in selection and then to meet the performer half-way by giving his whole attention to what is being broadcast". It is a sad commentary on popular tastes that the curtailment of the Third Programme received comparatively so weak an opposition. This programme made accessible to the listener music and drama which has an appeal to the more intelligent members of the public and has introduced them to lectures by prominent authorities in their respective subjects.

One important advantage which the broadcast lecture possesses is that it is available for listeners in isolated places where the formation of the ordinary classes would not be practicable. In many villages listening and discussion groups have been formed, and the B.B.C. through its staff and its pamphlets has been able to give them useful help in showing them how a discussion should be organised.

From the educational point of view the introduction of television has been a mixed blessing. Not only has it interfered in many instances with the studies of young people, but also there are a number of families whose routine is entirely governed by what is being offered by the television service. On the other hand, it can be said that the B.B.C. has seriously tried to find a mean between light entertainment and more worth-while features. Many folk would say that the concessions made to "show business" are more generous than they would advocate. The establishment of the Independent Television Authority was strongly opposed by the majority of teachers and university staffs. To be just, one can say that the agencies which contribute to independent television have been responsible for presenting to the public plays and musical items of value. The religious presentations have been exceptionally good. The unfortunate features are that they are punctuated by advertisements which are often so puerile as to set the viewer against purchasing any of the products recommended, *e.g.* soap powders and detergents and patent medicines, and the competitions appeal to one of the lowest human motives, that of monetary gain. In both programmes the appeals to sex attraction and the showing of scenes of violence could have a dangerous effect on the younger generation.

SUGGESTIONS FOR FURTHER READING

Much has been written on the subject of adult education, and the titles below represent only a short selection of publications which are most informative. Among the official publications of H.M.S.O., the following are recommended: —

The *Final Report of the Adult Education Committee*, Ministry of Reconstruction, 1919. This contains a concise history of adult education.

The Development of Adult Education in Rural Areas, 1922.

Adult Education in Yorkshire, 1927.

Pioneer Work and other developments in Adult Education, 1927.

The history of the W.E.A. is well represented in: —

A. Mansbridge, *An Adventure in Working-Class Education*, Longmans, 1913. This is a first-hand account of the formation and early years of the W.E.A.

University Tutorial Classes, Longmans, 1913.

T. W. Price, *The Story of the Workers' Educational Association, 1903-24*, Labour Publishing Co. Ltd., 1924. This is now out of print, but may be obtained from a good library.

S. G. Raybould, *W.E.A., The Next Phase*, W.E.A., 1949.

Mary Stocks, *The Workers' Educational Association—The First Fifty Years*, Geo. Allen and Unwin, 1953.

Studies in special aspects of the adult education movement are: —

C. Delisle Burns, *A Short History of Birkbeck College*, University of London Press, 1924.

L. J. Davies, *The Working Men's College*, Macmillan, 1904.

G. Currie Martin, *The Adult School Movement*, National Adult School Union, 1924.

R. Scott, *The Story of the Women's Institutes*, Village Press, Idbury, Oxon., 1925.

Moore G. C. Smith, *The Story of the People's College, Sheffield*, Northend, 1912.

The following studies in adult education may be consulted: —

H. C. Dent, *Part-time Education in Great Britain*, Turnstile Press, 1949.

Sir Richard Livingstone, *The Future in Education*, C.U.P., 1942.

R. Peers, *Adult Education in Practice*, Macmillan, 1934.

S. G. Raybould, *The English Universities and Adult Education*, W.E.A., 1951.

Ed., *Trends in English Adult Education*, Heinemann, 1959.

Sir M. E. Sadler, *Continuation Schools in England and Elsewhere*, Manchester University Press, 1907.

Basil A. Yeaxlee, *Spiritual Values in Adult Education*, 2 vols., O.U.P., 1925.

CHAPTER XV

THE UNIVERSITIES OF ENGLAND AND WALES

At the beginning of the nineteenth century the only English universities were the ancient foundations of Oxford and Cambridge, which during the previous century had suffered a decline similar to that which overtook the public and grammar schools. The first year of the new century witnessed the beginning of a movement which eventually was to bring them into line with modern developments. Although the medieval period had long since passed, the colleges of the universities, and even the universities themselves, were still bound by the customs and statutes which had been handed down from an earlier age and now had ceased to have value and meaning. It was during the nineteenth century that the ancient universities became adjusted to the demands of the modern world, and a convenient starting point in tracing this development is the year 1800, when the Public Examinations Statute of the University of Oxford introduced the practice of holding written examinations which were to replace the oral tests of medieval days, which by that time had become quite farcical.

The universities were only open to members of the Anglican Church, so that Dissenters and Roman Catholics were debarred from graduation. The curriculum was unsuited to modern needs, and the teaching of mathematics and science was completely out-of-date. It is true that Cambridge gave more attention to mathematics, but in both universities the curriculum was ill-balanced and overshadowed by the study of the classics. Before any curricular reforms on a large scale could be attempted, the constitution and government of the universities needed an overhaul.

The Public Examinations Statute not only introduced written papers, but it made a distinction between Pass and Honours. At Oxford the classical and mathematics honour schools were separated in 1810, making it possible for a candidate to secure a "double first". At Cambridge the original Tripos was in mathematics, but in 1824 a second Tripos in classics was established. Peel was the first to gain a "double first" at Oxford, and later he was followed by Keble and Gladstone. The reform of the examination system progressed slowly because of opposition from heads of colleges. By 1851, Cambridge had instituted Triposes in moral science and natural science, and by 1850 the Oxford honour schools included mathematics, natural science, law, modern history, and theology.

The reform of the examination system led to the demand for changes of a different character. Within the universities themselves there was a growing party in favour of reform, and considerable external pressure was brought to bear. The *Edinburgh Review*, which had been criticising the public schools, now turned its attention to the curriculum of the universities. Members of the University of Oxford were not slow in replying to the criticisms. In 1810 there appeared *A Reply to the Calumnies of the "Edinburgh Review" against Oxford containing an Account of Studies pursued at that University*. It was produced anonymously, but Newman claimed Edward Copleston as its author. Copleston was a Fellow of Oriel, who became Provost in 1814. He was a moderate member of the reform party, and couched his reply in terms which won general support.

The *Edinburgh Review*, in an article on Edgeworth's *Professional Education*, criticised the classical studies of the university and asked how they could be defended on the ground of utility. Copleston's reply was one of the finest vindications of the value of literary studies and a classical education that has ever been penned. He was not so successful in his answer to the criticism of the undergraduate course at Oxford. He and his critics were at cross purposes. He nobly defended the content of the honours courses, but the *Edinburgh Review* was mainly concerned with the studies of the pass man, and there is no doubt that at this period the attainments expected of him were extremely modest.

The attack then shifted to the question of religious tests. Previous attempts to open the universities to students who were not members of the Established Church had failed. Sir William Hamilton, the famous Scottish philosopher, was a vehement opponent of religious tests. He received much support from different parts of the country, which became evident from the number of petitions sent to Parliament. One petition from Skipton, Yorkshire, added the name of Durham to the ancient universities.

Some of the leading members of Cambridge University signed a petition for the abolition of religious tests. Thirwall, Fellow of Trinity (later Bishop of St David's), advocated the discontinuance of compulsory attendance at college chapel. This was opposed by Christopher Wordsworth, Master of Trinity (1820-41), who demanded the resignation of Thirwall. Dr William Whewell, still remembered as a logician of note, intervened in the dispute, with the result that Wordsworth became intensely unpopular. This was one reason amongst others which led to Wordsworth's resignation and the appointment of Whewell to the Mastership of Trinity. A Bill to permit Dissenters to proceed to degrees was presented to Parliament in 1834. The House of Commons was in favour of it, but it failed to pass the House of Lords. It was nearly forty years before the question was re-opened, although Hamilton, in the *Edinburgh Review*, tried to keep it alive. Failing to achieve this, he began to attack the statutes of the universities by asserting that the incoming student was forced to swear an oath to observe something he was unable to carry out. Hence he declared: "Oxford is now a national school of perjury".

Whewell was a carpenter's son who by dint of his intellectual ability and force of character was chosen on two occasions as Vice-Chancellor (1843 and 1855). Had he possessed more control over his temper and been more modest in manner, he would have wielded still greater influence. A story is told that being caught in a heavy shower, he sought shelter under the umbrella of an undergraduate. When the latter attempted to make a remark, Whewell reminded him that all communications must come through a tutor.

In his younger days, Whewell represented the reformers within the university. His answers to the attacks on the curriculum in *Thoughts on the Study of Mathematics as a part of a Liberal Education* (1835) and *The Principles of English University Education* (1837) were eminently constructive. He pointed out the distinction between lecturing and teaching, and emphasised that because of the constant interplay between the mind of the teacher and the minds of the students, teaching small classes was most effective in such subjects as mathematics and classics. He believed that lecturing to large audiences is apt to convert students into passive listeners. It should be remembered that in Scottish universities of that day the lecture was the principal means of instruction. At the present time, the modern provincial universities, who started by pinning their faith to the lecture system, are now agreed that the number of lecture periods ought to be reduced, and have planned more seminars and tutorial groups in which each student comes into intimate relation with his tutor. Whewell thought that the older universities had hit upon a happy compromise by providing both types—practical teaching in the colleges combined with professorial lectures in the university. He also believed that examinations should play the parts of a test and a means of instruction, but he disliked the external examination system which was adopted by the newly-formed University of London.

During the second quarter of the century, the most important influence at Oxford was the Tractarian, or Oxford movement. It began with Keble's Assize sermon on National Apostasy, and its early leaders were Keble, Newman, and Pusey. The majority of the university authorities were not in sympathy with the movement, and the minor persecutions which followed were one factor which undermined the faith of Newman and others in the Church of England and caused them to find satisfaction in the Church of Rome. Newman became a convert in 1845, but Keble and Pusey remained in the Anglican fold. Even those who cannot agree with the views of the Tractarians admit that the Oxford movement gave a new direction to the Anglican Church and transformed it from apathy into a lively spiritual force. In 1852, Newman published his lectures on the proposed "Catholic University of Ireland", in which he used many ideas, skilfully blended with his Catholic belief, which he had acquired at Oxford.

At the beginning of the century, Cambridge was given the opportunity of showing what a college would be like with statutes which conformed to the age on the occasion of the foundation of Downing College. It owed its existence to the will of Sir George Downing in 1717. Downing directed that if his issue failed, his trustees should establish a college at Cambridge bearing his name. The last member of his family died in 1764 and the university presented its claim. Legal difficulties delayed the decision until 1800, when the Lord Chancellor pronounced in favour of the university. It received its statutes in 1805, and the important feature of them was a clause directing that of the sixteen Fellowships, only two were to be for life. The remainder were tenable for twelve years and were to be given to laymen who intended to enter the legal or medical professions. Most Fellowships were conferred on those who were in Holy Orders. In another way, this was important because of the lack of facilities for studying these subjects in the university. Also provision for amending the statutes was included, if and when they became out of date. D. A. Winstanley, the distinguished authority for the history of Cambridge University, described the constitution of Downing as "an experiment in college reform".

Unfortunately, events did not turn out as intended. The Court of Chancery gave its approval to an ambitious building scheme, which could not be carried through with the available funds. The result was that Downing for some time was the only college in the university which could offer no prizes, scholarships, and exhibitions, and only three fellowships. It was not surprising, therefore, that the college was unable to attract a full complement of undergraduates. In place of serving as an encouragement for reform, it became a warning against it, and thus strengthened the other colleges in their opposition to reform. In spite of this, however, because of the efforts of Whewell, Trinity in 1848 and St John's in 1849 obtained new statutes, and in 1850 a committee was appointed to revise the statutes of the university and a second one to remodel the public examinations.

Royal Commissions on Oxford and Cambridge

Such slow progress did not satisfy the more enthusiastic reformers, and in 1849 a petition was presented to the Prime Minister, Lord John Russell, urging him to ask the Queen to appoint a Royal Commission. This was constituted in the following year, and issued a report in 1852. Both universities showed their annoyance at Government interference with their internal affairs, but when the Commissioners visited Cambridge they were received, if not with warmth, yet with some degree of courtesy. Those who visited Oxford experienced organised opposition, and every conceivable obstacle was placed in their way. The Vice-Chancellor declared that he would contest the legality of the Commission. Four leading lawyers supported him, but the legal advisers of the Government held the contrary view. Many heads of colleges and officials of the university gave the minimum of help, though some at Corpus Christi, All Souls', St John's, Merton, and Lincoln were more co-operative. Jeune, the Master of Pembroke, was a well-known supporter of reform, and had been chosen as a member of the Commission.

The Commissioners were greatly concerned with the question of the expense of a course at the older universities. Both the Newcastle and Taunton Commissions had considered that elementary and secondary education, respectively, were not available for all who needed them. The same consideration influenced the members of the University Commission. It appeared to them that many members of the upper middle class were prevented from taking advantage of the opportunities afforded by the older universities because of the expense involved, the restrictions of out-of-date statutes, and the religious tests. The Commissioners were advised not to press the last point. The report on Oxford was more drastic than that on Cambridge. The recommendations of the Commissioners formed the basis of the Oxford University Act of 1854 and the Cambridge University Act of 1856.

The supreme academic authority at Oxford was originally the Congregation of Masters (later Convocation), but the revised scheme of government set up by Archbishop Laud, Chancellor of the University from 1630, created the Hebdomadal Board, which was mainly an assembly of the Heads of Colleges. Its consent was necessary before any new statute could be discussed by Convocation, so that the powers of Convocation became curtailed and the Masters had less and less say in the government of the university. The Oxford University Act replaced the Board by the Hebdomadal Council, which contained a large number of elected members. The Laudian statutes were repealed and private halls or hostels were once more permitted. The colleges were given new constitutions which freed them from the restrictions which had previously bound them to particular families, places, or schools. Colleges were granted new constitutions and the professorial system was reorganised and strengthened. Fellowships were to be awarded on merit and scholarships were thrown open to free competition. Nonconformists were allowed to take the degree of B.A., but the Master's degree was still withheld. The Cambridge Act was on similar lines. The supreme governing body, the *Caput* or Council of the Senate, became to a great extent an elected body. The obligation for Fellows to be ordained was abolished, and in both universities ordinances were to be discussed in English instead of Latin. The Acts were an important step in bringing the older universities into line with modern needs.

When the Commissioners visited Cambridge, the Borough Council petitioned them to have their long-standing grievances removed. The town authorities complained that the university exercised certain antiquated privileges and did not pay its fair share in rates and taxes. The university paid a mere £100 a year as land tax, and the town £2,700. Most of the university buildings were not assessed for rates, but the university authorities, in reply, stated that they paid two-fifths of the cost of paving, cleaning, and lighting the streets. A similar grievance had existed at Oxford, but most of the points of disagreement had been settled by compromise before the appointment of the Commission.

The principal grievance was related to the powers of the Vice-Chancellor of Cambridge. Amongst others, he had the right to licence ale-houses in Cambridge and Chesterton, and could forbid the licensing of any theatre or other places of entertainment in Cambridge or within fourteen miles of the town. The university had the right of supervising weights and measures, and the Vice-Chancellor was empowered to be present when the university declared the markets and fairs at Cambridge, Barnwell, and Stourbridge to be open. The Mayor and Corporation claimed similar rights.

One of the chief grievances, however, was concerned with the jurisdiction of the Vice-Chancellor's Court, which extended within a mile of the town, over most civil and all criminal proceedings. The townsfolk, as was natural, made the most of their grievances to the Commissioners, who proposed a compromise agreement in which a number of the privileges of the university were retained. Thus, the Vice-Chancellor was to retain his right of issuing wine licences but without any charge, and this applied to the licence for theatres. The university was to be assessed for rates, but the proportion of the land tax was unaltered and the university now was only responsible for a quarter of the cost of paving, cleaning, and lighting the streets of the town. This ended the dispute for a time, but it broke out again later in the century.

The occasion was a number of cases which had been decided in the Vice-Chancellor's Court. The Court could not only inflict fines, but it had its own prison, which was known as the Spinning-House. The town authorities considered this to be slur on their ability to maintain law and order. As neither party was willing to make concessions, the town appealed to the M.P. for the borough. After an abortive Bill in Parliament, further negotiations followed which resulted in the Cambridge University and Corporation Act of 1894. The chief grievances of the townsfolk were removed; the Vice-Chancellor retained the right of issuing wine licences, and friendly relations between the university and the borough were restored.

Abolition of Religious Tests

The fight for the abolition of religious tests broke out anew, occasioned by the resignation of Sedgwick from the Fellowship of Trinity College, Cambridge, in 1869, and the charge of heresy which was brought against Benjamin Jowett at Oxford. The reason for Sedgwick's resignation was that he felt acutely that his religious opinions would not allow him to continue his membership of the Church of England. Jowett was Regius Professor of Greek at Oxford, who became widely known for his translations of the *Dialogues of Plato* and the *Politics of Aristotle*. As Regius Professor he received the statutory salary of £40 a year, and this was not increased for many years because of his views on the Atonement and his contribution to *Essays and Reviews* in 1860. He was summoned to appear before the Vice-Chancellor's Court on a charge of heresy, but the proceedings were eventually dropped. In 1863, Dr Pusey, in the spirit of Christian charity, proposed that Jowett's salary should be raised to £400 per annum. Pusey's proposal was rejected by Convocation, whose action was disapproved by the majority of undergraduates and the national Press. Eventually, in 1865, Dean Liddell persuaded the chapter of Christ Church to fix the salary at £500 per annum.

Incidents of this kind roused intense indignation in all parts of the country, and Mr Gladstone, who had previously upheld religious tests, changed his mind. The agitation became more vehement when at Cambridge the Senior Wranglers of 1860 and 1861 were refused fellowships because they would not subscribe to the Thirty-nine Articles. The result was that when a Liberal Government came to power in 1868, Mr Gladstone presented a Bill for the abolition of religious tests in the universities of Oxford, Cambridge, and Durham. It became law in 1871, and all degrees except those in divinity were thrown open to Dissenters. Compulsory attendance at college chapel was also abolished. In 1915, Cambridge removed all restrictions on degrees and fellowships and Oxford adopted the same policy in 1920.

Oxford and Cambridge Commission of 1872

The reforms which followed the Acts of 1854 and 1856 resulted in the introduction of a new vigour in university life and studies. The number of undergraduates increased; new studies were introduced, which led to the establishment of honour schools in natural science, law and history, oriental languages, English language and literature, and medieval and modern languages. In fact, many of the more obvious defects had been corrected, but there was a strong feeling that the reforms should be carried a stage further. Eventually, another Commission was appointed in 1872 which reported in 1874, and was followed by the Oxford and Cambridge Act of 1877. The Act set up Commissioners for both universities and gave them considerable executive powers. Thus they were able to deal with out-of-date college statutes. The previous Acts had been concerned mainly with university statutes. Each college was required to contribute a portion of its revenues for university purposes.

For several centuries the colleges had become increasingly independent of the university, but now a reverse process began to take place. Life fellowships were replaced by prize fellowships, which were non-residential awards for exceptional performance in the examinations. Fellows were permitted to marry, were given regular teaching duties, and the opportunity of becoming members of boards concerned with university administration. Their stipends were standardised and a pension fund was created. These changes freed a good deal of money which could be utilised for university purposes such as the establishment of additional professorships, readerships, and lectureships. It could also be used for the maintenance of buildings. The accusation that the older universities paid too little attention to research was remedied by the establishment of research fellowships. The obligation to lecture was laid upon the professors, but attendance at their lectures became voluntary for undergraduates.

The abolition of religious tests was followed by the foundation of new colleges and halls on a denominational basis. In association with the Church of England, Keble College was opened at Oxford in 1870 and Selwyn at Cambridge in 1882. The Free Churches and the Roman Catholics established halls which, although from a constitutional aspect were not an integral part of the university, were able to give their residents the benefit of university teaching. Perhaps the most important innovation of this period was the establishment of colleges and halls for women students, a topic which will be considered later in this chapter. One can sum up the changes by saying that the ancient universities now became institutions well organised and equipped to take an increasing part in the life and culture of the modern world.

The claims of scientific studies were now recognised and the monopoly of classical studies was broken. Greek as a compulsory subject was stubbornly retained until after the First World War, and in 1959 the University of Oxford considered the abolition of Latin as a compulsory subject for entrance. Cambridge followed suit shortly after. Several of the modern universities had abolished Latin for entrance purposes some years previously, and only retained it in the degree course for students reading those modern languages in which Latin was considered to be necessary.

In the later Victorian period, Oxford was dominated by Benjamin Jowett of Balliol and Dean Liddell of Christ Church. Jowett was not only a most accomplished Greek scholar, but was also one of the outstanding teachers of the century. He thoroughly understood the needs and interests of the young men he taught, and many of them who rose to occupy positions of national importance became his personal friends. Amongst his pupils were such prominent statesmen as Asquith, Milner, Curzon, and Grey. Jowett encouraged young men of ability irrespective of whether they came from wealthy families or not. When he became Master of Balliol in 1870 he commenced an ambitious rebuilding programme. He rebuilt a considerable part of Balliol, acquired grounds for the cricket and football of the college, and provided a hall for poorer students unable to afford the cost of living in college. Liddell rebuilt part of Christ Church, and his example was followed by many other colleges.

New examination-schools were built, and the Bodleian Library, which had become cramped in its original quarters, overflowed into the older schools. The library sprang from the collection of Duke Humphrey in the fifteenth century. It suffered greatly during the Reformation period when most of its books disappeared, and was restored by Sir Thomas Bodley (1545-1613), who endowed it and presented it with a new collection of books. He drew up statutes for its government, and, by his agreement with the Stationers' Company, the Bodleian was given the right of receiving a copy of every new book published in the kingdom. Other libraries which possess a similar privilege are the British Museum, Cambridge University, the National Library of Wales, the Scottish National Library, and Trinity College, Dublin. Cambridge is proud of the Cavendish Laboratory, named after Henry Cavendish, the famous chemist and physicist. It is one of the great research laboratories of the world, and is associated with the names of such outstanding scientists as Clerk Maxwell, Lord Rayleigh, Sir J. J. Thomson, Sir Ernest Rutherford, and Sir William Bragg.

Higher Education of Women

Two of the most important features of higher education in the latter part of the nineteenth century were the admission of women students and the rise of the modern universities. As soon as the provision of more places in secondary schools for girls began to develop, the need for a supply of teachers, well-trained academically and professionally, was bound to arise. The first step was to gain admittance for girls to examinations which would qualify for university entrance. They were allowed to sit for the Cambridge Local Examinations in 1865. In 1862, Miss Garrett applied to sit for the London Matriculation, but the Senate refused her request, and it was not until 1869 that girls were admitted to the examinations of the University of London. Oxford opened its examinations to girls in 1870, and ten years later women were admitted as degree candidates in the University of London and the newly-established Victoria University of Manchester. In the latter university it was some years before the practice was abandoned of admitting women only after adequate provision for men had been made.

In 1870 women were permitted to sit for the Tripos examinations at Cambridge, and two years later they were allowed to enter the Honour schools at Oxford, but neither of the older universities were prepared to confer degrees on them. In 1887, Miss Agnaton Ramsey, of Girton, was the only Cambridge student to obtain a first division of the first class in the classical Tripos. This success was followed by a memorial addressed to the Senate asking for the degree to be granted to women. The request was refused, and even when Miss Fawcett, of Newnham, was placed before the Senior Wrangler in 1890 the Senate rejected the proposal to admit women to full membership of the university. In 1896 a similar memorial was rejected by Oxford. Cambridge admitted them to the titles of degrees in 1921. Women were admitted to full membership of the university at Oxford in 1920, but Cambridge was more conservative and did not admit them until the Michaelmas Term, 1948.

The mention of Girton and Newnham introduces another important development; namely, the establishment of colleges for women in the older universities. The pioneers of the movement were Miss Emily Davies and Miss A. J. Clough. Miss Davies presented to the Schools Inquiry Commission a petition signed by twelve prominent women teachers asking for the foundation of a college for women connected with one of the ancient universities. The strong support given to the petition led Miss Davies to take a house at Hitchin in 1869, and she began her project with six students. The college moved to Cambridge in 1873, and was known as Girton.

Newnham will always be associated with the name of its first principal, Miss A. J. Clough (1820-92). She had previously taught in schools at Liverpool and Ambleside, and had been secretary of the North of England Council for Promoting the Higher Education of Women. With the help of Henry Sidgwick, the Cambridge philosopher, she started a house for women which was eventually moved to Newnham. In 1880 the foundation became recognised as Newnham College. At first the question arose whether the education of girls and women should follow lines similar to that of boys. Miss Beale and Miss Clough considered it should, but Miss Buss and Miss Davies took the opposite view and thought that women ought to be admitted to university examinations on the same terms as men. Miss Clough believed in special courses for women, and this policy was adopted at Newnham. Eventually, the policy of Miss Davies at Girton prevailed.

At the same time a similar development took place at Oxford. An Association for the Higher Education of Women was started, and in 1878 and 1879, respectively, Lady Margaret Hall and Somerville Hall (later Somerville College) were opened, each with nine students. Miss Wordsworth, principal of Lady Margaret, opened St Hugh's Hall in 1886 for twenty-five students who were unable to afford the higher fees demanded at Lady Margaret. This was followed in 1893 by St Hilda's Hall, which was associated with the Cheltenham Ladies' College.

The idea of establishing other universities in addition to Oxford and Cambridge was by no means new. In 1596, Gresham College was established in London by Sir Thomas Gresham, but although it had considerable influence during the Stuart period, it never developed into a university. In the same year, Elizabeth I was in favour of a university at Ripon, but in spite of powerful support the scheme did not mature. Another attempt at founding a university was made in 1656, when the Privy Council issued an order to apply the sequestrated revenues of Durham Cathedral for the establishment of a college. Two years later the college petitioned Richard Cromwell to grant university status, but the Restoration intervened and the endowments were returned to the dean and chapter of the cathedral.

University of Durham

The idea for a university at Durham was revived at the beginning of the nineteenth century. An Act of Parliament in 1832 authorised the dean and chapter to endow a university from the revenues of the see and the cathedral chapter, and the charter was issued in 1836. The university was of the residential type, and its curriculum was similar to that of the ancient universities. It also required a religious test at the admission of students. The latter were accommodated in residential colleges within the bishop's palace.

University of London

At the beginning of the nineteenth century there was a growing dissatisfaction with the ancient universities because of the religious tests, the high cost of the courses, and the nature of the teaching. The latter was predominantly classical and mathematical, and did not appeal to those interested in the sciences and the manufacturers who desired practical and technical instruction. The dissatisfied elements included Liberals, Nonconformists, Roman Catholics, Jews, and those who supported the scientific and secularist movement. Hence the demand for a new university from which religious teaching would be excluded and adequate attention given to modern and scientific studies.

This view was expressed by the poet Thomas Campbell in a letter to *The Times*, 9 February 1825, in which he urged the foundation of a "great London University". The idea was supported with much enthusiasm by Henry Brougham, Dr Birkbeck, Francis Place, Zachary Macaulay, Joseph Hume, and other members of the so-called "education-mad" party. The result was the formation of a joint-stock company under the name of the Proprietors of the University of London. A plot in Gower Street was secured, and the foundation-stone of London University laid by the Duke of Sussex in 1827. In the following year classes in arts, law, and medicine were started, but so far the new institution had not received a charter and its efforts to obtain one were opposed by Oxford and Cambridge.

The secular constitution of the new college aroused the opposition of the Anglicans, and as a counterblast they proposed the establishment of a second university in which religious instruction would be an essential part of the curriculum. George IV promised his patronage and the new college received the name of King's College. It was given a charter of incorporation in 1829 and opened in the Strand near Somerset House in 1831. The Gower Street college had to wait until 1836 before it was incorporated. In the same year the University of London was created as the body which had the power to confer degrees.

The events recorded above led to the anomalous position of a university which was merely an examining body without any teaching functions but with the power to grant degrees, while the two colleges, King's and University, which taught the candidates who entered for the examinations, were not integral parts of the university. The original charter had given the university power to affiliate other institutions. This policy was carried out in 1850, when a large number of institutions, some of which were nothing more than secondary schools, were affiliated to the university. Eight years later this practice was discontinued, and the University of London began to award degrees solely on the results of examination. This policy caused criticism, which grew to the extent that proposals were made for the establishment of a teaching university to be known as the Albert University. The threatened secession from the existing university led to Government intervention. A Royal Commission under the chairmanship of Lord Selborne was appointed, and its report was issued in 1889.

It is not necessary to enter into the details of the complications which followed, and one can sum up by saying that the findings of the Selborne Commission were not acceptable to University and King's Colleges, who decided to secede and establish a new teaching university to be called the Gresham University. The Government once more found it necessary to intervene in the dispute, and appointed the Gresham Commission in 1892. The Commissioners rejected the idea of two universities for London, and after two abortive attempts the London University Commission Act was passed in 1898 and new statutes were put into operation in 1900.

The next problem was to find administrative headquarters for the reconstituted university. This was solved by the acquisition of the Imperial Institute at South Kensington, which since its inauguration had encountered serious financial difficulties. The major part of the building was assigned to the University of London, and the Imperial Institute continued its work of research and propaganda in the remainder. Once again events were extremely complicated and only a brief summary need be given.

The Imperial Institute was in the midst of a number of institutions for higher education which were superintended by the Board of Education. Amongst these institutions were the Victoria and Albert Museum, the Science Museum and Library, the Royal College of Science, the Royal College of Art, the Royal School of Mines, the Royal College of Music, the Royal School of Art Needlework, the Natural History Museum, and the City and Guilds of London Institute for the advancement of Technical Education. In 1907 the Imperial College of Science and Technology was established and granted a Royal Charter. At the same time, the Board of Education transferred the control of some of these institutions to the governing body of the Imperial College. The colleges concerned resented the loss of their individuality. In 1906 the incorporation of the Imperial College with the University of London was proposed, but as soon as the Imperial College received its charter it began to agitate for recognition as an independent university.

Yet another Royal Commission, under the chairmanship of Lord Haldane, was appointed, and it issued its report in 1913. The Commission thought that the most effective means of bringing unity into the varied collection of institutions which comprised the University of London was to adopt a faculty organisation. The Government agreed with this recommendation, and the University of London Act, 1926, provided a new constitution for the university. The different institutions which made up the university were recognised as "schools of the university" in one or more faculties. The specialist teaching given in the different institutions made this organisation possible.

The Haldane Commission also drew attention to the need for providing a permanent building for the university. The Imperial Institute was no longer adequate for the purpose. It was considered that a great hall accommodation to promote the social interests of members of the university, additional lecture rooms, and a central library were urgently needed. There was difficulty about the most suitable site, but in 1920 the Government offered an area of about eleven and a half acres north of the British Museum. King's College insisted on remaining in the Strand.

The accommodation necessary for new buildings such as the University Institute of Education demanded an increased acreage, and in 1955 the County of London Development Plan approved an area of about thirty-five acres north of the British Museum and west of Russell Square as a University Precinct. Through the purchase of sites the university has now come into possession of more than four-fifths of the area. The plans for the development of the University Precinct have been prepared so that on the enlarged site University College, Birkbeck College, and the examination halls, together with other buildings, will be unified with the existing buildings.

The University of London is unique as being the only British university which grants degrees to candidates who are not resident members. The practice of granting external degrees has often been criticised on a number of grounds. It is urged that the institutions such as senior technical colleges, which prepare candidates for the London University examinations, have little control over the syllabus. There is also a large number of candidates who are not members of a recognised college, but prepare by means of private study or correspondence courses. Hence they miss two of the most important influences that a residential university brings to bear upon its students; namely, the close association with teachers of rich and varied experience and the daily contact with students in other faculties, which is so vital in broadening the mind and outlook of the student.

Against this, one must admit that the external degree system has two advantages which, in the opinion of many people, outweigh its disadvantages. In the first place, had it not been for the external degree system, many of the provincial universities which pride themselves on being residential would not have developed. Most of them began as university colleges, and it was only because they could enter their students for London University degree examinations that they were able to attract a sufficient number of students. In addition, it is important to remember that the external degree system has made it possible for many individuals to obtain a university qualification which otherwise would have been permanently beyond their reach.

Whether the system has now outgrown its usefulness at a time when facilities for obtaining a university education are more widespread is a matter of opinion. It has been stated that many candidates are ill-prepared for the examinations, and this accounts for the large number of failures amongst external students. The authorities of London University have paid attention to this fact, and there is now a scheme for guiding external candidates in their reading. Nevertheless, no other university has been willing to adopt the external degree system, and the provincial universities, which attach such high value to residence (though this often means no more than attendance at a limited number of lectures), always frown upon any proposals which seem to open the door to an external degree system.

Sometimes the University of London has been described as a modern provincial university. This is an error. The University of London is the university of the capital city of the British Commonwealth and provides special facilities for students from all parts of the Commonwealth and Empire.

The Provincial Universities

The oldest member of the confederation which became known as the Victoria University was Owens College, Manchester. John Owens was a prosperous Manchester business man who, in 1845, left the sum of £97,000 for the foundation of the college which bore his name. It was opened in 1851, but for some years it had a grim struggle to maintain its existence. After some difficult years it settled down to make slow and steady progress. In 1871 it received a new constitution which permitted the admission of women students, but an objection was raised on the grounds of John Owens's will. In 1874 women were admitted, but only on the condition that adequate provision was first made for all men who wished to study at the college. Owens College hoped for recognition as an independent university in 1875, but these hopes were frustrated by events which had occurred on the other side of the Pennines.

As early as 1826, proposals had been made for the establishment of a university in Leeds, but lack of funds prevented them from being realised. There were, however, in Leeds, three sources from which the present University of Leeds originated. The first of these was the School of Medicine. It started with the Old Infirmary, in which medical instruction was provided as early as the year 1800. Within a short time a private school of anatomy opened, and this, in turn, was superseded in 1831 by the Leeds School of Medicine. The latter had developed into an institution of considerable prestige because of the eminent medical men associated with it.

The second institution was the Yorkshire College of Science, which started off in rented buildings in 1874. Many factors contributed to its foundation, such as the influence of the Great Exhibition of 1851, in stimulating recognition of the value of a scientific and technological education; the interest awakened by the Leeds Mechanics' Institute and the Philosophical and Literary Society, and the new life which developed in the endowed grammar schools as a result of the Taunton Commission. A Yorkshire Board of Education was formed to foster the teaching of science in secondary schools, the establishment of evening courses in science, and to bring into existence a central science college. By 1869 the Board considered that it was now time to concentrate on its third objective, but it immediately came up against the chief difficulty—that of securing adequate funds. It did not, however, drop its aim, but hoping that the financial position would improve it rented the buildings mentioned above.

The college began with the purpose of supplying instruction in science and its application in the industries of the region, but it soon became evident that the curriculum would have to be widened by the inclusion of literary studies. The opportunity to do this was at hand. A University Extension Committee, sponsored by Cambridge University, had been set up in Leeds, and it decided that the most effective method of putting its work on a firm basis would be to hand over its functions to the College of Science. This plan was put into operation in 1877, and the Extension Committee gave a guarantee of sufficient funds to enable it to be carried out. The following year the college changed its title to that of the Yorkshire College. An arrangement was also made for students of the medical school to attend science classes at the college.

This was the situation on the eastern side of the Pennines when Owens College petitioned for the grant of a charter.

The Yorkshire College immediately opposed the memorial and asked the Lord President of the Council to advise the Queen not to grant a charter to a college which was associated with a particular city, but to create a new foundation in which Owens College and similar institutions might be incorporated. Negotiations between the two colleges began, and it was agreed that if Manchester abandoned the idea of a local name for the new university, Owens College should be designated as the first college constituting the new university and its president and principal should be appointed as its first chancellor and vice-chancellor, respectively. The Government agreed, but the Yorkshire College raised an additional point. It protested against the right of the university to grant degrees in the faculty of medicine. Once more the Government agreed, much to the disappointment of Manchester which possessed a flourishing medical school. The Victoria University received its charter in 1880, and Owens College was at once incorporated in it. Thus began the idea of a federal university.

University College, Liverpool, was founded in 1881 with strong support from the Corporation of the city. Its expressed intention was to seek incorporation in the Victoria University, and in 1884 it became the second constituent college of the university. The Yorkshire College progressed more slowly. In 1884 it was amalgamated with the Leeds School of Medicine, and three years later it was admitted as a member of the confederation.

For some years the federal university seemed to prosper, but eventually fresh disputes arose. For some time the professors of the Yorkshire College had grumbled about the waste of time in attending senate and board meetings at Manchester. The real dispute sprang from the proposal to establish a faculty of theology. Although this only affected Owens College, both Liverpool and Leeds had strong objections. The proposal was defeated, but was revived in 1900. The dispute was at its height when the news came that the University of Birmingham had been created by Royal Charter with the name of a provincial city as its title. The reaction of Liverpool was to petition for a charter to grant it the status of an independent university. The city authorities strongly supported the claim and added financial backing, with the result that both Manchester and Liverpool became independent universities in 1903. Leeds, alone, was left as a member of the Victoria University, and put in a claim to become a member, with Sheffield, of a federal Yorkshire university. The Privy Council decided otherwise, and in 1904 the University of Leeds received its charter. The only remnant of the federal institution to-day is the Joint Matriculation Board for the Northern Universities.

The University of Sheffield originated in the bequest of Mark Firth, a wealthy iron-master, who, in 1879, gave a site, a building to the value of £29,000, and an endowment of £10,000 for the foundation of Firth College. As happened with most of the modern civic universities, the early years were a period of struggle for Firth College, but with the assistance it derived from the medical school, the Corporation of Sheffield, grants authorised by the Technical Instruction Act, and its university extension work it was able to carry on. At one time it considered applying for membership of the Victoria University, but as the latter was beginning to break up it was decided to aim at independent status. The University of Sheffield was chartered in 1905.

The University of Birmingham was the result of the amalgamation of two separate colleges. The first was Queen's College, which possessed a theological and a medical school. The theological side disappeared, but the latter prospered. The second, Mason Science College, was founded in 1880 by Sir Josiah Mason, who had had an astonishing career. He began by selling cakes in the streets of Birmingham, and after a number of successful ventures he retired as a millionaire. He was also a successful pen manufacturer, and later in his career he founded a combined orphanage for girls and almshouses for elderly women. Mason College was intended to teach science subjects only, but as many of its students were preparing to sit for London degrees which demanded literary subjects, Mason was forced to modify his position. The title "Science" was dropped when, in 1892, the college merged with the medical faculty of Queen's College. Two years later the Birmingham Training College for Teachers in Elementary Schools was attached to Mason College, and in 1897 the college was incorporated as the Mason University College. Mr Joseph Chamberlain encouraged the college to seek the status of an independent university, and when, in 1898, Andrew Carnegie gave the sum of £50,000 it was thought that the time had come to petition the Privy Council for the grant of a charter. This was given in 1900.

The foundation of the University of Durham was mentioned on p. 341. It made little progress for some years, and by 1857 the number of students had decreased to such an extent that its closure was considered. Indeed, the situation had become so bad that in 1862 a Royal Commission was appointed to inquire into the prospects of the university. The Commission strongly criticised the government and curriculum of the university, and drafted a set of ordinances which brought about drastic reforms.

In 1834 a College of Medicine was founded in Newcastle-on-Tyne, which became associated with the university first in 1852 and then more closely in 1870. The following year the College of Science was opened, and like the Yorkshire College of Science and the Mason Science College at Birmingham it began to give instruction in the arts subjects. It received additional endowments, and from 1904 became known as Armstrong College. Thus, at the beginning of the present century, the University of Durham was of the federal type, consisting of three practically autonomous institutions, each of which controlled its own finance, appointed its own staff, and took responsibility for its teaching and discipline. With its strong clerical and arts element, the older section of the university, situated in the city of Durham, was reminiscent of Oxford and Cambridge. The Newcastle section resembled the civic universities of northern England.

The federal constitution did not work smoothly, so that the University of Durham Act was passed in order to revise the constitution and to unite the Durham colleges, Armstrong College, and the College of Medicine more closely. The Act failed to secure the unity of the university, and the controversies between the Durham and Newcastle divisions grew so bitter that they led to the appointment in 1935 of yet another Royal Commission, which resulted in a reconstitution of the university in 1937. All its constituent members were grouped under a single control for administration and finance; the Newcastle colleges were merged, and the united college was renamed King's College. This arrangement did not satisfy King's College which for some years had been hoping to become a separate university. The latter materialised in 1963 and the new University of Newcastle-upon-Tyne envisages a target of 6,000 students by 1970.

A third example of the federal type of university is the University of Wales. It came into existence as a result of a national movement led by the same men who had accomplished so much for Welsh elementary and secondary education. During the latter years of the eighteenth century the Established Church was declining in influence, and in 1803 Dr Burgess, the Bishop of St David's, suggested the provision of a Welsh college at which candidates for Holy Orders could obtain a liberal education at a moderate cost. As a consequence of his efforts, St David's College, Lampeter, was chartered in 1828. Sir Thomas Phillips was a keen supporter of Lampeter, which, he hoped, would become the foundation on which a national university for Wales might be built.

In 1852 the college obtained a charter enabling it to grant the degree of B.D., and in 1865 it was also empowered to confer the degree of B.A. Lampeter, however, was not destined to become the University of Wales. It was too closely associated with the Established Church to commend itself to all sections of the Welsh people, and, if anything, it proved an obstacle to the establishment of a national university. After failure to obtain recognition as a university, a scheme of sponsorship by the University College of South Wales and Monmouthshire was approved in 1960, and Lampeter is now eligible for Treasury grant.

According to Lord Aberdare a pamphlet published by B. T. Williams in 1853, later M.P. for Carmarthen Boroughs, struck "the first note" in the university movement. Sir Hugh Owen suggested the establishment in Wales of a number of colleges similar to the Queen's Colleges which had recently been founded in Ireland. The result of the ferment of ideas led to a vigorous campaign for a national University of Wales. The first steps in the scheme were the result of a fortunate accident. In 1867 a large hotel which was being built at Aberystwyth could not be finished because its promoter fell into financial difficulties. The opportunity was seized; the hotel purchased for the sum of £10,000, and in 1872 was opened as a college, which received its charter of incorporation as a university college in 1889. From the start residential accommodation was provided, and Aberystwyth is still more fully residential than any other Welsh college.

Its early financial struggles led the Welsh M.P.s to seek Government assistance. The result was the Commission of 1880 under the chairmanship of Lord Aberdare, which recommended the foundation of two colleges, both of which should receive a Government grant. While the position of the two colleges was being considered, Aberystwyth was given a grant which served as a precedent for the grants later made to English university colleges. Both Cardiff and Swansea made claims to be recognised as the university college for South Wales. The former was successful, and its university college was opened in 1883. North Wales chose Bangor as the site for its college, which was opened in the following year. Aberystwyth was forced to fight for its existence, and a compromise was effected which agreed to award a grant to all three colleges.

So far, Wales had achieved the foundation of three isolated colleges and much was required to be done before the national university could be constituted. This was an urgent matter because the Welsh Intermediate Education Act of 1889 was producing a large number of pupils who were able to benefit from a university course. A conference of the three colleges had already considered the creation of a federal university similar to the Victoria University.

With the support of Lord Aberdare and Viriamu Jones, the University of Wales was constituted in 1893. It consisted of the three constituent colleges of Aberystwyth, Bangor, and Cardiff, to which later were added the Technical College at Swansea and the National School of Medicine at Cardiff.

The remaining universities were of later origin. The Bristol Medical School was founded in 1833 and the University College in 1876. The University of Bristol received its charter in 1909. The university received considerable assistance through the generosity of Sir W. H. Wills.

Modern Problems

Both Reading and Nottingham present some interesting features in their development. Reading is a town situated in the middle of an agricultural district, and this exercised a twofold influence on the growth of the university. Unlike the larger cities of the north, Reading had no densely populated district in its neighbourhood and therefore has always been less provincial in its character than most of the civic universities. As well as from the town itself, it accepted its entrants from all parts of the country. Hence it developed its halls of residence, and is the most completely residential of the modern universities. Even the "town students" are members of St David's Hall. Because of its position, the university has always paid attention to agricultural studies and research.

In 1892 a University Extension College was opened at Reading and was associated with Christ Church, Oxford. Ten years later it was recognised as a university college. Lady Wantage endowed Wantage Hall as a residence for men students (1908), and this was followed by the erection of other halls of residence. The college received further endowments from the Palmer and Sutton families, and it received its charter in 1926. The original site has grown inadequate, and the university is now being transferred to the Whiteknights Park Estate, some short distance from the centre of the town and which offers facilities for its future development.

Nottingham sprang from the university extension work carried on in that city by the University of Cambridge. The college which developed from this was opened in 1881 in a building given by the Corporation, and thus grew up under municipal control. As the college developed, its governing body felt the need for controlling its own affairs, but this was not possible until it possessed adequate endowments. The generous benefaction of Sir Jesse Boot (later Lord Trent) enabled it to erect new buildings in 1928. The college had been recognised as a university college in 1903, and a charter of 1938 changed its constitution and freed it from municipal control. It became the University of Nottingham in 1948.

The remaining university colleges have received university status quite recently—Southampton (1952), Hull (1954), Exeter (1955), and Leicester (1957).

The beginning of the present century saw the growth of new problems, which both the older and the modern universities had to face. The Education Act of 1902 produced an increasing number of county and municipal secondary schools, whose pupils soon began to enter for the same university scholarships as members of the public schools. The free-place system enabled pupils of ability from elementary schools to enter secondary schools and eventually, by means of scholarships, to proceed to the older universities, the University of London, or to one of the provincial universities. For the first time, children of working-class parents were able to obtain a university training, and as many of the new undergraduates came from less wealthy homes the expense of residence at Oxford or Cambridge often prevented them from taking up a scholarship and forced them to accept places in the modern universities.

It was for this reason that in 1907, Dr Gore, then Bishop of Birmingham, moved in the House of Lords the appointment of a Royal Commission to inquire how the endowments of Oxford and Cambridge could best be used to benefit all classes of the community. The Commission was delayed until after the Armistice. Immediately after the close of hostilities, all the universities became crowded by students returning from national service. The modern universities found it extremely difficult to carry out their work effectively under post-war conditions. They made an application to the Chancellor of the Exchequer and the President of the Board of Education for increased grants. Plans for post-war reconstruction involved the appointment of additional teaching staff to cope with the increase in the number of students. The rising cost of living necessitated new salary scales, and the heavy cost of materials and labour placed restrictions on their development plans. The President of the Board of Education agreed to receive a deputation from the universities, including representatives from Oxford and Cambridge. The result was that the universities were asked to submit estimates to the Board to cover their immediate needs.

Oxford and Cambridge also asked for financial aid, and the Government considered that it was time that the long-delayed Royal Commission was appointed. The Commission was appointed in 1919 and issued its report in 1922. Meanwhile, as a temporary expedient, the sum of £30,000 a year was paid to the universities of Oxford and Cambridge. The recommendations of the Commission were embodied in new statutes which came into force in 1926. No drastic changes were suggested. The two universities were assured that the acceptance of a grant would not in any way prejudice their independence. The recommendations also suggested certain changes which would place the administration of the universities on a modern basis.

The modern universities found themselves in very great difficulties. As we have seen, nearly all of them in their early days were handicapped by lack of funds. They had managed to struggle on and even extend their buildings and their work through the generosity of local benefactors, but it was not until 1889 that the House of Commons voted the sum of £15,000 per year to be distributed amongst them and the university colleges. The condition of the grant was that each institution should perform an appreciable amount of advanced work, which was taken to mean provision for post-graduate research. The annual grant continued to rise, until in July 1919 a body known as the University Grants Committee was established. The grants were to be made through the Treasury on the recommendations of the Committee, and not through the Board of Education.

The members of the University Grants Committee are chosen because of their wide experience of the needs and work of the universities. The universities are represented on the Committee, and its members visit the universities each five years to discuss with the governing bodies and the heads of departments the needs of their particular institutions and their plans for development. The grant includes a non-recurrent grant for capital expenditure in addition to one for meeting current expenses. The control of each university over its internal affairs is respected, and it is free to decide what it will teach, the details of its syllabuses, and the organisation of its own examinations for degrees and diplomas. This arrangement has worked well and has avoided the unhappy results, due to centralised control, that have been characteristic of many universities on the Continent.

The grant for British universities rose from £800,000 in 1920-1 to over £70,600,000 in 1960-1, and will increase further in the future. In addition, most universities receive grants from the local education authorities. Thus, at present, more than 70 per cent. of the income of the universities comes from the Treasury and the remainder from L.E.A.s, fees, and endowments. In recent years a new body, the Standing Committee of Vice-Chancellors and Principals, has come into being. Strictly speaking, it is an unofficial body, but its work may be regarded as supplementary to that of the University Grants Committee by creating a close liaison between the different universities and the Government departments.

When the Second World War started the Government adopted a scheme for the call-up of university students and staff so that there was not the sudden fall in numbers that ocurred in 1914. Joint Recruiting Boards were established which considered each student individually, and those with specialist knowledge were either deferred or posted to the kind of national service in which their knowledge and experience could be utilised. Full-time members of the teaching staffs were at first reserved at 25 years of age, but later the age of reservation was raised to 30 and in some categories to 35. The three-years degree course was reduced to two years and three months, and in many universities standards were maintained by adopting a four-term arrangement which cut out the greater part of the long vacation. Men in the arts faculties and others who were not deferred, were attested, placed on the reserve, and permitted to complete their first year before their call-up, on the condition that they trained with the university Senior Training Corps or with the Air Training Corps.

During the intensive air attacks some universities suffered severely. Some had evacuated students and staff and shared the facilities offered by universities in less vulnerable areas. At London, University College was extensively damaged; Bedford College lost nearly a third of its buildings; Birkbeck College was damaged by fire; and the medical schools and other institutions of the university received varying amounts of damage. One of the worst incidents occurred at the London School of Medicine for Women only a short time before the war in Europe came to an end. The new wing of the school received almost a direct hit by a rocket. It was completely wrecked and three laboratories were rendered useless for some time. Bristol and Liverpool Universities also received heavy damage. In the former, the Great Hall and the anatomy wing were entirely destroyed by fire. At Liverpool the engineering laboratories were badly damaged. Other universities were either untouched or suffered only slight damage.

Considerations of space will only permit a brief outline of the problems the universities are facing in the post-war period. The most immediate one was caused by the return of large numbers of students to complete their degree courses and the entry of many others who had been awarded places under various schemes for further education and training. The universities, especially those which had suffered considerable war damage, found themselves in a difficult situation because of vastly increased numbers. This can be appreciated when one realises that the number of full-time students had grown from 50,246 in 1938-9 to 107,699 in 1960-1. As soon as the flow of ex-service students slackened, other candidates appeared to take their places. The nation had come to realise the value of university-trained men and women, and industry, as we saw in Chapter XII, was stepping up its demands for highly-trained technicians and technologists. The effects of the reorganisation of school education brought about by the Act of 1944 were beginning to be felt. The number of school-leavers qualified to enter institutions of university status is now much greater, and when the so-called "bulge" leaves the secondary schools numbers will be further augmented. The expansion of existing universities was clearly inadequate to meet the increasing demand for student places in the future. This could only be met by the foundation of new universities, and the University Grants Committee was requested by the Government to advise on the establishment of new universities in different parts of the country.

The first of the new universities was the University of Sussex at Brighton which received its charter in 1961. Lord Monckton was appointed Chancellor and Mr J. S. Fulton Vice-Chancellor. Its first students were admitted for the session 1961-2. They numbered fifty-two but this was increased to 400 in 1962-3 and by another 400 in October 1963. The next was the University of York which admitted its first 200 students in October 1963. Its target for 1972 is 3,000. The Earl of Harewood is Chancellor and Lord James of Rusholme, formerly High Master of Manchester Grammar School, the Vice-Chancellor. York is being developed on collegiate lines with eight colleges which will each accommodate about 300 students. At first the undergraduates of each college will consist of the same sex but the ultimate aim is to have equal numbers of men and women. The University of East Anglia at Norwich is in process of formation. Its administrative headquarters are situated in Earlham Hall, the birthplace of Elizabeth Fry. Its first students entered in October 1963 but when its permanent buildings are completed it will accommodate 3,000. A special emphasis is on the provision of halls of residence. Lord Mackintosh is the Chancellor and Mr Frank Thistlethwaite the Vice-Chancellor.

In May 1961, the U.G.C. was authorised to consider further claims for university status. Many applications were received but up to date the following have been accepted:—the University of Essex at Colchester, the University of Kent at Canterbury, the University of Warwick at Coventry, and the University of Lancashire and the North West. The list of applicants included Stamford, Gloucester, Bournemouth, Chester, Plymouth, and Swindon. Cornwall is campaigning to become the university of the southwest.

The University of Essex envisages a target of 6,000 students. Professor A. E. Sloman was appointed Vice-Chancellor in June 1962. The development plan for Essex rejected the traditional halls of residence in favour of a pre-fabricated village with the "apartment" as the basic unit. Each apartment will have its own common room and kitchenette and it is hoped that every undergraduate will be able to spend at least one year in residence.

The new University of Kent soon ran into trouble about the use of the title, University of Canterbury. The University of Canterbury, New Zealand, pointed out that the proposed title would cause considerable distress in New Zealand and this consideration was supported by the U.G.C. The name of the new university is now the University of Kent at Canterbury. The first Vice-Chancellor is Dr Geoffrey Templeman. The original target was set at 3,000 but because of the increasing number of applicants, it may be double this figure. The opening of the university was planned for 1965 but the pressure of applications may result in an earlier opening.

The University of Warwick is being developed on a site close to Coventry and it will probably be opened in 1965 when it will receive its first 200 undergraduates. Mr J. B. Butterworth, Fellow and Bursar of New College, Oxford, is its first Vice-Chancellor. The university hopes to accommodate 3,000 undergraduates at the end of its first ten years. The latest comer is the University of

Lancashire and the North West. Considerable discussion about its site developed but Lancaster was eventually chosen. The university is at present in the planning stage. Its first Vice-Chancellor is Professor C. F. Carter, formerly Jevons Professor of Political Economy at Manchester.

Two applications for new universities are specially interesting. One is Chester which is a city historically corresponding in the west to York in the east. The local authorities and leading industrialists in the area were in favour of its claims and a site of about 200 acres was reserved. Stamford's claim was supported by Dr R. Stopford, formerly Bishop of Peterborough and now Bishop of London Dr Stopford has had a long experience in education, especially as regards voluntary schools, training colleges, and universities. One plea of the supporters of Stamford is that for a short time in the Middle Ages, it was a university town. In 1334 a quarrel between the scholars and townsfolk of Oxford led to a migration of a considerable number of the former to Stamford. Oxford took this very seriously and up to 1827 no person could be awarded the M.A. unless he swore an oath that he would never lecture at Stamford. It was on this occasion that the famous knocker of Brasenose was left at Stamford and remained there until it was bought back by the College in 1890. The claim of Stamford is still under consideration and the verdict will probably be published some time after the Robbins Report. Stamford has collected a large sum for its scheme, selected a site of 236 acres and has stressed that a university in the town would serve the higher education needs of an area containing more than a million people.

A new policy has been adopted for these universities. Formerly, before an institution could achieve full university status, it passed through a period of "apprenticeship" as a university college, during which its students were prepared for the external degrees of the University of London. The first break with the traditional policy was the University College of North Staffordshire, which was given power to grant its own degrees. A further development with the new universities is to issue their charters at their foundation without passing through a period of sponsorship. It is thought that this will give them greater freedom in curriculum construction and allow them to adapt themselves to the needs of their particular districts.

The urgent demand for technological training and preparation for such professions as medicine, teaching, architecture, and others has raised its own set of problems. Will the universities of the future become overwhelmingly technological in character? Will the departments teaching the applied sciences tend to make those in the arts studies of less importance? Thinkers like Bonamy Dobrée have been well aware of this danger. His belief is that the universities must be more than centres of study and research. "They must in the future play an active part in the life of the community. There is only one way for them to do this if it is to be done radically and not merely by linking industry more closely with technological departments; that is by a thoroughgoing change in the curriculum of their Arts' Faculties, and a different approach to present subjects."

Ideas of this kind influenced the B.A. course of the University College of North Staffordshire[1] which was founded in 1949. This college wished to experiment with a curriculum less specialised in character than that of the degree courses in other universities. It was felt that the external degree system of London would not permit such an experiment, and the college obtained a charter enabling it to grant its own B.A. degree. The course extends over four years. The first year of the course is compulsory for all students and deals with the heritage of civilisation, present-day problems, and the methods and influence of the experimental sciences. In the remaining three years the student must choose not less than four subjects, two of which must be studied for three years and the others for one year. The principal subjects must include at least one from the Humanities and Social Studies and at least one from the Sciences.

Another problem is that of providing hostel accommodation for students. With the exception of Reading, a very large proportion of students in the modern universities who cannot live at home are forced to live in lodgings because of the lack of halls of residence. Even suitable lodging facilities are becoming more difficult to find. In the early days of the University Grants Committee, little attention was given to the provision of halls of residence. By 1936 the Committee became interested in the problem, but hoped that it would be solved by the universities themselves or through the generosity by private benefactors. Since the war the increase in the student population has made the problem more acute. At the older universities a large proportion of undergraduates are obliged to live in lodgings. The University Grants

[1] Now the University of Keele, 1962.

Committee have now realised the seriousness of the situation, and large sums of money have been set aside for building halls of residence.   Now that building restrictions have been relaxed, the universities are going ahead with their plans for securing adequate hostel accommodation.

SUGGESTIONS FOR FURTHER READING

The standard histories of the older universities are: Sir Charles Mallet, *A History of the University of Oxford,* 3 vols., Methuen, 1924-7, and D. A. Winstanley, *Early Victorian Cambridge,* C.U.P., 1940, and *Later Victorian Cambridge,* C.U.P., 1947.   B. Truscott, *Redbrick University,* Faber, 1943, is an interesting account of the life and studies of modern universities, and W. M. Childs, who was Principal and first Vice-Chancellor of Reading, in *Making a University,* Dent, 1933, gives the story of the early years of Reading University.   H. C. Dent in *Universities in Transition,* Cohen and West, 1961, deals with the future of the universities.

CHAPTER XVI

THE TRAINING OF TEACHERS

The Day Training Colleges

This topic has already been discussed in earlier chapters and it is now the intention to resume the story, starting with the period of the Cross Commission. The reader will remember that, as a consequence of its recommendations, day training colleges were established in association with universities and university colleges. The Cross Commissioners were divided on this point. Its critics pointed to the loss of much of value that residence conferred upon students, and feared that the religious influence upon young teachers would be weakened. The supporters of the step pressed so vigorously that their views prevailed, and in 1890 the Education Department issued its grant regulations for day training colleges. At first, the number of day students who were Queen's Scholars was limited to 200, but this restriction was removed in the following year. The basic idea was that these students would pursue their studies in the ordinary classes of the university or university college, but their professional training would fall within the province of the day training college.

In the first year, day training colleges were set up in connection with King's College, London, the Mason College, in Birmingham, the Durham College of Science (later Armstrong College and now King's College, Newcastle-on-Tyne), Owens College, Manchester, and the university colleges at Nottingham and Cardiff. In 1891, they were followed by the University of Cambridge and the colleges at Leeds, Liverpool, and Sheffield; in 1892, by the University of Oxford, and by Bristol and Aberystwyth; in 1894, by Bangor; and, finally, in 1899, Reading and Southampton established day training colleges.

At first they were not popular and the entry of students was small, but it was quickly realised that the new colleges offered important advantages. One of the complaints about the pupil-teacher and training college system was the lack of academic attainments possessed by the entrants to the teaching profession. This was now remedied, because the academic preparation was the business of the regular lecturers in the university institution.

369

In some places the academic staff took part in the training work, and this constituted the very real danger that it might entail that the training might fall into the hands of members of staff who had but little experience of the daily routine of the elementary school. The examination in academic subjects was controlled by the academic staff, but the Education Department (later the Board of Education) assumed responsibility for the professional training and examination of students. This dual control gradually disappeared until delegation became complete, and both the academic and professional training fell within the province of the University Institutes of Education.

One important feature of the new system was that in the day training college the segregation of the ordinary training college disappeared. The life cycle of the training college student started when he was a pupil in the elementary school and was selected to be a pupil-teacher. He taught in an elementary school under the care of the head teacher, and attended a pupil-teachers' centre where he was coached for the Queen's Scholarship Examination. If he passed this, he applied, and if successful, was accepted by a training college which contained other students, most of them with experiences similar to his. He attended lectures with them and carried out teaching practice in an elementary school. After passing the examination for the Teachers' Certificate, he obtained a post in an elementary school, and perhaps in the later stages of his career he was given the supervision of other pupil-teachers. All his career was centred round the elementary school and he never had the opportunity of associating with men who were training for other professions. If he had been a student in a day training college he would have mixed with people who were going to be engineers, doctors, civil servants, lawyers, and clergymen, with the result of broadening his outlook and giving him some understanding of the other aspects of life which lay outside the elementary school.

Another advantage was the outlook given by the university institution. There is little doubt that the student in a training college acquired a more detailed knowledge of the daily routine of an elementary school class. The student from the university probably knew little about the marking of registers and the adding up of attendances on Friday afternoons, but these were details he could master in the first week of his teaching appointment as an assistant-master. University institutions had a wider conception of teacher training. They regarded education as a subject worthy of study in its own right, and refused to consider that their work was completed when they turned out a competent practical teacher. They attached great value to forming the outlook of the student, and they realised that the study of the philosophy, history, and psychology of education offered great possibilities in extending his understanding of his pupils. This became part of practical politics when, at the end of the nineteenth century, the day training colleges became university departments of education.

A serious disadvantage showed itself in the early years of the day training colleges. Many of the entrants were unfitted for the discipline of study demanded by the university, and at first the number of failures in the intermediate examination was alarming. Many university departments admitted both two- and three-year students. Thus at Reading, the two-year students followed a course which led to the Associateship of the college in letters or science and at the same time studied education. Selected students who had previously matriculated, took a three-year course for an external degree of the University of London. Education was additional to the degree course. At Leeds, education was a degree subject which all intending teachers were obliged to offer.

A further disadvantage suffered by day students was that many of them lived at a considerable distance from the college and spent a good deal of time each day in travelling. At Leeds, students travelled from West Riding towns and villages, sometimes covering more than fifty miles a day. The alternative was for them to live in hostels. As we saw in the previous chapter, the University of Reading was unique in being planned as a residential university. Although the modern civic universities have greatly developed the hostel system, it will be some time before all students can be catered for in halls of residence.

Training for Secondary Schools

Some universities offered a diploma in secondary education. Previously, many secondary school heads tended to despise training because of its association with elementary school teaching. The possession of a university degree was thought to be all that was required for a schoolmaster. When the universities offered training for secondary school teaching, heads of schools gradually began to change their opinions. In 1883, the University of London offered a diploma in education to those who had graduated, and this example was soon followed at Oxford and Cambridge. The

College of Preceptors was a pioneer in providing training for secondary school teachers. It began to grant diplomas as early as 1854, and in 1873 it organised courses of lectures for intending teachers. In 1878, the Teachers' Training and Registration Society founded the Maria Grey Training College, which offered special courses for those who intended to teach in secondary schools.

Cross Commission and Teacher Training

The training colleges of this period were severely criticised by the Cross Commission. It was originally hoped that most pupil-teachers would enter for a three-year course of training. Actually, a large number did not enter a training college at all, and either gave up all desire of becoming teachers or continued as uncertificated assistants. The majority of those who entered a training college left after the completion of one year of training. In 1856, the Education Department accepted the inevitable and reduced the training college course to two years. The "pledge" was introduced at the same time. Entrants signed a declaration before a witness and declared that it was their *bona fide* intention to teach for a stipulated number of years in a recognised school. Although this was signed over a sixpenny stamp, since the candidates were usually under 21 years of age, it really had no legal validity, though the student incurred a moral obligation to repay his grant if he defaulted.

In the first year, the students were required to pass in practical teaching, religious knowledge, reading and recitation, music, arithmetic, English grammar (with a small amount of literature), geography, and history. Men offered elementary mathematics and women, needlework. The students were also examined in school management and could offer certain additional subjects with a view to obtaining extra marks. The second-year syllabus was similar, but science, political economy, and languages could be substituted for certain sections. The examinations of the Science and Art Department could also be taken. There was no specialisation, because each student was expected to be able to teach all subjects in the elementary school curriculum. Charles Dickens, in *Hard Times* (published 1854), described Mr Choakumchild, a product of the training college, as follows: —

"He and some hundred and forty other schoolmasters had been lately turned at the same time, in the same factory, on the same principles, like so many pianoforte legs. He had been put through an immense variety of paces, and had answered volumes of head-breaking questions. Orthography, etymology, syntax, and prosody, biography, astronomy, geography and general cosmography, the science of compound proportion, algebra, land surveying and level-ling, vocal music, and drawing from models, were all at the ends of his ten chilled fingers. He had worked his stony way into Her Majesty's most Honourable Privy Council's Schedule B, and had taken the bloom off the higher branches of mathematics and physical science, French, German, Latin, and Greek. He knew all about the watersheds of all the world (whatever they are), and all the histories of all the peoples, and all the names of all the rivers and mountains, and all the productions, manners, and customs of all the countries, and all their boundaries and bearings on the two and thirty points of the compass. Ah, rather overdone, M'Choakumchild. If he had only learnt a little less, how infinitely better he might have taught much more."

No doubt Dickens exaggerated in order to give effect to his criticisms, but in his accounts of mid-Victorian schools and train-ing of teachers he pointed out the prevailing faults of English education, in particular the idea that education consisted in the accumulation and memorisation of facts. One should remember that he was writing in the atmosphere of the Revised Code and Payment by Results. If the reader can obtain a copy from a library, he will find *Dickens as an Educator*, by James L. Hughes (D. Appleton and Co., New York, 1906), both amusing and instructive.

At the end of his training, each student was required to teach in the presence of an inspector and was tested in oral reading and recitation. Most training colleges possessed a Practising or Model School attached to them. Thus at York, the school in which students received their practical training in teaching is still often referred to as the Model School. A serious limitation was that students were restricted to teaching in the practising schools under rather artificial conditions and seldom had the opportunity for visiting other schools in order to widen their experience. Later, the same system applied to the university training departments and survived well into the present century. The writer remembers when he was tested in reading and recitation by H.M.I., and the test was a mere farce, developing into a discussion of the merits of Prag-matism, which was just becoming known in England, and he then was examined in the theory of music and singing. In the former, he obtained full marks, but in the practical test there was only time to select a sample of candidates. He was not chosen, and as he could not sing at all he was pleased to be missed. Nevertheless, he still possesses a Certificate of the Board of Education which qualifies him to teach music, both theoretical and practical, though it would be quite impossible for him to teach the latter. Lively descriptions of the student and his daily routine in the residential training colleges have been given by old students who were in training before 1884. See the *Report of the Board of Education*, 1912-13, pp. 47-69.

Weakness of the Pupil-Teacher System

The Cross Commission was extremely critical about the training of teachers, especially about the staffing of the colleges by old students who had little experience of the world outside the colleges. The weaknesses of the P.T. system were examined. The policy of entrusting the preliminary stage of the teachers' training to head teachers of schools was criticised on the ground that very few heads had either the time or the right kind of experience for undertaking this task. The general opinion was that P.T.s were overburdened, in spite of the fact that since 1884 they were required to teach only half-time in school and attended a P.T. centre for academic instruction during the remainder of the day. The establishment of the centres was an indication that the traditional methods of training were inadequate. The minority report of the Commission declared that P.T.s were badly taught and taught badly, but no members of the Commission suggested replacing the system. The report stimulated the Education Department to inquire into the preliminary training of teachers (1896-8), but the total abolition of the P.T. system was not recommended. It was considered that the age for entering the apprenticeship should be raised to 15, and as soon as possible to 16. It was also thought that the academic instruction given in the centres should approximate to that provided in the higher forms of secondary schools. The main difficulty was the inadequate number of secondary school places, and until this was remedied after the Act of 1902 little else could be accomplished.

In 1900 the period of apprenticeship was reduced to three, and later to two, years. The P.T. system still came in for a good deal of criticism, and this moved the Board of Education to provide an alternative scheme. Any secondary school pupil who had received instruction in the school for not less than two years (raised to three in 1910) could claim a bursary for a year, and afterwards either serve for a year as a student teacher or pass direct to a training college. The alternative system was adopted by many L.E.A.s, with the result that the number of P.T.s started to fall. In 1907, the Queen's (then the King's Scholarship) examination was abolished and its place was taken by the Preliminary Examination for the Certificate. The bursary system came to an end in 1921, and the decreasing number of P.T.s and student teachers was compensated by the growing practice of recruiting training college entrants direct from secondary school leavers. This had become possible because the local authorities, by using their powers under the Education Act of 1902, had now a sufficient number of municipal and county secondary schools. By 1938 the number of P.T.s in centres had fallen to fifty-one, and those in rural districts to 287. There were still 545 student teachers who were recognised by the Board. This is the last date when P.T.s were mentioned in official publications.

After the Second World War, P.T.s and student teachers gave place to direct entrants from the grammar schools. Some L.E.A.s require candidates for the teaching profession to spend a period, ranging from a fortnight to a month, in a primary school in order to obtain an introduction to the work of teaching. Most of the time is spent in observing the work of experienced teachers. Many training colleges and university departments of education encourage their entrants to gain contact with children outside the classroom through Brownies, Cubs, Scouts, Guides, Sunday Schools, Youth Clubs, and similar organisations.

L.E.A. Training Colleges

One of the important features of the Education Act of 1902 was the power given to L.E.A.s to establish county and municipal training colleges. The majority of the colleges built during the nineteenth century were denominational, but now the local authorities were encouraged to develop their own training colleges, and when, in 1907, a building grant of 75 per cent. became available the number of municipal colleges rapidly increased. By 1938 there were twenty-eight colleges provided by local authorities, including seven for domestic subjects. Most of the new colleges were residential. This development reacted on the voluntary colleges, many of which were rebuilt or their premises substantially improved.

University Training Departments

The new municipal training colleges not only served their immediate areas, but encouraged applications from candidates living in other districts. An important development also occurred in the university training departments. This was the introduction of a four-year course, which became the norm after 1921. Previously, the intending teacher had to read for his degree and take his professional training in three years, thus placing a heavy burden upon him. In some universities, such as Leeds, the student was able to offer education as one of his degree subjects in order to lighten his overcrowded timetable. The four-year system enabled him to spread the burden. The first three years were given over to his degree studies, and the bulk of his professional training was carried out in the fourth year. Some universities thought that the rigid separation of academic and professional studies was not to the benefit of the Recognised Student in Training, and introduced some preliminary instruction, visits to schools, and attendance at demonstration lessons during the first three years. The arrangements for practical teaching varied in different universities. As a rule, the students spent two or three weeks in school at the end of their third year. During the professional year, students at Oxford and Cambridge spent a whole term in school. This was not so much a set policy, but was forced upon these universities because of the lack of school accommodation in their immediate neighbourhoods. Some universities provided for practical teaching on certain days in the week, but many adopted a compromise arrangement by which the students spent half of the first and second terms in school.

The four-year system came to an end in 1951, and now graduate students wishing to enter the teaching profession can apply for a one-year course of training to a university department of education or to one of the training colleges which offer a post-graduate training course. The two-year training colleges were enabled to offer a third year of more specialised training to their most promising students. Because of financial considerations, only a small proportion of students elected to take this additional course. It was suggested that all training college students should pursue a three-year course, but at the time it was not considered to be in the realm of practical politics.

Departmental Committee on the Training of Teachers

In 1925, a Departmental Committee, under the chairmanship of Lord Burnham, reported on the training of teachers. The opinions of the Committee members were divided, which was a pointer to the divergent views about teacher training. Hence the report was not revolutionary in its recommendations. Nevertheless, some of the recommendations were important. Thus it was felt that the P.T. system and student teacherships should not be encouraged and that the normal avenue of entry to the profession should be direct from the secondary schools. This was in line with the general policy of the Board of Education. Although trained certificated teachers now formed the majority, there were still certain classes of teachers who were officially recognised, and it was thought that these should eventually be abolished. These consisted of non-trained certificated teachers, uncertificated, and supplementary teachers. The first group consisted of a number of ex-P.T.s who, because of their low academic attainments, had not been accepted by the training colleges. They were functioning as uncertificated teachers. After five years' experience in teaching they were permitted to sit for the Board's Acting-Teacher examination, and if successful were granted the Certificate. It was suggested that this avenue to the Certificate should be closed and that uncertificated teachers who wished to continue teaching should take a course of academic study and professional training for at least one year. Supplementary teachers should cease to be appointed. These were women employed in infant schools, mainly in rural districts, whose only qualifications were that they had reached the age of 18, possessed a good moral character, and had been vaccinated. The Board of Education immediately accepted these proposals. This meant that within a few years all teachers in elementary schools were trained and certificated, but the question of untrained teachers in secondary schools was not touched.

The Joint Board System

The Committee also suggested that the training colleges suffered from isolation and should be brought into closer relations with the rest of the educational organisation, in particular with the universities in their areas. After due consideration, the Board of

Education decided to adopt what was known as the Joint Board system. Previously, the examination of students in academic and professional studies and in practical teaching had been conducted by the Board of Education. In a few cases, the Board had approved alternative examinations. This had for many years been the policy in regard to university training departments. Students who passed the intermediate examination for the degree were accepted as having qualified in their academic studies for the Certificate, and at the close of their four-year course the professional examination conducted by the university for the Diploma in Education was accepted by the Board as qualifying for the Teachers' Certificate. The Board, however, retained their assessment of the practical teaching of students and the Board's inspectors assessed the students' work in such subjects as handicrafts, music, art, needlework, and physical training.

From 1930, ten Joint Examination Boards were established which contained representatives of the staffs of the training colleges and the universities. The result was not by any means satisfactory. The only co-operation was through the examination boards, and little progress was made in securing the closer relations with the universities which were desired. The outbreak of war in 1939 put an end, for the time being, to any further changes in teacher training. It was not until 1942 that the Board of Education felt that the time was now ripe for a thorough survey of the supply and methods of recruitment and the training of teachers and youth leaders. A committee, known as the McNair Committee, was appointed for this purpose and the report was issued in 1944.

McNair Report

The chief recommendations of the McNair Committee, named after its chairman, Sir Arnold McNair, were approved by the Government, but there appeared what at first seemed to be a serious divergence of opinion between the Committee members. One half of them proposed that the responsibility for teacher training in England and Wales ought to be shouldered by the universities. The other half thought that improvement could be attained by a development of the Joint Board system. Hence the Committee produced two solutions to the problem, which were known as Scheme A and Scheme B, respectively.

The first proposal was for the establishment of Schools of Education or Institutes of Education, as they were afterwards named. Those who favoured this view admitted that Scheme A involved a "major constitutional change" from the university point of view, but believed that it was well worth taking. The alternative opinion gave rise to a modification of Scheme B, which was generally known as Scheme C. This proposal objected to the Institute of Education being an integral part of the university, and maintained that it should be a separate entity financed by the Ministry of Education. Scheme A institutes would receive their grants through the University Grants Committee. The university, the local authorities, the university training departments, and the training colleges would be represented on the governing body of Scheme C institutes.

The majority of universities decided to adopt a Scheme A institute. Oxford remained outside the scheme altogether, whilst Cambridge, Liverpool, and Reading preferred Scheme C. Eventually, they changed over to Scheme A, and in 1951 Oxford decided to come into the system. The adoption of Scheme A did not involve a dead uniformity. Each university was able to express its own individuality by minor differences in the organisation of its institute and the title of the award made to successful students.

In some universities the Director of the Institute is also the Head of the University Department of Education, but more commonly the two posts are separate. The Department is a member institution, but not a member college of the Institute. In many universities the Director of the Institute is also a professor of education.

The Institutes of Education

The Institutes of Education are officially recognised as the Area Training Organisations, and one of their most important duties is the co-ordination of teacher training in each university area. They award certificates in education to candidates of the member colleges who have been successful in their examinations and recommend them to the Ministry for the status of Qualified Teacher. This is in accordance with the finding of the McNair Report. The latter had also suggested that the Diploma in Education issued to graduate students in the University Departments of Education should be discontinued. Some universities resented the abolition of the Diploma which they had conferred on successful candidates for more than a quarter of a century. In one university a compromise was reached, which awarded a graduate certificate under the authority of the Board of the Faculty of Arts. A neighbouring university at first accepted the certificate, but later decided to restore the Diploma. Some training colleges established a course of training for graduates, and those who are successful are awarded a graduate certificate.

The institutes also provide facilities for study and research in the field of education. They organise refresher courses for acting teachers and, in addition, give instruction of a more advanced kind which leads to diplomas in primary, secondary, and religious education, and for teachers of backward children. The courses may be of one, two, or three years duration. As a rule, the one-year courses are full-time and the three-year courses part-time. Many two-year courses are part-time, but include a full-time period of study for one or two terms. Many of the entrants are teachers with at least four or five years experience but who, because they are non-graduates, are not able to undertake research for the degrees of M.A. in Education, M.Ed., or Ph.D. Most institutes have a full-time teaching staff and also make use of the services of the staffs of the university departments and senior members of the training college staffs. In order to carry out these functions effectively, the institutes are housed in suitable buildings equipped with a library, lecture, conference, and seminar rooms. At first, they had to make do with what premises were available and later moved into more commodious quarters as these became vacant. Some institutes, such as London, possess modern buildings expressly designed for their needs.

The governing body is the Board of the institute, which is composed of representatives of the university, the training colleges and member institutions, and the local education authorities. The actual day-by-day business is carried on by the Professional Committee, and the discussion of the syllabuses of instruction provided by the different training colleges is the function of the various Boards of Studies. The teaching profession is represented on the Board and the Professional Committee, and two assessors are appointed by the Ministry of Education who have no vote but can contribute to the discussions. The Board and the Professional Committee usually have a number of sub-committees, which deal with such matters as lectures and courses, the library, research apparatus, and school textbooks. Most institutes issue a bulletin which contains topics and news of contemporary interest, and a quarterly journal containing longer articles concerned with research.

It is still somewhat early to make a full assessment of the value of these changes in the system of teacher training. At first, the institutes were regarded with some suspicion by the training colleges and the academic and education departments of the universities. The training colleges had developed a considerable degree of autonomy after the establishment of the Joint Boards, and now they wondered whether this would be maintained and even developed under the new regime. The resentment felt by many education departments at the substitution of a certificate for the Diploma as the first teaching qualification has been mentioned. This may have been one of the reasons why at first the universities tended to favour Scheme C, but pressure from the teachers and the local authorities was often too strong to resist. When the day training colleges (later university departments of education) were first established, they were regarded by the academic departments as poor relations, and this feeling affected the attitude of many of the students. Now, the departments of education are regarded with greater respect and the institutes are looked upon as poor, or, perhaps, new relations, who have to find their place in the university family.

Some academic departments had always deplored the fact that universities had accepted education departments, because many members of the academic staff considered that no type of vocational training was a function of a university. They only became reconciled to education departments when they discovered that the study of education was a university study in its own right, and that research in the fields of history, philosophy, and psychology, of education was really worth while. The fact that for many years the universities had been concerned with producing doctors, chemists, and engineers tended to be overlooked. This attitude was now transferred from the education departments to the new institutes. Some heads of departments felt that the introduction of the institutes compared unfavourably with the development of their own departments. One can sympathise with their point of view. For years they had fought for adequate funds for research apparatus or increases in teaching staffs, and now they found that the institutes appeared to be granted funds and facilities with the utmost readiness. It is only just to the institutes to mention that they were starting from scratch, and for some years they would need funds considerably in advance of those enjoyed by long-established departments. No doubt the heads of arts departments must have had similar feelings when they saw the amount of money which was being allocated to the science and technological departments.

These teething troubles are now lessening, and the institutes are foremost in acknowledging the assistance they have received from the older-established departments. On the whole, it can now be said that the institutes are settling down to a *modus vivendi* with other departments of the universities, and the spirit of co-operation between the institutes and the academic departments has developed considerably. The accusation that heads of institutes are "empire building" is less frequently heard. On the side of teacher training, the results are most promising. The departments of education and the training colleges have found that not only has their autonomy been respected but in some cases it has increased, and the feeling of isolation, so strong in some of the smaller colleges, is fast disappearing. They now feel that they have a meeting-point in the institute of their regional university. They have come to know their colleagues in other training institutions more intimately and also the staff of the university. One can forecast that the Institutes of Education will develop considerably in the future and will raise the status of the teaching profession.

Salary Scales

We have seen that the McNair Committee were also confronted with problems such as the recruitment and supply of teachers in the post-war period. Its members thought that not only the work and the prospects of the profession should be brought to the notice of senior pupils in the grammar schools, but that older men and women should be attracted to teaching. They had in mind members of the Forces who would be demobilised when the war came to an end. In order to secure the services of the latter, it would be essential that initial salaries should take into account the age and previous experience of the applicant. A basic scale of salaries should apply to teachers in all types of school, but special qualifications and experience should be rewarded by extra increments at the minimum and maximum of the scale. Special allowances ought to be made to teachers holding posts of special responsibility, *e.g.* senior masters and mistresses, heads of departments, etc.

Abolition of the "Pledge" and of Four-Year Training

The McNair Committee also made some other important recommendations. It was thought that the time had now come to abolish the "Pledge" system, under which entrants to training colleges and university departments of education received a two- or a four-year grant on condition that they declared in writing that it was their intention to enter the teaching profession. It was considered that an undergraduate on entering upon his academic course should not be restricted to any particular profession. The Ministry of Education was in agreement, and in 1951 the four-year system was discontinued. Students were not obliged to decide on their future profession until near the end of their degree course, and in 1956 the signed declaration was no longer required. The salary recommendations were discussed by the Burnham Committee and a new scale was adopted from 1 April 1945. Since that time, there have been frequent revisions of the scale to meet rises in the cost of living.

The Three-Year Training Course

The McNair Committee thought that the young person who entered a training college frequently found that two years in which to extend his academic studies, gain some useful experience in practical teaching and an adequate knowledge of the theory and practice of education, was overburdened, and a three-year course of training was recommended. Because of the acute shortage of teachers at the time, the Ministry, whilst approving the recommendation in principle, decided that they would be ill advised to make an immediate change, especially as the "bulge" threatened to accelerate the deficiency. The Ministry recently announced that from 1960 the normal training college course will extend over three years.

Opinions differ about how this extra year can be spent most profitably. The older generation of teachers seems to be in favour of a considerable extension of the time spent in practical teaching. The training colleges and the institutes have considered this problem, and have generally concluded that there should be no very significant change in the time devoted to teaching practice. The student would gain more by reflecting upon his own practical teaching and by obtaining a fuller insight into our modern social and industrial life and the nature of the child. After all, most students will spend over forty years in practical teaching. Many institutes have suggested that the third year would also give the students opportunities of widening their academic background.

Supply of Teachers

The problems connected with the increase in the supply of teachers was also considered. They had been developing since 1902, but it was not until 1918 that the effects of the First World War rendered them acute. The Education Act of that year resulted in a demand for more teachers, not only to make good the wastage consequent on the war but also to serve in the nursery and continuation schools and to meet the results of raising the school leaving age to 14. The Board of Education calculated that about 5,000 extra teachers would be necessary and that the annual number of entrants to the profession ought to be doubled. Training colleges and university departments of education were urged to increase their accommodation for intending teachers. Actually, the Board had over-estimated, and the result was an over-supply of teachers. Many students left their colleges to find that no posts were available for them and were forced to seek other employment.

Emergency Training Scheme

After the Second World War the shortage of teachers appeared in a still more acute form. This time, however, the Ministry had reckoned that about 70,000 teachers would be required, and after the critical stage of the war had been passed the Emergency Training Scheme was launched in 1943 to obtain men and women teachers from the Forces and other forms of national service. Emergency training colleges were opened in different areas, but an initial obstacle was encountered. As the war had not yet come to an end, most of the suitable buildings were occupied by Service personnel and it was not until they were vacated that the scheme really got going. The new colleges offered a one-year course of intensive training, and after completing his course the student was required to follow a scheme of directed reading to improve his academic and professional knowledge. The writer served on one of the interviewing boards and was greatly impressed by the maturity and personality of many of the applicants. Head teachers who received them after their training warmly praised their enthusiasm, character, and personality.

There were some criticisms of the scheme. The period of training was short and in most cases the academic background of the students was below the normal standard. Some teachers spoke of the scheme as a dilution of the teaching profession, but some such temporary expedient was necessary at the time until the ordinary training could be restored and augmented. Emergency training came to an end in October 1951. Some of the colleges were retained as two-year training colleges, but the majority were closed. Out of 124,000 applicants, 54,000 were accepted for training, and the net result was an additional 35,000 teachers, of whom 23,000 were men. In addition to this effort, the training colleges and university departments of education were pressed to increase their intake.

In spite of the advantages the teaching profession was able to offer, the shortage of teachers still presents a problem. Although the number of teachers in all types of school had increased in 1954 by about 7,600 on the previous year, and again by a similar amount in 1955, it was realised that a steady increase of 6,000 to 7,000 teachers a year was insufficient to cope with the "bulge" in the birth-rate which was now affecting the secondary schools. In 1957 the increase had fallen to 4,400, and only reached 5,200 in the following year. The number of full-time teachers in all types of school in England and Wales was about 316,000 in 1959, nearly 100,000 more than in 1947. The demand for teachers in scientific and technical subjects was growing, and the situation as regards graduate teachers was so serious that the Government granted indefinite deferment to graduate students in certain subjects so that if they had been appointed to teaching posts they could accept them in place of entering upon their National Service.

The situation for the future became more complicated when the information about the number of births in 1958 became available. It was evident that the increasing school population would necessitate a revision of the forecast of the number of teachers required from 1964 onwards. In September 1958 the Minister announced a programme of training college expansion to accommodate an addition of 12,000 students. This included the expansion of sixty-six existing colleges and the opening of four new colleges for men and women students at Nottingham, Walsall, Brentwood, and Cardiff. Provision was made for additional courses in mathematics and science. The fresh information about the increasing school population led the Minister to decide to increase the number of student places by another 4,000. A new Church of England college at Canterbury was also approved. The Church of England colleges agreed to enlarge the accommodation they could offer, and their new buildings are well on the way to completion. To assist the voluntary training colleges the Minister raised the grant for approved extensions to existing colleges to 75 per cent., and for the first time a similar grant became available for building new colleges.

An interesting development in 1959 was the opening of a new day training college by the Leeds L.E.A. Its aim is to meet the needs of older students, especially those with family commitments which prevented them from attending a residential college. The number of applicants was much greater than the places available. Some students were content to travel thirty or forty miles to attend classes. Amongst the applicants were married women whose children were in their early teens and some men who had retired from the Services.

The University Grants Committee increased the grants to university departments of education to make available 600-700 new places. The number of graduates in mathematics and science has grown. The Ministry decided that since the need for teachers would be much greater after 1964, September 1960 would be the most favourable time to launch the third-year training scheme in the colleges.

Because of the rapid increases in the cost of living since the War, the salary scales of the teachers were revised from time to time. In spite of this, teachers found that the increases they received did not match the increased salaries of those employed in industry. At the beginning of 1961 a proposed salary scale drawn up by the teachers' professional associations was presented to the Burnham Committee. The L.E.A. panel of the Committee was sympathetic and the whole of the Committee approved the new scale which would cost £47,500,000.

The agreement was sent for the approval of Mr Selwyn Lloyd, the Chancellor of the Exchequer. His policy limited pay increases to 3 per cent. and in order to check the movement towards inflation, he had already introduced some tax increases in his Budget. Both panels of the Committee and the teachers were exceedingly angered at his rejection of the total claimed and the substituted scales drawn up by himself. In addition he stated that Sir David Eccles would propose legislation in the autumn fixing the total amount at

£42,000,000. He also declared that he would amend Section 89 of the 1944 Act to give the Chancellor of the Exchequer powers similar to those possessed by the Secretary of State for Scotland to modify salary agreements. The Burnham Committee strongly protested but had to admit that they were powerless. Sir William Alexander, the secretary of the authorities' panel declared, "The Burnham Committee as constituted ceases, as I see it". His prophecy was quite true.

When negotiations between the teachers and the Chancellor and the Minister of Education broke down, token strikes occurred in different parts of the country. The N.U.T. wished to avoid a national strike and decided on a one day token strike and notified that teachers would cease to supervise school meals after 1 November. The National Association of Schoolmasters refused a compromise offered by Mr Selwyn Lloyd and Sir David Eccles to postpone the new legislation and it staged a number of token strikes. The N.U.T. accepted the compromise with reluctance because they considered that the cuts were not sufficiently severe to warrant the wholesale distress that would accompany strike action.

When the Burnham Committee met to consider the scale which would be operative after 1 April 1963, it was hoped that negotiations would be peaceable. The Committee recommended an increase of £50 to operate throughout the basic scale. This would amount to £21 million. The L.E.A. panel and the N.U.T. agreed but the N.A.S. rejected the recommendation as inadequate. The successor of Sir David Eccles, Sir Edward Boyle, was willing to accept the total amount which he considered was very generous but he objected to sanction further expenditure on salaries and he disagreed about the distribution of the money. He believed that a uniform increment throughout the basic scale would deter new recruits to the teaching profession. They would be looking ahead to the salary they would receive after a number of years of experience. He was convinced that the proposed form of distribution would not give satisfaction to graduates, holders of graded posts, and others who had posts of special responsibility and experience.

The N.U.T. would agree that the more experienced and more highly qualified teachers ought to receive higher awards but this would entail an increase in the total sum recommended and the Minister had declared that he was not ready to accept this. In contradiction to the Minister's statement, it would be the Minister's proposal which would deter new recruits. Young teachers were more in need of additional money in the first few years of their service when they were buying their houses and bringing up young families. The Burnham Committee refused to compromise and a deadlock followed.

The problem is not an easy one to solve. Like most problems there is much to be said on either side. It is doubtful whether the Minister has the legal right to reject a recommendation before it has been officially presented to him. The intervention of the Minister is that of an individual who is not a member of the Burnham Committee, and the negotiations which take place at the meeting are between the representatives of the teachers and their employers who are the L.E.A.s. The principles of procedure in Section 89 of the Education Act need very careful examination. Sir Edward Boyle has notified that he will present legislation to give the Minister a place on the Burnham Committee.

Another problem connected with this is one which began to appear after the Education Act of 1902 but which is more formidable now. It is the burden on the rates due to education. This is exceptionally severe as the result of the new valuation. We need to keep in mind that the ratepayers contribute nearly half the cost of teachers' salaries. It has been suggested by the Liberal party and by some in the other political parties that education ought to be taken off the rates and become the concern of the central government. This might lead to a breakdown of the partnership of the central authority, the local authorities, the teaching profession, and the parents which has existed since 1902. Obviously it seems that the Burnham Committee will be replaced or, at least, there will be a major change in its functions.

SUGGESTIONS FOR FURTHER READING

Much useful and interesting information about progress in teacher training will be found in R. W. Rich, *The Training of Teachers in England and Wales during the Nineteenth Century,* C.U.P., 1933, and the Annual Report of the Board of Education, 1912-13. A full account of the Emergency Training Scheme will be found in *Challenge and Response,* Ministry of Education Pamphlet No. 17, H.M.S.O., 1950. R. W. Rich, *The Teacher in a Planned Society,* U.L.P., 1950. M. V. C. Jeffreys, *Revolution in Teacher Training,* Pitman, 1961, gives a full account of teacher training in the post-war period.

CHAPTER XVII

THE COMING REVOLUTION IN ENGLISH EDUCATION

The coming revolution in English education was foreshadowed by the publication of the White Paper of 1958 *Secondary Education For All: A New Drive* (pp. 208-9). At the same time special investigations into different parts of the educational field were in progress, namely, the Albemarle and Beloe Reports which were concerned with the Youth Service and the problem of examinations in nonselective secondary schools, respectively. It was also apparent that systematic inquiries into the whole of our educational system would be necessary. These really began with the Crowther Report and were continued in the Newsom and Robbins Reports, and in the future, by the Report of the Plowden Committee which started its inquiry in October 1963.

The Crowther Report

The Crowther Report of the Central Advisory Council for Education (England), entitled *15 to 18*, is without doubt the most complete survey of the education of the older adolescent that has been produced. The main Report was published as Volume 1 in 1959, and Volume 2, which followed in 1960, contains a number of special surveys and statistics which provide detailed information about young people between the ages of fifteen and eighteen. They comprise a Social, a National Service, and a Technical Courses Survey. The two volumes cover more than 750 pages, so that in a short chapter one can do little more than draw attention to the major topics and recommendations of the Report.

The main Report is divided into seven sections, entitled Education in a Changing World, The Development of the Modern School, Secondary Education for All, The Way to County Colleges, The Sixth Form, Technical Challenge and Educational Response, and Institutions and Teachers. The last chapter contains a summary of the principal conclusions and recommendations of the Report, and Appendix III is an interesting account of technical education and vocational training in western Europe. The Glossary, giving definitions of terms used in the Report, is in a form which is useful to the non-expert reader.

The first two chapters of the Report consist of an historical summary which sketches the great changes in education since the days of the Bryce Commission, and the comparisons made are most illuminating. The Report then draws attention to the "bulge" in the birth-rate. In 1959 there were 2,318,000 boys and girls in the age group considered. The peak year is expected to be 1965, by which time this number will have increased by about 700,000. Another "bulge" of seventeen-year-olds is expected in the middle 1970s. If the Education Act of 1944 had been put fully into operation (school leaving age of sixteen and establishment of county colleges), about 1¾ million boys and girls would now be receiving full-time or part-time education in day schools. The actual number in 1957-8 was only two-fifths of this figure. The number of boys and girls receiving full-time education was approximately equal, but part-time education presented quite a different picture. There was a natural decrease after the age of fifteen, but this was most marked in the case of girls. Most boys obtained part-time release during the day, but only 5 to 6 per cent. of the girls got this. There was also a considerable number who attended evening classes or who took correspondence courses, but a much larger number was practically untouched by educational activities. Children of manual workers seldom remained at school after fifteen. The percentage remaining for an additional year varied according to districts. In the north-east it was about 16 to 17 per cent., but in the southwest it reached 28 per cent. At present, day release is a privilege granted by the employers, and on the whole is granted to skilled workers in training and almost exclusively to boys.

On the other hand, the number of pupils in secondary schools has shown a tremendous increase. In 1894 only about four or five pupils per 1,000 in elementary schools were able to proceed to grammar schools, compared with the 200 per 1,000 who are in grammar schools at the present day. The number of those obtaining part-time education has grown more slowly, and even in 1911 only about 45,000 of all ages received such education, but the number of those attending evening classes increased considerably. The closure of the day continuation schools of the 1918 Act slowed down the number receiving part-time day instruction, so that it had only increased over 1911 by about 6,000 in 1938. The raising of the leaving age to fourteen in 1918 and to fifteen in 1947 removed those under these ages from industry, but little has been done for those over fifteen. What should be done for them is the main topic of the first half of the Report.

Of about 2,550,000 boys and girls in secondary schools, only about 320,000 are above the age of fifteen. Although greatly reduced in number, there are still over 2,000 all-age schools. The majority of secondary schools are organised on the tripartite plan, and the remainder are new types of school—multilateral, bilateral, and comprehensive.

The Report states that in 1938 about 38 per cent. of modern schools were co-educational and this percentage has increased to about 53. Most of the co-educational secondary modern schools are located in rural districts in which there is insufficient population to warrant single sex schools. The proportion of co-educational grammar schools has not changed to any extent, and is still under 30 per cent. The increase in the number of sixth form pupils is a welcome sign. The technical high schools have broadened their curriculum, and the lower age of entry and later age of leaving are to the good. The Report queries the term "tripartite system". "We do not now have, and never have had a tripartite system" (para. 34). In a truly tripartite system there would be as many technical as grammar schools, but over 40 per cent. of L.E.A.s do not provide technical schools, though in many bilateral and comprehensive schools technical streams exist.

The historical outline is followed by a brief discussion of the changing social and economic conditions of the country. On the family side, men and women live longer and marry earlier than in the last century. Earlier marriages tend to become the rule, and about half the women in this country are married before the age of twenty-five. The result has been smaller and earlier families and an increasing number of women have found it necessary or helpful to take up full-time or part-time employment. Earlier in the century the professions, trades, and industries open to women were limited, but this is no longer the case. Statistics show that children from large families are more likely to leave school at the statutory age of fifteen. The birth and care of children now tends to be merely a break in the employment of women and not the end of it, and the earlier age of marriage has important repercussions on the nature of the education best fitted for girls.

The Report then refers to the emancipation of young people and the prevalence of less rigid moral codes. This has both good and bad aspects. Public ideas about right and wrong are often indeterminate, so that young people easily fall into personal bewilderment and disaster. It is not altogether the fault of the young, for, as the Report remarks, "it was the adults and not the teenagers who first cast doubt on the rules". The prevalence of juvenile delinquency is greater in some districts, especially in the declining and impoverished areas near the centres of large cities, but new housing estates can be equally deadly if there is a lack of communal life and social leadership. In such districts the teacher should be both an educator and a social worker. It has been suggested that it is not those born during the war as much as those who were infants at that time and whose education was upset and who are now in the early twenties who swell the ranks of delinquents. The last year at school is the peak age of juvenile delinquency, and therefore more thought should be given to the conditions of life amongst boys and girls during the last year before leaving school.

There have been rapid economic changes since 1938. Materially, the country is richer and the standards of living have risen, especially in the lower income groups. The earnings of young people have increased more rapidly than those of adults, with the result that they have to decide whether to remain at school or leave at fifteen to reap the benefits of a high immediate wage. On the whole, those who stay at school longer catch up and pass the latter after the age of twenty. Industry is demanding special qualifications more and more, and a good general education enables the young to choose between a larger number of occupations. Young people need to learn how to live in a technological society, and those who do not qualify as scientists, technologists, or technicians need to develop "general mechanical intelligence".

The Report draws attention to the distinction between two different ways of viewing education; namely, that which regards it as a duty owed by the State to its citizens and that which sees it as a national investment. The two aspects are really complementary, and the answer given is that the benefit to the individual is the more important, but only by a very short lead. It may appear that the expenditure on education has grown out of all proportion, but when examined more closely it is seen that, excluding the cost of the social services of education and the grants to universities, the amount expended just about keeps pace with the increase in the national income. The recommendations offered by the Advisory Council will not seem to be so costly if compared with the money spent on housing and capital investment on plant and machinery or the total expenditure on drink or tobacco.

Part II of the Report deals with the development of the secondary modern school. There now exists a widespread demand for a longer school life, and extended courses should be available for all modern school pupils. The problem of external examinations calls for careful consideration. It is important to cater for the minority of abler pupils, but the interests of the majority must not be neglected. Some pupils can justify themselves by their record in selected subjects of the G.C.E. examination. The Council realised the dangers of large-scale external examinations. About a third of the pupils of fifteen plus can benefit by a lower grade examination, but before adopting a national scheme further experience and inquiry is necessary. Hence it is recommended that regional experiments should be studied and leaving certificates on local or regional lines should be examined before setting up a national system.

It is essential that neither L.E.A.s, nor school governors, nor the general public should judge the modern schools on the basis of successes in external examinations. One must keep in mind the large number of pupils who are immature or below average, and special responsibility payments should be available for members of the school staff concerned with this group. There is another group of children who are less dull, but are physically well developed and are burning with the desire to leave school. Hence the modern school should be in a position to offer a variety of courses, but small schools are unable to do this. Hence the recommendation for larger schools.

In Part III, the Report strongly advises the extension of the school leaving age to sixteen, and the most favourable period for doing this will be between 1965 and 1969, which lies between the two "bulges" which affect secondary schools. The extension of the leaving age is of benefit to the individual and is in the national interest. As a preliminary step, there should be two, in place of three, leaving dates in the school year—Easter and July. It is essential that the actual date of raising the leaving age should be chosen well ahead so that arrangements for accommodation and an adequate supply of teachers can be made. Which should have priority—the raising of the leaving age or the introduction of compulsory county colleges? The Council had no doubt about the answer. The former should have priority.

Part IV of the Report considers the county colleges. "The majority of the boys and nearly all the girls who leave school as soon as they are entitled to do so are without that help in growing up which is acknowledged to be necessary" (para. 261). Most boys and girls during the period in which they are at school belong to some type of youth organisation, but after they leave they gradually drift away. The conclusion is that the Youth Service fails to attract and retain the lower quarter or third of young people. The Report regrets that the present position is so unsatisfactory, but can offer no promise of improvement. No specific recommendations are made since these fall within the province of the Albemarle Report. Young folk at the age of seventeen or eighteen are beginning to be affected by four new kinds of experience: they earn money; they have more spending money; they are "going steady"; and it will not be many years before they think of marriage, pay taxes, and become voters. In what ways can the county colleges be of assistance to them? The very newness of these experiences causes them to think, and the welfare of the community demands straight thinking about these matters. Hence one object of the county college is to lead them to discover how to employ both their time and their money in the best possible way. The stability of a democratic society depends on the possession of such knowledge and discrimination amongst its members. The problem of values is a more difficult one. These young people will soon come up sharply against the divergence between the moral values taught in the schools and those practised by many adults in the outside world. The more intellectual individuals who continue full-time education will develop in maturity and the ability to stand on their own feet in the new world they are entering. Those who leave school at fifteen are immature, and this justifies compulsory attendance at the county college, which can be most effective in giving these young people assistance if it works in association with a strong Youth Service.

When the Act of 1944 stipulated attendance at county colleges it did not lay down details about the nature of the curriculum. No doubt it was realised that the curriculum would vary from district to district and could be constructed at a later stage. The Crowther Report suggests four strands in the curriculum. (1) The task of helping young workers to live successfully in the adult world, *e.g.*

spending their money sensibly, understanding the ways in which the welfare state can help them, how to play their part as responsible citizens, etc. (2) Training them to define, in a form which they can understand, a standard of moral values by which they can conduct their lives. (3) Enabling them to carry on with those worthwhile leisure pursuits and hobbies which the majority abandon after leaving school. (4) An opportunity of making good the deficiencies in their formal school education.

One general criticism may now be mentioned concerning the Crowther Report. Though it speaks at some length on the topic of moral education, it seems hesitant in regard to religious education and does not mention the place of religious worship nor the teaching of the Bible. Possibly the hesitation was due to denominational differences, but one should remember that the 1944 Act has provided for religious worship and instruction in all schools, primary and secondary, county and voluntary, and this provision has, on the whole, worked quite smoothly. The Student Christian Movement, which has accomplished successful work in secondary modern schools and in technical schools and colleges, could be of assistance in the county colleges. The university chaplains of the different Christian bodies have got into touch with the technical colleges, and could be equally helpful in regard to students in the county colleges.

The Report does not agree that a national system of county colleges should be established in one move. Careful preparations are necessary for success. The Advisory Council had in mind the fate of the continuation schools of the 1918 Act. Adequate buildings are essential and also teachers who have been trained in the methods of approaching these young workers. Makeshift arrangements must be avoided at any cost. It recommends that certain districts should be designated in which compulsory day release to experimental colleges should operate, and this scheme would provide a good deal of useful experience. The county colleges also depend for their success on gaining both the support of employers as well as that of the employees. In addition, there are a number of complicated administrative problems which have to be tackled, *e.g.* the respective values of a day-a-week attendance and of a block release for a whole month.

The next subject considered in the Report is the sixth form. So far, the great majority of sixth form pupils are to be found in the maintained grammar schools, the direct grant schools, and the recognised independent schools, but this proportion may change in the near future when the technical high schools, the comprehensive, and other new types of school are able to make their contribution. This part of the Report deals with quite a different set of problems. So far, the average and below average pupils have been considered, but this section of the Report is concerned with the more able boys and girls. Attention is drawn to the alarming waste of talent through those pupils who are withdrawn from the grammar school at the age of fifteen or sixteen. Of those who remain to seventeen or eighteen, the largest proportion—over 60 per cent. —are in maintained grammar schools. The problems relevant to the sixth form are examined in much detail, but in the compass of a short chapter it is only possible to mention a few salient points.

The Report refers to "express routes" to the sixth form which are more common in the independent and direct grant schools. The course is organised to enable the most able pupils to sit for "O" level G.C.E. at fifteen rather than the usual age of sixteen, but the number of candidates presented at fourteen should be restricted to exceptional cases. It is important that the majority of pupils should experience the curriculum as a whole before they decide on the subjects in which they wish to specialise. Early specialisation often entails a reduction of the time spent on such studies as English, history or geography, religious knowledge, and the arts and crafts. If these are retained the sixth form time-table becomes overcrowded. Thus pupils who desire to be specialists in languages are often asked to study Latin and two modern languages, and this throws a heavy strain upon them. "This downward pressure is more marked in boys' schools than in girls' " [para. 329 (e)].

Historically, the sixth form has always been closely linked with the universities, and this link should be retained, but attention should also be given to pupils who do not wish to enter a university or a college of higher education. Other characteristics of the sixth form are "subject-mindedness" and specialisation, training in independent work, and a more intimate relation between pupils and teacher. It is also important that the sixth form pupils should acquire a sense of social responsibility.

The problem of the staff of the sixth form is a very serious one. As the Report phrases it, "we are living on capital". The number of men and women with first-class degrees who wish to enter the teaching profession is declining, and it is therefore necessary to do more than has been done in attracting such people into teaching.

Although specialisation is approved, there is a tendency for pupils to tackle too many subjects at "A" level so that insufficient time is left for non-specialist subjects. An endeavour should be made to render science specialists literate and arts students "numerate", *i.e.* to give them some understanding of scientific method and an acquaintance with the achievements of science.

Chapter 26 is concerned with the "obscure and controversial" problems of university entrance. The Report suggests that it is wrong to separate off potential university candidates, even if possible, from others and that "A" level should be regarded primarily as a school leaving examination. Many pupils qualified to enter a university have difficulty in being selected. One reason is that some universities and departments are preferred to others and the entrance requirements of different universities and of the faculties and departments within them vary greatly. The result is that potential entrants usually apply for entrance to a number of universities. All this puts a great strain on sixth formers, and the Report recommends a great expansion in the number of university places available and a more uniform and expeditious method of selection. There should be an overhaul of the method of allocating financial grants from the L.E.A.s. Since the Crowther Report, more university places are becoming available, and the Anderson Report has recommended a revised scale of parental contributions so that 40 per cent., instead of the previous 25 per cent., of university students can obtain full Government grant. The latter came into force in October 1961.

We now approach an extremely important section of the Crowther Report, Part VI, entitled "Technical Challenge and Educational Response". So far, the Report had been dealing with groups of young people and the educational problems they present, which are generally well defined. The boys and girls who leave school at about fifteen years of age constitute approximately one-half of the age group considered in the Report. Those who are in grammar and technical schools or in the selective streams of comprehensive schools comprise a little less than a quarter of the young people aged fifteen. Some of these will remain at schools for at least another year, or even longer. This leaves the last quarter, whose full-time education stops at fifteen or sixteen but who continue to spend a proportion of their time in further education. The majority of these are working as apprentices and trainees in various industries and follow part-time courses at technical colleges.

The remainder is scattered across a number of different courses, including non-technical industries and commerce.

These young folk are not necessarily inferior in intelligence to those in the higher forms of the grammar schools. Some, indeed, entered further education from the sixth form. The kind of education considered is not of an inferior but rather of a different type to that experienced in the sixth form. All these represent what the Report terms "neglected education territory", which has never been reviewed as a whole and constitutes the next major problem to be tackled in English education. Two main challenges, which are not entirely distinct but rather overlapping, have to be met. The first is constituted by the nature of the technological age which we, in common with other civilised communities, have now entered. The grammar school does make a significant contribution, but not only pure scientists and technologists are urgently needed, but also far greater numbers of technicians and craftsmen for industry and agriculture. Thus the White Paper on Technical Education (1956) pointed out that five or six technicians are needed for every technologist. Hence a definite expansion must take place if we are to meet future requirements successfully.

The other challenge is that of numbers. Only one in eight of young people of sixteen to eighteen are following full-time educational courses. We should aim at raising this proportion to one-half. Not all of these will be full-time in school, but they will devote the major portion of their time to "continuing in education". Attendance at a county college would not meet this requirement, though a well organised sandwich course would be satisfactory. Not all part-time further education will be technical. The teenager needs general as well as technical education, and the two overlap.

The Report gives a list (excluding universities and private institutions) of agencies which supply further education. In addition to the "major establishments" there are over 8,000 evening institutes containing nearly 400,000 students under the age of eighteen. The past contribution of evening classes is praised, but the Report considers that the future of the evening institutes will tend to lie in the field of non-vocational adult education. Most part-time day students attend for a day a week on release from their work, which is mainly engineering or building. Appendix A to Chapter 29 quotes the definitions of technologist, technician, and craftsman given in the White Paper, but the Report adds a fourth category—that of operative.

A critical account of the characteristics of the present state of further education is given in Chapter 30. The twelve significant observations are: (1) Only a few industries have apprenticeship schemes involving a day-a-week release, and these are for boys alone; (2) There should be consistent provision for the three ability grades of technician, craftsman, and operative; (3) Further education has grown up "as the handmaiden of employment" and day release is dependent on apprenticeship; (4) There is, however, little connection between the organisation of apprenticeship and further education, a factor which presents the boy with two different objectives; (5) The smooth transition from full-time school to part-time further education is often lacking; (6) The largest group of boys entering upon courses in further education are those who left school at fifteen, but at the higher stages the number of those with longer full-time education is growing; (7) Examinations are organised in stages, and a student must pass in all subjects at one stage before he can enter upon the next—this causes a considerable amount of retardation; (8) Because of the different nature of girls' employment, there is too little day release for girls; (9) Attendance of students at evening courses is irregular, and a high proportion fail to complete the courses; (10) Full-time courses in further education are at present mostly short commercial courses for girls or courses to make good deficiencies in G.C.E. qualifications; (11) Sandwich courses are spreading into the fifteen to eighteen age-range; (12) The teaching staffs are mainly part-time and untrained, and include few women.

Day release is increasing, but not rapidly enough to keep pace with the increasing number of fifteen-year-olds. By 1964, day releases should increase by about 28,000 to avoid falling back to the position of 1956. The percentage of passes in comparison with the number entering upon a course is unsatisfactory. Thus, of students starting on a five-stage course for the National Certificate, only 26 per cent. gain the Ordinary and 10 per cent. the Higher Certificate. The two main causes of failure are reliance on evening classes only and an inadequate knowledge of mathematics. Little or nothing is known about the position in other professional examinations, and this calls for similar investigation.

The Report recommends three principles for future development. There must be greater integration between school and further education. To reduce the rate of failure, more time should be allowed in all courses. No young student should rely exclusively on the preparation given through evening classes. Most important, our eventual aim must be to replace the varied collection of plans for vocational education by a comprehensive and well-organised national scheme. There should be closer contacts in each area between the schools and institutions for further education. School-teachers should be well informed about what further education can offer and technical colleges need to be aware of recent developments in secondary education. When new students enter, colleges should separate them from those who are returning for a course. A full-time induction course, about a month in duration, should be instituted in the autumn term for all new students. This would be valuable for the selection of courses suitable for them. Some universities have organised short courses for their entrants, and these have proved to be of considerable value. A tutorial system would improve relations between students and staff, and the division of students into small groups would help them in their learning of mathematics.

The problem of time is discussed in Chapter 34. The length of year laid down by the Education Act of 1944 for county colleges (forty-four weeks or 330 hours) should be introduced into technical colleges through an agreement between them and the employers. Wherever possible, "block release" should replace release for one day a week. Students failing in one subject at one stage should be permitted to proceed to the next stage and repeat that subject by means of a subsidiary examination. Sandwich courses should be the norm for technicians, and every effort should be made to secure the replacement of part-time by sandwich courses. At present, boys and girls of fifteen and sixteen have only two alternatives—the full academic course for which they may not be suitable, and the arduous and wasteful part-time course. One of the major tasks for English education is to develop a new type of "practical" education which is free from the defects of the academic and part-time systems, but which is technical but not solely technical. The problems of further education for agriculture are discussed in an Appendix to Part VI. The recommendations of Lord De La Warr's Committee on "Further Education for Agriculture provided by Local Education Authorities" (1958) should be carefully considered.

Part VII of the Report is entitled "Institutions and Teachers", and deals with problems, many of which are highly controversial.

The suggestions offered are not dogmatic, but an effort is made to produce a workable *via media* between the conflicting points of view. We should aim at securing that the present 12 per cent. of seventeen-year-olds in full-time education (including sandwich courses) becomes 50 per cent. by 1980. To attain this end we shall have to keep until eighteen, by persuasion, all who enter the grammar school at eleven and about one-third of those in non-selective schools, and an alternative route for the non-academic—the new type of "practical" education mentioned above—should be provided. What should be the size of a school? The answer, in broad terms, is that the older the pupil the larger the school can be. This would give the teenager an adequate choice of courses. Many of the present grammar and modern schools are not large enough to make the courses economic after the age of sixteen. Technical schools (entrance age eleven or thirteen) should be distributed throughout the country and ought to be planned with a large sixth form in view. This would involve transfers from the modern schools and some of the grammar schools.

As regards the comprehensive school, the Report takes the view the writer expressed in an earlier chapter of this book. They are still in the experimental stage, and it would be premature to arrive at a definite decision until we have accumulated more experience about them. The disadvantage of size (1,200 to 2,000 pupils) could be avoided by adopting two single sex schools instead of one co-educational or by organising two schools to divide between them the age-range eleven to eighteen. L.E.A.s are experimenting to discover the most effective kind of organisation. One point is imperative. The comprehensive school must be housed in suitable buildings. Makeshift accommodation cannot be tolerated. Also the comprehensive school should not be established in an area in which it would harm an efficient existing grammar school.

There are, however, certain situations in which a comprehensive school can best cater for local needs, *e.g.* densely populated areas, new housing estates, thinly populated rural districts which could not support a grammar or modern school of adequate size, and small, self-contained industrial townships where one good all-purpose school is the only alternative to two poorly equipped and inadequately staffed separate schools. A case can be made for junior colleges, parallel with but not replacing the sixth forms, and experiments in this direction should be encouraged.

Educational advance along the lines recommended by the Report ultimately depends upon the teachers. There must be "teachers with the right qualities and in the right numbers to carry it out". Obviously, the raising of the leaving age to sixteen will require many more teachers. One should note that a longer school life widens the field from which teachers can be recruited. The Report outlines the characteristics of the good teacher, but apart from the essential personal qualities one must consider qualifications. Hence the statement that the modern schools need more graduates and the grammar schools could pretty certainly do with some college-trained general teachers. It is recommended that the National Advisory Council on the Training and Supply of Teachers should be asked to advise on the additional number of teachers that will be required to raise the school leaving age. The standards reached by training college students should become higher as the result of the third year of training. One problem concerns graduates with high qualifications. There should be an energetic campaign to obtain first-rate graduate teachers, but "no campaign, however, will succeed unless the material rewards of teaching compare favourably with those of other professions open to the graduate".

The Report concludes with the admission that the Central Advisory Council has drawn up "a formidable list of recommendations, some of which are more urgent than others". One paragraph is quite frank. "We do not believe that there is any hope of carrying out the measures we have outlined—or any other list of proposals adequate to the needs—unless they are worked out and adopted as a coherent, properly phased development plan, extending by timed and calculated steps a long way into the future. Nothing of this sort has ever hitherto been possible in English education. There has been no lack of aspiration, or of definitions of objectives; but the attainment of them has been left to the mercies of the parliamentary time-table and of financial exigences. Nothing more than this has been possible because there has not been support in public opinion for anything more" (para. 696).

The observations raised above were important because there existed a fairly widespread feeling that the Report stood the risk of being put into cold storage. Sir David Eccles seemed to be aware of this when he wrote in the Introduction to the Report of the Ministry of Education, *Education in 1960*, "The recommendations of the Crowther Report, covering a wide range of complex and controversial issues, took some time to study and many outside interests had to be consulted before the Government could formulate their views. But, as recorded in the Annual Report, the Government are taking action on many of the Crowther recommendations and as time passes it will be seen that this outstanding Report has influenced the thinking of the Ministry on a wide variety of subjects, including the supply of teachers, external examinations, school leaving dates, the integration of school and further education, and courses for technicians."

A Bill was introduced at the end of 1961 and became law in March 1962 which carried out the recommendation of the Crowther Report for only two leaving dates each year. The object of this was to lead to a more worthwhile fourth year in non-selective schools for those pupils who were ready to remain at school beyond the statutory leaving age of fifteen. Thus pupils who reached the age of fifteen in 1963 have to stay at school until Easter 1964 and those who would have left at Easter 1963 have to remain at school until the beginning of the summer vacation 1964.

At the request of the Ministry, Sir Geoffrey Crowther agreed to continue in office as Chairman of the Central Advisory Council for Education (England). He relinquished office in November 1960 and was succeeded by Viscount Amory who had retired from the office of Chancellor of the Exchequer. In June 1961 he was selected as United Kingdom High Commissioner in Canada and was succeeded by the Vice-Chairman of the Advisory Council, Mr John Newsom.

The Newsom Report, August 1963

The terms of reference given to the Central Advisory Council for Education (England) were as follows:—"To consider the education between the ages of thirteen and sixteen of pupils of average or less than average ability who are or will be following full-time courses either at schools or in establishments of further education. The term education shall be understood to include extra-curricular activities".

Since the majority of pupils in this age group are in non-selective secondary schools, the emphasis is on those in modern and comprehensive schools. Some pupils of this age may be in the lower or middle forms of grammar schools or institutions of further education, who have left school or are members of a youth organisation. The majority, however, will constitute approximately half of the population of England and Wales in the future. Hence the title of the Report, *Half Our Future,* and the last sentences of the Introduction supply the aim of the Report: "Half our future is in their hands. We must see that it is in good hands".

Before a report of this type can be drawn up and issued, the facts about the schools, the pupils, and the education provided must be ascertained. This was the task of the survey carried out for the Council in 1961 in modern and comprehensive schools. It was out of the question to deal with every school because of cost and time and therefore representative samples were obtained. By careful sub-sampling within the selected schools the sample was reduced to about 6,000 pupils. Care was exercised in choosing the samples so that they would give reliable information.

The Council confessed that the terms average and below average caused difficulties. Although it is difficult to find a sharp line of demarcation between the two categories yet for practical purposes they do classify two large groups of pupils. There is a danger that below average ability may carry emotional overtones and can easily suggest "below average people" who are inferior to the more able pupils and are less worth educating. This is a consequence that the Council would not accept. The average is not a fixed classification but can vary and during the last twenty-five years it has been steadily rising. "The mysteries of one generation become the commonplaces of life to their grandchildren. In this sense standards do rise."

Developments in the education of the average and below average will cost a great deal of money. Can we afford this? The answer to this question is that we need many more skilled workers for existing jobs and a better educated labour force to meet the demands of the future. There are reserves of ability among our children and these can be tapped. One of the means is a longer school life. Since 1958 the number of pupils remaining in modern schools has doubled and in the future we may find some secondary modern pupils remaining at school until seventeen or even eighteen.

At the present time this is a voluntary choice but we cannot be satisfied by this, especially when some countries such as the United States and France have raised the school-leaving age. The Crowther Report had suggested that the most convenient time for such a measure in this country would be in the years 1966-9 when the secondary schools would be less crowded. Delay in implementing the advice offered by the Crowther Report has made it almost too late to change at the most apt time. Hence it is recommended that an immediate announcement should be made that the school-leaving age will be raised to sixteen from 1965. This would mean that it would come into force in 1969-70. It is further recommended that full-time education for this group should be school-based but this would not prevent some part of the school course in the final year being taken in a college of further education.

In describing the schools and their pupils, the Report not only made use of the survey of 1961 but obtained additional information from the National Service Survey given in Vol. II of the Crowther Report. These sources of information enabled the Council to give a rough classification of the environment of the pupils. "A third of them live on housing estates, which may be bright and modern, like those of the new towns, or drab and ageing, as are some of those built in the early years between the wars. Just under a fifth live in the old and overcrowded centre of some big city or industrial area, where there are few amenities and often a concentration of social problems; for brevity we later refer to these as 'problem' areas. Another fifth of the pupils is made up of boys and girls from rural and from mining districts; and the remainder come from areas which do not fit into any one of these categories and are generally mixed in character."

Many of the pupils attend schools which have attractive modern buildings but a large number of these new schools are hopelessly overcrowded. Two-fifths of the schools in the sample carry on in very inadequate buildings. There is often a great many changes in the teaching staff. The teachers reported that on the whole the pupils are co-operative and only a minority in the fourth year raise serious problems of class control. The less able pupils more often are absent from school without adequate reason. Nearly half of the boys but a minority of the girls take up part-time paid employment. The latter help their mothers in the household duties. There is no evidence that the school work suffered from pupils taking up part-time work.

Many of the schools are housed in old buildings and others suffer from lack of books and inadequate equipment. The picture drawn by the Report bears out the evidence presented by the N.U.T. survey, *The State of Our Schools*. The Report states that the 1944 Act changed the name and status of the old Senior Elementary Schools to Secondary Modern Schools, but at first changed little else. One difficulty is, that unlike established grammar schools, they have no tradition or reputation to help them. When the building programmes described in the White Paper of 1958 are completed in 1965, the majority of pupils will be attending new schools or older ones which have been enlarged, but from the opening day, a large number of these schools were greatly overcrowded.

One of the reasons which has led to a considerable number of pupils remaining at school after the age of fifteen is the development of extended courses. Many of these do not necessarily lead to an external examination. The Report stresses the extra-curricular activities in the newer schools and believes that these should be more publicised. If the general public knew more about these the lurid accounts of misbehaviour and delinquency described by the press would be seen to be exaggerated. As the Report says, "Education needs a better communications service".

Some pupils declare that the work in the school bores them whilst others say that they do not see the value of what is being taught. It is essential to make boys and girls more active partners in the educational process. Often linguistic inadequacy or the disadvantage of the pupils' social and physical environment are responsible for their poor attainments in school.

The Council recommends more attention to the deficiencies mentioned above. Some of these are the result of overcrowding rather than old buildings. The Ministry should organise a programme of research to assist pupils in their linguistic or environmental difficulties. The establishment of an experimental school working in close contact with a teacher training college in which specially selected members of staff are appointed for this purpose, is strongly recommended.

A very vivid description of the environment of boys and girls who are unfortunate enough to live in the slum areas in London, Yorkshire, Lancashire, and the industrial Midlands is given. In many of these areas there has been a considerable influx of coloured people from India, Pakistan, and the West Indies. In most modern schools disciplinary and social problems generally arise with the children of a few families but in a slum district the school has to meet the challenge of the whole neighbourhood. It is stimulating to know that sometimes the achievements of pupils in these schools are equal to or even better than in schools in better areas.

The staffing of schools in slum areas is so important that the Report recommends the setting up of an interdepartmental Working Party to deal with general social problems including education. An increase in the number of teachers will not by itself be sufficient for the needs of these schools unless the right kind of teachers are selected. "Whatever happens in the schools depends on the men or women who staff them." Some teachers with a strong sense of vocation volunteer to work in these difficult areas but they are far too small in number. The Crowther Report had recommended that "the bad areas, which pay much more than their fair share of the price for a shortage of teachers, need a direct attack upon their problem". Many of the teachers appointed to schools in slum districts have accepted the posts because their applications to schools in more pleasant surroundings have been rejected. They are looking out for posts in schools which are more agreeable to them and this produces constant changes in teaching staffs in the very schools which need stability. The Council confessed : —"We can at present see no alternative to some solution involving the recruitment of a special body of teachers who are ready to go where they are needed in return for financial compensation, whether under schemes centrally operated through the Ministry or by groups of local education authorities working on a consortium basis. What is quite certain is that this is a matter of urgent educational concern which must be faced."

The Report then passes on to discuss the ultimate objectives of the education of pupils between the ages of thirteen and sixteen in secondary modern and comprehensive schools, and recommends that the basic tool subjects should be reinforced through the whole of the subjects and activities of the curriculum. More demands should be made on the pupils, both in the nature and in the amount of work required. The value of the educational experience should be judged in terms of its total impact on the pupils' skills, qualities, and personal development, not by basic attainments alone. The Report is in agreement with the Hadow Report (1926) on the Education of the Adolescent when it stressed the importance of a practical and realistic approach in framing the curriculum of modern schools. As a result of the Hadow Report, the Senior Schools of pre-1944 and the secondary modern schools after them, gave a considerable amount of time to practical pursuits. The survey of 1961 showed that many schools were more generously provided with practical rooms than with libraries, which goes to signify that the need for the former was recognised before the need for the latter. At the present the pendulum has swung to a middle point and the need for each is recognised.

The Newsom Report falls into line with the Hadow Report which complained that there was too great a tendency by some schools to regard the school as an isolated unit and education as something apart from the main stream of life. The Newsom Report does not reiterate the advice of the Hadow but corrects its misinterpretation. "Unimaginative exercises can be as dully repetitive in woodwork as they can be in English." During the last two years of school life, a new look should be given to the curriculum, and the general idea should be that of a preparation for adult life.

Pupils in the last two years of school should have some choice in the programmes of work. It follows that a generous variety of courses should be available many of which should be broadly connected with occupational interests. This calls for a more advanced technical equipment than is usually found in modern schools—training in worthwhile ways in which boys and girls can spend their leisure time. These would include different hobbies or imaginative experience through the arts. Two interesting examples of courses for pupils of very limited abilities are given on pp. 38-40 of the Report.

Chapter 6, "The School Day, Homework, Extra-Curricular Activities", breaks new ground. A rather longer school day is recommended for pupils in their last two years at school. Several reasons are given for this recommendation. Most pupils of fourteen to fifteen spend no longer time at school than they did at the age of seven. "A disturbing number appear to leave school under-equipped in skills, knowledge, and personal resources. A characteristic complaint of this group is that they are 'bored'—with school, with life outside school, and later with their jobs."

The Newsom Report is in agreement with the Crowther that the last year before pupils leave school is the peak period for juvenile delinquency. The latter Report had stated (vol 1. para. 63), "There is one aspect of juvenile delinquency with which the schools must be very closely concerned—it is the fact that the last year of compulsory education is also the heaviest year for juvenile delinquency, and that the steadily increasing rate in the secondary school years is reversed when a boy goes to work. . . . When the school-leaving age was raised from fourteen to fifteen in 1947 there was an immediate change over in the delinquency record of the thirteen-year-olds (who until then had been the most troublesome age-group) and the fourteen-year-olds, who took their place in 1948 and have held it consistently ever since . . . there is nothing in the state of affairs . . . to make any thoughtful person doubt the value of being at school; indeed, the delinquency may arise, not because boys are at school, but they are not at school enough."

The Newsom Report goes a step further. In addition to its recommendation about the raising of the school-leaving age, it makes some suggestions which may startle some pupils and parents. What are generally known as extra-curricular activities should become an integral part of the educational programme. Moreover, it suggests that some of the pupils' time could be used for homework. Grammar school boys and girls are expected to do homework which increases when they begin to study for the G.C.E. Some of the more able pupils in modern schools are also required to do homework which again may grow in extent when the C.S.E. is in operation. "But large numbers of pupils and the majority of 'our' pupils, commonly do none." The Report had some reluctance in using the term, homework, and confessed that another name would be more appropriate for the kind of activity the members of the Council had in mind. In the earlier days of this century the homework required from the pupils was at first an extension of the work in class and later, intensive study for passing an examination. Often it consisted of tasks which could better be done in school.

The homework recommended is work for the pupils themselves outside the class work of the school, and it should take various forms. The writer has visited a modern school near his home the headmaster of which has considerable interest and ability in music. In addition to the school choir and school orchestra, a desire to have an organ was expressed. Aided by the headmaster and some members of the staff, the pupils constructed a two manual organ which is used in school assembly and for special functions such as speech days, open days, and school concerts. Obviously a great deal of the construction had to be done outside school hours but the boys were most enthusiastic.

Whenever it is practicable homework activities should take place in the home itself. This has the virtue of bringing parents into touch with the work in the school. Some headteachers have reported that parents have demanded more homework for their children. Reports from schools in congested urban conditions emphasise that in some areas it is difficult for children to have privacy and quiet in order to concentrate on what they are doing. Some authorities have recognised such difficulties and have provided quiet rooms in public libraries or in the school itself.

One suggestion is that of a three-session school day. There are several ways in which this could be organised. Possibly the institution of a morning and early afternoon session and followed on one or more days by an evening period during which pupils could follow up hobbies, or some individual work or take part in different informal group activities is probably the most practical. Experiments in such schemes should be encouraged. Teachers have been exceedingly generous in giving their time but if the three-sessional pattern is developed on a large scale it would be unfair to saddle them with such a heavy burden especially while the shortage of teachers continues.

A somewhat similar situation occurred when plans were being discussed for the staffing of the Day Continuation Schools of the 1918 Act. The number of teachers available was quite inadequate and the Board of Education asked retired teachers, clergy, graduates, and others with sufficient knowledge and experience to give their assistance. The Newsom Report suggests that people with special experience and skills might be invited from time to time to contribute to the courses for older pupils. Others with special interests could help in the extra-curricular activities. "If a group of boys and girls want to take up photography or badminton or learn a musical instrument, persons other than qualified teachers may be well capable of instructing and inspiring the group."

In different parts of the country experiments on joint appointments of teacher/youth leaders or teacher/wardens are taking place. Such people spend part of their time teaching in school and carry on their work with adolescents in youth organisations in the evening. Another development worthy of notice is an experiment in group living which takes different forms such as school journeys or expeditions and camps or residential courses varying from a week-end to a month. Some of the latter emphasise strenuous outdoor physical activity and some schools have combined this with school work for the Duke of Edinburgh's award. The Report recommends that a short survey by the Ministry and the L.E.A.s should be undertaken with the object of discovering the scale on which provision of residential courses is available. One would also need to ascertain whether the demand for such courses is being met and what would be the cost if they were extended to a larger number of pupils.

The following chapter on Spiritual and Moral Development is again a very important one. The Report is mainly concerned with county schools in which the teachers may be committed Christians belonging to different denominations or at the other extreme, agnostics. Between the two is a middle group whose members are not associated with any special Church but who have a respect for the traditional Christian outlook on life and feel that it should be preserved.

On the other hand one must consider the boys and girls who from about thirteen to sixteen are in what is generally described as being in the middle stage of adolescence. This period has been termed the age of criticism and this is shown by the kind of questions they ask. The primary school child, unless he is precocious, accepts the views presented by his teacher and when he asks questions he is more concerned with obtaining information about persons and their actions, but at 11 plus he begins to open his questions with the word "what?". He is still seeking information but at thirteen to fifteen his characteristic question begins with "why?". This does not mean that he is necessarily hostile and critical towards what he has been previously taught but he wants to see how Christianity applies to the problems of the world in which he lives and in which he is going to work.

Pupils of this age "become increasingly aware of the differences of opinion between adults, and of the gulf between practice and profession". The aim of religious and moral teaching in the voluntary school, whether Anglican or Roman Catholic, is to train the pupils to be worshipping members of the Church. The county school does not seek to make converts to Christianity. Its duty is to present to its pupils the traditional standards of this country which are based on the Christian way of life.

There is, however, a problem which springs from the opposing differences in society about pre-marital intercourse and the permanence of marriage. The Report very sensibly advises the educator: "We can only say that we believe it to be wrong to leave the young to fend for themselves without guidance, and wrong to conceal from them (as if we could) the differences on this issue which separate men and women of real moral sensitivity. For our part we are agreed that boys and girls should be offered firm guidance on sexual morality based on chastity before marriage and fidelity within it. . . . It is also important that boys and girls should realise that 'going off the rails' does not involve for Christians losing the fellowship of the Church, still less of forfeiting the love of God. There are other, and often graver sins than those against chastity."

The religious instruction given in the schools should go beyond moral teaching. The Act of 1944 required that religious instruction should be in accordance with the local authority's Agreed Syllabus of instruction in the Christian religion. This has given rise to some controversy and some schools have sought a way of escape by confining religious instruction to Bible reading with the very minimum of comment possible. The Report describes this as a sure way of losing the attention of most boys and girls. "A teacher cannot help his pupils unless he can put into words their ill-formulated problems and show them how Christians would set about solving them. He must know his Bible and its teaching, he must have thought about the relation of religion and religious knowledge to other fields of human activity and ways of knowing. . . . His scholarship must be up to date, and he must move on the Christian frontiers of to-day."

It is then essential that for religious instruction there should be an improved supply of suitably qualified teachers and adequate time must be allowed for this instruction in the schools. For over a century the differences between the Church of England and the Free Churches made religion a very dangerous subject for what are now county schools. This has now changed and the 1944 Act was based on the conviction that denominational differences could be overcome in a way that would not cause obstacles to a real Christian education in county schools. This greater tolerance and understanding between the denominations was made possible by the use of Agreed Syllabuses. Each syllabus has received the unanimous consent of the local education authorities, the teaching profession, and the Church of England and the Free Churches. The faith expressed in the Act has been fully justified.

Many of the Agreed Syllabuses were drawn up during the period between the two world wars and were revised at the time the school leaving age was raised to fifteen. They attempted the method of study starting with the Bible and leaving the teacher to build up his Christian teaching from this basis. The result was that the pupils in the age range considered by the Report tended to think that the Bible has no significance for modern times. The Student Christian Movement in Schools reversed this procedure and beginning with modern problems led the way back to the Bible. The writer has supported this method for many years. When the West

Riding of Yorkshire Syllabus of Religious Instruction was adopted in 1947, he was asked to draw up the secondary school syllabus for the age group twelve to eighteen. For the secondary modern school pupils of the age fourteen to fifteen he included a section dealing with Christianity and modern problems.

The aim of this section was explained in the syllabus. "In dealing with these problems, the teacher should endeavour to develop in the pupil certain essential attitudes of thought: (a) To think honestly and sincerely, but to treat with respect the opinions of those who differ from him if they are also sincere and honest in their thought. (b) To preserve an open mind, not rejecting any point of view because it is new or rashly adopting it for the same reason. (c) In thinking about these problems, to apply the knowledge and experience he has about the nature of God and the example of Jesus Christ. (d) To make his personal decision and live up to it."

The kind of problems he recommended fell into three categories—personal and moral, e.g. Why is it wrong to swear, to eat or drink or smoke too much, to think and speak impurely about sex?; social, e.g. What should be the Christian's attitude to the use of atomic weapons, to war, slums, gambling, unemployment, sharp practice in business, observance of Sunday, propaganda, scandal, sex, and divorce?; and intellectual and religious, e.g. If God is all-powerful, why does he not put an end to war, crime, and violence? What difference does being a Christian make to a man? This syllabus was drawn up when most secondary modern school pupils left school at fifteen. Now, when the number of pupils who remain at school after fifteen is rapidly growing, more attention needs to be paid to religious and moral instruction for the average and under average boys and girls. The Newsom Report quite rightly recommended that local education authorities should think about the revision of the Agreed Syllabuses along the lines suggested in this chapter. One might also add that there is a definite need for diocesan authorities to consider a revision of their syllabuses in the direction of providing a more realistic basis for religious teaching in the voluntary schools.

The chapter closes with some remarks about the value of corporate worship in schools. The corporate life of the school has a tremendous influence upon the moral growth of its pupils. Corporate worship has a similar effect upon their spiritual development. It is in the school assembly that pupils are able to realise its unity. The Report says: "Corporate worship is not to be thought of as an instrument of education—though it is that—but as a time in which pupils and teachers seek help in prayer, express awe and gratitude and joy, and pause to recollect the presence of God". Educators will agree gladly with the recommendation of the Advisory Council: "We reaffirm the value of the school act of worship as a potent force in the spiritual experience of the pupils".

Chapter 8 of the Report deals with the relations of boys and girls with their teachers as reflected in discipline and care for the pupils' personal welfare. The views of the Council are largely based on the evidence supplied by the heads of schools in the survey and on a collection of essays by girls who had recently left school at the age of fifteen. It is a long chapter which gives rise to a number of practical recommendations. These are summarised on page 71 of the Report.

(a) Every effort should be made to emphasise the status of the older pupils, through school organisation and in the design of school buildings.

(b) We welcome interest in developing group responsibilities, and see a particular value in community service projects.

(c) Corporal punishment for the older pupil is likely to delay, rather than promote, the growth of self-discipline. It is humiliating for both the pupils and the staff. We especially deplore such punishment for adolescent girls.

(d) There is an urgent need to strengthen all existing links between home and school, and in difficult areas to create new ones, as, for example, in the appointment of members of staff with special liaison or home-visiting responsibilities.

(e) Positive and realistic guidance to adolescent boys and girls on sexual behaviour is essential. This should include the biological, moral, social, and personal aspects. Advice to parents on the physical and emotional problems of adolescents should be easily available. Schools of whatever type should contrive to provide opportunities for boys and girls to mix socially in a helpful and educative environment.

(f) It is of the greatest importance for schools to build up a knowledge of individual pupils and to devise some system of supervising their future welfare.

If the school is to provide a training for life in the greater world outside the school, then it follows that in the last year of its programme there should be a concentration on the preparation of the pupils for entry to the adult world of work and leisure. In other words, the programme ought to be deliberately outgoing. The pupils should mentally and physically be taken outside the school walls and people from the greater world should be brought into the school. Television constitutes a new resource in the hands of the teacher and its value consists in extending the knowledge of the pupils and developing their sympathies. Films also serve the same purpose and are more readily available at any time.

It is recommended that the educational value of television and the film should be more appreciated by the schools and the training colleges. Both B.B.C. and Independent Television should give special attention to the extension of school television and L.E.A.s should base their plans on the recognition that television receivers are part of the necessary equipment of education. Training colleges and university departments of education should, if they have not already done so, include in their programmes the value of films and television as social and educational forces, and practical instruction should be given to students to enable them to make use of school broadcasts in sound and television.

Some countries are experimenting in schemes of release-from-school to provide pupils with a limited experience of different types of employment. Some schools in this country are launching out with experiments along similar lines and have secured the co-operation of the youth employment service and industrial and commercial firms. Such experiments should be carefully studied and further information should be obtained on these activities through the Ministry of Labour, industry, and the trade unions.

Pupils over fifteen should know about facilities for further education not only through pamphlets on the local courses available, but also by visiting institutes of further education. Invitations to visit the schools should be issued to the principals and staffs of these colleges. A closer touch with the youth service and the youth employment service is recommended, and the personal advisory and welfare services should be extended. The teachers should be able to gain familiarity with industry since all secondary schools need teachers of special responsibilities in career work and should be allowed time and facilities to do it effectively. The training colleges could consider how their students can obtain this kind of knowledge. The British Employers' Confederation has instituted "Introduction to Industry" schemes for serving teachers and similar experiments should be considered for teachers in training.

Pupils who remain at school until sixteen or over need some kind of leaving certificate which combines an assessment with a record of their school careers. "An assessment of the pupil by the school is essentially what we have in mind. Unfortunately, one of the most sought after forms of assessment, though one that is often misunderstood, is a public examination. We say unfortunately, because we are convinced that for large numbers of the boys and girls with whom we are concerned public external examinations are not likely to offer a suitable means of assessment." It is important to realise that these examinations are not intended for all pupils. Newsom is in agreement with Beloe that the C.S.E. should not be taken before the fifth year and it must not shape the curriculum in the way that the old School Certificate did. Oral work to test candidates' use of spoken English should be included and the teacher's assessment of the candidate should be taken into account.

If the advice proffered by the Report is to be implemented, two factors are essential without which the revolution in the secondary school will be impossible. The first is the problem of school buildings. Few schools at the present have adequate facilities for the social needs of the older pupils. A great amount of new building will be necessary and the heavily built-up areas need special consideration. Chapter 11, "Building for the Future", contains a number of diagrams which are most informative and which have been made available by the Development Group of the Ministry's Architects and Building Branch. In addition to buildings, developments in educational method require new equipment or more extensive use of the existing equipment including all the audio-visual aids.

The other essential is an adequate number of teachers of the right type. The difficulty in acquiring good teachers for schools in slum and highly built up areas has been mentioned in the earlier part of the Report. When the school leaving age is raised, new demands will be made on the teachers and this must be taken into account in their training. Most teachers in addition to offering one main subject which they teach throughout the school, should also be able to offer one or preferably two subjects which they are competent to teach over a more restricted range. These should include such subjects as housecraft, handicraft, art, music, drama, and physical education. When drawing up the programme of training colleges this principle should be kept in mind.

The training of all teachers should include sociological and environmental studies with special reference to the problems of pupils in culturally deprived areas. A few joint training courses should be organised for intending secondary school teachers and for those who desire to enter other services such as the youth and youth employment services or who seek social worker posts. The conditions of teaching will become more attractive if non-teaching ancillary staff responsible for clerical work, servicing and maintaining workshops, craftrooms, and laboratories were appointed and if expensive audi-visual equipment was supplied in a more generous way.

One recommendation seeks to terminate an anomaly which has existed for too many years. At the present a graduate can be accepted as a qualified teacher without any training in the art of teaching. The Report quotes the statement of the 8th Report of the National Advisory Council on the Training and Supply of Teachers. "Here (in the primary and secondary modern schools) teaching methods and techniques with all the specialised knowledge that lies behind them are as essential as mastery of subject matter. The prospect of these schools staffed to an increasing extent by untrained graduates is, in our view, intolerable." The Council was convinced that a training requirement for graduates should be introduced as soon as possible and a date be fixed in advance. As an emergency measure, untrained graduates should attend in-service courses to help them to deal more effectively with the teaching problems they will meet.

Part II of the Newsom Report deals with the "Teaching Situation". For space reasons it cannot be included in a summary of this kind but the reader is advised to read it and think about its suggestions concerning the curriculum and teaching method. Part III provides details of the 1961 Survey and includes a useful description of typical (imaginary) pupils who are to be found in secondary modern and comprehensive schools. Appendix II on Sex Education is helpful and Appendix V is a statistical detail of the Survey.

The Robbins Report

The Robbins Report is unique in several ways. In the first place the Committee was instructed to consider the pattern of full-time education in Great Britain and dealt with institutions for higher education in Scotland as well as in England and Wales. No previous committee has been called upon to investigate higher education as a whole. In the past there have been Royal Commissions concerned with particular universities, *e.g.* Oxford, Cambridge, London, Durham, and St Andrews. Other committees have dealt with different aspects of higher education, *e.g.* technical education, the training of teachers. The Robbins Committee was appointed by the Prime Minister and not by the Ministry of Education.

The weakness of our education system has been that it has developed piecemeal, and there has been, as the Bryce Commission of 1895 pointed out, no consideration as a whole. Elementary education was the first to be organised in England and Wales through the Elementary Education Act of 1870, and in Scotland the Education (Scotland) Act of 1872. Subsequent developments led to free and universal elementary education which with a few exceptions was achieved in 1902. A demand for secondary education started in Scotland and Wales. The Scottish Act of 1872 was concerned with both elementary and secondary education, and the Welsh Intermediate Education Act of 1889 organised secondary instruction in Wales. The Education Act of 1902 led to an expansion of secondary schools in England and Wales. The same occurred in Scotland by the Scottish Education Acts of 1908 and 1918. It was not until the Education Act of 1944 (England and Wales) and the Scottish Act of 1945 that the foundation of a secondary school system for all children was laid and was completed by the raising of the school leaving age in 1947 when school fees in maintained secondary schools were abolished. Higher education was the only field left untouched at the commencement of the Educational Revolution.

The terms of reference at the appointment of the Robbins Committee in 1961 were: "to review the pattern of full-time higher education in Great Britain and in the light of national needs and resources to advise Her Majesty's Government on what principles its long-term development should be based. In particular, to advise, in the light of these principles, whether there should be any change in that pattern, whether any new types of institution are desirable, and whether any modifications should be made in the present arrangements for planning and co-ordinating the development of the various types of institution." The Report, therefore, was convinced that the needs of the present and still more of the future, demanded a system of higher education, but one in which the freedom of individuals and institutions should be respected.

After the historical introduction the Report gives four objectives which are considered essential to a well balanced system of higher education. (1) Instruction in skills necessary to play a part in the general division of labour. This aim is placed first not because it is of prime importance but because it has so often been neglected. A good general education is important but it is often insufficient to solve the many grave problems of the present. (2) The aim of producing cultivated men and women must be more important than the creation of mere specialists. (3) Views differ in regard to the respective values of teaching and research in institutions of higher education. The search for truth and the advancement of knowledge must always be one of the important functions of higher education. (4) The function of transmitting a common culture and common standards of citizenship is fundamental. It must not restrict individuality, but like school education, it should provide in partnership with the family a background of culture and social habit which will ensure a healthy society.

This function is especially important at the present when the idea of equality of opportunity has been accepted. "It is not merely by providing places for students from all classes that this ideal will be achieved but also by providing, in the atmosphere of the institutions in which students live and work, influences that in some measure compensate for any inequalities of home background. These influences are not limited to the student population. Universities and colleges have an important role to play in the general cultural life of the communities in which they are situated."

The functions described will vary in different institutions of higher education as well as in the methods of discharging them. In some the vocational emphasis will be more evident. More stress on research and the advancement of knowledge will be found in the postgraduate stage than in the undergraduate, but these principles should be present in all the different institutions of higher education, and local circumstances will shape the amount of participation in the life and culture of the community.

These objectives lead to certain principles upon which the recommendations of the Report are based. First is the general principle that higher education should be available to all who are qualified to profit by it and who wish to do so. It is essential to make the maximum use of the talent of our people if we are to compete successfully with other highly developed countries in this age of rapid technological and social advance. "But beyond that, education ministers intimately to ultimate ends, in developing man's capacity to understand, to contemplate, and to create. And it is a characteristic of the aspirations of this age to feel that, where there is capacity to pursue such activities, there that capacity should be fostered. The good society desires equality of opportunity for its citizens to become not merely good producers but also good men and women."

The principle of equal academic awards for equal performance is assumed. The grading of individuals for the purpose of higher education should depend on academic accomplishments rather than upon the status of the institution in which they have studied. There is a need for a variety of institutions with differing functions and with differing emphasis. The Report accepts the inevitability that some institutions will be more eminent than others. The history of education bears this out. "It is in the nature of things that talent should attract talent and that where famous intellectual exploits take place, there should develop some concentration of staff and students especially interested in the subjects concerned.[1] Moreover, such concentrations are not only profitable but also desirable." The Report gives the warning: "There should be no freezing of institutions into established hierarchies; on the contrary there should be recognition and encouragement of excellence wherever it exists and wherever it appears". The differences in level and function will persist among institutions and are only acceptable if a student is able to transfer from one institution to another when his intellectual attainments and educational needs warrant it.

The principle of allowance for free development of institutions must be retained. Existing institutions must be free to experiment without limitations except those which safeguard their essential functions. At the same time there must be freedom to experiment with new kinds of institution when it is desirable. There must be, however, some co-ordination, commonly accepted principles of policy, and an organisation for a reasonable allocation of resources.

Nevertheless, a system must maintain a standard. A sound educational system must include full scope for all kinds of talent at all levels. Historically, our universities have tended to set a standard for other institutions and it is probable that they will continue to do so in the future. It is hoped that their reputation will be sustained and while they broaden the education they provide for first degrees, they will achieve higher standards for those who are capable of postgraduate work.

[1] The reader will find examples of this in the pre-eminence of the University of Paris in the 13th century and the older universities of Britain in the 19th century.

Chapter III of the Report, "The Growth of Higher Education in Great Britain", is largely historical and shows that in the space of sixty years the number of full-time students in institutions of higher education has increased more than eight times. Chapter IV summarises the different types of institutions which provide higher education. It begins with the universities which are classified into seven groups. There is no need to summarise the description of the universities in each group. The reader can gather these if he turns back to Chapter XV of this book. The categories into which the universities fall are:—(1) The ancient universities of Oxford and Cambridge which are collegiate universities founded in the 12th and 13th centuries respectively. (2) The four ancient Scottish universities of St. Andrews, Glasgow, and Aberdeen founded in the medieval period, and Edinburgh in the 16th century. Many of their customs and traditions resemble those of Continental universities rather than those in England. With the exception of St Andrews, few of the undergraduates are accommodated in hostels or halls of residence. These universities are of a similar type which was laid down in the Universities (Scotland) Act, 1889. (3) The University of London. This is the only university which grants external degrees. (4) The older civic universities which in order of foundation are Durham, Manchester, Birmingham, Liverpool, Leeds, Sheffield, and Bristol. (5) The federal University of Wales. (6) The younger civic universities of Reading, Nottingham, Southampton, Hull, Exeter, Leicester, and Keele. Newcastle which separated from Durham in 1963 should be added to the list given in the Report. (7) The new universities described in Chapter XV. In the Robbins Report they are identified by the place in which they are situated.

The next type of institutions to be considered consist of the Training Colleges in England and Wales and the Colleges of Education in Scotland. The earliest training colleges were established in the 19th century. They were organised by voluntary bodies, the majority of which were the religious denominations. The Education Act of 1902 empowered L.E.A.s to open training colleges which now number 98 of the total of 146 colleges. A new Anglican college was opened in 1963 and will receive its first students in 1964. The training colleges were gradually established and this accounts for the number of colleges with less than 500 students. This number became twenty in 1962-3 when the demand for more teachers had necessitated the enlargement of the college buildings. The links with the universities through the University Institutes of Education and the introduction of the three-year course have been described in Chapter XVI.

There are also specialist colleges for training teachers of physical education and domestic subjects. Four colleges for the training of technical teachers have been opened. A small number of colleges offer a one-year course for graduates but the majority of graduates enter the University Departments of Education. Four colleges offer a four-year course which leads to the external degrees of London and includes the professional training of the students.

In Scotland all graduate teachers must be trained. The training colleges are known as Colleges of Education which are seven in number including two Roman Catholic colleges. Only three of the colleges contain less than 450 students. The colleges are supervised by the Scottish Council for the Training of Teachers and receive direct grant from the Scottish Education Department, and also grants from the education authorities. Their link with the universities consists of university representatives on their boards of governors.

In the 19th century most of further education was provided by evening classes. Towards the end of the century the courses were extended to meet the needs of students who wished to obtain a degree or a professional qualification. The majority of students were still in the evening institutes and it was not until after the second world war that there was a rapid increase in the number of advanced day courses both full-time and part-time. There are now about 150,000 students following advanced courses which lead to a degree or to a qualification of degree standard.

The four categories of colleges of further education as defined in 1956 have been described in Chapter XII. In addition to technology and science, there are Art Schools which contain about 8,000 students taking advanced full-time courses. Departments of Regional and Area Colleges provide business studies and there are a few Colleges of Commerce. Most of the instruction is given in the evenings but there has been a marked increase in the number of part-time and full-time day students. There are also certain colleges which receive direct grant from the Ministry of Education. Most of them are specialist colleges such as the Royal College of Art and the College of Aeronautics at Cranfield. There are also six National Colleges. (See Chapter XII.)

Full-time advanced further education in Scotland is carried on in fifteen Central Institutes, the larger of which correspond to the

C.A.T.s. They are handing over to Further Education Centres part-time work which is below the level of higher education. The Further Education Centres correspond broadly to the Area and Local Colleges of England and Wales. The Royal College of Science and Technology, Glasgow, has now acquired university status.

Chapter V of the Report compares British higher education with that in Continental countries, the United States, and the Soviet Union. The facts about the latter were acquired from the Embassies and the British Council. This initial inquiry indicated the topics in which the Committee was interested and led to visits to seven countries. Space forbids an extended description of the differences found but there are several points which stand out as very important. Thus in Western Europe technology was not on the whole accepted in the universities whereas in this country technological studies entered the universities during the 19th century.

The European universities have not acquired the prominence that Oxford and Cambridge have here. The exception is France where the Sorbonne has a commanding position, though the Report suggests that the attraction of Paris contributes to this. The real analogy in French higher education to Oxford and Cambridge is to be found in the Grandes Ecoles, such as the Ecole Normale Supérieure and the Ecole Polytechnique. Another difference is that the training of primary school teachers which is carried out in "normal schools" is really an extension of secondary education. In Western Europe colleges of education are not as a rule considered to come under the heading of higher education.

Only a few American States have made efforts towards a co-ordinated development of the institutes of higher education. California is one exception which has made a clean break with American tradition. The State University plans to have 120,000 students on its eight campuses by 1975. California also proposes to concentrate post-graduate studies in the University. The Soviet Union presents a different pattern. The universities account for only about 10 per cent. of enrolments in higher education. There are many specialised institutions some of which possess a reputation equal to that of the universities. The tendency in the universities is to concentrate on arts and science in their "pure" forms and to exclude law, medicine, and economics.

Quantitatively the comparison reveals that France, the Soviet Union, and the United States greatly exceed Britain in the number of students following full-time courses in higher education. The Report summarises as follows:—"The output in Britain is equal or superior to that in most of the Western European countries shown. We suspect that a full comparative investigation would reveal that, on its chosen ground, the British university system is among the most efficient and economical in the world. But the output of British higher education is, in very important respects, smaller than that of the Soviet Union or the United States."

So much for the present but what about the future? In France what is known as the *explosion scolaire* has been taken into account and the official plans look forward to 1970 when the increase of university students will raise numbers to about two and a half times over 1960. The Soviet Union has an equally ambitious programme. It is clear that immediate action is called for in order to improve the situation in Britain. "Both in general cultural standards and in competitive intellectual power, vigorous action is needed to avert the danger of a serious relative decline in this country's standing."

In Chapter VI, the future demand for higher education and the places needed to meet it are considered. There are two ways of estimating the number of places required. The first is to estimate the national need for the number of individuals who have passed through courses of full-time higher education. This way was rejected because of the incertitude of calculating the national need over a long term. The alternative is a reasonable estimate of the demand for places in higher education. This seemed to be a more practical approach to the problem. The principle in Chapter II, that all young people qualified by ability and attainment to follow a full-time course in higher education should have the opportunity of doing so, should be the guiding one in solving this problem.

One frequently hears the statement that we are not making full use of the pool of ability which is at hand. This is often followed by the suggestion that when the pool of ability in the higher professional group becomes exhausted there remain the children of the parents employed in skilled manual work, a group which has not been fully used. It is a truism that between the two groups of those who by their natural qualities would attain highest success and those if they were taught by the best teachers would never reach the required standards, there is a third group whose future depends largely on how they have lived and have been taught before entering upon higher education.

The Committee surveyed a sufficient number of both sexes aged twenty-one in August 1962 and the results were tabulated in Table 21. The Robbins Committee agreed with the Crowther Report that there is a close correlation between the occupational level of the father and the achievements of his children at school. Thus, 45 per cent. of the children whose fathers were in the higher professional group enter full-time higher education in comparison with the 4 per cent. of children whose fathers are in skilled manual occupations. Table 22 shows that children going forward to higher education and whose fathers had continued their own education until eighteen or after, were eight times more numerous than those whose fathers left school before the age of sixteen.

It might be suggested that the great increase of pupils in recent years who leave school with good qualifications is to be found among those whose parents are manual workers. The Tables show that the desire for education which results in improved performance in school is to be found in all classes. The Report states that it is reasonable to conclude that this trend will continue. The statistical tables show that in comparison with the 195,000 places required in 1962-3, the number is likely to rise to 507,000 in 1980-1. To this last figure must be added the number of overseas students. The data available for these makes it more difficult to forecast their number. At present they occupy about 10 per cent. of the places in higher education but it is probable that this proportion will remain for some years ahead; but within this group the number of postgraduates is likely to increase. The total demand for places in full-time higher education indicates that about 390,000 should be available in 1973-4 and about 560,000 in 1980-1.

The relations between the schools and the institutions of higher education are considered in the next chapter. Since the war the pressure to enter universities and training colleges has grown so great that many who are qualified and acceptable are not able to gain a place. The situation in Scotland is not so grave but entry to a university tends to grow more difficult. In other institutions of higher education the pressure is not so great, but even in this sphere there are some shortages of places. "It is not necessary to enlarge at length on the unhappiness and frustration bred in the applicants by this state of affairs. The apprehension among the more gifted boys and girls as they approach eighteen is coming to be as serious as the tension and anxieties caused by the 'eleven plus' examination."

To ease the pressure on the schools there must be a great expansion of places in higher education. At present many schools in their anxiety to help their more able pupils, do all they can to give them the best chances of gaining university entrance and do not take full advantage of the flexibility of the G.C.E. Competition to gain a place in "Oxbridge" is more intense than that for other universities. The suggestion that Oxford and Cambridge should become postgraduate institutions is definitely rejected by the Robbins Committee. It was considered that the attraction of "Oxbridge" should be lessened by making generous capital grants for the development of other existing universities. There ought to be a closer relation between the colleges at "Oxbridge" and the schools maintained by the local education authorities. Institutes for higher education should consider with the Minister of Education and the Scottish Education Department ways in which better information can be supplied to pupils and their parents with regard to the range of courses available.

Faculty and departmental requirements for entrance should be made more uniform so as to widen the choice for candidates and the schools. Selection procedures are discussed in some detail and the hope that "Oxbridge" and the C.A.T.s will join the university clearing house scheme is expressed. In the selection of entrants more use should be made of school records and recommendations and research into methods of selection should be undertaken by a suitable independent organisation. The schools should collaborate with the teachers in the institutes of higher education in the improvement of their syllabuses and the revision of textbooks. "There is still much dead wood in many of these in current use, especially perhaps in physics, mathematics, and languages."

Chapter VIII reviews the present courses provided by the universities and recommends means for future development. One important recommendation is that the universities should consult together in the establishment of new undergraduate courses and the provision of more varied facilities for postgraduate study. There "should be some attempt to secure a measure of uniformity in the nomenclature of degrees". An article in *The Times Educational Supplement*, 12 October 1962, pointed out some of the anomalies in the titles and the contents of the degree courses which are misleading to potential employers and more also to the general public.

Thus the initial degree in most of the English civic universities is that of bachelor but in Scotland since 1858 the M.A. has been the first degree and awards such as B.Ed. are for postgraduate study. The M.A. of "Oxbridge" is not awarded for postgraduate study as is the custom in the English civic universities. The Oxford degrees of B.Sc. and B.Litt. are postgraduate awards. The degree of Ph.D. is not confined to philosophy but can be awarded for postgraduate work in most subjects. As an example of the confusion that may be caused, a few years ago the writer was a member of an appointing committee for a senior post in a grammar school. His fellow members supported the application of a candidate who held a Pass M.A. of a Scottish university and on academic grounds were going to turn down another candidate with a good Honours degree awarded by an English university. He was able to prevent this from happening by informing the committee about the different nomenclature of initial degree in Scotland and England.

The Robbins Committee received a number of criticisms about the present first degree courses. They fell into two main classes— the overloading of many of the courses and that they often do not satisfy the needs of many students who can take them. There is a tendency to add new knowledge to a curriculum which is already full. "The essential aim of a first degree course should be to teach the student how to think. In so far as he is under such pressure to acquire detailed knowledge that this aim is not fulfilled, so far the course fails of its purpose." There is need to thoroughly revise most of the present courses. Those which specialise on a very narrow front are unsuitable for many students. They would receive greater benefit by following broader courses which would prepare them for their future careers.

Undergraduates fall roughly into two categories : those who have the ability and desire to specialise in one or two subjects, and others who would benefit from a wider course. Thus those who wish to teach in secondary modern schools or the lower forms of the grammar school would find their purpose suited by a study of two or three subjects at less depth. Some universities have realised this.[1]

[1] Thus in the University of Leeds the courses for initial degrees in art or science are either for general or special studies. The term "honours degree" has disappeared and courses are for a degree in general or special studies. The term "honours" has now its proper meaning. Students following both types of course can obtain honours if their attainments warrant this. Thus an arts student in either type of course can be awarded first class Honours or second class (first or second division), third class or the simple B.A. A similar scheme applies to science, applied science, and law. Some of the special courses include two main subjects.

Students whose earlier promise does not become realised should be transferred to less exacting courses. The Committee did not favour the extension of the three-year course to four years. It thought the general first degree in Scotland should be retained. Because students can only master the rudiments of their subjects in the first degree course, extension of facilities for postgraduate study is needed. The Committee thought that some Ph.D. theses cover too narrow a field. In some subjects "discussion of central problems at a high level is probably more rewarding to the young graduate than intensive investigation of one problem". This is specially applicable in social science and the humanities. Arrangements for the supervision of postgraduate students should be improved and it is often advisable for many graduates to take their postgraduate course in a university other than that in which they obtained their first degree.

The next chapter is concerned with colleges for the education and training of teachers. Although the arrangements for this work differ markedly in Scotland from those in England and Wales the same essential problems apply to both. The colleges feel that they are not fully recognised as institutions of higher education despite that the standards they reach constitute them as such. At one time the colleges concentrated on training non-graduates as school teachers but in recent years they have accepted a small number of graduates for professional training. In Scotland most of their students take a combined course of education and training.

Some students prefer to graduate first and then follow it with professional training either in a university department of education or in a training college. Other graduates do not make up their minds to become teachers until the end of the graduate course. The introduction of the three-year course in the training colleges has given the students a better education than was possible in a two-year course. Nearly half the students now entering the colleges possess the minimum qualification for university entrance. The establishment of the University Institutes of Education has forged closer links with the universities since the work completed in the three-year course approximates to the standard of a Pass degree. The Scottish colleges feel they can claim to be universities in their own right.

Looking to the future, some colleges will wish to broaden their curricula by introducing courses giving entrance to a variety of professions in the social services or general courses in the arts and science subjects. The urgent need for teachers will restrict these developments for at least ten years but in the 1970's there will be more opportunities for experiments with these kinds of courses and some colleges may become constituent parts of a university. Others could combine with larger technical colleges to form a new university. The recommendations for future developments must vary according to the different positions of the colleges in England and Wales and those north of the Border.

In England and Wales many of the colleges are too small and eventually a college with less than 750 students should be an exception. The McNair Report had proposed the establishment of University Schools of Education. The present federation of the regional colleges and the University Departments of Education in the University Institutes of Education only goes part of the way. The next step should be the institution of University Schools of Education financed through the grants committee system. In addition to the three-year course, a four-year course leading to a degree and a professional qualification should be open to suitable students. In some cases students should be able to transfer, after a period in a college, to a university to graduate in the subject of their choice. Students who wish to teach at the end of their professional training should have opportunities to complete their qualifications for a degree by part-time study.

A B.Ed. degree of the university with which the college is linked should be awarded after a successful conclusion of the four-year course. The training colleges should be renamed Colleges of Education. Each School of Education should be responsible to the university senate for degrees awarded to students in the colleges. The colleges should be financed by earmarked grants from the grants committee made through the Schools of Education. With certain modifications the voluntary colleges should be included in the Schools of Education.

The Scottish Colleges of Education should provide four year courses for suitable students leading to a degree and a professional qualification. The teaching staff should be represented on the governing bodies of the colleges and the universities represented on their boards of studies for each subject in which degree level is established. University graduates who intend to become teachers should normally take the course for the university Diploma in Education,

Chapter X deals with institutions for technological education. It includes a large number of recommendations which if implemented will be one of the most significant factors in the educational revolution. Since 1945 progress had quickened through the stimulation of the Percy and Barlow Reports and the White Paper on Technical Education in 1956. At the higher level two complementary policies have emerged, the expansion of technology in the universities and the vigorous encouragement of colleges outside the universities. The outstanding features have been the selection in 1953 of the Imperial College of Science and Technology and other university centres for special development and the designation of the first C.A.T.s in 1956, but more needs to be done.

In Britain less attention is directed to technology and more to pure science than in the other countries which the Committee investigated. In Britain pure science attracts greater numbers of students and of higher quality than does technology. Very few girls study applied science in contrast to countries like the U.S.S.R. Steps should be taken to attract a greater number of students of first-class ability into technological courses and this involves a considerable expansion of postgraduate work. In our country technology lags behind as concerns numbers involved in technological research although our best research is equal in quality to that of any other country.

The Report recommends that as soon as possible we should aim at five special institutions for scientific and technological education and research. At present the Imperial College, the Manchester College of Science and Technology, and the Royal College of Science and Technology at Glasgow, which is now an independent university, form the nuclei of three. With all possible speed, two others should be selected and should receive financial aid similar to that given to the Imperial College. These two new Special Institutions should be constitutionally independent and contain about 3,500 to 4,500 students, half of which should be postgraduate.

The C.A.T.s have made good progress but, "They lack many of the attributes of university self-government; they have not full power to award their own qualifications, and in particular cannot award degrees, despite the fact that their curricula, staffing, and facilities are adjudged by the National Council for Technological Awards to be appropriate for work for honours degrees". They should be designated as technological universities with power to award both initial and higher degrees.

The Scottish Central Institutions differ considerably and hence a varied pattern of development is recommended for them. The larger colleges might form close links with an appropriate university and if this is not practicable, they should have the same status proposed for the C.A.T.s. The smaller ones might adopt a form of academic association with the Royal College, now designated as the University of Strathclyde or the proposed arrangements for the English and Welsh Regional Colleges should be extended to them.

Whilst welcoming the developments now taking place in some universities and colleges, the Committee recommended that two post-graduate schools of management studies should be developed on a larger scale. They would have to employ a proportion of part-time staff and would therefore need to be situated in large cities, and in order to have available the best specialists in their work, they should be associated with university institutions. Another recommendation is for suitable courses in modern languages to be provided in some of the technological universities and Regional Colleges.

The latter, twenty-five in number, provide much of the full-time and sandwich courses of first degree level. Many of them concentrate on the degrees of the University of London. They are not so exclusively concerned with science and technology as the C.A.T.s but also have departments of business studies, architecture, and other special studies. Some of the more developed Regional Colleges may eventually attain university status.

In the Area Colleges the advanced part-time students greatly outnumber the full-time and less than two-thirds of the former are studying science and technology. These colleges are the prime providers of courses for National Diplomas and Certificates and for many other qualifications. They include a small number of Colleges of Commerce which in co-operation with business firms are developing full-time and sandwich courses. As their advanced work grows some of these will become eligible for designation as Regional Colleges. Area Colleges should continue to be maintained by the L.E.A.s and offer courses connected with local industries. Transfers of suitable students should be available to advanced courses in Regional Colleges, and, at the postgraduate stage, to universities and technical universities.

A strengthening of the links between university and institutions and government research establishments, freer movement of staff, and expansion of joint arrangements for research and its supervision are recommended. Colleges outside the London area provide courses for the external degrees of London. The external degrees have had a major influence upon the development of higher education. At present an alternative system has worked well. The National Council for Technological Awards is one of the factors which has produced the high standard of work of the C.A.T.s. The Diploma in Technology is of the standard of higher degrees and the work for National Diplomas and Certificates has approximated to the Pass degree. These awards are usually made for a successful sandwich course of three years.

The situation will be changed when the C.A.T.s become technological universities with power to award their own degrees. The Report recommends the replacement of the present Council by a Council for National Academic Awards applicable to the whole of Great Britain. Its prestige would be raised if it could be established under Royal Charter. Some colleges may prefer to continue to offer courses for external degrees and the London external degree will continue to play an important part especially in satisfying the needs of part-time students.

If these recommendations are accepted they will cause degrees to be more widely available than ever before in this country, but it is essential that the standards of degrees should be fully maintained. The Report calls attention to the state of the present law which does not restrain unauthorised bodies or persons from awarding degrees. "Unless fraud is to be proved, a 'degree' can be conferred after studies of trivial content, or indeed after no study at all. . . . Action is difficult, not only against those who confer worthless degrees, but also against those who falsely lay claim to genuine qualifications. We recommend legislation to remedy both deficiencies. In future the power to give degrees should be vested only in authorised bodies or persons and abuses should be capable of speedy and effective remedy." This is an important point. The writer has had several experiences of both the types mentioned.

The Report recommends that the Royal College of Art should be treated administratively in the same way as the C.A.T.s. Other colleges which provide advanced courses should develop along the lines of Regional and Area Colleges. In Scotland, the four Central Institutions providing education in art should develop along one of the alternatives proposed for the other Central Institutions. The College of Aeronautics at Cranfield should be financed through the system for university grants. If it remains at its present size and wishes degrees to be available to its students, it should form a link with a university. Degrees should also be available to students who are taking courses of degree level at the six National Colleges.

The Agricultural Colleges, five in England and Wales and three in Scotland, provide two-year courses with a minimum qualification at the "O" level of school leaving examinations. From April 1964 they will come under the Ministry of Education instead of the Ministry of Agriculture, Fisheries, and Food. The Scottish colleges are part of the group of Central Institutions, and each has, or is developing, close links with the university in its area. Those in England and Wales may raise their entry qualifications to the "A" level of G.C.E. and develop courses of degree standard.

The future pattern of higher education recommended is discussed in Chapter XI. It was agreed that on the whole if the existing institutions are developed along the lines recommended, the establishment of new types would not be necessary. The 560,000 places required by 1980 should be distributed between different kinds of institutions. This would ease the pressure on the schools and allow the universities to increase their share of entrants from the 55 per cent. of 1962 to 60 per cent. in 1980. Immediate action is necessary and 350,000 places in the universities will be needed in 1980. The present number of students is about 130,000 but the development of institutions to university status would increase the number to about 300,000.

One must take into consideration that new universities require a number of years to fully establish themselves. Although most of the places required in the next ten years can be supplied by the expansion of existing universities, the immediate foundation of six new universities is essential. One of these should be in Scotland and another would be the new Special Institution for Scientific and Technological Education and Research. By 1980 this would account for about 30,000 new places and the remainder would be provided by the grant of university status to about ten Regional Colleges and Colleges of Education. There are indications that the demand for places after 1980 will continue to increase and the Report once again emphasises that the expansion must not result in the lowering of the standards of degree or the qualifications of the teaching staff.

The new universities founded at the request of the U.G.C. were largely in cathedral and other smaller cities but those of the future should be in the great cities for two reasons: the advantages derived from the environment and those they can confer. There are now two universities in Glasgow and this precedent should be followed in other great cities. The Report has on the whole made few recommendations about the content of courses in particular studies. These should be worked out within and among the different institutions. In general the number of students studying science should be increased and the quality of those following different types of technological courses should be improved, but the proportion taking courses in arts should not be reduced.

The Report very sensibly points out that higher education is not confined to young people but many adults find a need for refresher courses to keep them up to date with new developments. The Crowther Report showed that the age for marriage has fallen and the expectation of life has lengthened. Now more than half the women employed in industry are married and a new career pattern has emerged: a short period of work before marriage and another period starting about fifteen years later and continuing for twenty years or more. This pattern will probably become more common. Hence the increasing demand by adults for further education which in many cases will be for part-time courses.

Apart from those who have a level above that of the "A" level of the G.C.E., there are many who desire courses in liberal adult education. The Report mentions the work done in such full-time institutions as Ruskin College and Coleg Harlech and suitable students should be assisted by capital grants and other means. There is also the work carried out in the Extra-Mural Departments of the universities, the W.E.A., and the classes provided by the L.E.A.s, and there is a further development in conjunction with the television services. The hope is expressed that the universities and other institutions will co-operate with this part-time further education.

The problem of staffing is considered in Chapter XII. The present student/staff ratios in universities, especially in regard to research and postgraduate training, should be maintained and, if possible, improved. Conditions of service should be such as will attract suitable recruits and there should be no disparity between the salaries and prospects of teaching in similar institutions. Superannuation and facilities for the movement of staff between higher education, government, and other research establishments and industry should be provided. Part-time staff in higher education should be more generally used with the proviso that the proportion of full-time staff is not reduced. More extensive residential facilities for students should be provided and the tradition of only one professor to a department is out of date and more appointments at this level are recommended.

Naturally there must follow an expansion of the teaching and research staff and the present number of 16,750 must rise to about 45,000 and in other colleges it should be increased from 5,750 to about 14,000. This expansion would not have a harmful effect on the upper forms of the schools. The newspapers have drawn attention to the emigration of well-qualified specialists to countries overseas. This can be checked by more generous salaries, more secretarial assistance, and wider facilities for research.

The next chapter is concerned with teachers and students and approves the present balance between teaching and research. These activities are complementary and overlapping. In the appointment and promotion of staff more weight ought to be given to other qualities such as ability in teaching as well as distinction in research or publication. Differences in salary and status between senior lecturers and readers ought to be abolished and in some universities this has happened. The two main discussions in this chapter are concerned with methods of teaching and student wastage. It is possible to possess a competent knowledge of one's subject but little ability in teaching it. Some time ago the Students' Union of the University of Leeds recommended that all new and inexperienced lecturers should attend a course on teaching method in the education department. Actually some heads of departments had used this idea for some time. The writer was requested by certain departments to give such short courses to newly appointed staff.

Teaching methods in the universities were reviewed in 1962 by a Committee on University Teaching Methods appointed by the U.G.C. under the chairmanship of Sir Edward Hale. This committee also investigated the use students made of their vacations. Methods varied from the large lecture attended by several hundred students to the traditional tutorial in which the tutor discussed the essay written by a single student. Varieties between these extremes are smaller lectures, tutorial groups and seminars of different sizes, and practical laboratory work. The lecture system was common to the Scottish universities and the older civic ones in England. There is a tendency to give lectures to smaller groups of twenty to thirty students. The tutorial system once the mainstay of "Oxbridge" has been adopted by the newer universities. Even at "Oxbridge" tutorial groups of three to five students are becoming more common but in the civic universities where the student/staff ratio is greater a group often varies from seven to ten.

The Report does not condemn the large lecture if the audience is not too large and if the lecturer is not content with presenting information that students can obtain from their textbooks. An able lecturer can stimulate his audience and even inspire it. The merit of the tutorial is that it promotes a closer link between the tutor and the students.

Wastage is a term to describe those who enter an institution of higher education and leave without obtaining the qualification for which they enrolled. Some degree of wastage is inevitable but it is good to know that the average wastage in Britain is much less than in France and the U.S.A. in which the wastage rate varies between 40 to 50 per cent. In our universities it is about 14 per cent. Some students leave early because they discover their choice of studies has been wrong. Others are unable to develop to the intellectual standard necessary, and others again withdraw through illness or disturbing personal or financial troubles.

The statistics given in Table 50 of the Report show considerable differences between universities and between different faculties in the same university. The Committee could not avoid thinking that a significant factor affecting wastage in some faculties and departments is the custom to expect a fairly fixed number of failures. "It should be an essential part of the responsibility of any university department towards its students to investigate this problem carefully, both in regard to the general level of wastage over a period of years and in regard to the individual students who fail in any given year to complete a course successfully."

In the training colleges and the Scottish Colleges of Education the wastage rate among non-graduates is about 7 per cent. Several reasons account for this: the difference in standards, the fact that students are committed to a profession and that the closer contact between students and teachers makes it possible for less able students to receive more help. In the C.A.T.s and other institutions of higher education the wastage is much higher. Among full-time candidates for the Diploma in Technology in 1961 it was 37 per cent. and among those reading for a degree of the University of London it was 62 per cent. A high wastage rate for external degrees is to be expected. The Committee thought that the growing competitions for places in the C.A.T.s is leading to higher standards of selection and it is probable that wastage rates will decrease.

The way in which students spend their vacations is of great importance. The Hale Committee in "The Use of Vacations by Students" (an interim report of the Committee on University Teaching Methods, 1963) showed that during the long vacation, in general, little work is done which is relevant to the students' studies. The Robbins Committee believe that students should be occupied with their studies during ten months of the year. For many students strictly academic work would not be the most appropriate for the whole of the ten months. Different activities are appropriate to different studies, e.g. the arts student may need access to libraries, the biologists can extend their work in a wider setting, the modern language student can visit the country in which the language he is studying is spoken and can extend his knowledge of the institutions and cultural heritage of that country, and those who are taking courses in applied science or in the social sciences can gain much from a period in a related industry or through vacation training schemes.

The chapter ends with the truth that both teachers and taught form a privileged class. They possess a freedom which brings with it a great responsibility. "Public opinion will not support the cost of higher education unless teachers are actuated by a high sense of professional obligation and students are actuated by a corresponding sense of the obligation to work."

The recommendations of the Robbins Report if put into practice will undoubtedly cost a large amount. The financial and economic aspects are examined in Chapter XIV. In assessing the cost of the expansion proposed, the Committee worked under two assumptions. The first is that incomes in general will only rise with increases in productivity and result in a constant overall price level. Secondly, an average increase of productivity of $3\frac{1}{4}$ per cent. per annum can be assumed. The Report wisely states, "We are not predicting that these assumptions will be fulfilled; we adopt them simply as a suitable basis for calculations". When we consider the growing increases in prices set against the increase in productivity, many of us are apt to be sceptical. On these assumptions the total expenditure on full-time education which in 1932-3 was £206 million will become £742 million in 1980-1. The Report states, "Needless to say, such estimates have an appearance of precision that is false, but they indicate the orders of magnitude involved". The first thought that comes to the reader is, can the country afford such an enormous sum? The Report thinks that it is not a matter of "can" but rather that of "must". It is quite honest in acknowledging that there is no means of measuring the rate of return on the expenditure. "It is just not true that the rate of return on investment in education is measured adequately by the same yardstick as investment in coal and electricity", but, "on a broad view of history . . . the communities that have paid most attention to higher studies have in general been the most obviously progressive in respect of income and wealth". The conclusion is that it is possible to spend more on higher education without imposing intolerable strains on the budget or the economy.

The Committee made no recommendations on loans for buildings and equipment but those to students fall into a different category. Loans in place of grants is an alternative which has almost as many supporters as adversaries and therefore is not recommended at present. The decline in tuition fees is regretted and it was agreed that they should be increased to meet at least 20 per cent. of the expenditure of institutions. At the same time, gifts and endowments by private persons should be encouraged.

The next chapter discusses the internal government of institutions of higher education. The present majority of lay representation on governing bodies is supported provided that the academic representatives are sufficiently numerous to prevent interference in purely academic matters. The Report acknowledges the importance of Vice-Chancellors especially during a period of rapid expansion. There is need to relieve them of superfluous duties. The repeal of the Universities (Scotland) Act of 1889 is necessary and there should be an independent inquiry into the problems of the University of Wales, London, Oxford, and Cambridge unless these are able to solve their own. A modification of the Committee of Vice-Chancellors is needed to put it on a wider basis. To secure this, each university should be represented by its chief administrator and a member of the academic staff elected by the senate.

The scope of academic freedom is discussed in Chapter XVI. This is a principle which has been jealously guarded by universities for many centuries and the Committee believed that academic freedom is essential to a healthy system of higher education. At present the institutions concerned are mainly dependent on State grants instead of endowments and fees. Academic freedom depends on a balance between the necessary freedom of institutions and the equal necessity to serve the needs of the nation. It was a stroke of genius which produced the idea of the U.G.C., but it now needs revision since the expansion of institutions of higher education will require a Grants Commission of a wider type than the present U.G.C.

We now reach the controversial problem of the Machinery of Government in Chapter XVII. The principle accepted is that "once institutions have become almost wholly preoccupied with advanced education and research and recruit on a national basis, they are most likely to perform these functions efficiently if they are allowed as far as possible to govern themselves and develop their own policies". Their activities, however, must be guided and co-ordinated to serve national needs. This problem is solved by the grants committee principle. The present U.G.C. is " a committee independent of politics and not subject to ministerial direction, yet maintaining close contact with the organisation of government, which advises the Chancellor on the magnitude of the amounts needed and distributes the funds made available".

If this principle is extended to all autonomous institutions, it would not be appropriate for the Chancellor of the Exchequer to be responsible for the new Grants Commission which will have a wider scope than the present U.G.C. The enlarged Commission would have a standing committee and a number of committees dealing with varied aspects of higher education. Matters of broad policy must remain with the Government and Parliament. This raises the problem of which minister should be responsible for the Grants Commission. It will become increasingly difficult for the Chancellor and the Treasury to be at once guardians of the public purse and claimants on it.

Many suggestions have been made, one of which is that the Lord President of the Council or some other minister without portfolio should be responsible for the universities. This was rejected along with the other view that there should be one Secretary of State responsible for higher education and research as well as education in the schools. The Committee decided that there should be a separate Minister of Arts and Science responsible for the Grants Commission, the Research Councils, and other autonomous state-supported activities.

Responsibility for the other institutions of higher education in England and Wales should remain with the Minister of Education and generally with the L.E.A.s, and in Scotland with the Secretary of State. The three ministers concerned with higher education should establish a small Consultative Council.

Chapter XVIII, "The Short-term Emergency", considers the immediate problem. The Report points out that in the years 1965-6 to 1967-8 we will be confronted with an emergency which demands swift action now. In these years a very large number of boys and girls born just after the war will have reached the age of entry to higher education. If there is no immediate action, the long-term aims of the Report will be more difficult of attainment. Apart from improvised measures, it is recommended that the Council for National Academic Awards should be established at once and the Minister of Arts and Science should be appointed without delay.

The Report is rounded off by a short Conclusion. It states: "We are aware that the magnitude of this need will come as a surprise to many. But we have been conservative in our assumptions and, if we had to guess at the probable direction of error, we think it the more likely that we have set our sights too low."

We conclude this summary of the recommendations of the Newsom and Robbins Committees by a brief review of the criticisms that have been made. While the Newsom Report was approved in principle the Government has been tardy in accepting the main recommendation that the raising of the school leaving age should be announced immediately.[1] Professor H. C. Dent accused the Government of refusing to commit themselves. He believed that the raising of the leaving age would add about £60 million to the annual cost of secondary education and to carry out the necessary school buildings would add £10 to £15 million a year for a limited period.

Sir John Newsom who received a knighthood in the New Year Honours List of 1964, in a speech delivered at the N.U.T. headquarters, said it would be wicked and foolish to neglect the majority of children to turn out an elite of eggheads without a very large number of skilled people working for and with them. "If we say we can afford Robbins, by heaven we can afford Newsom." *The Times Educational Supplement,* in a leading article of 13 December 1963, took a similar point of view. "In spite of all the *Aides-mémoires* which have been showered upon them, the Government remain remarkably costive on the question of raising the school age. It will be recalled that it has been before them for a long time. When the Crowther Report came out, a decision was promised before the end of the Parliament. Some weeks after Newsom it has still not been made. The only possible conclusion is that the Government lack

[1] The announcement has now been made (Feb. 1964).

enthusiasm for the reform. It could, of course, be ascribed to caution, but no caution at all was shown over the Robbins crash programme. . . . Whatever the reason the delay in the declaration of Government policy seems to indicate a lack of stomach for the job." On the other hand, the Minister of Education, Sir Edward Boyle, declared that the fears that the Newsom Report would be overlooked were groundless.

The Church of England Board of Education set up a group to receive and consider the Newsom Report. It reported most favourably to the Schools Council which sent their approval to the Board. The group said: "The importance of this report is that it is concerned with attitudes before administration, with persons rather than programmes, with love and not law . . . Convinced Christians and those who do not share our beliefs can, to a very large extent, join together in the task of seeing that these children of average and below average ability are enabled to realise their potentialities, and leave school well equipped to take their place in adult society. . . . Many have already contented themselves with expressing a benevolent and non-committal approval of Newsom, rapidly passing on to speculation about the exciting and costly prospects which Robbins holds out. Robbins has a greater news-value than Newsom and will almost certainly continue to attract greater publicity. But the measure of the integrity with which higher education is expanded and developed will be the determination with which justice for the other half of our future is pursued. And it is the duty of Christians to ensure that Robbins and Newsom become equal partners in one process. This is so because we know that in the mind of God there are no second-class human beings."

In the first edition of the writer's *History of Education in Great Britain,* 1948, he drew attention to the mistake in the sequence of the Hadow Reports. ". . . logically, the Committee should have considered the education of infants and juniors before that of the adolescent. It must be admitted that the order was unfortunate. since in most areas priority was given to the adolescent. . . . Meanwhile, a good deal of damage had been done. The scholarship examination had taken possession of many junior schools and the whole of their work was orientated to obtaining as many entrants to grammar schools as possible." Governments are often slow in discarding the errors of their predecessors. The logical timing of the recent reports should have been Plowden, Newsom, Crowther, and Robbins. The 1944 Act had impressd the public with the truth that education is a continuous process within which there are the three stages of primary, secondary, and further education. What occurs in the ultimate stage is dependent to a considerable extent on what has happened at other levels.

The Times Educational Supplement, 4 October 1963, put a similar criticism. "Next Monday the Plowden Committee starts its long, hard look at the primary schools. That section of the system which we have always complimented and then ignored comes under scrutiny at last. . . . It is, of course, ironic that before we hear from Lady Plowden and her colleagues—almost, indeed, before they begin—major reports on other sections of the system will have come and gone. It is evidence of the piecemeal way in which we set about reform that the primary schools have come last. The Plowden Committee could quite conceivably make recommendations about them that would materially affect the subsequent stages of education; but the definitive reports on those stages are being made in advance."

The most drastic attack on the Robbins Report is that of A. J. P. Taylor, Fellow of Magdalen and Lecturer in Modern History in the University of Oxford, made in an article contributed to the *Sunday Express,* 27 November 1963. He described the Report as "feeble in its arguments, mistaken in its conclusions, and dangerous in the consequences which follow from them . . . Its recommendations will lead to the useless spending of much public money and will distort the lives of many admirable young people who will go to universities without being fitted to go there." He challenged the assumption of a great pool of first-class ability running to waste. "The pool is only of third-class ability or not even that."

The main criticism of the Report is concerned with the recommendation to place higher education under a separate minister. One member of the Robbins Committee, Mr H. C. Shearman, a former Chairman of the L.C.C., did not agree with the recommendation, and his view is given in the Note of Reservation, pp. 293-6 of the Report. He summed up his conclusion: "I submit therefore that a single Minister for Education . . . with one or two Ministers of State to assist him is the more satisfactory answer. He would take over the present sphere of responsibility of the Minister of Education and that of the Chancellor in respect of the University Grants Committee, and conceivably some of the other functions alluded to in Chapter XVII, but he would be at the head of a new department from which a forward-looking outlook might be expected."

In the debate in the House of Lords a heated attack was made on the proposed change by Lord Eccles, who said that he was astonished that someone with Lord Robbins's experience should prefer two weak Ministers to one strong one. In his reply, Lord Robbins based his case on the distinct and separate functions of the school and university. The former imparts knowledge, the latter advances it as well. On the whole the Labour Party was in favour of a single Minister of Education and this was supported by the T.U.C. The representatives of the Association of University Teachers suggested that there was a difference of opinion amongst the staff of the universities but the majority seemed to favour the view of the Report. Lord James of Rusholme, Vice-Chancellor of York, described himself as being alone among Vice-Chancellors and a member of the minority amongst university opinion which believed in control by one Minister. Sir William Alexander, Secretary of the Association of Education Committees, agreed with Lord James.

The Government eventually decided to appoint Mr Quintin Hogg (formerly Lord Hailsham) Secretary of State for Education and Science with responsibility over the whole field of education. His department would include two administrative units, one concerned with the schools of England and Wales, the other with science and, through the University Grants Commission, with institutions of university status. The Secretary would be supported by two Ministers of State. The Prime Minister, Sir Alec Douglas-Home, announced that the present Minister of Education, Sir Edward Boyle, would be one of the Ministers of State and continue to be a member of the Cabinet. Mr Hogg announced that the recurrent grants for existing universities would be increased in each of the three remaining years of the present quinquennium to make a total increase of £20,500,000 by 1967. One practical result was the request of the U.G.C. for claimants to the proposed new university foundations to come forward. Claims which were previously unsuccessful would be considered. Stamford, Chester, Plymouth, Swindon, Gloucester, Cornwall, Shropshire, and Wolverhampton presented their claims. Claimants for a sixth Scottish university were considered and in July 1964 Stirling was accepted. The Heriot-Watt College, Edinburgh, which was similar to the Royal Technical College at Glasgow, has been promised university status but it will probably have to seek a site outside the capital city for its expansion. Queen's College, Dundee, is to be separated from the University of St Andrews and become an independent university by August 1967. The Plowden Committee has continued its inquiry but its report is not expected until 1966. Lady Plowden followed Sir John Newsom as chairman of the Central Advisory Council for Education. Sir John is now vice-chairman.

The General Election of October 1964 resulted in a Labour Government (with a precarious majority) headed by Mr Harold Wilson. Mr Michael Stewart was appointed Secretary of State for Education and Science and the two Ministers of State in the Department of Education and Science were Lord Bowden, Principal of the Manchester College of Science and Technology, and Mr R. E. Prentice. Mr Frank Cousins was appointed Minister of Technology. Within a short space of time a Cabinet shuffle became necessary because Mr Patrick Gordon Walker, who was defeated at Smethwick, was also rejected at Leyton early in 1965. Mr Stewart replaced him as Foreign Secretary and Mr A. Crosland was appointed in place of Mr Stewart. Lord Bowden resigned his office and his work was taken over by Mr Prentice who is responsible for further education and the training of teachers. Mr E. Redhead, formerly Minister of State at the Board of Trade, is responsible for schools.

Mr Stewart had already expressed his belief in comprehensive education and his views were also accepted by Mr Crosland. In April 1965 he issued a confidential draft circular to local authorities and others connected with education, obviously to ascertain their views on the Organisation of Secondary Education. On 12 July 1965 the Circular 10/65 was addressed to L.E.A.s and the governors of grammar and direct grant schools, voluntary aided and special agreement schools. There are some alterations in the text of the Circular, some of which are merely verbal and others which indicate more clearly the objectives of the Secretary of State. L.E.A.s are requested, if they have not already done it, to prepare and submit to him their plans for reorganising secondary education in their areas on comprehensive lines. The Circular is somewhat lengthy and only a brief account is given below.

Mr Crosland reiterated the Government's motion in the House of Commons in January 1965. This declared that the selection at eleven plus would be ended together with separatism in secondary education. The eleven plus selection needed a careful investigation on account of serious weaknesses which had developed. One of these was that its form varied according to the different local

authorities. Most teachers feel that the test needs a drastic reform
or it should be replaced by some other system. The Circular points
out that comprehensive education can be organised in at least six
main forms but Mr Crosland is not prepared to adhere to any one
form as being universally applicable.

(1) There is the "orthodox" comprehensive school with an age
range from 11-18. Mr Crosland believes that there are strong
arguments for its adoption. On the other hand he realises that
the majority of present school buildings are too small to adopt
this form. In areas in which new schools are being built this is
the simplest and best solution.

(2) A two-tier system by which all pupils enter a junior comprehensive school at 11 and at 13 or 14 they transfer to a senior
comprehensive school.

(3) A two-tier system under which all pupils leave the primary
school and transfer to a junior comprehensive school. At the age
of 13 or 14 some go to a senior comprehensive school while the
remainder stay in the same school. There are two variations of
this system. In the first the comprehensive school does not provide
a course ending in a public examination and the pupils remain in
the school until 15. In the other the school provides courses for
the G.C.E. and the C.S.E., and the pupils remain at school to at
least 16 and they are encouraged to transfer at the appropriate
stage to the sixth form of the senior school.

(4) A two-tier system in which all pupils leave the primary
school for the junior comprehensive school and at 13 or 14 can
choose to enter a senior school for those who expect to remain well
beyond the compulsory age or go to a senior school which caters
for those who do not.

(5) Comprehensive schools with an age range of 11 to 16
combined with sixth form colleges for pupils over 16.

(6) A system under which pupils transfer from the primary
school at 8 or 9 to a comprehensive school with a range of 8 to 12
or 9 to 13. From this middle school they will enter a comprehensive school which has an age range of 12 or 13 to 18.

The Circular states that the most appropriate system depends
on the local circumstances and an authority may decide to adopt
more than one form of organisation in its area. Mr Crosland
does not conceal his ultimate objective. His Circular points out
that types 1, 2, 5, and 6 produce fully comprehensive schools. On

the other hand, forms 3 and 4 are only partly comprehensive because they involve the separation of pupils of differing aims and attitudes into different schools at 13 and 14.   Hence these schemes can only be accepted as interim solutions because of the limitations of existing buildings and are only stages to a fully comprehensive organisation.   One is tempted to ask what will happen if after some years of experience of both types of organisation it is found that the latter schemes produce results equal to or more effective than the completely comprehensive solutions.   Mr Crosland's Circular reminds one of the old saying that the man from Whitehall always knows best.

The Circular moves on to a discussion of a number of problems such as the difficulties which arise from the existence of older school buildings which are not easy to adopt as comprehensive schools. The voluntary schools, whether aided or special agreement, and the direct grant grammar schools present their own particular problems. Mr Crosland admits that there will not be a single and easy solution to them.   He expresses the hope that the schools, denominational authorities, and the local education authorities will be able to nego-tiate solutions which ensure that while selection is eliminated, parents will not be deprived of places which meet their religious wishes, and on which they have hitherto been able to rely.   He looks to both local education authorities and governors of direct grant grammar schools to consider ways of maintaining this co-operation in the context of comprehensive education.   The govern-ing bodies of many of these schools, which are among the most efficient schools in the country, are finding it difficult to agree with the Secretary's hopes.   The voluntary denominational schools, aided and special agreement, are much concerned with Mr Cros-land's policy.   Most of them are Anglican or Roman Catholic and largely depend upon the generous support of the churches.   It would be difficult for them financially to meet the demands for a wholesale rebuilding.

In this criticism of the Government's policy I wish to make it clear that I am not tied to any political party.   I recognise that in many areas some form of comprehensive school is the best solution of their educational problems.   When the London County Council shortly after the passage of the 1944 Act decided to adopt the comprehensive idea, it was thought that in order to have a vigorous sixth form the school would be a large one containing 2,000 pupils or over.   The objection was made that the head could not possibly know all his pupils and would become a mere administrator. Since then, experience has shown that a much smaller school could be effective, especially if it developed an adequate house system. I have come across certain rural areas in which the grammar school contained only about 100 pupils and the sixth form was so small that it had little influence on the rest of the pupils. In such circumstances, if there is a county secondary school in the neighbourhood, the two schools could be combined either as a bilateral or a comprehensive school. Again, in the new towns a comprehensive school is probably the best solution, and, in the larger cities, there seems to be no reason why the existing grammar schools should not remain side by side with a comprehensive school.

The Circular does not say what will happen to the existing grammar schools and does not discuss whether the comprehensive school can be co-educational. One, however, can conclude that the grammar school will be merged in a comprehensive unit. I believe that no grammar school which is thoroughly efficient should be closed especially if the inhabitants of the area wish it to be retained. There is no reason why a grammar school should harbour class distinctions. The grammar schools cater for pupils who come from the primary schools and any snob ideas about the grammar school are due to foolish parents and should not be supported by the school. My criticism of the Circular is that it intends to force the comprehensive system upon pupils and parents who do not wish it. One of the important points in the philosophy of democracy is that consideration ought to be given to the beliefs of minorities. The Government should remember that its existence hangs upon a shoe string since the precarious majority shows that the views of the country are nearly equally divided.

Some direct grant grammar schools are considering independence, and more will probably take this decision in the future. One of the earliest which has decided to go independent is the Colston's Girls' School at Bristol and considerable financial assistance has been promised. The governors of the Leeds Girls' High School have decided that if necessary the school will revert to the independent status it had from 1945 to 1957. The Parents' Association of Sheffield's oldest grammar school is fighting to prevent it from being turned into a comprehensive school. Drax Grammar School, which loses its maintained status with the West Riding County Council, is seeking to become an independent boarding school. The National Association of Governing Bodies of Aided Grammar

Schools has declared that under the Act of 1944 an aided Grammar School can break off its connexion with a local authority.

The County Borough Council of Bournemouth is the first L.E.A. to challenge Mr Crosland's Circular. By 39 votes to 10 the Council stated that "A change to a system of comprehensive schools was unnecessary and undesirable in Bournemouth". It is likely that some other councils will follow Bournemouth.

The Government is still uneasy about the supply of teachers in spite of the increased number of students entering the colleges of education and the education departments of the universities. Mr Crosland has made another appeal for married women to return to teaching when possible. The problem of the supply of teachers has led to increasing use of visual aids, closed-circuit radio and television and the development of programmed learning and the employment of teaching machines. These devices can assist the teacher by giving more time for attention to individual students and also enable him to teach larger classes. These aids do not take the place of the teacher.

The Queen's Speech at the opening of Parliament in November 1965 stated that a public schools commission will be set up to advise on the best way of integrating the public schools with the state system.

Sir John Newsom has been appointed Chairman of the Public Schools Commission. The Commission will not be concerned with the direct grant schools since their future was considered in Mr Crosland's Circular.

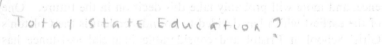
Total State Education ?

INDEX

INDEX OF NAMES AND TITLES MENTIONED IN THE TEXT

(Major references are shown by numerals in heavy type)

For writers on education, the lists on pages 128-30, 159-61, 243-5, 275-80, and the Suggestions for Further Reading at the end of each chapter should be consulted.

PRINTED IN GREAT BRITAIN BY UNIVERSITY TUTORIAL PRESS LTD, FOXTON
NEAR CAMBRIDGE